T0319901

CREATING WEALTH AND POVERTY
IN POSTSOCIALIST CHINA

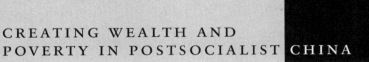

# CREATING WEALTH AND
# POVERTY IN POSTSOCIALIST CHINA

*Edited by Deborah S. Davis and Wang Feng*

STANFORD UNIVERSITY PRESS
STANFORD, CALIFORNIA

Stanford University Press
Stanford, California

Printed in the United States of America on acid-free, archival-quality paper

Library of Congress Cataloging-in-Publication Data
    Creating wealth and poverty in postsocialist China / edited by Deborah S. Davis and Wang Feng.
        p. cm. — (Studies in social inequality)
    Includes bibliographical references and index.
    ISBN 978-0-8047-5931-1 (cloth : alk. paper) —
    ISBN 978-0-8047-6116-1 (pbk. : alk. paper)
    1. Income distribution—China   2. Wealth—China.
3. Poverty—China.   4. Social stratification—China.
I. Davis, Deborah   II. Wang, Feng.   III. Series.
    HC430.I5C73 2009
    339.20951—dc22

                                    2009020017

Typeset by Publishers' Design and Production Services, Inc. in 10/13 Sabon

CONTENTS

PART IV Interpreting Postsocialist Wealth and Poverty

# ILLUSTRATIONS

## ACKNOWLEDGMENTS

As this project moved from a conference at Yale University to published book, we have benefited from the intellectual encouragement of many colleagues and financial support of several organizational sponsors. We gratefully acknowledge grants from the Center for Asian Studies at the University of California, Irvine, the Council of East Asian Studies at Yale University, the Ford Foundation, and the American Sociological Association Fund for the Advancement of the Discipline that supported the January 6–8, 2006, conference and an additional publication grant from the Yale Council of East Asian Studies. We also wish to thank Mimi Yiengpruksawan, then chair of the Council of East Asian Studies, and staff member Abbey Newman for their superb logistical support and leadership during our meetings in New Haven as well as Kate Wahl, our Stanford University Press editor, and her editorial assistant, Joa Suorez, for their expert guidance at all stages of manuscript preparation.

During the conference, discussants Dalton Conley, Sarah Cook, Bonnie Erickson, John Logan, Jesper Sørensen, and Iván Szelényi pushed authors to place their arguments in broadest comparative perspective, and in the final stages of manuscript preparation we benefited from critical reading by Dorothy Sollinger, two anonymous reviewers, and the superb translation work by Xuan Gui (Chapters 6 and 9) and Laura Burian (Chapter 8). The final manuscript gained substantively from these intellectual contributions.

*Deborah Davis and Wang Feng*
*January 2008*

CONTRIBUTORS

JENNIFER ADAMS, Assistant Professor, School of Education, Stanford University

YANJIE BIAN, Professor, Department of Sociology, University of Minnesota, Chair Professor and the Director of Survey Research Center, Hong Kong University of Science and Technology

YONG CAI, Assistant Professor, Department of Sociology, University of Utah

PHILIP N. COHEN, Associate Professor, Department of Sociology, Fellow, Carolina Population Center, University of North Carolina, Chapel Hill

DEBORAH DAVIS, Professor, Department of Sociology, Yale University

PETER EVANS, Eliaser Professor of International Studies and Professor of Sociology, Department of Sociology, University of California, Berkeley

QIN GAO, Assistant Professor, Fordham University Graduate School of Social Service

CHUNPING HAN, Ph.D. student, Department of Sociology, Harvard University

EMILY HANNUM, Associate Professor, Department of Sociology, University of Pennsylvania

CHING KWAN LEE, Professor, Department of Sociology, University of California, Los Angeles

LIU XIN, Professor and Chair, Department of Sociology, Fudan University

EILEEN M. OTIS, Assistant Professor, Department of Sociology, University of Oregon

CARL RISKIN, Distinguished Professor of Economics, Department of Economics, Queens College, CUNY, and Senior Research Scholar, Weatherhead East Asian Institute, Columbia University

SARAH STAVETEIG, Ph.D. student, Departments of Demography and Sociology, University of California, Berkeley

WANG FENG, Professor and Chair, Department of Sociology, University of California, Irvine

R. BIN WONG, Director, Asia Institute and Professor of History, University of California, Los Angeles

MARTIN KING WHYTE, Professor, Department of Sociology, Harvard University

ZHANG JING, Professor, Department of Sociology, Peking University

ZHOU FEIZHOU, Associate Professor, Department of Sociology, Peking University

XUEGUANG ZHOU, Professor, Department of Sociology, Stanford University

# CREATING WEALTH AND POVERTY
## IN POSTSOCIALIST CHINA

# PART I
# POVERTY, WEALTH,
# AND STRATIFICATION:
# THE INTERCONNECTIONS

# Poverty and Wealth in Postsocialist China: An Overview

*Deborah Davis and Wang Feng*

China today is an economic giant deeply embedded in global trade and production. In 2006, China's nominal gross domestic product (GDP) exceeded two and one-half trillion U.S. dollars, larger than that of France and approaching that of Germany. Calibrated in the metric used by the World Bank to capture comparable real standards of living, China's GDP in 2006 reached 10.21 trillion purchasing power parity (PPP) dollars, thereby placing its economy second in the world only after the United States.[1] In the three decades since 1979, when it began to dismantle the socialist planned economy, China has become the number one recipient of global capital flow among all developing countries, and the Shanghai Stock Exchange, which reopened in 1990, had by 2007 become the sixth largest stock exchange in the world.[2] In May 2007 eight million new accounts were opened in a single month. For the first time in its history, the combined stock market capitalization in China's two stock exchanges surpassed its GDP.[3] By any metric China is a central player in global capitalism, and the practices and institutions of socialism appear to have receded into a distant past.

Communist capitalism has not only produced an economic miracle but also glaring inequality. In 2005, *China Daily* reported that 236,000 citizens were millionaires and that the number of individuals with at least one million U.S. dollars in assets grew at the sixth fastest pace in the world (Wilson 2005). At the same time, per capita incomes are low and a majority of citizens live on less than two dollars a day. Moreover, simultaneously with sustained macro level growth, levels of income inequality are now comparable to those in the United States and greater than those in India and Indonesia.[4] Thus, within the story of global growth and new affluence are social, political, and economic dynamics that produce both wealth and poverty.

One can argue that the most central process in China's postsocialist transformation is the "reallocation of labor and capital" that transformed other former socialist economies (Mitra and Yemtsov 2006: 25). Yet in almost every parameter China's postsocialist trajectory does not parallel those of Russia and Eastern Europe in initial outcomes or pace of change. Instead of suffering a devastating economic downturn in its initial retreat from socialist autarky, China experienced two decades of double-digit growth and a dramatic drop in poverty. In contrast to the "shock therapy" that characterized postsocialist transformations in Europe and Central Asia, China followed a gradualist reform approach that not only avoided sudden economic contraction but also kept the state firmly at the helm. In addition, even as China has emerged as a giant in the global capitalist economy, the communist one-party system that engineered both the socialist and the post-socialist revolutions retains its political monopolies. In 2007, twenty-four Chinese companies made the list of the Fortune 500;[5] all were either owned or controlled by the Chinese state. China's postsocialist economic surge, therefore, in many ways more closely resembles the trajectory to relative affluence in the 1970s of such authoritarian East Asian developmental states as Taiwan and Korea rather than duplicating the experience of the former Soviet Union or Eastern Europe.

Prevailing meta-explanations for rapid transformation typically privilege dichotomized pairs of economic and social stratification regimes, highlighting the shift from an agrarian to an industrial society or from a planned to a market system. But China's transformation does not accord easily with either an abrupt transition to an industrial society or sudden abandonment of a command economy. Central to China's emerging dynamics of social stratification is the interaction between institutional practices of the socialist decades and deep engagement with the market rules of global production. For example, twenty-five years after the demise of the People's Communes, there is still neither private ownership of agricultural land nor total freedom to move permanently from a village to the city. Equally important is the coherence and power of the Chinese Communist Party. In 1991, just prior to Deng Xiaoping's intensification of market reforms, the Communist Party had 51 million members, or 4.4 percent of the entire population; by 2005 membership reached 70.8 million or 5.5 percent of the population (Xinhua 2006b). Furthermore, although there have been reports of declines in the number of Young Communist League branches, League membership remains an essential stepping-stone for career advancement, and recruitment efforts have recently intensified on university campuses (Rosen 2004).[6] No one would dispute that the Chinese economy has "grown out of the (socialist) plan" (Naughton 1995), but it is equally true that the party organizations and officials close to party-state power continue to hoard income-generating opportunities and extract major rents. Extensive expropriation of collectively owned agricultural land for state infrastructure projects and commercial real estate development have created vast profits for officials and place party-state agents at the center of profit seeking. Consequently, to understand the current distributions of poverty and wealth as well as the underlying processes that stratify Chinese society, we emphasize institutional context and historical legacies.

For example, to understand the situation of industrial workers in a post-socialist China, we must consider China's long history of sustained investment in industry. From the very first years after the establishment of the People's Republic in 1949, the Chinese Communist Party (CCP) leadership was committed to rapid industrialization. Thus, the industrial capitalist practices in recent decades have evolved both from three decades of Soviet style urban industrialization and the evolution of rural township-village-enterprises (TVEs), whose origins are in part in the five small industries sponsored by the People's Communes when subcontracting to urban state-owned enterprises (SOEs). The current receptivity to global investment in Chinese industry and massive spending on industrial infrastructure, therefore, do not represent a new commitment to either manufacturing or industrial organization.[7] Rather, the most distinctive shift in industrial institutions since 1980 has been a radical spatial redistribution of industrial labor from north to south and from large cities to an industrializing countryside.

Contributors to this volume address many different dimensions of inequality as well as the institutional processes that have generated wealth for a minority and kept others mired in poverty. The specific location or population varies by chapter, but each author goes beyond arguments about efficiencies of marketization and lowered transaction costs to analysis within a particular institutional and historical context. Cai (Chapter 10), for example, explores how recommodification and privatization of social welfare goods such as medicine have improved quality of services but increased the risk that illness will push a family into poverty. Xueguang Zhou (Chapter 7) and Zhou Feizhou (Chapter 8) examine how recommodification of land remains a highly politicized process that creates pockets of great wealth amidst relative poverty. Zhang Jing (Chapter 9), Han and Whyte (Chapter 13) and Ching Kwan Lee (Chapter 14) analyze popular understandings of equity and justice and ask how the legacy of socialist practices creates patterns of inequality that differ from those in capitalist societies without a socialist past. Most broadly, the authors ask how generic capitalist institutions and practices interact with China's historical, political, and cultural institutions to allocate life chances. Like Gerber (2006) in his work on postsocialist Russia, we offer no overarching explanation. Rather we find that it is the social and political context and the interaction of individual attributes within particular organizational settings that define current patterns of social stratification.

In this overview essay we first summarize the distributional outcomes in terms of income inequality, poverty, and wealth, and then look in more detail at the configurations of political and economic power that have increased returns on political power and such capital assets as farm land but depressed returns to manual labor in the service sector and manufacturing.

## INEQUALITY

In the case of Taiwan and Korea, two early Asian "tigers" who leapt ahead of their neighbors economically through export-led industrialization, macro-level economic gains initially left almost no poor household worse off than before and even reduced income inequality among households (Fei, Ranis, and Kuo 1979). In high-growth, postsocialist China, however, greater affluence has dramatically reduced the incidence of subsistence poverty but increased income inequality, resulting in a pattern of rising inequality similar to that found in Brazil, Mexico, and Indonesia.[8]

Prior to market reforms, China had a distinctive pattern of inequality because of a rural-urban divide that essentially created two forms of socialism within one country (Davis 1995 and Whyte 1996). In towns and cities the socialist revolution created historically unprecedented security as well as an industrial proletariat whose standard of living approached that of managers and professionals. During the 1970s, average city incomes were triple those in the countryside and urban income inequality was one of the lowest in the world (Davis 2000; Parish 1984; Walder 1986; Wang 2008).

Rural residents, however, gained meager rewards from the socialist revolution. Regardless of whether they grew grain or nongrain crops, farmers could only sell to the government procurement stations at prices fixed by central ministries to provide cheap food in the cities. Prohibited from engaging in private trade or handicraft production and denied the opportunity to leave farming for industrial work, those working in rural areas were necessarily condemned to the lowest income strata. Only the small minority who held administrative or professional jobs at the commune level had access to cash salaries that approached those of the lowest-paid urban factory workers. The collectivization of rural land during the 1950s had reduced within-village inequalities. However, because the Maoist blueprint for the rural sector eliminated self-employment, artisan sidelines, and petty trade, the same policies that leveled income differences also institutionalized village self-sufficiency, which over time created inequalities between villages that were as great as—if not greater than—those of the precommunist years. Thus, in one of the ironies of history, the communist victors of the 1946–1949 civil war not only built a collective economy with an unusually harsh rural-urban divide but also decimated one of the most commodified and commercialized preindustrial economies in human history (see Chapter 15 by Wong as well as Hamilton 2006; Naquin and Rawski 1987; Pomeranz 2000; Wong 1997) and transformed tens of millions of rural craftsmen and traders into land-bound peasants (Davis 1995; Friedman, Pickowicz, and Selden 1991, 2005; Knight and Song 1999; Oi 1989; Watson 1984).

Reliance on export-led industrialization and recommodification of goods and services after the elimination of the People's Communes radically altered the earlier socialist rules of the game for rural residents. Households no longer pooled labor, and by 1993 grain sales and decisions on cropping were left almost entirely in the hands of individual farmers. As early as 1980, the government encouraged rural households to start family enterprises and become individual entrepreneurs and traders. Even as a system of household registration continues to restrict full access to urban services and permanent registration, rural labor now flows to city jobs in response to market signals. As a result, although village incomes still lag behind those in cities, real per capita incomes rose nearly six-fold between 1978 and 2004. Simultaneously, however, income inequality at the national level and between rural households is higher than it was during the socialist decades.

In cities, there was neither a single institutional "big bang" comparable to the rapid dismantling of the People's Communes nor as rapid an inflow to self-employment and private sector employment. However, by the time China had entered the WTO in 2001, urban labor markets resembled those in other capitalist economies, and the compressed urban wage structure of earlier decades had disappeared. In 1988 the Gini coefficient for urban family income was 0.227; in 1995 it reached 0.336 and by 2002 had risen to 0.345. See Chapter 2 for a discussion of how inclusion of cash value of benefits increases the gap.

Rising inequality in China cannot be divorced from the international political economy within which China has engineered its impressive economic growth. China's economic growth both fueled and has been fueled by the most recent expansion of global capitalism. Increasingly engaged in global manufacturing and trade, both state and nonstate employers maximize their comparative advantage of cheap manual labor. The decision to enter the WTO and adopt an export-led growth strategy recalibrated the reward structure across sectors. Particularly in manufacturing enterprises that had previously operated under soft budget constraints, international competition pushed managers to widen the potential labor pool and adopt new criteria for setting wages. Multinationals—first from Taiwan and Hong Kong; later from Japan, Korea, the United States, and Europe—moved production to greenfield sites in southern provinces that had had little or no industry. Their new shop-floor employees were millions of young rural migrants, not established industrial workers. Initially wages exceeded those in farming but were lower than those paid in the state manufacturing sector. By the late 1990s, a national labor market for unskilled and semiskilled labor had emerged, and wages for manual jobs began to converge across

ownership sectors and geographic regions. By contrast, credentialed professionals and experienced managers who were in short supply commanded a
premium and the blue-collar–white-collar income gap that had been trivial
in socialist cities rapidly increased (Research Group for Social Structure in
Contemporary China 2005).

Macrolevel growth and rising profits over the 1990s, however, did not
greatly increase the percentage of jobs in manufacturing or consistently raise
the wages of industrial labor. On the contrary, the percentage of the labor
force working in manufacturing declined after 1995, and wages for manual
workers stagnated (Research Group for Social Structure in Contemporary
China 2005). As Peter Evans and Sarah Staveteig explain in Chapter 5, rather
than replicate the English experience, in which manufacturing continued to
absorb excess farm labor for half a century, China has already turned to
capital-intensive manufacturing. Therefore, some have estimated that manufacturing is unlikely to ever employ more than 15 percent of the labor force
and that, like developed capitalist economies, China must rely on a hetero-
geneous service sector to provide the bulk of new jobs. Moreover, Evans
and Staveteig predict that these new service jobs will be bifurcated between
knowledge jobs with high incomes for an educated minority and semiskilled
jobs with low rates of return on labor for the majority (see Chapter 5 for a
full discussion). Recent wage disparities by sector and occupation support
such predictions. Between 1986 and 2000, the average wage in mining and
quarrying industries dropped from 16 percent above the national average to
11 percent below, whereas in the real estate sector average wages in 2000 exceeded the national average by 35 percent, in banking and insurance sector
they exceeded by 44 percent, and in scientific research and technical services
by 45 percent (Wang 2008, Chapter 2).

Nor has the rapidly expanding economy benefited men and women
equally. As Philip Cohen and Wang Feng explain in Chapter 3, male-female
wage gaps have widened as a result of expansion of the market economy
and changes in state policies, with the largest disparities appearing in private
sector jobs in cities with highest incomes and fastest growth rates. In China's
shrinking public sector, however, state controls continue to equalize income
between men and women.

At the end of their analysis, Cohen and Wang suggest that to identify
the actual mechanisms of segmentation and differentiation that intensify
gender inequalities in market-dominated employment, scholars should look
to the microcontext of specific occupations. In Chapter 4, Eileen Otis does
precisely that by drawing on her ethnography of service workers in one
Beijing luxury hotel to illustrate how the employment practices of postsocialist workplaces systematically heighten distinctions and disparities of
gender. Thus, like Charles and Grusky (2004), Otis finds that manual jobs

are horizontally segregated by sex and guided by gender essentialism that "legitimates unequal access to skills, wages, and organizational mobility" and valorizes vertical managerial-professional trajectories as associated with male authority (see Chapter 4 for a full discussion).

## POVERTY

Regardless of the exact metric one uses to measure poverty, one of the most positive results of China's economic reforms has been the dramatic drop in the number of people living in extreme destitution (Sen 2006). For example, using a Chinese government definition of poverty as per capita income of less than 101 yuan ($12.50 by official exchange rates) per year in 1978 and 626 yuan ($77.90) per year in 2000, the poverty count fell from 250 million people (or 31 percent of the population) in 1978 to 32 million (just under 4 percent) in 2000 (Park and Wang 2001). Raising the poverty threshold to that of the World Bank's one PPP dollar a day, the results are still impressive. In 1980, 76 percent of the rural population lived on less than a dollar a day; by 1988 the percentage had plummeted to 23 percent, and by 2003 only 9 percent lived at such hardship (World Bank 2005). One qualifier to this story of dramatic improvement, however, is that approximately half the decline since 1980 occurred in the first few years of the reform. Had the rates of economic growth been more balanced across urban and rural China after 1988, it would have taken ten years, not twenty, to bring the rate down below 10 percent (Ravallion and Chen 2004). Thus, while the aggregate trends document a major reduction in poverty, the uneven pace of progress highlights the complexity of the causal explanations and suggests that institutional impediments and policy choices were as integral to understanding poverty reduction as were macroeconomic growth or structural change in labor markets.

In government reports, urban poverty remains statistically trivial. However, as temporary layoffs of state industrial workers have hardened into long-term unemployment and as urban labor markets for semiskilled service and construction jobs open up to rural migrants, a significant segment of the urban population now confronts persistent economic hardship and insecurity.[9] While the absolute decline after 1978 is substantial, it appears that after two decades of nearly double digit macroeconomic growth, China has settled at an overall poverty rate that some economists believe exceeds that of Egypt and Indonesia (Khan 2005). Moreover, we would note that a focus on absolute poverty ignores both the critical situation of the near-poor—whom some estimate are two times as numerous as the official poor (Hussain 2003)—and the issues of social exclusion and reproduction of inequality.

In the Chinese countryside, where poverty is still most concentrated, the poor and near-poor are members of households in regions where prices for grain are falling or where low prices for natural resources have depleted local investment in nonfarm jobs (Khan 2005). More jobs and higher paying jobs are the keys to eliminating poverty, but over the decade of the 1990s, even as national GDP surged, lackluster job growth in the poorest counties prevented the most desperate from moving beyond subsistence. In addition, households in better-endowed and economically dynamic regions have recently become impoverished because of natural disasters or personal catastrophes for which postsocialist China provides no meaningful safety net. In particular, the newly impoverished rural residents of the twenty-first century often come from families who fall into penury because they have exhausted savings to pay high medical charges in the now dominant, for-profit, fee-for-service health care system (Wang 2004).

In urban areas, the poor live in households headed by less-educated men who work outside the state sector and in households with unemployed members (Wang and Tai 2006; Meng et al. 2007). Between 1995 and 1999 urban state and collective enterprises reduced their payrolls by more than 41 million, and by 1999, 29 percent of the 1995 jobs in the public sector had disappeared, largely because of ownership reorganization (Khan 2005). Initially, it appeared that the primary losers would be women over the age of forty, but as privatization intensified and barriers to rural migration fell, urban men of all ages lost jobs to healthy and ambitious youths who had left farming (Khan 2005; Hussain 2003; Park et al. 2006). As in rural areas, another group of newly poor comes from households with heavy medical expenses. In sum, the individual and household pathways to destitution appear to be converging across the rural-urban divide with a speed that was unimaginable even ten years ago.

At the turn of the twenty-first century, a child born in the city still had a better chance to reach university. Wages from farm work were below those of industry, and rural migrants faced economic discrimination and social exclusion in the cities (Davis 2005; Khan and Riskin 2005; Liang and Ma 2004; Research Group for Social Structure 2005). Nevertheless, the material circumstances of urban and rural residents no longer were as distinct as in the socialist era and those on the lower rungs of the urban ladder no longer uniformly stood above all those in the villages. In 2002, 11 percent of those in the wealthiest income decile lived in rural areas, as did 26 percent of those in the eighth highest decile (Li, S. 2003). The upwardly mobile rural citizens now surpass the emerging underclass of urban China.

As the postsocialist state retreated from management of the economy, it also authorized privatization and commercialization of education and medical care previously provided as decommodified social services. For the poor and near-poor, this recommodification created new forms of exclusion and disenfranchisement. During the 1970s China was the premier example of how low-cost but comprehensive public health could reduce mortality rates close to those of a middle-income country (Sen 2006). By 2000 total spending on health care reached 5.7 percent of GDP, a share that slightly exceeded the world average of 5.2 percent of GDP. Medical infrastructure and the training of medical professionals were superior to the standards of the 1980s, and in coastal cities many hospitals offered care comparable to that of the United States or OECD countries (Wang 2004). However, despite increased spending and higher quality medical care, gains in mortality rates and life expectancy lagged behind the gains made by a poorer country like Sri Lanka, and the incidence of infectious diseases such as tuberculosis, viral hepatitis, gonorrhea, and schistosomiasis actually rose (Wang 2004). As Yong Cai notes in this volume, WHO recently ranked China at 141 out of 191 nations in terms of overall performance of health care (see Chapter 10 in this volume). In postsocialist China, inequality of health outcomes also increased. Between 1982 and 2000, national estimates of life expectancy at birth improved but the gap between provinces remained high and the variation at county level was particularly pronounced. In 2000 the gap between counties with the highest life expectancy (80.8 years) and those with the lowest (46.0 years) rivaled the global gap between Japan (81.6 years) and Niger (46 years) (see Chapter 10 for a full set of comparisons).

Rising disparities in access to educational opportunities and in quality of education are among the root causes of social inequality and poverty in China, as elsewhere. Moreover, reducing the disparities in the quality of education or removing the financial barriers to access have no simple or quick solutions. In Chapter 11 Emily Hannum and Jennifer Adams use detailed surveys on school children in rural and migrant communities to demonstrate how children living in the poorest communities face multiple disadvantages. Not only can their parents rarely afford the fees for secondary education, but their communities also cannot provide the quality of equipment and teaching staff necessary to succeed in the competitive exams that allocate access to further education. Furthermore, because children in the poorest communities soon surpass their parents' level of education, they are additionally handicapped in comparison to wealthier rural children and most urban children in terms of parental guidance and advice. The educational barriers to children from the poorest families did not originate in the economic reforms. Nor has the Chinese government ignored the disparities. In fact, during the 1990s, government funding increased substantially, and by 2004 the government had significantly reduced fees charged for the first nine years of school. However, direct costs to parents are not the only barriers to educational success, and the postsocialist economy of rural and urban

China increasingly rewards those with the best educational credentials and highest educational achievement. Unlike the inequities in access to affordable medical care, marketization and privatization did not create new barriers, but they did greatly increase the rewards to the winners in educational competitions.

WEALTH

During the socialist era, Chinese families and individuals had few opportunities to accumulate wealth. In fact, because the regime explicitly collectivized or expropriated real estate, artwork, or objects of significant monetary value, we assume that variations in wealth narrowed more quickly than those in income after 1949 and remained low across the socialist era. Although no national-level data reliably calibrate the distribution of wealth, changes in the rental value of housing can serve as proxies for changing concentration of wealth, and scrutiny of the processes by which land and dwellings are recommodified can identify the institutional practices that shape accumulation of wealth in the context of communist capitalism (see Chapters 2, 6, 7, 8, and 9 for more detailed analysis).

In the first decade of decollectivization, families in rural areas invested heavily in home construction, and national survey data document a major increase in the Gini ratio for rural property income from 0.543 in 1995 to 0.777 in 2002 (Khan and Riskin 2005). However, while the Gini coefficient for property income increased, there was little change in the Gini coefficient for either net farm income or net income from household nonfarm activities, suggesting that as the rural economy abandoned socialist institutions, rural wealth became more unevenly distributed (Khan and Riskin 2005).

In urban China, value of homes as personal property or in terms of rental value also provides a metric for assessing the distribution of wealth. Between the mid-1980s and 2000, the share of urban households in owner-occupied units rose from about 10 percent to over 75 percent (Davis 2003; Wang 2003). But because the primary routes to ownership were sales of publicly owned flats to sitting tenants, home ownership initially reset the clock of wealth distribution and equalized rather than polarized household wealth (Khan and Riskin 2005; Meng 2007). More recently, as the real estate market matured, new inequalities have clearly emerged in terms of resale value.[10] In 2005, the Blue Book of the Chinese Academy of Social Sciences reported that urban households in the top income decile owned 50 percent of the wealth in 2004, while those in the bottom decile held only 1 percent (Lian 2005: 21). We would predict that further accumulation brought by a booming stock market and escalating urban housing prices in recent years will further distinguish the Chinese population between a wealthy strata whose wealth derives from ownership of capital or property and a majority who rely on their labor.

Urban home ownership is only one example of how ties to organizations and relationships originating in the socialist era shaped subsequent inequalities of wealth in the capitalist era. In the countryside, the best example has been the capitalization of land owned collectively by village residents. Between 1987 and 2001, more than 7 million acres of previously arable land moved into nonagricultural use and an estimated 40 to 60 million farmers lost their land-use rights. Local governments, businesses, village organizations, and rural families all participated in the process of the transformation, but local officials reaped a disproportionate share of the profits. Using data collected in Zhejiang province between 2001 and 2003, Zhou Feizhou describes how local officials exploited their political control over land transfers to expropriate the profits from fellow villagers who were legally entitled to a share of the profits on a per capita basis. (See Chapter 8 for full discussion.) In one county, he found that compensation to villagers and rural collectives accounted for only 7 percent of the total offering price. Whereas some households benefited subsequently from renting out houses and participating in nonagricultural activities, most became landless urban residents. In a parallel fashion, many urban workers have lost out to managerial cadres and new capitalist owners during the sale of previously publicly owned industrial assets to individuals under the mantra of property rights reform. In the absence of a Russian-style privatization, China has generally avoided the creation of an oligarch class. Yet the differences in the pace between China and other formerly socialist countries in their respective processes of privatization should not obscure an important similarity in the advantaged access to acquiring valuable "public" property from the socialist economy among the politically powerful.

## PROPERTY, OPPORTUNITY, AND THE DURABLE PARTY STATE

Even as privatization, commodification, and integration into the global economy have transformed the Chinese society, one critical structural parameter of the socialist era continues. Thirty years after the death of Mao, China remains a "durable Communist party-state" (see Chapter 12 for discussion of how the party-state still shapes occupational mobility). Thus, contrary to the early predictions of the decline of economic returns on political influence (Nee 1989), data through the late 1990s document continued economic returns to individual-level political capital in both urban and rural China (Bian, Shu, and Logan 2001; Davis, Bian, and Wang 2005; Walder 1995a, 2002; Zhou 2004). It is also noteworthy that the party has recently focused recruitment among the wealthiest industrialists and among students at universities while generally ignoring farmers and manual workers (Rosen 2004). Indeed, the emerging alliance among political, economic, and intellectual elites under the mantle of "stability" has prompted some Chinese scholars to predict a social structure that will become ever more clearly bifurcated between the powerful and the powerless (Sun 2006).

How does the persistent political power led by the Communist Party adapt itself in China's postsocialist economy? Two studies in this volume, one at the macrotheoretical level and the other at the microempirical level, address the question. In his extension of Aage Sorensen's concept of rent derived from property right transactions, Liu Xin (Chapter 6) argues that the relationship between state political power and property rights continues to be the central mechanism of social stratification even in a postsocialist economy. Concurring with those who have advanced the argument for power persistence (Bian and Logan 1996; Rona-Tas 1994), Liu finds that a cadre class of party officials occupies a privileged status in postsocialist China. But in contrast to previous scholarship, Liu identifies the causal mechanism as contractual principal-agent relationships that allow those in positions of bureaucratic authority to extract excessive rents, an argument that finds ample empirical support and further elaboration in a recent book on urban inequality (Wang 2008). For Liu these administrative principal-agent relations coexist with market power and markets are actually so embedded in the socialist bureaucratic authority structure that they set market entry rules and create rent-seeking space. Especially at the local level, officials directly manage the private sector, and in the absence of democratic supervision or rule of law, they exercise their "self-serving rent-seeking ability." Therefore, the Chinese system of stratification can best be understood as a multidimensional system that includes redistributive power, rent-seeking ability, and market power.

The durable party-state rule also rests on its ability to improvise in face of fragility and internal contradictions, as demonstrated in Xueguang Zhou's case study of five villages in north China (see Chapter 7). Focused on political processes by which village-level cadres negotiate central government payments to farmers who agree to take land out of corn cultivation to reduce soil erosion and stabilize slopes, Zhou, like Liu, finds that corporatist institutions are still the major organizing basis for resource distribution and mobilization. However, he doubts their long-term survival because he finds that the accelerating privatization of collective firms and new freedoms to migrate from the villages fundamentally alter the group boundaries and identities that sustain corporate state institutions. In particular, he finds the ties of kinship that are not "dictated by the principles of state socialism" are particularly central. Unlike Liu's own empirical work (not presented in this volume), which focuses on urban surveys, Zhou relies entirely on ethnography in one rural county. One possible interpretation of their different explanations, therefore, is that, whereas a rent-seeking model that places the political class at the apex may identify the fundamental processes of stratification in Chinese cities, it does not apply as well to village communities where family farms and self-employment dominate the opportunity structure. People living in rural areas where power and resources operate at household and village levels may experience what Zhou calls "institutional involution," in which kinship loyalties and identities replace the socialist corporatist basis of redistribution.

## CLASS FORMATION AND CLASS CLOSURE IN POSTSOCIALIST CHINA

As the economic, political, and social institutions of postsocialist China continue to evolve, the increasing income gap and the altered pathways to wealth have revived interest in class identities and the process of class formation, a subject that many Chinese tried to erase after the discrimination and horrors of the state-dictated class labels and the orchestrated class struggles of the Cultural Revolution. During the Mao period bureaucratically assigned class labels identified every individual in China, creating the basis of social and political control and functioning as tools of political persecution. In a sharp reversal of Maoist criteria of political stratification, the post-Mao leadership renounced the earlier system of class labels. With relatively little fanfare, twenty years of politically defined social stratification disappeared; henceforth, politicized class labels would no longer determine life chances.[11]

Most previous work on social stratification in postsocialist China, including our own, has focused on explaining income inequality, most notably the relative returns on education and political position (Bian and Logan 1996; Davis 1995; Gerber and Hout 1998; Nee 1989, 1991, 1996; Rona-Tas 1994; Wu 2002; Zhou 2004.) Unequal incomes, not the processes of class formation and closure, received most of our attention. In part we privileged debates over income because there had not been time for intergenerational shifts in class position to solidify and because we lacked extensive data on career mobility for the years after 1998 (Bian 2002a). However, now that the postsocialist era has lasted as long as the socialist, it is possible to identify core elements of the new social order and the emerging institutional dynamics of social stratification. Three elements stand out.

First, China has shifted from a status-ranked society toward one in which economic assets trump. Second, the sharp urban-rural divide has eroded, and for the first time since the mid-1950s, those on the lowest rungs of the urban income ladder stand below those at the top of the rural ladder. Third, income is highest for those who have access to capital, and the previously favored socialist proletariat has emerged as a relative loser. In short, China appears to be converging toward a pattern of inequality found throughout other market economies in which the returns to capital exceed those to labor and capital is more mobile than labor.

At the same time as the outline of the postsocialist system of stratification converges toward those of more established capitalist economies, three features of contemporary Chinese society serve to slow the solidification of a new order. First, rapid economic growth has created and continues to create multiple opportunities for social mobility. In a nationwide survey in 2001, researchers from the Chinese Academy of Social Sciences found that among those who started work before 1980, 32 percent achieved higher occupational rank than their fathers; among those who started work after 1980, 41 percent were upwardly mobile. Of those employed between 1980 and 1989, only 30 percent changed jobs and only 19 percent gained status in the move. Of those employed between 1990 and 2001, 54 percent changed jobs and 30.5 percent gained in status (Research Group for Social Structure 2005: 217). While job mobility remained somewhat lower than in other market economies, the acceleration over the 1990s created significant gains among the youngest cohorts in urban labor markets (Bian, Chapter 12 in this volume). Nationwide, millions of rural-born youths continue to leave their villages each year for new lives in the cities (Liang and Ma 2004). At the same time the success of the one-child policy among urban couples will continue to reduce the relative proportion of new entrants of urban origins for another 20 years (Wang 2005). For the immediate future, therefore, we would expect rural newcomers to transcend the social and economic status of their parents. The fate of those born to urban manual workers who fail to gain college education, however, is less optimistic because they are forced to compete with their rural peers for low-skill service jobs.

Second, continuities with socialist practices embedded in the durable party-state and a hybrid property rights regime maintain social categories and group memberships that cut across class divisions (Wang 2008). These categories and memberships not only shape distribution of job opportunities and access to capital but also create identities and loyalties that segment Chinese society. One such group is the rural migrants to large cities. Two decades after the initial liberalization of migration controls, rural migrants continue to face economic and social discrimination. In terms of welfare benefits and political rights, most remain "floaters" on the surface of China's urban society (Solinger 1999a; Wang, Zuo, and Ruan 2002); economically, they occupy a middle position between the urban born and those still working in villages (see Gao and Riskin, Chapter 2). In addition to the broad social distinctions of urban, rural, and migrant, the population is also segmented by geographic location, economic sectors, and work organizations that partially homogenize access to political power and economic resources (Wang and Wang 2007; Wang 2008). Chinese citizens therefore confront a paradox. At one level, they map and acknowledge the sharp income inequalities for society as a whole. At another, they recognize and often accept the smaller degree of inequality in their workplaces or neighborhoods (see Han and Whyte, Chapter 13 in this volume; Wang 2008).

Third, for several reasons the sense of class-consciousness crucial for a class to transform from "a class in itself" to "a class for itself" remains weak, and the two features of the postsocialist Chinese society just described both contribute to undermining class-consciousness formation. As shown by the survey results analyzed in Chapter 13, those economically at the bottom of the society are not those most likely to reject the reforms or express anger at current levels of inequality. To the contrary, those in the bottom deciles express more optimism than those with higher incomes, in part because their reference frame is with their own past and in part because of microlevel equality. Case studies in rural China similarly find those who have been "losers" refuse to see themselves as voiceless or victimized. In Chapter 9 Zhang uses land disputes in Inner Mongolia, Hebei, and Zhejiang to identify the claim makers and their logics of entitlement. In contrast to legal and economic criteria that privilege clear property rights, she found that cadres and villagers negotiated in a fluid sociopolitical framework in which claims to property are central to the postsocialist order, and local interests rather than universal rules determine what is considered just or fair. In a less optimistic reading of perceived injustice, Ching Kwan Lee (Chapter 14) concludes that it is inequity, not inequality, that fuels discontent. While aware of the large gap in incomes, her Beijing respondents were most concerned about the immoral ways in which certain groups of people have gained their new wealth and how the new postsocialist order has created new inequalities in access to medical care and education. Also of note is that across the income spectrum Lee's respondents looked for redress from the state, not from horizontal solidarities forged in the market or voluntary associations. Certainly the continued control of the Communist Party over public media and its opposition to any alternatives to party-controlled organizations reduce the opportunities for formation of oppositional class-consciousness. But Lee's results suggest that many citizens also continue to accept a world in which they first turn to the party-state for redress.

Contemporary patterns of poverty and wealth have their roots in China's socialist period. But viewed in longer historical perspective, the rapid economic expansion since 1978 represents only one brief interlude in China's long history. Furthermore, as we are reminded by R. Bin Wong's sweeping review of China's experiences since the eighteenth century (Chapter 15), there are intriguing parallels with a more distant past that further temper expectations of convergence toward a more generic twenty-first century postsocialist society. Intense commercialization, global trade, rural-urban economic integration, and a unified economic and political elite are not unique to the contemporary period; these elements also characterized the Chinese political economy during the late imperial era. Relevant to understanding dynamics of class formation and class closure in those centuries was the absence in China of the sharp class divisions that had emerged during the commercialization of English agriculture as well as the absence of clear social differentiation between those who worked the land and those who worked in rural industry. Thus, in contrast to the English case that was so central to the nineteenth- and early twentieth-century Western theories of class formation, Chinese society revolved around a family economy in which craftwork remained in households that simultaneously engaged in farming. At the same time few legal-institutional barriers stood between people of different economic or social positions, and traditional Chinese elites were also more integrated with nonelites than elites in either northern European societies or Tokugawa Japan. In addition, officials in premodern China actively promoted agriculture in poor areas of the empire and systematically regulated migration to balance regional disparities and alleviate absolute poverty (Wong, Chapter 15 in this volume). Thus, the patterns we see today of support for the state as an investor and as a redistributor, tolerance of inequality in the face of opportunities for upward mobility, and strategies of advancement built around enduring groups of networked kin may be as rooted in China's long history as in thirty years of socialism or current economic and political configurations of communist capitalism.

China's postsocialist economic growth has drastically altered the worldwide mapping of wealth, poverty, and inequality. At the same time, the social and political processes shaping and defining the dynamic redistribution provide fertile ground for us to rethink the theoretical approaches to the study of poverty and wealth. The earlier wave of research in postsocialist societies focused overwhelmingly on determinants of income inequalities and revolved around the question of what types of *individual* characteristics were rewarded more during the transition to markets than under the socialist redistributive regime (Bian and Logan 1996; Gerber and Hout 1998; Nee 1989, 1991, 1996; Nee and Cao 1999; Rona-Tas 1994; Wu 2002; Zhou 2000a). In contrast, in explaining the emerging trends of poverty and wealth in China, authors in this volume go beyond questions about income inequality and debates over market transition. They focus instead on multiple outcomes, multiple actors, and the complex processes embedded in the larger institutional context. Inequality is generated as individuals arrive at a particular social position within a preexisting structure and then evolve as they progress across the life course within changing social and economic institutions. Such structures are products of historically and culturally defined processes created by contemporaneous political, economic, and social forces. It is such historical and structural forces that make inequality durable.

## CHAPTER TWO

# Market versus Social Benefits: Explaining China's Changing Income Inequality

*Qin Gao and Carl Riskin*

During the late twentieth and early twenty-first centuries, much of the world experienced increased economic inequality. The increase occurred among countries of the OECD (Atkinson 2003), as well as in such capitalist developing nations as India, Nepal, Bangladesh, and Sri Lanka in South Asia (World Bank 2006) and the major postsocialist economies such as Russia (Kislitsyna 2003) and China (Chen and Ravallion 2004; Khan and Riskin 2005). The Chinese case, however, is distinctive because after income inequality surged exceptionally fast, it appears to have plateaued or even slightly declined. For example, using the national China Household Income Project (CHIP) survey data, Khan and Riskin (1998, 2005) found that after sharp increases between 1988 and 1995, income inequality between 1995 and 2002 declined slightly in urban areas and quite substantially in rural areas.

The CHIP data used by Khan and Riskin contradicted earlier findings by the Chinese National Bureau of Statistics (NBS) and by others who have used NBS official data. For instance, Ravallion and Chen (2004) found that income inequality within both urban and rural populations had continued to rise between 1995 and 2001. The NBS data, however, disregard important (and rapidly changing) components of real income, such as rental value of owner-occupied housing and employer and government subsidies. By contrast, the CHIP data that document increase followed by decrease incorporate these additional income components. In this chapter, we return to analysis of the most recent CHIP data to demonstrate the value of developing more comprehensive measurement of per capita household income both to estimate trends over time and to identify the sources of change. In particular, unlike the studies that draw on the NBS data, we examine how changes in the relative importance of market and nonmarket sources of income account for the initially counterintuitive finding of reduced inequality among rural households and only slightly increased inequality in the cities since 1995.

In this chapter, we focus on the respective roles of market economy and social benefits in explaining changes in income inequality in urban and rural areas of China. Conceptually, these two central driving forces of changing income inequality could reinforce or offset each other's impact: If market reforms widen income gaps and if social benefits are distributed regressively, benefits will strengthen this market effect and further enlarge gaps. In contrast, if social benefits are distributed progressively, they will offset the market impact and narrow income gaps.

Riskin (2007) tentatively concluded that social policy was primarily responsible for at least temporarily halting the march toward greater inequality in China's cities and towns. We now take a more detailed look at social policy, and in particular at the impact of changes in social benefit programs. To date, the literature on income inequality has privileged the impact of the overall growth rate and microlevel elements of the structure and characteristics of the market economy. The important redistributive role of social benefit transfers has rarely been considered. In one of the first papers to assess the impact of social policies, Gao (2006, 2008) found that although specific urban social benefits (mainly cash transfers, including pensions, Minimum Living Standard Assurance [MLSA] subsidy and unemployment subsidy) significantly reduced income inequality in both 1988 and 2002, they were unable to close the rising income gap. By contrast, social benefits were minimal among rural households and had little impact on income inequality for this population during the same time period.

To build on prior work (Gao 2006, 2008; Riskin 2007), this chapter brings together the two sets of key factors—market developments and social policy changes—in explaining China's income inequality. We estimate the magnitude of their respective impact as well as their interaction. We will present changes in levels and composition of household per capita income and the contributions to it of market earnings and social benefits over time. To achieve this, we make fuller use of the CHIP data by including the previously underutilized data on various in-kind social benefits, including health, housing, food, and other in-kind transfers. We include their cash value in estimates of total household per capita income package and explore how each type of transfer impacts income inequality.

However, it is important to note the complex nature of both market economy and social policy in the Chinese context, as well as the interdependent relationship between the two forces. First, social policies have market consequences. For instance, the state decision in the late 1990s to invest heavily in infrastructure in backward western regions created wage-earning jobs among the rural population. The income from these jobs shows up as "market income" despite its source in state policy. Indeed, the market economy itself in China is far from being a laissez-faire model and has been guided and shaped by government policies and interventions in a myriad of ways.

Second, social policy reforms since the early 1980s have been heavily driven by economic reform objectives. They were initiated mainly to facilitate market economy reforms and to stimulate economic growth and efficiency through reducing the heavy financial burdens of welfare provision borne by the state-owned and collective enterprises. For example, the provision of pensions and health insurance was shifted from being the sole responsibility of state-owned and collective enterprises to being shared among employers, employees, and the government. Urban housing has been privatized over time, also to relieve the housing provision responsibility of state-owned and collective enterprises, but has favored the more privileged in this process.

DATA AND METHODS

This chapter uses all three waves (1988, 1995, and 2002) of data from the CHIP project, a national cross-sectional study collectively designed by a team of Chinese and Western scholars and conducted by the Institute of Economics at the Chinese Academy of Social Sciences. Samples of the CHIP study were drawn from larger NBS samples using a multistage stratified probability sampling method. The CHIP study is arguably the best publicly available data source on household income and expenditures and includes sample provinces from eastern, central, and western regions of China. The CHIP urban sample includes 9,009 households in 1988, 6,931 households in 1995, and 6,835 households in 2002; the rural sample includes 10,258, 7,998, and 9,200 households in the three years, respectively (Khan and Riskin 2005; Riskin, Zhao, and Li 2001).

We adopt a comprehensive measure of total household per capita income, which includes "market income," cash and in-kind social benefits, and private transfers, less taxes and fees paid. In urban areas, "market income" (hereafter used without quotation marks) is made up of wages, income from private enterprises, property income, and rental value of owner-occupied housing. In rural areas, market income includes wages, income from family farming and nonfarm activities, income from property, rental value of owner-occupied housing, remittance income sent back by members working outside the household, and other miscellaneous income.

Rental value of owner-occupied housing is included because it is a standard component of the conventional definition of income throughout the world. Owned housing is a valued asset whose services would be costly if rented in or out. Still, the reader should be aware of the somewhat tenuous basis for the estimates of this income component, which were made either by residents themselves or from calculations based on house value. Such estimates may be imperfect reflections of the actual market value of housing service, especially in an incompletely marketized economy.

In both urban and rural areas, social benefits are composed of cash transfers and in-kind benefits, including health, housing, food, and other in-kind benefits. The inclusion of health benefits changes the conventional definition to one broader than that used in earlier analysis of CHIP data by Khan and Riskin (1998, 2005). Cash transfers are further divided into three subtypes: social insurance (mainly pensions, sometimes also living subsidies to older persons), supplementary income (price and regional subsidies in urban areas), and public assistance (living hardship subsidy, relief benefits, living subsidy for the urban laid-off, and the MLSA subsidy). Household per capita income is calculated to take into consideration household size and the economies afforded by resource pooling among household members. Official urban and rural Consumer Price Indices (CPI) are used to convert 1988 and 1995 values to constant 2002 values, for urban and rural areas respectively.[1] See Table 2.1.

INCOME INEQUALITY TREND REVISITED

We first explore whether or not our expanded definition of household income generates the same trend of income inequality among CHIP respondents as reported by Khan and Riskin (1998, 2005). Note that the only difference between our definition of household final income and theirs is the inclusion of the medical care expenses covered by the work unit, government, or collective, and the cash value of in-kind health services, as reported by survey participants.[2] When these various social benefit transfers are considered, we find that, in contrast with the pattern uncovered by Khan and Riskin (1998, 2005), in which urban inequality decreased slightly after 1995, our urban Gini for total income keeps increasing—although only very slightly—from 0.34 in 1995 to 0.35 in 2002, after a much sharper rise from 1988 (see Table 2.2). Such a change in urban income inequality trends therefore suggests

TABLE 2.1

*Changes in household per capita income and social benefits in urban China*

|  | LEVELS (¥) | | | COMPOSITION (%) | | |
|---|---|---|---|---|---|---|
|  | 1988 | 1995 | 2002 | 1988 | 1995 | 2002 |
| Market income | 2,480 | 4,744 | 8,054 | 54 | 73 | 78 |
| Social benefits | 1,997 | 1,738 | 2,559 | 44 | 27 | 25 |
| Cash transfers | 433 | 721 | 1,570 | 9 | 11 | 15 |
| Social insurance | 280 | 684 | 1,443 | 6 | 10 | 14 |
| Supplementary income | 153 | 34 | 81 | 3 | 1 | 1 |
| Public assistance | 1 | 2 | 46 | 0 | 0 | 0 |
| Health | 186 | 325 | 684 | 4 | 5 | 7 |
| Housing | 862 | 629 | 246 | 19 | 10 | 2 |
| Food assistance | 510 | 43 | 47 | 11 | 1 | 0 |
| Other in-kind | 6 | 19 | 12 | 0 | 0 | 0 |
| Private transfers | 108 | 120 | 170 | 2 | 2 | 2 |
| Taxes and fees | −9 | −80 | −450 | 0 | −1 | −4 |
| Total household income | 4,576 | 6,521 | 10,333 | 100 | 100 | 100 |

that health subsidy, the social benefit included in our measure but not in that of Khan and Riskin, was distributed more regressively in 2002 than in 1995, which led to wider gaps in final household income. Indeed, market income, which omits health benefits as well as other social benefits, private transfers, and taxes, follows the Khan and Riskin trend, with inequality almost constant between 1995 and 2002 with a Gini ratio of 0.31 in both years.

The rural inequality trend estimated by our measure, however, remains consistent with that of Khan and Riskin. The rural Gini for total income declined quite significantly from 0.42 in 1995 to 0.37 in 2002, but remained higher than that of 1988 (0.36). With social benefits amounting to less than 1 percent of income in all three years, the close correspondence between the concentration ratios for market income and the Ginis for total rural income (see Tables 2.3 and 2.4) confirms that income inequality trends in rural China have been driven by changes in the market economy and that the redistributive role of social benefits has been marginal.

URBAN INCOME INEQUALITY

Between 1988 and 2002, urban per capita household incomes increased and the relative share of different market and nonmarket sources shifted (see Table 2.1). The CPI-adjusted total household per capita income increased from ¥4,576 in 1988 to ¥6,521 in 1995, and then jumped to ¥10,333 in 2002. In terms of income components, however, the most dramatic shift was from 1988 to 1995. In 1988 market income made up 54 percent of total income, social benefits contributed 44 percent, and urban families paid virtually no taxes. By 1995, the share of market income had increased to 73 percent of total income, social benefits dropped sharply to only 27 percent, and families paid 1 percent of their income in taxes. From 1995 to 2002, the share of market income increased slightly to 78 percent, social benefits fell to 25 percent, and tax payments rose to 4 percent of total income.

Table 2.2 details the effect of each income source in shaping urban income inequality over time. Column (1) of the top panel shows the share of each market income component in total household per capita income in the three years. Wage income, the largest component, increased from 49 percent in 1988 to 60 percent in 1995 and then fell back slightly to 58 percent in 2002. The other notable change from 1995 to 2002 was the sharp increase in rental value of owner-occupied housing, from 11 percent to about 17 percent of total income. This was a consequence of the implementation of housing reform, which privatized ownership of most urban housing. The increase in rental value of housing is mirrored by the fall in in-kind housing subsidy (from 10 percent in 1995 to 2 percent in 2002) going to renters, as the number of renters sharply declined.

TABLE 2.2
Urban income inequality and its sources

| Source | (1) Share of total income (%) | | | (2) Gini/concentration ratio* | | | (3) Contribution of income source to overall inequality (%) (col. 1) × (col. 2)/G | | |
|---|---|---|---|---|---|---|---|---|---|
| | 1988 | 1995 | 2002 | 1988 | 1995 | 2002 | 1988 | 1995 | 2002 |
| **Market income** | | | | | | | | | |
| Total market income | 54.18 | 72.74 | 77.94 | 0.20 | 0.31 | 0.31 | 48.01 | 66.17 | 69.64 |
| Wages | 48.99 | 59.98 | 58.31 | 0.18 | 0.24 | 0.30 | 39.59 | 43.68 | 50.77 |
| Income from private enterprises | 0.79 | 0.51 | 2.59 | 0.39 | 0.01 | 0.04 | 1.34 | 0.01 | 0.29 |
| Property income | 0.50 | 1.23 | 0.52 | 0.43 | 0.47 | 0.45 | 0.94 | 1.72 | 0.68 |
| Rental value of owner-occupied housing | 3.90 | 11.03 | 16.68 | 0.36 | 0.63 | 0.37 | 6.13 | 20.75 | 17.75 |
| **Social benefits** | | | | | | | | | |
| Total social benefits | 43.65 | 26.65 | 24.76 | 0.25 | 0.41 | 0.46 | 48.10 | 32.75 | 33.03 |
| Total cash transfers | 9.47 | 11.05 | 15.20 | 0.33 | 0.32 | 0.33 | 13.62 | 10.66 | 14.36 |
| Social insurance | 6.12 | 10.49 | 13.97 | 0.42 | 0.33 | 0.34 | 11.48 | 10.32 | 13.61 |
| Supplementary income | 3.33 | 0.52 | 0.78 | 0.15 | 0.19 | 0.40 | 2.14 | 0.29 | 0.91 |
| Public assistance | 0.01 | 0.04 | 0.45 | -0.04 | 0.43 | -0.12 | 0.00 | 0.05 | -0.16 |
| Total in-kind transfers | 34.18 | 15.61 | 9.57 | 0.23 | 0.48 | 0.67 | 34.48 | 22.09 | 18.67 |
| Health | 4.07 | 4.99 | 6.62 | 0.19 | 0.45 | 0.83 | 3.43 | 6.73 | 15.89 |
| Housing | 18.83 | 9.65 | 2.38 | 0.30 | 0.51 | 0.31 | 25.08 | 14.54 | 2.12 |
| Food | 11.14 | 0.67 | 0.45 | 0.12 | 0.27 | 0.40 | 5.73 | 0.53 | 0.53 |
| Other in-kind | 0.14 | 0.30 | 0.12 | 0.41 | 0.32 | 0.39 | 0.25 | 0.29 | 0.13 |
| Private transfers | 2.36 | 1.84 | 1.65 | 0.40 | 0.38 | 0.37 | 4.14 | 2.06 | 1.77 |
| Taxes and fees | -0.19 | -1.23 | -4.36 | 0.29 | 0.27 | 0.35 | -0.24 | -0.98 | -4.43 |
| Total income | 100 | 100 | 100 | 0.23 | 0.34 | 0.35 | 100 | 100 | 100 |

*The "Gini/Concentration Ratios" for total income are Gini ratios; for all income components they are concentration ratios.

Column (2) shows the concentration ratios of income sources, along with the Gini ratio for total income. The concentration (or "pseudo-Gini") is a measure of the inequality of distribution of a particular income source (e.g., wages). It is measured analogously to the Gini itself, except that it measures the distribution of an income source over all income recipients, rather than just over recipients of that source (which would be a true Gini). It has the convenient property that, when multiplied by the source's share of total income and then summed over all sources, it yields the Gini for all income.[3] Thus, the product of the concentration ratio (shown in column 2) and income share of an income source can be interpreted as the absolute contribution of that source to total inequality.

For components of market income, the most striking aspect is the great jump in inequality of rental value of owner-occupied housing between 1988 and 1995, followed by an equally sharp decline in inequality in 2002. The reason for this pattern is discussed below. The concentration ratio of total social benefits begins in 1988 (0.25) at a level about equal to the overall Gini coefficient (0.23); however, it then rises well above the Gini in 1995 and 2002, which implies that, contrary to the usual expectation that social benefits are to be targeted to the poor and vulnerable, in urban China they became a disequalizing component of income, in the sense that an increase in their share of income, ceteris paribus, would raise overall inequality. We discuss this further below.

The relative contributions of each source to the urban Gini are shown in column (3) of Table 2.2. The contributions of each source (top panel) indicate that market income inequality was dominated by wage income, whose contribution to overall inequality rose over time, reaching 51 percent in 2002. Rental value of owner-occupied housing also increased its contribution to overall inequality sharply between 1988 and 1995, but the ensuing years saw a decline both in inequality of this income source and in its contribution to the overall Gini coefficient.

Such a transition largely reflects the course of housing privatization in urban China. After a series of housing reform trials in different cities, the government started nationwide housing reform in 1988, including rent increases and the sale of public housing mostly to its occupants (Gao 2006). Therefore, in 1988, few urban residents (18 percent in the CHIP sample) owned their own housing while the majority still lived in free or heavily subsidized public housing. As the reform progressed, by 1995, a bigger group of privileged urban residents had been given priority to purchase housing from their work units at heavily subsidized prices, yielding both a higher share of housing value in final income and a much higher inequality of distribution of this income source. The government began to build generally affordable and functional housing in 1998 and introduced the publicly accumulated housing fund nationwide in 1999. These reforms, as well as the spread of subsidized purchase opportunities more widely among the urban population, greatly increased urban housing ownership while sharply reducing inequality in rental value of housing by 2002.

Changes in tax policies in urban China accompanied the changes in market income. As shown in the bottom panel of Table 2.2, urban taxes in 1988 were slightly progressive, being distributed more unequally (concentration ratio = 0.29) than total per capita income (Gini = 0.23). However, they constituted only a very small share of total income (–0.19 percent) and thus had little impact on overall income inequality. By 1995, taxes had risen to over 1 percent of income and were distributed somewhat less unequally (concentration ratio = 0.27) than total income (Gini = 0.34), signifying that taxes were now regressive. By 2002, the ratio of taxes to total per capita income came to over 4 percent and they were distributed proportionally to income (concentration ratio and Gini both equal to 0.35). This made their impact on the Gini ratio essentially equal to their share of income (–4.4 percent).

A designated redistributive mechanism, social benefits have an important impact on urban income inequality, and the major social welfare reforms carried out in late 1980s have had a major impact on the changing levels and compositions of social benefits across the three different CHIP surveys (Gao 2006, 2008). While overall absolute value of all social benefits rose, the relative share dropped significantly and the relative importance of different types of benefits varied quite dramatically. For example, housing benefit, which is the difference between estimated market rent and rent actually paid, dropped from 19 percent of total income in 1988 to 10 percent in 1995 and only 2 percent in 2002. Food benefits, the second largest component of in-kind benefits in 1988, similarly became insignificant by 2002. "Other in-kind benefits" were minimal in all three years. Similarly the total value of supplementary income (i.e., price and regional subsidies) decreased from ¥153 in 1988 to only ¥34 in 1995 before rising to ¥81 in 2002, and its share in total income dropped from 3 percent in 1988 to only 1 percent in 1995 and 2002.

By contrast, the value of cash transfers increased from ¥433 in 1988 to ¥721 in 1995 and ¥1,570 in 2002, and their share in total income grew greatly from 1988 (9 percent) to 2002 (15 percent). The value of health benefits also increased from ¥186 in 1988 to ¥325 in 1995 and ¥684 in 2002, and its contribution to total household per capita income increased from 4 percent to 5 percent and then to 7 percent. The welfare policy reforms, however, actually had cut the levels and coverage of health benefits. Such an increase in amounts, therefore, most likely reflects the dramatic rise in health care costs and increased health consciousness among the public (Gao 2006).

The value of public assistance also increased dramatically from its original minimal level (¥1 in 1988 and ¥2 in 1995 to ¥46 in 2002). Although public assistance still contributed only a very small portion of final per capita income, such an increase reflects the beginnings of government's effort to provide a basic safety net to the newly emerged urban poor since the mid-to-late 1990s, mainly through the MLSA program and unemployment living subsidy.

Both cash transfers and health benefits can be conceptualized as "equity-oriented" benefits, but do the above results indicate that the welfare reforms improved this set of benefits? One could argue that cash transfers were less necessary in premarket reform days, so that their increase in value represents less of an improvement in benefits than a cost of coping with the new levels of personal insecurity associated with the market. Moreover, the inequality of distribution of health benefits became quite extreme by 2002, which is not what one expects in a successful social benefits program. A closer look at benefits can distinguish the "intended" and "unintended" aspects of equity promotion. The biggest increases were in pensions and health, which were largely the unintended consequences of demographic trends, in the one case, and of health care price increases, in the other. Public assistance is the only component that can be clearly identified as an "intended equity-oriented" benefit, serving as a safety net for the poor. Another embedded goal of public assistance, of course, is to prevent social unrest and ensure political stability. Nonetheless, many progressive policies have found their origin in practical political motives, which should not detract from their progressive identity. It is less clear whether changes in supplementary income were "intended" or not.

The middle panel of Table 2.2 further explores the distributions of each social benefit component over all income recipients and their relative contributions to total inequality. Overall, total social benefits were distributed more and more unequally over time, both absolutely and relative to overall income inequality, as indicated in column (2). Compared to the overall Gini of 0.23 in 1988, the concentration ratio of total social benefits was 0.25 in 1988; in 1995, it was 0.41 (Gini = 0.34), and in 2002, 0.46 (Gini = 0.35). Contrasting cash and in-kind benefits, we find that the changing distribution patterns of the three types of cash benefits largely offset each other, yielding an almost constant concentration ratio for total cash benefits over time. More specifically, the inequality level of social insurance decreased after 1988 and that of supplementary income increased in 2002. Public assistance is the only category displaying a negative concentration ratio (except for the somewhat anomalous value in 1995), which signifies that more of it, appropriately, went to the poor than the rich. When it comes to in-kind benefits, all except for housing became more unequal over time, resulting in much increased concentration ratios for total in-kind benefits (from 0.23 in 1988 to 0.48 in 1995 and 0.67 in 2002). The concentration ratio of total in-kind benefits in 1988 was the same as the Gini for total income, while they were distributed much more unequally in later years (concentration ratios larger than Gini coefficients). Particularly striking is the very high concentration ratio for health benefits (0.83) in 2002, which all by itself explains 16 percentage points of the 19 percent contribution of all in-kind benefits to the overall Gini.

The contribution of total social benefits to overall inequality was 48 percent in 1988, and 33 percent in both 1995 and 2002, as shown in column (3) of Table 2.2. In 1988 total social benefits were contributing the same share (48 percent) of income inequality as was market income. However, as economic and social welfare reforms progressed, the relative contribution of market income to overall inequality grew rapidly, reaching 66 percent in 1995 and 70 percent in 2002, pushing that of social benefits lower (33 percent in 1995 and 2002).[4] Among social benefits, in-kind benefits constantly contributed more to inequality than cash transfers although the difference between the two contributions declined over time.

RURAL INCOME INEQUALITY

Rural income inequality, regardless of which definition is used, increased significantly from 1998 to 1995 but then dropped between 1995 and 2002. It was mainly driven by changes in wages, income from family farming and nonfarm activities, rental value of owner-occupied housing, and taxes.

Table 2.3 presents the changing patterns of household per capita income levels and structure in rural China. Per capita market income increased from ¥1,874 in 1988 to ¥2,500 in 1995 and ¥3,187 in 2002. At the same time, per capita social benefits for rural families remained at a minimal level, despite a slight increase from ¥11 in 1988 to about ¥20 in 1995 and 2002. Taxes and fees paid by families increased from ¥39 per capita in 1988 to ¥99 in 1995 and then declined to ¥85 in 2002, and their share in total income remained marginal and largely constant (from –2 percent in 1988 to –4 percent in 1995 and –3 percent in 2002). As a result, the positive (social benefits and private transfers) and negative transfers (taxes and fees) offset each other in contributing to the total income package, leaving market income the dominant income component. Therefore, even before considering the distribution of benefits and taxes, it is clear that market income played the dominant role in shaping income inequality in rural China, and the redistributive roles of social benefits and taxes were very small.

Table 2.4 details the distribution patterns and contributions to inequality of various components of total household per capita income. Overall, market income was distributed slightly more equally than total income across all years, as indicated by slightly lower concentration ratios as compared to

TABLE 2.3
*Changes in household per capita income and social benefits in rural China*

|  | LEVELS (¥) | | | COMPOSITION (%) | | |
|---|---|---|---|---|---|---|
|  | 1988 | 1995 | 2002 | 1988 | 1995 | 2002 |
| Market income | 1,874 | 2,500 | 3,187 | 100 | 102 | 99 |
| Social benefits | 11 | 21 | 20 | 1 | 1 | 1 |
| Cash transfers | 9 | 14 | 17 | 0 | 1 | 1 |
| Social insurance | 6 | 6 | 16 | 0 | 0 | 0 |
| Supplementary income | 0 | 0 | 0 | 0 | 0 | 0 |
| Public assistance | 3 | 8 | 2 | 0 | 0 | 0 |
| Health | 0 | 1 | 1 | 0 | 0 | 0 |
| Housing | 0 | 0 | 0 | 0 | 0 | 0 |
| Food assistance | 1 | 0 | 0 | 0 | 0 | 0 |
| Other in-kind | 1 | 6 | 2 | 0 | 0 | 0 |
| Private transfers | 34 | 22 | 83 | 2 | 1 | 3 |
| Taxes and fees | –39 | –99 | –85 | –2 | –4 | –3 |
| Total income | 1,881 | 2,444 | 3,205 | 100 | 100 | 100 |

overall Gini coefficients in column (2). Conversely and notably, social benefits were more unequally distributed than total income, especially in 2002. Private transfers grew relative to total income and became more unequal. Taxes were regressive (with very low concentration ratios) in all three years, becoming slightly less so in 2002. This and a decline in the tax rate in that year were the only aspect of tax policy that eased the burden on poorer peasants.

The separate components of market income had quite different effects on overall inequality. First, wages, which had been highly disequalizing in 1988 and 1995, became much less so in 2002 as its concentration ratio dropped sharply even as its share of income grew. Wages contributed 27 percent of overall inequality in 1988, 39 percent in 1995, and 36 percent in 2002. The reduction from 1995 to 2002 was a major contributor to the overall decline in rural inequality during that period (Riskin 2007).

Second, between 1995 and 2002, income from family farming activities both fell substantially as a share of total income and became somewhat more equally distributed. Both changes worked to reduce sharply the relative contribution of this income source to the overall Gini ratio (from 27 percent to 22 percent). The opposite happened to income from family nonfarm activities: it both increased as a share of total income and became even more unequally distributed than it had already been.[5] These changes caused the relative contribution of family nonfarm income to overall inequality to grow from 12 percent of the Gini in 1995 to 18 percent in 2002.

TABLE 2.4

Rural income inequality and its sources

| Source | (1) Share of total income (%) | | | (2) Gini/concentration ratio** | | | (3) Contribution of income source to overall inequality (%) | | |
|---|---|---|---|---|---|---|---|---|---|
| | 1988 | 1995 | 2002 | 1988 | 1995 | 2002 | 1988 | 1995 | 2002 |
| **Market income** | | | | | | | | | |
| Total market income | 99.64 | 102.29 | 99.43 | 0.35 | 0.40 | 0.36 | 97.12 | 98.63 | 95.99 |
| Wages | 12.53 | 21.93 | 29.22 | 0.75 | 0.75 | 0.45 | 26.48 | 39.21 | 35.51 |
| Farm activities* | 70.77 | 47.47 | 38.98 | 0.28 | 0.24 | 0.21 | 54.84 | 26.87 | 21.84 |
| Nonfarm activities* | | 9.92 | 11.94 | | 0.49 | 0.55 | | 11.49 | 17.61 |
| Income from property | 0.17 | 0.44 | 0.60 | 0.52 | 0.54 | 0.77 | 0.24 | 0.57 | 1.24 |
| Rental value of owned housing | 9.34 | 11.86 | 14.03 | 0.29 | 0.32 | 0.37 | 7.51 | 8.93 | 13.91 |
| Remittance income | 0.87 | 2.68 | 1.03 | 0.40 | 0.36 | 0.49 | 0.97 | 2.30 | 1.34 |
| Other income | 5.97 | 7.99 | 3.63 | 0.42 | 0.49 | 0.47 | 7.07 | 9.25 | 4.54 |
| **Social benefits** | | | | | | | | | |
| Total social benefits | 0.60 | 0.86 | 0.63 | 0.37 | 0.44 | 0.71 | 0.63 | 0.90 | 1.20 |
| Total cash transfers | 0.47 | 0.56 | 0.55 | 0.35 | 0.26 | 0.72 | 0.47 | 0.35 | 1.05 |
| Social insurance | 0.33 | 0.24 | 0.50 | 0.36 | 0.30 | 0.75 | 0.33 | 0.17 | 0.99 |
| Public assistance | 0.14 | 0.32 | 0.05 | 0.33 | 0.22 | 0.42 | 0.13 | 0.17 | 0.05 |
| Total in-kind transfers | 0.13 | 0.30 | 0.09 | 0.44 | 0.78 | 0.67 | 0.16 | 0.55 | 0.15 |
| Health | 0.01 | 0.06 | 0.03 | 0.70 | 0.65 | 0.72 | 0.03 | 0.09 | 0.05 |
| Food | 0.04 | 0.00 | 0.00 | 0.56 | NA | NA | 0.06 | 0.00 | 0.00 |
| Other in-kind | 0.08 | 0.24 | 0.06 | 0.34 | 0.81 | 0.64 | 0.07 | 0.47 | 0.10 |
| Private transfers | 1.80 | 0.90 | 2.59 | 0.47 | 0.46 | 0.54 | 2.37 | 0.98 | 3.74 |
| Taxes and fees | -2.06 | -4.05 | -2.65 | 0.02 | 0.05 | 0.13 | -0.12 | -0.50 | -0.93 |
| **Total income** | 100 | 100 | 100 | 0.36 | 0.42 | 0.37 | 100 | 100 | 100 |

*Incomes from farm and nonfarm activities in 1988 cannot be differentiated, because the survey question lumped their production inputs.

**The "Gini/Concentration Ratios" for total income are Gini ratios; for all income components they are concentration ratios.

Third, and very importantly, the share of rental value of owner-occupied housing in total household per capita income grew continuously from 9 percent in 1988 to 12 percent in 1995 to 14 percent in 2002. As the same time, the distribution of this income component became more and more unequal over time: Its concentration ratio (0.29) started well below the overall Gini (0.36) in 1988 and, while rising, remained lower than the faster rising Gini in 1995. By 2002, however, its concentration ratio increased to 0.37, identical to the overall Gini. Correspondingly, the rental value of owner-occupied housing accounted for more and more of overall income inequality over time, contributing 8 percent of the Gini in 1988, 9 percent in 1995, and 14 percent in 2002. Such a changing pattern reflects the great value placed by rural people on home ownership since the economic reforms, the ability of wealthier households to invest more in housing than less wealthy ones, and the increasing (and increasingly differentiated) prices of land and houses in rural areas.

Fourth, income from property and remittance income sent back by members working outside the household were distributed much more unequally in 2002 than in 1995. However, their contributions to overall inequality changed differently during the period: The contribution of income from property increased while that of remittance income decreased. Both remained a very small portion of final income and thus did not have a major impact on overall inequality.

Table 2.3 also presents the levels and composition of social benefits in rural China over time. The most significant characteristic is the lack of both cash and in-kind benefits to rural residents. There were minimal cash transfers (making up 1 percent of total household per capita income or less) in all three years—although their value increased over time from only ¥9 in 1988 to ¥14 in 1995 and ¥17 in 2002—and almost none of the important in-kind forms of support that urban families routinely received for health, housing, and food. The value of public assistance, a benefit targeting the very poor, increased slightly from a minimal ¥3 in1988 to ¥8 in 1995, but dropped to ¥2 in 2002.[6]

The middle and bottom panels of Table 2.4 show the effects of social benefits and taxes on overall income inequality. As pointed out earlier, social benefits contributed less than 1 percent of total rural income in any of these three years. The small difference between cash and in-kind benefits converged between 1988 and 1995 and then diverged again between 1995 and 2002. By 2002, in-kind benefits were negligible, making up only 0.09 percent of total income as compared to 0.55 percent for cash benefits. Nevertheless, they were disequalizing in all three years (i.e., concentration ratios higher than overall Gini) and very disequalizing in 2002 (with a very high concentration ratio of 0.71). The reasons for this are unclear. The benefits with the highest concentration ratios are those available mostly to government employees.

Civil service worker wages have more than doubled since 1999, as the government has strived to maintain social stability (Wong 2007). It is possible that benefits have risen hand in hand with wages paid to this small, favored component of the rural population. More specifically, total cash transfers, driven by social insurance income including pension and elder living subsidies, changed from quite equalizing in 1995 to very disequalizing in 2002. Thus, their contribution to overall inequality also increased from 1995 to 2002, but they still contributed only about 1 percent of overall inequality in 2002 because of their very small share of income. Other benefits, as we discussed, were minimal and contributed little to overall inequality.

Rural taxes were distributed very regressively (i.e., much less unequally than total income), although the tax structure moved in a slightly more progressive direction in 2002. Table 2.5 shows just how regressive the rural tax structure has been. In 1995 the richest decile paid only 1.3 percent of its income in taxes and fees, whereas the poorest paid almost 17 percent of its income. All deciles but the richest had lower tax bills (as a share of income) in 2002 than in 1995 but the biggest drop occurred for the poorest decile. Even so, that decile still paid over four times as high a share of its income in taxes as did the richest decile.

## INCOME AND SOCIAL BENEFITS AMONG MIGRANTS

Since the early 1980s an increasing number of those who hold rural household registration status actually live in the towns and cities. The number of rural to urban migrants increased from 11 million in 1982 to 18 million

TABLE 2.5
*Share of tax payments in total household income
by decile in rural China (%)*

| Decile | 1988 | 1995 | 2002 |
|--------|------|------|------|
| 1 | 15.69 | 16.85 | 6.78 |
| 2 | 3.25 | 7.95 | 4.80 |
| 3 | 3.13 | 7.74 | 4.07 |
| 4 | 2.54 | 6.74 | 3.99 |
| 5 | 2.40 | 6.40 | 3.58 |
| 6 | 2.21 | 5.68 | 3.31 |
| 7 | 2.03 | 4.80 | 2.94 |
| 8 | 1.73 | 3.84 | 2.41 |
| 9 | 1.44 | 2.89 | 2.06 |
| 10 | 0.95 | 1.34 | 1.37 |
| Total | 2.07 | 4.05 | 2.65 |

by 1989 (Liang 2001). Official estimates indicate that there were about 70 million rural migrants in 1993, and that number had doubled by 2003 (Zhu and Zhou 2005). If this is accurate, the 140 million migrants in 2003 made up about 11 percent of the national population and more than 20 percent of the actual urban residents.

In the 2002 survey, the CHIP project for the first time included a subsurvey of 2,000 migrant households. Table 2.6 presents the levels, composition, and distribution of income among migrants in 2002 (Khan and Riskin 2005). In terms of per capita total household income, migrants' average of ¥6,365 was nearly double that of those in the rural areas (¥3,205), but only two-thirds that of urban residents (¥10,333). Moreover, migrants' income is more unequally distributed (Gini = 0.38) than that of either full-status urban residents (0.35) or rural residents (0.37).

The leading component (60 percent) of migrant income was derived from individual enterprises. Wage income provided an additional third, while rental value of owner-occupied housing in total income (5 percent) and other income (including pensions) (2 percent) provided the balance. Among these income components, rental value of owner-occupied housing was the most disequalizing item; its concentration ratio was 0.658, much higher than the Gini (0.38). This reflects the fact that only a very small advantaged group of migrants own their homes in the cities where they currently reside. Rental value contributes about 9 percent of overall migrant income inequality. The other two disequalizing income sources were income from individual enterprises and "other income," the concentration ratios of which were somewhat higher than the Gini (0.43 for income from individual enterprises and 0.41 for "other income"). Income from individual enterprises, the main in-

TABLE 2.6

*Composition and distribution of income of rural migrants in 2002*

| | Level (¥) | Composition (%) | Gini/concentration ratio | Contribution to overall inequality (%) |
|---|---|---|---|---|
| Wages | 2,189 | 34.40 | 0.250 | 22.63 |
| Individual enterprise | 3,758 | 59.04 | 0.429 | 66.65 |
| Property | 8 | 0.29 | 0.189 | 0.14 |
| Net subsidies | −60 | −0.95 | 0.208 | −0.52 |
| Rental value of housing | 311 | 4.88 | 0.658 | 8.45 |
| Other (including pensions) | 149 | 2.34 | 0.408 | 2.51 |
| Total income | 6,365 | 100.0 | 0.380 | 100.0 |

SOURCE: Khan and Riskin (2005, p. 373). Column 4 calculated by authors based on figures in columns 2 and 3.

come source for migrants, contributed two-thirds of overall inequality, while "other income" accounted for only 3 percent of it. Wages were the main equalizing item, contributing only 23 percent of overall inequality despite their 34 percent share of total income.

The "net subsidies" received by migrant families (equal to subsidies received less taxes and fees paid) were negative ¥60 on average (1 percent of total income), indicating that taxes and fees paid by migrants exceeded any sums they received from the government. This net tax was distributed regressively, with a concentration ratio of 0.21, much lower than the overall Gini (0.38).

Our calculations from the CHIP migrant data show that migrants received minimal social benefits in 2002. Less than 5 percent of the migrant sample received pension benefits, or health or unemployment insurance. The CHIP survey did not ask about the exact values of most kinds of benefits, perhaps on the general assumption that they did not exist for migrants. Fewer than 8 percent of migrants enjoyed housing benefits from their employers. Note that even if housing is provided to migrants, as in the case of construction sites or rooms for live-in nannies, the quality of such housing is likely to be lower than that of full-status urban residents and attaching a value to it would be very difficult. Migrants were also ineligible for the MLSA subsidy due to residency requirements (Gao 2006). Therefore, the redistributive role of social benefits among the migrants is negligible.

## CONCLUSION AND DISCUSSION

This chapter has examined the contributions of market income and social benefits to overall income inequality in urban and rural areas to advance current debates about the degree and causes of income inequality since China moved from a planned to a market economy. Using all three waves of the CHIP survey data, we find that urban income inequality increased significantly from 1988 to 1995, and rose again very slightly to 2002, while rural inequality rose rapidly between 1988 and 1995, and then declined to a level below 1995 but above 1988 by 2002. The difference between these results and those of Khan and Riskin (2005) is primarily in the findings about urban China and the additional new findings on migrants in 2002.

In regard to the urban trends, we find that our differences from the Khan and Riskin (2005) analysis is due entirely to our inclusion of health benefits, which became highly unequal by 2002. Health benefits, which used to be universal for urban workers, have been increasingly linked to employment status, sector, and type. Those with higher market earnings from better employment also gain more from health benefits.

We also find that the cash value of urban social benefits has become more unequally distributed than market income and therefore displays higher Gini coefficients than those for total income. Between 1988 and 1995 benefits fell as share of income but increased slightly in 2002 because of higher concentration ratios. Initially market income primarily in the form of wages drove the new patterns of inequality. Wage income rose relative to total income and became increasingly unequal. But the effect was offset in 2002 by the decline in inequality of rental value of owner-occupied housing. Over time urban social benefits have had an uneven effect. Cash transfers, particularly public assistance, turned from largely regressive in the early stages of the reform to slightly progressive more recently, whereas in-kind benefits with the exception of in-kind housing subsidy were distributed more and more regressively over time and contributed to the rise in overall inequality.

In rural China, overall income inequality decreased from 1995 to 2002, after a sharp increase from 1988 to 1995. In contrast to urban China, market income from wages reduced inequality as did even more equally distributed income from family farm production. Other income sources, including income from nonfarm production, property, remittances, and rental value of owner-occupied housing, were disequalizing from 1995 to 2002. Rural social benefits remained minimal since the economic reforms and did not play any significant role in changing income inequality. If anything, the level of cash transfers increased slightly over time but became more regressive. Finally we should note that rural taxes were reduced after 1995 and were distributed less regressively, contributing to the fall in rural inequality.

Among rural to urban migrants, income inequality by 2002 was greater than among either urban or rural families. Income from individual enterprises was disequalizing and contributed about two-thirds of overall inequality. Rental value of owner-occupied housing was the most disequalizing item, reflecting the fact that only a very small and privileged group among the migrants enjoys home ownership in the cities. On the other hand, wages were an equalizing item. Migrant families received only minimal social benefits which thus had no significant effect on overall income inequality.

As expected, "market forces" have driven the major trends in income inequality. However, public policy has also influenced outcomes. For example, policies that deliberately privileged coastal areas increased inequality after the mid-1980s while others that created jobs in poor areas and reduced rural taxes reduced inequality. On the other hand, most social benefit programs with the exception of public assistance have been highly and increasingly disequalizing. Social benefits as a whole have yet to play a significant progressive role.

## CHAPTER THREE

# Market and Gender Pay Equity: Have Chinese Reforms Narrowed the Gap?

*Philip N. Cohen and Wang Feng*

In the process of creating wealth and poverty, China has also simultaneously created a new social and economic structure under which rewards and penalties are assigned. One important component of the changing social structure is the relationship between men and women. Pursuing gender equality was one of the main goals and achievements under socialism, but it is no longer high on the policy agenda of the postsocialist state.[1] Instead, allocation of resources and rewards is increasingly left to the economic market, which many presume will result in more efficient allocation of resources as well as a greater degree of equality in the long run. Almost three decades after the start of China's transition away from the socialist planned economy, the time has come for assessing changes in gender equality.

Gender inequality manifests in numerous forms, and changes in gender dynamics should not be generalized in a simplistic way (Whyte 2000). The focus of this chapter is economic inequality, as seen in reported income inequality at work, among China's officially registered urban population.[2] We first examine the trajectory of gender income inequality, and then ask what role the emerging market economy has in the development of this inequality, as seen in income trends on the one hand, and variation between cities at different levels of market development on the other.

The market transition, as it has been called, does not necessarily increase or decrease the level of inequality (Parish and Michelson 1996; Walder 1996). Instead, it alters the context of the production and reproduction of inequality, which in turn results in changes in the level and trends in inequality. Although we will show growing gender inequality in China, several Eastern European countries provide a counterexample, in which market reforms did not result in worsening gender income inequality, in part because educational and occupational advantages women accrued under socialism were more highly rewarded after market reforms (Heyns 2005).

Chinese society at the turn of the twenty-first century presents an ideal setting to examine the role of economic change in gender inequality. Economic reforms have resulted in the coexistence of an emerging private sector and the older, state-owned economic organizations. This hybrid provides almost a natural experiment for comparing inequality patterns between two economic sectors in the same society during the same historical period. In other words, it allows us to observe the legacy of a socialist stratification regime and to detect the emergence of a new system of gender inequality in the market economy. The remaining state sector in China, while operating differently now than it did during the Mao years, in some respects still represents the legacy of that system. China's transition in the last two decades thus provides an opportunity to reexamine the old claims that the socialist state offers better protection for women and the new claims that the market is a more equitable adjudicator. Such claims would be supported if in the recently created non-state-owned sectors there is less gender discrimination.

This chapter is organized as the follows: first, we present trends in income inequality over a fifteen-year period, between 1986 and 2000. Second, we examine the role of the emerging market by focusing on gender differences within three important contexts of gender economic inequality: ownership sectors, occupations, and industries. Third, we use data from a cross-section of cities in 1999, taking advantage of variations across the country in the role of the market economy. Finally, we discuss the implications of our analysis for a comparative understanding of gender inequality.

ONE- AND ONE-HALF DECADES OF GENDER INEQUALITY

In contrast to the general consensus that there have been steep increases in income inequality in urban China after 1980 (e.g., Chapter 2 in this volume), there is no agreement with regard to changes in economic gender inequality. Using multiprovince survey data collected for urban China in 1988 and 1995, for instance, Shu and Bian (2003) find "no longitudinal change nor city-level variation in the gender gap in earnings." At the same time, however, they report increased educational and occupational segregation during this time period, and note that such changes are, "occurring largely only in the most marketized cities" (1107). This suggests a market-driven increase in economic gender inequality, which is consistent with the evidence we present below.

We use data from China's annual Urban Household Income and Expenditure Survey, conducted by China's National Bureau of Statistics. Specifically, we use survey data for the urban population in three provinces: Liaoning, Sichuan, and Guangdong. This dataset contains over 4,000 urban employees for each year from more than 2,500 urban households scattered across more than two dozen cities in these provinces.

Among urban Chinese employees in the three provinces, there has been a clear trend toward worsening gender inequality in income. In Figure 3.1 we present trends in the gender income penalty between 1986 and 2000, in

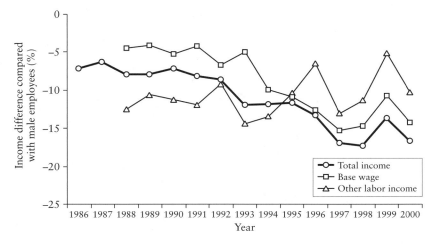

*Figure 3.1.* Gender penalty in income, urban China, 1986–2000 (adjusted)

terms of percentage difference between female and male urban employees in annual income. The pay inequality trends plotted in this figure are based on statistical analyses that control a number of commonly seen factors of income determination and can be viewed as the "net" effect of gender discrimination in income. It is "net" only in the sense that this difference is the income disadvantage for women compared with men with the *same* seniority, *same* educational attainment, holding the *same* position (occupation), and working in the *same* industries.[3]

In less than a decade's time, the net gender penalty in income rose from 7.3 percent in 1986 to 12 percent by 1993. It increased further in the late 1990s, to over 15 percent in most years.[4] Whereas there has always been a gap in the degree of gender penalty between base wages and other labor income, with the latter being twice or more than the former, the degree of deterioration in gender equality is more noticeable in base wages, over which the state used to exert a direct influence in promising women the same pay as men in the same jobs. Prior to 1993, in areas over which the socialist state had more direct influence, namely in basic wages and salaries, the gender gap was only around 5 percent after controlling for other factors. This represents a decent record of gender economic equality—though not a perfect one, given the government's promise of equal work, equal pay. After 1993, the gap in this income source suddenly enlarged, to as large as 15 percent, contributing directly to the overall worsening in gender equality in income in the 1990s.[5] Increasing inequality in this income source indicates a shift toward a hands-off policy by the state with regard to gender equality in the workplace; it also contains the effect of an economic reorganization by which an increasing share of the urban labor force is now employed in non-state-owned organizations.

CHANGING CONTEXTS OF INEQUALITY

Inequality is an outcome of socially and economically structured processes. Institutions, not individuals, structure and sustain inequality. Individuals participate in the process of generating and maintaining inequalities as social actors in accordance with their personal interests and preferences (Killingsworth 1983). But individual actions alone, if not organized and institutionalized, hardly matter in the long run for creating and sustaining inequalities (Tilly 1998). This is particularly the case with the most long-lasting and permeating form of inequality in all human societies: the inequality between men and women (England 1992). Thus, understanding the economic and institutional contexts of gender and work is crucial. To place the worsening gender income inequality of postsocialist urban China in its proper context, we briefly describe the gender composition of ownership sectors, occupations, and industries.[6]

Under the socialist planned economy, the state-owned sector was privileged over the collectively owned and private sectors, with better rewards for employees (Naughton 1997; Wang 2008). Throughout the decade of our study, women consistently outnumbered men in the collectively owned sector of the economy, where average incomes were 20 to 30 percent below the overall mean. In contrast, the sector that had the highest average income was that labeled "joint-venture," in which average incomes were 40 to 80 percent higher than the overall mean—and in which women held a declining share of positions over the 1990s. The changing gender composition across economic sectors provides a glimpse into the emerging new contexts of gender inequality in the economy.

Gender segregation across sectors contrasts with occupational segregation (Bauer et al. 1992), which in China is low by international standards, and remained relatively constant over the 1990s. Based on broad occupational categories, only 15 to 17 percent of men or women would have to change occupations to achieve an equal gender distribution. In comparison, we calculate the U.S. level of segregation in 2003, based on 10 major occupation groups, at 45 percent (U.S. Bureau of Labor Statistics 2005). Detailed examination of major occupations shows that women were especially underrepresented among senior engineers and professionals, and low- and middle-level government officials (cadres)—the three occupations with the highest average incomes.

Finally, gender segregation by industry is persistent in urban China. Chinese reforms have led to a drastic industrial reorganization, with industries favored under the planned socialist industrialization (such as manufacturing and mining) no longer paying premium wages, while others (such as banking, telecommunication, and real estate) have gained prominence. Women remain concentrated in health and social welfare services—in which incomes fell to below the overall average in the second half of the 1990s—and under-represented in science and technology. The science sector had no more than 40 percent female workers by the late 1990s, and workers there had incomes more than 20 percent higher than the national average.

In some ways, this picture of economic gender segregation is familiar to those who study gender inequality across societies, with concentrations of women in lower-paid, lower-status positions—albeit with less segregation than was seen in capitalist market economies. However the emerging segregation by ownership sector is particularly interesting given women's low representation in the highest-paid sector of joint-venture businesses. In the next section, we assess the effect of this segregation on the income gap between men and women.

HAVE MARKET REFORMS WIDENED THE GAP?

At the end of the 1990s, following two decades of economic reforms and the evident rise in gender economic inequality, how can structure or context be used to explain increasing inequality? In particular, while gender pay in-equality has increased over the course of market reforms, have these reforms themselves changed the structure of gender pay inequality?

To address these questions, we turn to a larger dataset, a survey of urban households in China's 35 largest cities conducted in 1999 by China's National Bureau of Statistics. This survey included all provincial capital cities of China, plus a selected few other large cities that experienced rapid economic growth, such as Shenzhen, Xiamen, Qingdao, and Dalian. The sample consists of 150,251 individuals from 48,801 urban households, of which about 65,000 individuals are currently employed and are used in our analyses of income inequality. In this section, we focus on the effects of ownership sector, occupation, and industry contexts on gender inequality. In the next section, we examine the effect of market economy development by modeling city-level variation.

*Ownership Sector, Occupation, and Industry*

Results from the national survey of large cities mostly confirm the gender segregation patterns described in the previous section based on data from three Chinese provinces. As shown in Table 3.1, women are overrepresented in the collectively owned sector, which also has the lowest mean earnings of all sectors. Similarly, women are seriously underrepresented in the high-paying

TABLE 3.1
*Descriptive statistics, urban household survey, 1999*

| | N | % | MONTHLY INCOME (RMB YUAN) | | % Female |
| --- | --- | --- | --- | --- | --- |
| | | | Mean | S.D. | |
| **Educational attainment** | | | | | |
| University | 6,873 | 10.5 | 1,157 | 1,308 | 35.1 |
| 3-Year college | 10,971 | 16.8 | 996 | 1,679 | 44.9 |
| Vocational school | 6,860 | 10.5 | 853 | 2,491 | 51.0 |
| Senior high school | 17,666 | 27.1 | 797 | 1,482 | 45.5 |
| Junior high school | 19,055 | 29.2 | 701 | 1,193 | 41.2 |
| Elementary school | 3,305 | 5.1 | 612 | 609 | 46.0 |
| Other | 493 | 0.8 | 605 | 760 | 56.0 |
| **Ownership sector** | | | | | |
| State | 41,276 | 63.3 | 811 | 752 | 41.8 |
| Collective | 6,469 | 9.9 | 567 | 595 | 55.6 |
| Other organization | 3,837 | 5.9 | 1,123 | 1,094 | 47.2 |
| Individual/owner | 6,999 | 10.7 | 1,184 | 4,050 | 41.9 |
| Individual/employee | 4,592 | 7.0 | 710 | 1,105 | 43.8 |
| Post-retirement hire | 639 | 1.0 | 1,056 | 752 | 43.5 |
| Other | 1,411 | 2.2 | 574 | 1,004 | 45.8 |
| **Occupation** | | | | | |
| High level official | 176 | 0.3 | 1,351 | 627 | 7.4 |
| Mid-level official | 1,779 | 2.7 | 1,227 | 1,315 | 17.3 |
| Low-level official | 4,038 | 6.2 | 1,048 | 921 | 29.1 |
| Senior professional | 1,498 | 2.3 | 1,197 | 1,165 | 31.4 |
| Mid-level professional | 4,348 | 6.7 | 1,069 | 1,346 | 43.2 |
| Low-level professional | 3,069 | 4.7 | 909 | 794 | 55.2 |
| Technician | 4,566 | 7.0 | 888 | 1,054 | 48.5 |
| Staff members | 9,533 | 14.6 | 873 | 929 | 49.0 |
| Commerce/service workers | 13,955 | 21.4 | 790 | 1,961 | 55.5 |
| Agriculture related workers | 227 | 0.3 | 770 | 746 | 42.7 |
| Industrial workers | 19,484 | 29.9 | 663 | 1,598 | 37.0 |
| Military personnel | 319 | 0.5 | 1,010 | 461 | 13.8 |
| Other | 2,231 | 3.4 | 790 | 2,783 | 44.6 |
| **Industry** | | | | | |
| Agriculture related | 532 | 0.8 | 782 | 751 | 37.8 |
| Mining | 245 | 0.4 | 725 | 727 | 36.3 |
| Manufacturing | 16,783 | 25.7 | 667 | 920 | 41.9 |
| Power, gas and water supply | 1,743 | 2.7 | 897 | 550 | 33.6 |
| Construction | 2,501 | 3.8 | 888 | 1,251 | 27.5 |
| Geological survey/water management | 484 | 0.7 | 726 | 513 | 33.1 |
| Transportation/telecommunication | 6,004 | 9.2 | 971 | 1,514 | 30.6 |
| Commerce, food services | 13,602 | 20.9 | 854 | 2,661 | 52.5 |
| Banking, insurance | 1,878 | 2.9 | 1,133 | 879 | 50.5 |
| Real estate | 694 | 1.1 | 1,123 | 900 | 38.0 |
| Social services | 4,711 | 7.2 | 784 | 879 | 48.9 |
| Health, social welfare | 2,585 | 4.0 | 861 | 564 | 61.8 |
| Education and media | 4,657 | 7.1 | 903 | 839 | 53.7 |
| Science research | 1,832 | 2.8 | 1,023 | 1,437 | 37.2 |
| Party, government, other organization | 4,825 | 7.4 | 949 | 682 | 33.5 |
| Other | 2,147 | 3.3 | 757 | 1,952 | 43.6 |
| **Total** | 65,223 | | | | 43.7 |

occupations of officials and are overrepresented in low-level professionals and service workers, which are among the lowest-paid occupations. Women are overrepresented in food service industries and in social welfare services, which are low-paying industries.

The relationship between gender composition and average monthly earnings by sector, occupation, and industry is shown by the scatterplot in Figure 3.2. Occupation shows the clearest relationship between gender and earnings ($r = -.72$), followed by sector ($r = -.50$); industry shows no overall correlation. In addition, not shown in this figure, we also observe a disparity in educational attainment by gender. Among urban Chinese, the ratio of university-educated employees between men and women is roughly two to one.

Ownership sector, occupation, and industry all serve as important contexts for gender pay inequality at the turn of the twenty-first century in urban China. Across the board, female urban Chinese employees earned 22 percent less than their male counterparts. This is shown in the first model of Table 3.2, which presents results of regression analysis, using the natural log of income as the dependent variable (the regression coefficients can be read as roughly the percentage difference in income). When variables representing the contexts of gender income stratification are introduced into the analysis, we observe that combined they reduce the magnitude of the female pay penalty by about 22 percent, from $-.2198$ (Model 1) to $-.1735$ (Model 6). In other words, about one-fifth of the overall gender inequality in income can be accounted for by ownership sector, occupation, industry, and personal characteristics such as age and educational attainment.

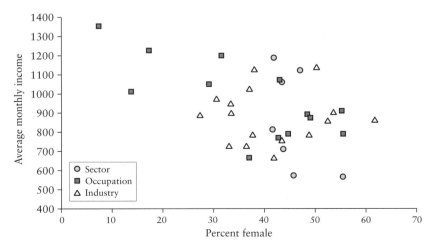

*Figure 3.2.* Gender composition and average income, by sector, occupation, and industry, urban China, 1999

TABLE 3.2

*Effects of gender and other factors on income, urban China, 1999 (OLS results, Ln income)*

| | MODEL 1 | | MODEL 2 | | MODEL 3 | | MODEL 4 | | MODEL 5 | | MODEL 6 | |
|---|---|---|---|---|---|---|---|---|---|---|---|---|
| | b | s.d. | b | s.d. | b | s.d. | b | s.d. | b | s.d. | b | s.d. |
| Female | -.220 | .006 | -.208 | .005 | -.194 | .005 | -.215 | .005 | -.179 | .005 | -.174 | .005 |
| Age | .012 | .002 | .020 | .002 | .031 | .002 | .022 | .002 | .034 | .002 | .027 | .002 |
| Agesqrd | -.00008 | .00002 | -.00016 | .00002 | -.00028 | .00002 | -.00022 | .00002 | -.00034 | .00002 | -.00028 | .00002 |
| **Education (university=reference)** | | | | | | | | | | | | |
| 3-year college | — | | -.135 | .010 | -.133 | .010 | -.084 | .011 | -.082 | .011 | -.064 | .010 |
| Vocational school | — | | -.248 | .012 | -.238 | .011 | -.144 | .012 | -.126 | .012 | -.132 | .011 |
| Senior high school | — | | -.385 | .010 | -.380 | .009 | -.206 | .012 | -.188 | .011 | -.188 | .010 |
| Junior high school | — | | -.520 | .009 | -.524 | .010 | -.307 | .012 | -.294 | .012 | -.275 | .011 |
| Elementary school | — | | -.659 | .014 | -.695 | .015 | -.431 | .017 | -.446 | .016 | -.439 | .015 |
| Other | — | | -.742 | .032 | -.777 | .031 | -.515 | .033 | -.529 | .032 | -.497 | .029 |
| **Ownership sector (state ownership = reference)** | | | | | | | | | | | | |
| Collective | — | | — | | -.252 | .009 | — | | -.194 | .009 | -.209 | .008 |
| Other organization | — | | — | | .304 | .011 | — | | .351 | .011 | .248 | .010 |
| Individual/owner | — | | — | | .254 | .009 | — | | .333 | .011 | .347 | .010 |
| Individual/employee | — | | — | | .005 | .011 | — | | .061 | .011 | .063 | .010 |
| Post-retirement hire | — | | — | | .293 | .028 | — | | .374 | .027 | .430 | .025 |
| Other | — | | — | | -.243 | .018 | — | | -.145 | .019 | -.142 | .018 |
| **Occupation (high-level official = reference)** | | | | | | | | | | | | |
| Mid-level official | — | | — | | — | | -.092 | .052 | -.093 | .050 | -.135 | .046 |
| Low-level official | — | | — | | — | | -.173 | .051 | -.174 | .049 | -.261 | .045 |
| Senior professional | — | | — | | — | | -.124 | .053 | -.130 | .051 | -.170 | .047 |
| Mid-level professional | — | | — | | — | | -.198 | .051 | -.211 | .050 | -.273 | .045 |

| | (1) | | (2) | | (3) | | (4) | | (5) | | (6) | |
|---|---|---|---|---|---|---|---|---|---|---|---|---|
| Low-level professional | — | | — | | — | | −.245 | .052 | −.260 | .050 | −.339 | .046 |
| Technician | — | | — | | — | | −.245 | .051 | −.252 | .050 | −.376 | .046 |
| Staff members | — | | — | | — | | −.248 | .051 | −.273 | .049 | −.388 | .045 |
| Commerce/service workers | — | | — | | — | | −.365 | .051 | −.469 | .050 | −.564 | .046 |
| Agriculture related workers | — | | — | | — | | −.346 | .068 | −.301 | .068 | −.480 | .062 |
| Industrial workers | — | | — | | — | | −.487 | .051 | −.439 | .050 | −.519 | .045 |
| Military personnel | — | | — | | — | | −.220 | .062 | −.162 | .060 | −.204 | .055 |
| Other | — | | — | | — | | −.497 | .053 | −.493 | .052 | −.524 | .047 |
| Industry (agriculture related = reference) | | | | | | | | | | | | |
| Mining | — | | — | | — | | — | | .044 | .051 | .076 | .047 |
| Manufacturing | — | | — | | — | | — | | −.034 | .031 | −.055 | .028 |
| Power, gas and water supply | — | | — | | — | | — | | .234 | .034 | .240 | .031 |
| Construction | — | | — | | — | | — | | .098 | .033 | .064 | .030 |
| Geological survey/water management | — | | — | | — | | — | | −.023 | .042 | .025 | .038 |
| Transportation/telecommunication | — | | — | | — | | — | | .276 | .032 | .242 | .029 |
| Commerce, food services | — | | — | | — | | — | | .057 | .032 | .017 | .029 |
| Banking, insurance | — | | — | | — | | — | | .321 | .034 | .273 | .031 |
| Real estate | — | | — | | — | | — | | .311 | .039 | .199 | .036 |
| Social services | — | | — | | — | | — | | .083 | .032 | .037 | .030 |
| Health, social welfare | — | | — | | — | | — | | .120 | .033 | .122 | .030 |
| Education and media | — | | — | | — | | — | | .088 | .032 | .088 | .029 |
| Science research | — | | — | | — | | — | | .088 | .034 | .072 | .031 |
| Party, gov., other organization | — | | — | | — | | — | | .097 | .032 | .082 | .029 |
| Other | — | | — | | — | | — | | −.020 | .035 | −.035 | .032 |
| Constant | 6.283 | .036 | 6.417 | .036 | 6.158 | .037 | 6.625 | .060 | 6.246 | .067 | 6.762 | .062 |
| City | | | | | | | | | | | Yes | |
| Adjusted $R^2$ | .032 | | .105 | | .145 | | .124 | | .183 | | .321 | |
| N | 63167 | | | | | | | | | | | |

Results in Table 3.2 also allow an examination of the effects of various contexts and factors separately. In Model 2, results show a clear and positive association between educational attainment and income. Employees with less than a senior high school education, who account for about one-third of the urban Chinese labor force, suffered at least a 50 percent pay penalty compared with those who have university educations. Results in Model 3 report the effects of ownership sector. In comparison to those in the state-owned sector, employees in collectively owned organizations made 25 percent less income in 1999, whereas those in "other organizations" (mostly joint-venture) or who were owners of private businesses reported 25 to 35 percent higher income. There is no statistically significant difference in income between those in the state sector (reference group) and those who are employees in privately owned businesses. Adding ownership sector does not have any noticeable effect on the role of educational attainment, but it did reduce the overall gender penalty by about 13 percent (from −.2198 to −.1943). Adding occupational context (Model 4) reveals the expected occupational differences in income, but it does not change the magnitude of the gender penalty. Model 5 includes all three contexts: ownership type, occupation, and industry. Combined, they reduce the overall gender penalty by about 23 percent (from −.2198 to −.1791). The last model, Model 6, introduces cities as dummy variables. Adding this factor significantly increases the overall explanatory power of the model ($R^2$ increases from .18 to .32), but does not alter significantly the magnitude of the gender penalty compared with Model 5.

A central question, raised at the start of this chapter, is the emerging structure of gender inequality following China's economic transitions. Specifically, we seek to address this question by examining the relative role of the state versus that of the market in reproducing gender income inequality. Following two decades of economic reforms, was the Chinese state still playing a protective role with regard to income equality between women and men? Or, was the newly created market sector more gender blind, governed mostly by the criteria of efficiency and merit? We do not have direct and ideal measures for the state or market, but we can explore answers to these questions by modeling the interaction effects between gender and ownership sectors. If the Chinese state continues to serve as a protective force, we would expect a weaker gender penalty in this sector than in other sectors. Alternatively, if the newly emerged market sector is less gender discriminatory, we would expect a smaller gender penalty in this sector.

China's emerging market economy is by no means gender blind. Moreover, the emerging market sectors do not discriminate against female employees any less. In Table 3.3, we provide regression results to examine the two alternative hypotheses raised in the paragraph above. When interaction

TABLE 3.3
*Effect of gender on income by sector, urban China, 1999*

|  | MODEL 1 | | MODEL 2 | |
|---|---|---|---|---|
|  | *b* | *s.d.* | *b* | *s.d.* |
| Female | −.194 | .005 | −.147 | .007 |
| Age | .031 | .002 | .030 | .002 |
| Age$^2$ | −.000 | .000 | −.000 | .000 |
| Education (university = reference) | | | | |
| 3-year college | −.133 | .010 | −.136 | .010 |
| Vocational school | −.238 | .011 | −.242 | .011 |
| Senior high school | −.380 | .009 | −.381 | .009 |
| Junior high school | −.524 | .010 | −.524 | .010 |
| Elementary school | −.695 | .015 | −.692 | .015 |
| Other | −.777 | .031 | −.763 | .031 |
| Sector (state ownership = reference) | | | | |
| Collective | −.252 | .009 | −.188 | .013 |
| Other organization | .304 | .011 | .326 | .015 |
| Individual/owner | .254 | .009 | .323 | .012 |
| Individual/employee | .005 | .011 | .067 | .014 |
| Post-retirement hire | .293 | .028 | .318 | .037 |
| Other | −.243 | .018 | −.183 | .025 |
| Female * sector interactions (state ownership = reference) | | | | |
| Collective | | | −.128 | .018 |
| Other organization | | | −.052 | .022 |
| Individual/owner | | | −.170 | .018 |
| Individual/employee | | | −.146 | .021 |
| Post-retirement hire | | | −.078 | .053 |
| Other | | | −.138 | .036 |
| Constant | 6.158 | .037 | 6.153 | .037 |
| Adjusted R$^2$ | .145 | | .147 | |
| N | 63167 | | 63167 | |

terms are added to the model, as shown in Model 2 of Table 3.3, the market sectors that in general provided higher incomes (as seen in Model 1 of Table 3.3, as well as in Model 2, as "main effects") also did so more for men than for women. Among all sectors of the economy, those in the state-owned sector suffered the least gender penalty. Whereas women as well as men in the emerging private sectors mostly enjoyed higher incomes than those in the state-owned sector, and especially more than those in the collective sector, the gender difference is smallest in the state-owned sector. Compared with employees in the state-owned sector, the gender pay gap between women and men is about 5 percent more pronounced for those working in joint-venture companies ("other organization"). The gender penalty is especially noticeable for those listed as private business owners or employees, where the difference from those in the state-owned sector is 17 and nearly

15 percent respectively. Our results therefore suggest that among the sectors of the existing mixed economy, the state sector is the least discriminatory.

### Market Development and Gender Inequity

Because market economy development has been uneven across China, we can take advantage of regional variation to further examine how China's development pattern might be associated with gender inequality (Shu 2005; Shu and Bian 2003). We assess the pattern of inequality across 31 of the cities in the 1999 data (four cities were excluded because of missing data). This analysis takes an explicitly contextual approach, in that local development levels and patterns are used to model gender inequality for *all* workers in the sample, not only those directly employed by, for example, joint-venture organizations.

We combine data collected on individual workers, used in the regression analysis above, with published statistics on population size, the size of the economy (per capita gross domestic product), per capita foreign direct investment, and the recent rate of economic growth (1998 GDP per capita divided by 1992 GDP per capita). Local GDP per capita is a good indicator of development, and given the rapid pace of urban development in the postsocialist period, the change from 1992 to 1998 may adequately identify those cities with steeper or less-steep development trajectories. Further, foreign direct investment (FDI) may be associated with different employment practices positively or negatively related to gender inequality.[7] As a test of the structural arguments outlined above, then, we model variation in the effect of being female across cities as a function of these city characteristics.

As these data are logically nested—individual workers within cities— we use two-level hierarchical linear models (Raudenbush and Bryk 2002). Conceptually, hierarchical linear models (HLM) are similar to estimating the linear regressions above separately for each city, and then examining the variation in the 31 model intercepts and gender coefficients that result. However, these models fix the effects of the control variables across cities. They also permit us to decompose the variance in incomes into that which occurs within cities (between individuals), and that which occurs between city means.[8]

One of the unique utilities of the models we employ here is that we can decompose the total variance in income into variance between cities (i.e., in the intercept, $\tau_0$) and within cities—the individual-level variance, $\sigma^2$ (Raudenbush and Bryk 2002). We show in Table 3.4 the proportion of the variance in income that occurs between cities, labeled as the intra-class correlation. From a fully unconditional model (not shown), we calculate an intra-class correlation of 11.9 percent. This finding is substantively important, because it reveals the extent to which incomes vary *between* rather than

TABLE 3.4
*Hierarchical linear models for total income (Ln) on individual and city characteristics*

|  | (1) | (2) | (3) | (4) | (5) | (6) |
|---|---|---|---|---|---|---|
| Intercept | 6.570*** | 6.566*** | 6.542*** | 6.567*** | 6.543*** | 6.543*** |
| Population (Ln) | — | — | — | .019 | .032 | .021 |
| GDP / capita (Ln) | — | — | — | .403*** | .397*** | .548*** |
| FDI / capita (Ln) | — | — | — | −.005 | .002 | −.013 |
| GDP growth 1992–98 | — | — | — | — | — | −.081* |
| Gender wage effect | −.227*** | −.215*** | −.168*** | −.218*** | −.169*** | −.169*** |
| Population (Ln) | — | — | — | .024*** | .011 | .011 |
| GDP / capita (Ln) | — | — | — | −.068** | −.051* | −.043+ |
| FDI / capita (Ln) | — | — | — | .015* | .016* | .015* |
| GDP growth 1992–98 | — | — | — | — | — | −.004 |
| Level-1 controls | None | Age only | All | Age only | All | All |
| Variance components |  |  |  |  |  |  |
| Intercept ($\tau_0$) | .047 | .046 | .049 | .019 | .019 | .017 |
| Female | .0009 | .0008 | .0004 | .0002 | .0002 | .0003 |
| Level-1 variance ($\sigma^2$) | .328 | .326 | .256 | .326 | .256 | .256 |
| Intra-class correlation | 12.4% | 12.3% | 16.0% | 5.4% | 7.0% | 6.1% |

+ $p < .10$; * $p < .05$; ** $p < .01$; *** $p < .001$ (two-tailed tests).

within cities. For example, in the United States, the intra-class correlation for income across metropolitan areas in 1990 was much lower, only 4 percent (Cohen and Huffman 2003). In China, therefore, it matters much more than in the United States what city a worker lives in, regardless of his or her other characteristics—reflecting the radically uneven nature of China's development and a pattern of inequality that is based on group membership (Wang and Wang 2007). Further, these intercity differences persist when individual characteristics are controlled (Model 3), with 16 percent of the remaining variance in income occurring between cities.

If what city one lives in is of paramount consequence for Chinese workers, how does this extreme variation affect women and gender inequality? The bottom panel of Table 3.4 shows that one-half of the cross-city variance in the effect of gender is explained by all the individual controls (Model 3 versus Model 2). However, a significant amount of variance remains.[9] Before discussing how the models predict that variance, let us illustrate the "net" gender gap in income across cities. Figure 3.3 shows the income gap between men and women (expressed by women's income as a percentage of men's income), derived from empirical Bayes estimates of the intercept and level-1 gender coefficient for each city, net of individual-level controls. We see that women have a high of 87.1 percent of men's income in Zhengzhou, and a low of less than 82 percent in Yinchuan and Fuzhou. In the figure, we plot

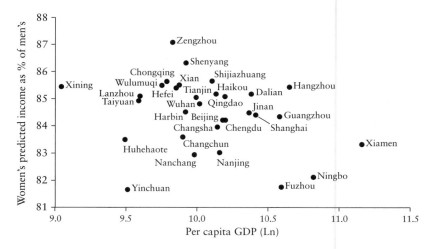

*Figure 3.3.* Gender gap in income, by city GDP (empirical Bayes estimates, with person-level controls[1])

NOTE: Data from 1999. Samples of 890–3,897 employed workers ages 18–70 per city.

[1]Controls include age, education, occupation, industry, and sector.

that gender gap against logged GDP per capita. The scatterplot suggests a negative relationship between economic development and women's relative income. It is interesting to note that three of the cities with high incomes and large gender gaps—Xiamen, Ningbo, and Fuzhou—are "special economic zones," areas slated by the central government for market-based reforms and outside investment.[10] The figure suggests that the level of economic development might help explain the pattern of gender inequality.

In the final three models we test whether the level of development (GDP), the nature of development (FDI), and the pace of development (GDP growth) are associated with the gender gap across cities, with population size as a control. The results are quite consistent across models. The strongest effect in the table is of GDP on the intercept. This shows that average incomes are dramatically higher in cities with larger GDP per capita. Of course, it is not surprising that incomes are higher in cities with higher per capita GDP, since GDP is essentially a measure of average income. However, the effect is almost unchanged when individual controls are added to the model (comparing Models 4 and 5). Thus, the advantage of living in more-developed cities does not occur only because workers there are more likely to have higher education or work in better occupations, industries, or sectors. (We note, however, that Model 6 shows that this effect is tempered in cities with rapidly growing economies, as there is a negative effect of GDP growth on the intercept.)

In addition to raising the overall income level, GDP is associated with greater gender inequality in income. The cross-level interactions show that women receive approximately 90 percent of men's benefit from higher local GDP. In Model 6, for every one unit increase in GDP, average income increases by .548 for men, but only .505 for women (.548–.043). The effect of FDI is different, however. Although it has no effect on the intercept, the models show that FDI is associated with a significantly smaller gender gap.

CONCLUSION

Postsocialist economic reforms in China have resulted in a clear reversal in one of the proudest accomplishments under socialism: pay equity between female and male urban employees. Economic reforms and economic growth have dramatically raised the standard of living of the urban Chinese population, but have done so unevenly, as economic inequality also increased substantially. Part of the overall increase in economic inequality is the income inequality between women and men. In our analyses of urban Chinese employees, we find that (1) the gender gap in income has increased sharply over recent years; (2) women are consistently more likely to work in lower-paid occupations, industries, and sectors of the economy; (3) the gender gap is smallest in the state sector; and (4) the gender gap is larger in more-developed cities. As a caveat, we note that the income gap is smaller in cities with higher levels of current foreign investment.

At the start of full-fledged economic reforms, female urban employees in China received on average about 15 percent less income than male employees. By the turn of the twenty-first century, the gap enlarged to about 25 percent. Some of this difference can be attributed to differences in individual and structural characteristics of the female and male employees. After taking into account gender differences in educational attainment, sector of employment, and occupational and industrial locations, the net gender income penalty showed a similar rising trend, from 7 percent to 17 percent. These increases in income inequality, while substantial, still place urban Chinese female employees in a more favorable position in comparison to female workers in other transitional societies, where the gap was as large as 37 to 51 percent (Domański 2002).

What also has emerged is a new structure of gender income inequality embedded in both the old and the new. A segregation and stratification regime created under the socialist planned economy persists and perhaps worsens. Women concentrate in the less-privileged economic sectors, lower-ranked occupations, and lower-paying industries. Gender segregation in the workplace by occupation and industry is not dissimilar to that in capitalist market economies, albeit at much lower levels.

What sets China apart from capitalist market economies is the coexistence of a remaining state sector and an emerging market sector, which structures the patterns of gender economic inequality. China's economic transition away from socialism has resulted in a hybrid economic system. By the end of the 1990s, nearly 30 percent of urban employees in major Chinese cities worked in nonstate and noncollectively owned sectors, in contrast to two decades ago, when nonpublic sector employment was virtually nonexistent. Our study shows that the remaining state sector still serves as the most benign and protective economic sector for women, at least regarding the gender gap in income. Such a pattern is also reported for the city of Moscow in Russia and in a number of settings in Eastern European transitional societies, such as the Czech Republic and Slovakia (Heyns 2005).

The newly emerged market sectors, contrary to the beliefs of some, are in fact also the ones where the gender income penalty is more extreme compared with the state-owned sector. Across major cities in China, locales with more vibrant economies and higher income levels on average also have greater gender income inequality. Overall, these results suggest that the creation of a market economy has not been accompanied by a lesser degree of gender economic inequality.

It is premature for us to draw conclusions from our results in this chapter about the mechanisms or processes that led to the gender inequality pattern we observe here. However, we consider some possibilities. Some scholars have suggested that capitalism, because it rewards rational and efficient, profit-driven decision making, is destined to undermine gender discrimination, which is based on ascriptive qualities and irrational biases (Jackson 1998). However, China has a cultural legacy of extreme gender inequality, which 30 years of socialist leadership could not hope to purge completely. Therefore, increasing gender inequality may reflect that underlying disposition toward gender discrimination, which is only becoming more freely expressed in the increasingly unregulated market. That argument would be consistent with our finding that the state sector has the lowest levels of gender discrimination.

Gender bias also could be expressed through an increasing tendency to relegate women to more nurturing roles, whether by families or by employers.[11] Increased economic uncertainty and less government assurance of support (albeit in the context of rising incomes) could have two effects on gender. Within urban families, some may be compelled to devote more of their own resources to household-based care work, for example taking care of sick family members. And in the urban labor market, a growing service economy—in the nonstate sector—could pull women into nurturing roles, where they earn lower incomes and have fewer opportunities for advancement. Our data are consistent with these explanations, but we do not have sufficient occupation and industry detail to test this possibility.

Finally, we note that in everyday life, the reproduction of gender inequality in income takes place in a more confined and concrete context, within jobs in specific establishments and labor markets. The inequality-generating mechanisms or contexts discussed above—local area, sector, occupation, and industry—only serve as the broad contours for capturing the overall structure of gender inequality. Ideally, we would be able to study patterns within specific establishments. However, without such data, we may create a proxy for jobs by examining groups of workers at the intersection of occupation by industry by city, as has been done for U.S. data (e.g., Cohen and Huffman 2003). One of the defining characteristics of China's emerging market economy is the large variation in local labor markets. Rates of foreign investment, employment, economic growth, and change in standard of living all vary dramatically from city to city. Incorporating such local contexts, especially at the job level, should constitute the next step in understanding the mechanisms of rising gender pay inequality in postsocialist urban China.

## CHAPTER FOUR

# The Labor of Luxury: Gender and Generational Inequality in a Beijing Hotel

*Eileen M. Otis*

China's urban employment structure has been transformed by a vast expansion of the service sector. In 1952 the service sector employed just over 9 percent of the urban population and over the next 25 years tertiary sector employment never exceeded 11 percent (China Labor Statistics Yearbook 2001:5). Since the beginning of economic reforms in 1979, however, urban tertiary sector employment has grown to 66 percent and generates almost one-third the national GDP (China Labor Statistics Yearbook 2005:119). The service sector is now the mainstay of new urban employment.[1]

This booming service sector is a locus of dramatic new inequalities forming in urban China. Not only does the service sector bifurcate into well-paying professional jobs and low-wage, low-skill jobs, but service sector employment also enforces fundamental social asymmetries between employees and customers as service employees display deference as a part of their employment (Hochschild 1983). To illustrate how such new modes of inequality form and become acceptable, even palatable, to workers, I apply an ethnographic microscope to organizational processes of labor segmentation in one Beijing luxury hotel. I compare three types of jobs: contract-based interactive jobs, contract-based manual jobs, and contingent custodial jobs.[2] Workers in these jobs labor side-by-side, but they experience profoundly divergent conditions of work, with dramatically different opportunity structures. This chapter untangles two conceptual knots regarding workplace inequalities: First, why do workers assent to new forms of workplace inequality, and second, why is gender central to defining work inequalities for some workers, but not others? The data show that a set of boundary-forming mechanisms bind workers by gender and generation to specific categories of work.

Job-boundary forming mechanisms are organizationally enforced, relationally defined meanings and values assigned to categories of people and types of work. Managers draw on assumptions that certain categories of workers embody skills, attributes, and dispositions that are appropriate to specific types of work. These assumptions become organizationally embedded logics that channel workers into job niches depending on their gender and generation. Once in these jobs, workers acquire different competencies and outlooks that naturalize the logic of job assignment. In other words, gender and generation become proxies for skills, attributes, and dispositions that are, in fact, acquired on the job.

As workplace boundaries are sustained through daily practice, they become a part of workers' sense of selfhood and dignity. Workers gain a stake in constructing and defending the gender and generational boundaries enclosing their work, even when those boundaries consign them to lower status and insecurity. Hence, these boundary-forming mechanisms explain how hierarchies of prestige, security, and remuneration solidify in the service workplace. The chapter sheds light on micro-organizational processes that limit occupational mobility and income of women and veteran workers laid off from state owned industries. In so doing, it unearths mechanisms of gender and generational inequality in urban China

## TRANSLUXURY HOTEL

The Beijing Transluxury[3] (hereafter BT) is a 300-room boutique hotel with a staff of 500 serving mostly Western businessmen. Affiliated with one of the largest hotel conglomerates in the world, BT is jointly owned and operated by the "Galaxy Corporation," and a central state ministry, that I will call "Beijing Inc."

As a "home away from home," luxury hotels manage virtually every dimension of "reproductive work" (Glenn 1999), developing a complex division of labor. "Front-of-the-house" positions, which involve working in the presence of hotel guests, include hostess, foodserver, bartender, butler, receptionist, concierge, housekeeper, banquet worker, bellman, security worker, and hairdressers. "Back-of-the-house" positions in which employees work mostly out of the sight of customers, include cook, launderer, housekeeper, custodian, dishwasher, administrator, and union personnel. This chapter focuses predominately on three types of jobs, which are highly segregated by gender and generation, with young women channeled into work that requires regular interaction with customers, young men performing manual labor, and middle-aged workers consigned to custodial labor.

A primary goal of the Transluxury hotels is to create a familiar atmosphere for Western travelers. Employees, most of whom are from working-class backgrounds, are explicitly tutored in hygienic practices, comportment, language, etiquette, and modes of interaction that management considers essential to win customer loyalty. However, in reproducing Western luxury service the BT relies on organizational strategies distinct to the Chinese setting and despite objections from Galaxy's home office, local management has insisted on continuing many of the personnel practices of Chinese state enterprises (Pearson 1992).

The Chinese Communist Party maintains a branch at the hotel. One manager simultaneously serves as leader of the party branch, director of security, head of the union, and chairman of the executive committee. The party convenes monthly meetings attended by administrative managers and higher-level middle management. Managers tend to view party membership in instrumental terms; advancement into high levels of management requires party membership.

In the Mao era, the union's role was to ensure worker compliance to the CCP, the state, and unit leaders; now the union works to organize activities that support hotel management. The branch leader of the union explained, "We [the union] help to realize management goals." The union does not hold meetings among its membership, but it does negotiate benefits and wages with the human resources department and the Galaxy Corporation.

In contrast to other hotels in China, the BT offers most workers two-year contracts, competitive wages, bonuses, health care, unemployment insurance, and housing subsidies. After serving an apprenticeship and a two-month probationary period, workers receive two-year contracts with a salary of 1,200 yuan per month ($150 U.S.). In 1999 the staff members formally attached to the hotel earned the equivalent of four additional months of salary in bonuses, and Beijing Inc. contributed half of each worker's salary to benefits. The workers' union organizes frequent entertainment, including parties for special occasions like festivals and birthdays, collective weddings, and trips to attend plays. Workers receive meals in the staff canteen, lockers, subsidized haircuts, and showers (which most would otherwise pay for at a local bathhouse). Middle managers enforce the family-planning policy, distributing condoms to sexually active female workers and also inquiring into their sexual activities.

Methods of recruiting staff also exhibit some continuity with the Mao-era work unit. In the Mao era, workers were assigned to factories upon graduation from school, and rural workers were, for the most part, excluded from urban employment (Whyte and Parish 1984). BT also confines recruitment to urban residents and has close ties to city schools. Eighty percent of frontline contract labor are graduates of one of the four nearby vocational schools that require all students to spend their third year in a hotel apprenticeship, during which time students receive one-third the normal starting wages, but continue to pay tuition. BT cherry picks the most promising graduates, and many students who interview are not hired.

The benefits and bonuses provided by the hotel, along with the prestige of the Galaxy Corporation, strengthen the managerial, union, and party "triad" of control. They also hold employees to their jobs. Thus, even though employees view service work as a low-status occupation, affiliation with a luxurious five-star hotel linked to a high-ranking central state ministry mitigates the social degradation of service. Most called the BT a good work unit.

## YOUNG AND EXTROVERTED

The vast majority of the front-of-the-house, contract staff members are between the ages of 17 and 27, working on two-year renewable contracts. Almost all live at home and turn their paychecks over to their parents in exchange for a monthly allowance. Many parents of workers once worked in state-owned factories and are now facing layoffs or salary cuts. The children often blame the rigid and inefficient state-run enterprise system for their parents' economic insecurity and accept the enterprise profit motive as a remedy for past inefficiencies as well as a legitimate rationale for the unequal mobility opportunities they personally experience at the BT.

Managers describe young workers as blank slates (*baizhi*), compliant, easily trained, and readily disciplined. The term *blank slate* suggests an implicit comparison with former factory workers whose history of dependence on the Mao-era enterprise is taken to be indelibly marked on their capacities. These older workers are widely viewed as slow and inflexible. By contrast, managers believe that young workers can be trained to be flexible, entrepreneurial, and efficient. One manager claimed that she trains her staff in the art of becoming "human beings."

With few attachments and responsibilities outside of work, young staff members readily adapt to the hotel's unpredictable scheduling and frequent demands for overtime. Young workers are considered strong, capable, and adaptable to changes in the workplace. When lapses in discipline occur, managers attribute them to immaturity (readily redressed by training and discipline). By contrast when middle-aged, "veteran" workers fail to meet work requirements, managers fault their poor work habits as deeply rooted in their former dependence on the socialist "iron rice bowl."

Managers develop caring if manipulative ties with their young workers. The managers, usually addressed as "older brother" or "older sister" by young staff, rarely penalize workers with formal misconduct slips and fines, preferring to iron out work problems individually. Managers socialize after work with employees, encouraging them to share personal problems. One worker compared her manager favorably to her own mother.

Managers frequently praised young workers for being proactive and socially gregarious with customers and each other. I discovered that these interventions enabled workers even to revalue their "poor" academic credentials and take pride in service. "I'm an extrovert," a young banquet worker announced to me in an interview. He elaborated:

> Just because you're a good student at school doesn't necessarily mean that you can become a good person in society. . . . I wasn't a good student but here I'm a much stronger worker than [other students]. I can speak, I dare to ask questions. Good students are introverted types, not very lively; they're rigid and awkward, not natural.

I discovered a consensus among managers and staff members that accomplished students lack the "people skills" to perform service work. Without prompting in interviews, staff members proudly described themselves as extroverts (*waixiang*), or with some embarrassment, as introverts (*neixiang*). Young workers who otherwise might be humbled by their vocational school background took pride in being "extroverts," a point of reference that offers poor academic performers an alternative source of respectability. In the service sector, personality itself has become an alternate standard of evaluation, apart from the measures of school testing. The human resources manager told me that she intentionally recruits mediocre students, who are thought to have the ideal personality characteristics for service work. At the BT, the moniker "extrovert" allows those who followed vocational tracks to measure success by personality and view their frequent socializing at the local MacDonald's and at the disco as a by-product of a valued set of characteristics. Yet, by spending their time and money munching burgers and dancing, forgoing further education, workers seal a future in the consumer service sector.[4]

While management praises both its young male and female extroverts, managers carefully sort men and women into distinctive task types. Women are assumed to be ideally suited to positions requiring interaction and deference that are appealing to male customers; men are assigned to jobs that require physical strength. As a result, although young men and women labor together, they perform tasks that endow them with different skills, sensibilities, and dispositions. Thus, even though men and women begin their careers at the hotel with similar vocational education and backgrounds, once at the hotel they acquire divergent skills and aptitudes, endowing them with unequal chances for mobility.

FEMALE WORKERS: THE SMILING FACE OF LUXURY

Young, female contract staff members are the smiling face of the hotel. Women fill the ranks of "frontline" work, interacting with customers as hostesses, waitresses, operators, and business center secretaries. Women account for just over half of the butlers and front desk receptionists.[5] When found in the managerial ranks, women are most likely to be assistant managers, shift leaders, or deputy executive managers. Half of the hotel's shift leaders and about a quarter of the outlet managers are women, while just under half of deputy executive managers are female. The single female executive manager heads the human resource department. The board of directors includes no women.

Managers employ nubile women to appeal to the hotel's male clientele. Female employees must be at least five feet four inches tall, slender, with light, unblemished skin and straight white teeth. One manager announced to me, after an interview with a job candidate, "I will hire her for her body." But managers also select women who look virtuous. The human resources department rejected a job candidate described as a "fox fairy," the mythical seductress of Chinese folk tales. The public often associates hotel work with prostitution and indeed, sex workers operate in many of urban China's new service venues (Hyde 2001). Thus, to protect the reputation of the hotel's high-profile clientele, BT managers explicitly work to eliminate any traces of sexual commerce. To demarcate a boundary between prostitutes and their own female workers, they stress the dress and comportment of their frontline staff.

For women, enacting extroversion therefore means walking a tightrope between congeniality and sexual availability. "Extrovert" is freighted with potential sexual overtones for women, many of whom were raised to avoid eye contact with men. The point was illustrated when three managers explained to me the importance of hiring workers who are outgoing. After I observed an employee evaluation, one manager complained about the worker, "She's not confident enough when talking to guests." He explained to me that traditionally Chinese women are taught to be shy and modest. He then quipped, referring to the female assistant manager sitting next to him, "But not Li Xin." Everybody laughed, including Li Xin. But the double entendre suggesting sexual availability was clear; she leaned back in her chair, her face reddened. Managers grumbled about the challenges of training women to smile and make eye contact with male guests. At the same time, because of the government-imposed one-child campaign, management is actively involved in implementing family planning. Female managers regularly take women workers aside to discuss their dating and relationship status, handing out condoms and encouraging sexual monogamy. Unlike men's sexuality, women workers' sexuality is a subject of managerial concern.[6]

In addition to monitoring of women's sexuality, hotel managers also exercise control over their appearance. The hotel's personnel handbook specifies detailed rules for hair, makeup, jewelry, and manicures. Women's fingernails are not to exceed ".5 centimeters beyond the fingertip." Earrings are not to be larger than 1.5 centimeters. Watches must be of a "conservative style." Makeup (which was required) should "create a natural appearance." Lip liner, tattoos, and second earrings are prohibited. At preshift lineups managers inspect workers fingernails, makeup, and general appearance, warning women workers not to swagger and "walk like men."

Management trains female frontline workers to execute the Transluxury's customization protocols, requiring them to address guests by name and title, while making eye contact and smiling. Furthermore, they are trained to notice and record in computer files the preferences of each guest. If a guest requests extra foam on his cappuccino, a particular type of fruit, or a special blanket or pillow, the employee records the details in the guest computer file so that the preference may be replicated in the future. Housekeepers keep records of how guests place their personal effects around the room, so as to reproduce this organization when cleaning. If the guest left his shaver on the left-hand side of the sink, and the wastebasket next to the bed, these items are placed accordingly by housekeeping.

Ongoing training programs perfect the interactional skills of female workers, offering discipline in the art of deference and training to respond to infinitesimal predilections of customers. Managers train workers to watch customers' minor gestures and facial expressions so as to preempt vocal requests for service. In the process they learn new Western emotional styles and etiquette. Managers train workers to use formal phrasing when interacting with guests, "certainly" instead of "yes" or "ok," or "no problem," "good morning," "good afternoon" or "evening" instead of "hello" or "hi."

They are also taught to apologize for any guest complaint, no matter who is at fault. New staff members are resistant to apologizing, fearing that by "taking the blame" they will be penalized. In a training role play, a manager played a guest and a waitress served him a fictitious "Bloody Mary." He erupted, "This is yellow, it's not a Bloody Mary!" The waitress retorted, "Yes, it is a Bloody Mary." After he insisted that it was defective, she explained, "It's a *"Beijing* Bloody Mary." At the end of the unscripted role play, he criticized the waitress for contradicting the customer and urged workers to apologize and affirm the customer. Managers relentlessly teach workers concerned about "losing face" to apologize when customers quibble. Workers memorize the emotion formula, "apologize, show empathy, resolve the problem, and follow up."

Managers repeatedly train women staff when to smile, how to smile, how to make eye contract, how to walk, and how to speak confidently so that they can be heard. For some workers showing empathy—or pleasure or displeasure in what American guests consider to be the proper manner—proved elusive. A manager's commentary during an evaluation reveals the standards of femininity used to discipline workers:

If you don't refine your service, you'll never improve. Think about it, does it have to do with your personality? You do your work quickly, but you need a kind of softness, especially as a girl. You need to smile more, especially as a girl. You can smile away the guests' problems.

When women workers fail to perform, they are accused of compromising their femininity, so that femininity itself becomes a disciplinary tool. In the course of another evaluation, a manager inventoried a waitress's defects:

She has no feeling, she's too severe. The quantity of work she performs isn't bad. She knows how to talk but she doesn't really do her makeup well. And there's a problem with her smile. She should learn how to interact with guests. Also [when she directs customers] she points like this [pointing index finger, which workers were instructed to avoid].

An assistant manager instructed a worker in the subtleties of smiling:

[I]f you have eye contact with a guest, then you have to smile. Of course, don't always smile. If a guest has a complaint, don't smile. You should listen to the guest attentively and try to think about how to use your smile flexibly. Your smile is a tool.

Paradoxically, managers tend to link emotional skills to women's biological capacities, concealing the organizational and disciplinary origins of the skills (Skeggs 1997; Bourdieu and Wacquant 1992). Managers repeatedly explained to me that women are ideal for frontline work because, compared to men, they are inherently "soft," mature, and cooperative. By viewing emotional skills as inherently feminine, managers devalue the skills, suggesting they are inbred features of the female gender rather than learned competencies. Managers also tend to view the skills as an expression of natural feminine deference, an attribute that disqualifies women for managerial positions.

The presumed effects of age also disqualify women from jobs as managers. Women over 30 years old are labeled "old lady" by male workers and managers, and they are considered too old to appeal to the hotel's male clientele. As female frontline workers approach the age of thirty, their contracts are allowed to expire. Pervasive uncertainty about future employment prospects induces a deep "sense of crisis" (*weijigan*). It remains to be seen if women pushed out of service work in their late twenties will move to different, most likely less-prominent and lower-paid positions in the service sector or exit the labor force altogether.

MALE WORKERS: THE SWEAT AND BRAWN OF LUXURY

While women workers struggle to decipher emotional cues, young male workers toil in jobs requiring physical labor. For three reasons, however, such jobs still position men as candidates for management. First, these jobs tend to involve some autonomy, access to tips, and more authority than women's work. Second, management routinely equates the physical requirements of men's work with authority and managerial aptitude. Finally, these jobs are easier to evaluate. Hence, male contract workers received higher job evaluation scores.

Young men account for the vast majority of staff in the banquet department, the security department, and the concierge department as bellmen. A few men are hired as food runners and bartenders in the restaurants. These workers rarely take guest orders; they perform manual tasks such as lifting boxes of supplies, carrying large trays of food to guest tables, and moving and adjusting dining tables. Nevertheless, they make one hundred yuan more than the highest-paid female frontline worker. Bellmen are allowed to keep their tips, while waitresses must pool them. Bellmen and security guards also enjoy considerably more autonomy than female frontline staff. Carrying guest bags, they move freely throughout the hotel. Security guards rotate through multiple posts on each floor. They monitor fellow workers punching the time clock, they search employee bags and lockers for stolen items, and invisibly watch over workers at their posts in the video surveillance room. By contrast, female staff rarely supervise anyone.

Male security personnel also act as class gatekeepers to the luxury hotel, authorized to eject those who do not look like paying customers of the hotel. A security guard describes how he learned to identify legitimate guests.

> We can tell by how they walk and their bearing (*qizhi*). Sometimes we can tell from their clothing. . . . Sometimes if they go to the cafe and order very few things and sit there for a long time, this will attract our attention. . . . Usually it's mostly migrants from other provinces. After 11 p.m. it's women who are wearing scanty clothing. These are usually "those kind" of women [prostitutes]. If the guest tries to bring them [prostitutes] to his room we don't let them go.

I found male security staff members to be particularly apt to see themselves as superior to guests, who are constantly under their surveillance. They had particularly harsh attitudes toward petty thieves, vividly illustrated when security apprehended a male migrant from the countryside who attempted to steal a hand towel from a lobby bathroom. As the culprit waited for at least an hour to be taken to the public security bureau, he was made to stand facing a busy corner outside the security office. When security staff members passed, they openly insulted and derided him.

Managers routinely urged male staff members to set their sights on management. I did not once observe a manager offer women this kind of encouragement. During a food service employee's evaluation, the manager suggested, "Maybe after a couple of years, you can be a shift leader, and then become a manager." A manager in the Italian restaurant told a young male food service worker, "You need to think about when you can be a manager or a shift leader." In the Chinese restaurant, a manager queried a bartender, "Have you thought about someday being in charge of this restaurant?" In interviews, men more frequently mentioned aspirations to become managers.

In evaluations, managers did not assess the emotional skills of male workers as they did those of female staff. Instead, evaluations assessed male staff members' capacity for "hard work," measured in terms of moving boxes, luggage, and tables, which often could be physically exhausting. Of course, compared to evaluating the emotional labor of women workers, this standard of assessment is straightforward to measure. After observing several back-to-back evaluations of male and female staff members, I found that managers unrelentingly criticize women workers for deficient emotional work skills. At the same time there is a strong overall tendency to praise male workers for their more manually oriented work. When male workers faced negative assessments, it was usually for "immaturity," and managers expressed certainty they would grow out of the phase. As a result, the job evaluation scores of young male workers tend to be higher than those for female workers; thus male workers have a better shot at obtaining raises and promotions.

Workers themselves patrol the borders of gender-appropriate work. Male workers defend the valorization of their physical labor, describing the work in glowing terms, like this banquet department staff member:

> We have to move things all the time. . . . This is the most exhausting department. The hotel won't let the women do this kind of work. So the men in the department are very strong.

Most female staff members also defend the gender boundary constructed around physical labor. In the words of a waitress, "Guys can handle more work; they have more energy."

The pressure felt by the sole female security guard to shift to "gender-appropriate" work also illustrates how workers enforce gendered work boundaries. Huaming is a highly trained martial arts expert. She works along-side twenty-nine male security guards, performing the same work. She complained of male co-workers who repeatedly inquire if she needs a replacement, concerned that she might suffer fatigue from standing long hours. Interestingly, no one seemed to demonstrate such concern for waitresses or hostesses. She lamented:

> My fellow staff members tell me I should be a waitress and ask me why I'm doing this work. One or two of these questions I can take, but everyone asks me, everyone. I always feel that they feel that women are inappropriate for

this kind of work. Or they wonder, Why is a woman doing the same job as a man? I feel they discriminate against me. They don't admire that I do this work.

By entering a world offering authority and potential for mobility, she perhaps inflicts injury on fellow workers consigned to feminized work in dead-end jobs. In sum, the work young men perform offers greater autonomy and authority than female frontline positions. Men's enactment of physical labor tends to be conflated with managerial potential. As a result, male workers are encouraged to become managers, while female workers are heavily criticized for deficient emotion work skills. While workers patrolled a managerial-constructed gender boundary, management also exploited age as yet another mechanism of workplace stratification.

## THE TEMPS: DOING THE DIRTY WORK

If young staff members are "blank slates," older, former state workers bear an indelible imprint of their past. No matter what their individual merit or skill, their previous employment qualifies them for temporary employment only and they function as a low-wage, reserve army of labor who perform the "dirty work" in the back stages of the service economy. BT maintains a pool of twenty-five to thirty temporary workers, all of whom have been laid off or retired early from posts in state-owned enterprises. Slightly over half of these workers are women. They perform custodial labor in the lobby, public bathrooms, restaurants, bars, and employee locker rooms. They wax and mop floors, clean toilets and ashtrays, polish crystal chandeliers, and iron and fold laundry. A few work in the housekeeping department, cleaning guest rooms. They rarely interact with younger staff and sit with other older workers when dining in the staff canteen.

As temporary employees (*linshigong*), they have little access to benefits, wage increases, and training. Unlike contract employees, who work five days a week, the temporary staff members work six days a week, earning 576 yuan monthly (about $72 U.S.). Management assumes most receive pensions and that their hotel wages are supplemental. However, only two of the six workers I interviewed receive pensions; the remaining four survive on their hotel wages, in addition to a spouse's wage. Without a contract, these workers could be refused employment at a moment's notice. Some had worked at the BT for three years, but had no contract and could be fired summarily.[7] While management is generally supportive of the younger hotel workers, the contingent workers experience the despotic face of the luxury hotel.

Among this cohort, gender distinctions do not systematically structure workplace rewards and opportunities. Older men and women wear the same uniform (white pants and a white jacket with a mandarin collar), rotate through similar job tasks, and are subject to similar work restrictions and requirements. Although the job tasks of younger workers are fixed by a gender binary, management treats older men and women as interchangeable. A minimization of visible distinctions between men and women, characteristic of the gender neutrality of the Mao era (Yang 1999), brand them with the imprimatur of now obsolescent, unproductive collectivism.

The older workers also provide a disciplinary foil against which to differentiate workers. Managers view veteran workers as a generation whose work ethic is crippled by their association with Mao-era collectivism, the antithesis of the "modern," motivated, entrepreneurial worker. The comments of the Beijing Inc.'s chairman of the board are typical:

> Of course, there are advantages to these older workers; they are mature and have lots of experience, but they also operate according to the old mentality by which it didn't really matter how well you worked. No matter what, you were guaranteed employment. Today we use younger workers . . . they are adjusted to the new economic environment so they work differently. We really need younger people in every position, including management; people who . . . haven't been raised in the environment where everything was guaranteed.

Even if veteran workers represent a workforce made indolent by the inefficient bureaucracies of the Maoist past and unfit for modern service work, the hotel preserves their obsolescence by excluding them from training opportunities. These workers are excluded from training in comportment, behavior, and etiquette, and this exclusion from training can lead to lapses in behavior. For example, one worker spat on the marble floor of the lobby after clearing his throat. He was immediately dismissed. These workers were also barred from attending language training offered by the hotel; managers assumed they are too old to learn new skills. The laid-off workers comprise a workforce that is socially, culturally, and organizationally isolated from the core activities of the hotel.

Most temporary workers are desperate to find work not only for economic survival but also to restore their dignity. Some were forced to retire early, before the legal age of retirement, 45 for women, 55 for men. Others had been formally laid off. Without the work that had previously given them identity and social honor, many suffer from a deep sense of purposelessness. At the same time, these workers often blame the lack of efficiency and entrepreneurship at their original work units for their loss of work. Liming was laid off from a yarn factory, at the age of 42 years. One year later her husband was laid off from his job. She explained:

> After I was laid off things were really quite difficult for me (*tongkude*). I said, work . . . no matter what work you do . . . it's the same, right? That's the

way it is. It doesn't matter if my position is high or low, it's all to serve the people. You give what you can of your self and the country will pay you back (*huibao*).

After reflecting on the wealth of hotel customers, the following laid-off worker displays a commitment to work as a source of meaning and identity:

> If my husband made a lot of money so we could buy a villa, and I had everything I wanted, including a little dog to pull about on a leash, and a maid to do all the housecleaning, I would not be happy. I would feel that life had no meaning. I must work.

Yet, temporary workers find labor at the hotel grueling and managers severe. A temporary worker describes adjusting to the regime of work:

> When I first started I found the work really exhausting. I'd never encountered a hotel. I found that the rhythm of work was very fast, much faster than the factory. I had to go through a process of adaptation. . . . They supervised me very strictly. Sometimes you might feel that you're not being lazy or slow but the supervisor will say you're being lazy and slow and then tell you off . . . and your heart feels unsettled (*xin bu pingheng*). If you argue with them, they still tell you off. Then you learn to be silent when they criticize you. If you argue there's just really no point. You're just a temporary worker and at any moment they can fire you. I don't want to do anything that would threaten my job, because today it's not easy to find work. I have to support my family, and I can't lose my job. So I learned to tolerate this.

At the age of 40 Xiuhua was "internally retired" (*neitui*), or retired early, from her state-owned work unit, a cloth-dyeing factory. She too expressed discomfort typical of the veteran workers at the hotel:

> The management is cold and severe . . . if you clean something wrong or inadequately or if you overlook something, they will fire the temporary workers without warning. They don't let us talk or rest or chat for even a moment at work. The other temp workers don't dare talk to you at work.

Indeed, these workers are subject to the close scrutiny of management. When a custodial worker took a moment out of her work to invite me to her apartment for dinner, she furtively whisked me into the double doorway between the front area and the back area of the hotel. This was one of the few hotel areas free of camera surveillance. No sooner could I accept her invitation than a shift leader appeared, from nowhere it seemed, criticizing her for abandoning her post shining the marble lobby floors.

Despite the backbreaking labor and low wages, the temps value their attachment to the hotel. A number of the temps complained bitterly of previous employers who refused to pay them at the end of the month. Even if BT wages are low, workers know they will get their paycheck at the end of the month. Furthermore, the BT provides temps with some of the fringe benefits enjoyed by contract employees. In 1999 they received the equivalent of $147 dollars in bonus money and gifts. They do not receive housing subsidies or medical insurance, but they find the other benefits received from the hotel quite generous. Participation in the fringe benefit regime is the only way these workers are not excluded from the workplace community.

A number of the temp workers adopted the profit-motive rhetoric of the hotel, actually referring to the financial failure of the state-run factories that once employed them as proof of the effects of poor business management and of poor motivation on the part of workers:

> If the hotel doesn't perform well, then our pockets will be empty. Just like at the factory, if business is bad, managers tell you to go home and they don't give you a penny. You must find money. If our factory would have been effective and organized, I would have avoided being laid off. I still love my factory, but the factory didn't love me. It performed poorly, didn't do things well, so they had to lay me off.

As if to fit into the new profit-oriented world, some laid-off workers accepted and internalized the critique alleging Mao-era factory workers to have grown lazy and dependent. But no matter how vigorously these workers try to overcome their history of attachment to the Maoist collectivist project, management systematically excludes them from opportunities for long-term employment.

CONCLUSION

The consumer service sector generates new forms of inequality, not only between managers, workers, and customers (Macdonald and Sirianni 1996; Leidner 1993) but also among different categories of worker, each with distinct avenues of mobility, each positioned differently within a continuum of reward, risk, and (in)security. In this chapter I use an ethnography of service workers in a luxury hotel to explore the management strategies that create and reinforce these distinctions and to understand how workers come to accept workplace inequalities. By contrasting the work experience of two generations of male and female service workers, I demonstrate how age and gender become two primary axes of differentiation.

Managers and workers utilize gender and generational meanings to construct the boundaries between job categories. Organizational processes of recruitment, training, and promotion mobilize and manufacture distinct job hierarchies for men and for women, for the young and for the middle-aged. The recruitment of workers into service jobs creates new cleavages between male and female workers and between neophyte and veteran workers, who are invested with distinct skills which, in turn, legitimate unequal access to managerial positions and long-term attachment to the service workplace. Neophyte workers experience considerable workplace hegemony; they have access to workplace contracts, welfare benefits, and opportunities to learn new skills with fairly supportive managers. Veteran workers experience a despotic side of hotel work: they are subject to frequent managerial penalties, easy dismissal, and are routinely blamed for the inefficiencies of Mao-era factories. In the process of reinventing themselves for the new economy, veteran workers adopt the profit-motive rhetoric of managers and, to some extent, internalize the generational critique by viewing their own former factories as flawed and inefficient. While veteran workers take pride in their work for its service to "the people" and the nation, young service workers draw on a psychological discourse, linking pride in work with their capacity for extroversion. In this way, they distinguish themselves within contemporary hierarchies of stratification that link educational opportunity to life chances. But extroversion has different connotations for male and female workers, as women tread a tightrope between virtue and vivaciousness.

Gender and generation are "connective tissues" binding young women and men as well as veteran workers to specific jobs, legitimating boundaries of opportunity and risk between workers. The gender essentialism operative in sorting men and women into different tasks illuminates how horizontal gender divisions of labor generate vertical segregation: male strength and youth become proxies for managerial competence, female youth and beauty for interactive competence and deference. Veteran workers stood outside the gender binary and were hobbled by associations with Mao-era loyalties to collectivist ethics, dependency, entitlement, and overall lassitude. As managers construct work boundaries based on gender and generational differences they legitimate unequal access to skills, wages, and organizational mobility. In an era of increased labor contention (Lee 2002), dividing new working classes who labor in the consumer service sector erodes the possibility for making unified demands of management and the state.

## CHAPTER FIVE

# The Changing Structure of Employment in Contemporary China

*Peter Evans and Sarah Staveteig*

China is the twenty-first–century's "workshop of the world," absorbing natural resources from Africa, Latin America, and the rest of Asia and exporting manufactured goods, much as England did during its nineteenth-century heyday. China's extraordinary position in the contemporary global political economy raises the question, "What are the implications of being the twenty-first century 'workshop of the world' for the future trajectory of wealth and poverty within China?" Optimistic answers to this question rely implicitly on Marx's famous dictum that "backward" countries can envision their future by looking at the trajectories of the more "advanced." In this view, China's industrial prowess would be the harbinger of a more egalitarian social future in which productivity gains spread to the broad mass of the citizenry.

We would like to question this assumption, arguing instead that the implications of becoming the "workshop of the world" are quite different in the twenty-first century than they were in the nineteenth and twentieth centuries. Our argument is simple. In a world where manufacturing technology has become global, the capital intensive "state of the art" quickly becomes the global norm, regardless of the cost of labor in particular locales. This is even more rigorously the case in countries like China, where ensuring the competitiveness of manufactured exports is a central developmental goal. Such technologically advanced manufacturing cannot absorb the bulk of the nonagricultural labor force, regardless of export success.

In the economic and technological context of the twenty-first century, industry ceases to be an effective vehicle for spreading the returns from development, and the service sector becomes the destination for the bulk of those fleeing arduous, low-return jobs in agriculture. Unfortunately, the service sector is characterized by extreme disparities of income, with most service sector workers relegated to low-wage jobs. In the service sector, "symbolic analysts" receive growing premiums while the gap expands between their remuneration and that of public sector workers, even those who deliver key services like health and education. Those engaged in "informal" service jobs revolving around petty commerce fall even farther behind.

If our argument is correct, it suggests that China's further industrialization is likely to generate wealth but be accompanied by a development trajectory that will exacerbate inequality. Any strategy for more equitable development must begin from the difficult problem of distributing service sector returns more equitably. This, in turn, suggests that more equitable development requires political dynamics quite different from either those that drove the emergence of the welfare state in the original industrializers or those implied by current neoliberal models of globalization.

China is the archetypal test case for understanding the effects of contemporary industrialization on social transformation, as well as a case whose evolution will, in itself, have a profound effect on the rest of the world. China is unquestionably the most successful exemplar of expanding manufactured exports during the final decades of the twentieth century and appears almost certain to continue to be the exemplar during the current century. On the one hand, its competitiveness vis-à-vis other countries in the global South meant the availability of markets has not limited its expansion. At the same time, the conviction of global corporations that they must have a presence in the world's largest country has unleashed a flood of foreign direct investment that virtually eliminates the constraints that might be imposed by an inadequate supply of new capital.

In short, if export-oriented manufacturing appears insufficient to deliver decent employment and improved well-being for the broad mass of the population in this exemplary case, it is hard to imagine that it will do so anywhere in the global South. If China must focus policy on the expansion of decent jobs in other sectors in order to provide employment and well-being, then other countries of the global South will have to do so as well. China is a crucial case in itself and a bellwether for other countries trying to develop their own strategies.

We will start with a brief review of the "classic syllogism" of traditional development theory in which the route to increased well-being runs from capital accumulation through increasingly productive industrial employment to broad expansions of income. We will then examine comparative data on changes in employment structure over the course of industrialization, first in England, then in Korea as a contemporary case of industrial success, and finally in China.

Our basic empirical argument is straightforward. In the classic English case, manufacturing did indeed absorb a large share of the labor force, enabling a broad swath of the population to gain a share of the dynamic and continuous productivity increases associated with machine-assisted production. In contemporary developing countries, even in small, highly successful industrializers like Korea, this pattern no longer holds. In China, manufacturing employment seems unlikely to ever absorb more than about 15 percent of the workforce. In 1995, the official percentage of the labor force in manufacturing reached its highest level: 14.4 percent. It has been declining since (National Bureau of Statistics [China] 2005b). Worldwide, manufacturing jobs declined by 22 million from 1995 to 2002 (Baum 2003).

Having set out this empirical proposition, we now turn to the question of implications for social structure and policy. Will increased reliance on service sector employment result in increased inequality and higher potential levels of social conflict? Such a conclusion would be consistent with Gao and Riskin's observation (this volume) that "China's rise in income inequality has been especially sharp." Other major developing country cases, such as Brazil, where industrialization has gone forward without absorbing workers from agriculture and where levels of inequality have remained extreme, would also be consistent with this conclusion. Yet, Korea has experienced modern, service-dominated employment growth without strong secular increases in inequality. The connection between a more service-dominated employment trajectory cannot therefore be taken for granted.

Political effects are equally important. Employment structures are intimately connected to social contention and political change. One of the key elements of the classic syllogism was the idea that industrial employment provided workers with structural leverage to press for redistributive demands. It is generally assumed that service employment does not provide the same mobilizational leverage. The structure of employment is one of the elements that must be taken into account when thinking about how the "palpable and wide presence of critical and rebellious sentiment" that C. K. Lee observes [this volume] might (or might not) be translated into effective political action.

There are policy implications as well. Replacing the "classic syllogism" with a vision of development in which services dominate employment growth is one more reason to emphasize the centrality of active state policy as a key element in development strategy. The state activism required cannot be designed to simply support private capital accumulation but must instead focus on counteracting the inegalitarian tendencies inherent in a "bit-based" model of growth in which new knowledge and ideas play a central role[1] and on providing ordinary citizens with the capabilities necessary to take advantage of service sector jobs. In short, current patterns of employment growth reinforce the value of a policy framework built more on the foundations of Amartya Sen's (1999) "capability approach" to development theory.

In order to set all of this in a comparative and theoretical context, we return to what we call the "classic syllogism" of conventional development theory: the supposed chain of logical connections that ran from investments in machines through employment in industry to increased well-being for the broad mass of the population. Understanding how this logic has been undercut by the current technological character of manufacturing is essential to understanding why industrialization will not, in itself, enable China to follow the sociopolitical trail blazed by the original workshop of the world.

In the conventional twentieth-century vision of how development occurred in the rich countries of the North, machine-assisted production plays a starring role, especially in the more positive versions of the conventional vision. In a simplified (and slightly caricatured) form, the story runs something as follows:

A massive shift of employment from agriculture to manufacturing takes workers out of a sector characterized by declining marginal returns to labor inputs and into one in which learning by doing, spillover effects, and greater possibilities for technological transformation of the productive process enable long-term secular increases in labor productivity.

At the same time, machine-assisted production lends itself to political organization both because workers are socially concentrated and because they are in a position to hold hostage the machines on which profits depend. Political organization in the form of unions and associated political parties enables a substantial part of the workforce to capture a share of the productivity gains generated by machine-assisted production and secure relatively broad increases in incomes.

The neat logic of this "classic syllogism" gives machine-based production the power to create broad-based expansion of incomes by means of two simple, plausible propositions: (1) If you can move a substantial number of people out of agriculture into manufacturing and continually give them better machines with which to work, their productivity will increase. (2) Marx was correct in suggesting that machine-assisted production lends itself to political organization, leading to partially successful demands for a more equitable share of this increased productivity.

Both premises make sense in relation to the historical experience of the original industrializers from the nineteenth century through the first two-thirds of the twentieth century. Moving people from the fields to the mills did enable them to become more productive, their initial inability to capture a share of their increased productivity for themselves and the consequent misery of the original "satanic mills" notwithstanding. Likewise, the labor movements that eventually emerged out of these new industrial settings played a key role in constructing a twentieth-century capitalism that shared more widely the gains from the more productive industrial economy.

However, we have reason to distrust this connection now. By the late twentieth century, manufacturing was going the way of agriculture in the rich countries of the North, leaving the service economy as the dominant source of employment. The most important feature of the service sector is its heterogeneity and a corresponding divergence of incomes.[2] As Torben Iversen (1999) has explained, a primary driver of inequality is the bifurcation between the private and public sectors. The private part of the service sector is characterized by high and growing levels of inequality. The public service sector, in which levels of wage equality are more like the old manufacturing sector, is starved for funds, limiting the possibility of wage gains for public sector workers.

Another way of understanding the bifurcation of returns to workers in the service sector is in terms of the divide between what could be called "bit-based" intangible production on the one hand and directly delivered interpersonal services on the other. Bit-based intangible production is great from the point of view of accumulation. Robert Lucas (1993) and Paul Romer (1986) and the others who developed new theories of endogenous growth 20 years ago forced us to pay attention to the fact that the returns from ideas (that is, intangible assets that are arrangements of bits instead of being arrangements of atoms) increase indefinitely, without the diseconomies of scale that eventually characterize physical production.

Of course, even before the sophisticated models of endogenous growth theory, the advantages of bit-based growth were intuitively apparent. We could see that Bill Gates was in a much more lucrative position than General Motors. And we knew that Snow White and Mickey Mouse were the true producers of golden eggs. As long as you can establish your legal ownership of ideas and images and effectively maintain your rights to exclusively appropriate the returns from them, you are in an enviable position, especially in a global economy in which the scale of potential returns is almost boundless.

The possibilities for concentration of income and economic power among those who own ideas and other intangible assets are, to use an appropriately contemporary term, "awesome." Bit-based profits also generate a range of opportunities for elite professionals. The upper reaches of the financial sector are the most highly remunerative. What are called "business services" can also be very rewarding, as are some of the jobs that Robert Reich calls "symbolic analysts" (1991:193).

The vast majority of workers in the new intangible economy, however, are not symbolic analysts but are engaged in delivering interpersonal services. These services may be crucial to our well-being as well as to the enhancement of human capabilities, but they don't necessarily produce high returns to those who provide them. Childcare is the most obvious example.

In short, we have a brave new bifurcated economy in which accumulation is bit-based and the sources of both people's employment and their well-being are increasingly located in arenas that simply don't lend themselves to the old link between accumulation and incomes via dynamically changing manufacturing technology and the productivity increases that could be embodied in machines.

Some will, of course, say that this analysis is North-centered and rooted in the fact that the production of tangible goods has shifted from the North to the global South. They will argue that this analysis does not apply to the successful industrializers of East Asia, and certainly not to the twenty-first–century's "workshop of the world." What we would like to argue is that, to the contrary, this argument applies at least as much to the long-term future of China as to the future of the rich countries of the North. The case for the diminished importance of the classic syllogism and increased relevance of the convoluted logic of the service economy rests first of all on the contrast between the classic pattern of sectoral shifts in employment and current patterns of structural change.

## COMPARATIVE PERSPECTIVES ON THE SHIFTING STRUCTURE OF EMPLOYMENT IN CHINA

If one starts by looking historically at the shifting employment structure in the original industrializer—the United Kingdom—during the nineteenth and twentieth centuries, as in Figure 5.1, the conventional vision of the classic syllogism holds up reasonably well. By the 1830s manufacturing had taken over from agriculture as the principal source of employment. Over the course of the nineteenth century, agriculture was transformed from being the modal form of work (employing about 40 percent of the population) to being a marginal form (employing closer to 10 percent). A growing population getting diminishing returns from working on a fixed amount of land was no longer a problem for the English economy. While the service sector soon became more important than manufacturing, jobs rooted in machine-assisted production remained sufficiently central (about one-third third of total employment) to anchor processes of social and political change and shape the distributional character of England's economy until the end of World War II. For more than a century, manufacturing and service employment were essentially coequals in the definition of the English economy. Thus, it is plausible to think of English development as driven by the sociopolitical logic of machine-assisted production.

England is the clearest case for the classic syllogism. In the United States, a relatively sparsely populated, continental-sized country, which industrialized later, manufacturing employment never reached English proportions.

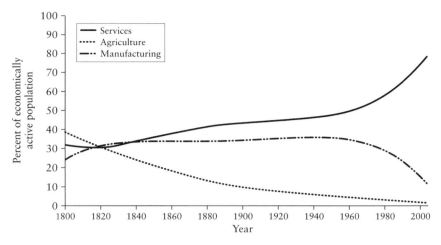

*Figure 5.1.*   Economically active population by sector, United Kingdom, 1800–2004

SOURCES: Data from 1801 to 1951 are from Deane and Cole (1967). Data for 1971 onward from Table 1c of International Labour Organization (1971–2005). Data from 1952 to
1970 were interpolated.

NOTE: Curves are smoothed representations of data trends. The percent of population in
mining, construction, utilities, and "other unclassified" industries is not shown. These industries employ a small percentage (generally between 6 and 11%) of the economically active
population in the United Kingdom. The unemployed have been excluded from the economically active population.

The share of agricultural employment did not fall below that of manufacturing until the end of the 1920s. Manufacturing gradually rose to a peak above
20 percent in the mid-twentieth century at which point the service sector was
on its way to employing the majority of the workforce.[3]

When we shift from historical patterns of development in the North to
contemporary cases of successful industrialization in the South, the plausibility of the classic syllogism as a fundamental mechanism for broad increases
in income breaks down. Korea is an excellent case in point. As Figure 5.2
shows, Korean manufacturing never came close to being the dominant form
of employment. When Korean industrialization took off during the 1970s,
the share of employment in manufacturing was still below that in the United
Kingdom at the beginning of the nineteenth century. Furthermore, manufacturing employment in Korea peaked at only half the English levels.

Finally, and perhaps most striking is the brevity of the period during
which the manufacturing employment accounts for a growing share of
employment in Korea. In the United States, manufacturing constituted a
share of employment comparable to its share in Korea throughout the latter half of the nineteenth century and continued to expand its share of total

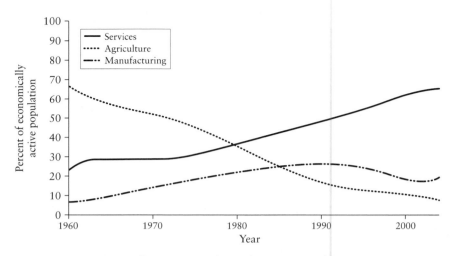

*Figure 5.2.*   Economically active population by sector, South Korea, 1960–2004

SOURCE: International Labour Organization (1960–2005). Table 1c.

NOTE: Curves are smoothed representations of data trends. The percent of population in mining, construction, utilities, and "other unclassified" industries is not shown. These industries employ a small percentage (between 3 and 10%) of the economically active population in South Korea. The unemployed have been excluded from the economically active population.

employment through the middle of the twentieth century. In England manufacturing's heyday was even more prolonged, lasting almost 150 years. In Korea, manufacturing passed its peak within the span of 40 years.[4]

If we look at Korea, the hypothesis that the North's share of manufacturing employment declines in response to increases in manufacturing employment in the global South is difficult to sustain. More convincing is the competing hypothesis of a global shift in which capital-intensive manufacturing combines with a global economy dominated by services and intangible goods production. By the beginning of the twenty-first century, Korea's employment structure begins to resemble that of OECD countries, but it does so without ever passing through a long formative period in which manufacturing shares pride of place with services as it did in the United Kingdom. Interestingly, the Korean trajectory looks more like that of the continental-sized United States than that of the more geographically comparable United Kingdom, supporting the idea that the historical timing of industrialization drives employment patterns.

Data from other successful industrializers in the global South reinforce the thesis. Brazil is a good case in point. Brazil has one of the most impressive industrial economies in the global South and exports a highly diversified range of manufactured goods, including airplanes. Yet, as Brazil's rural population fled low agricultural wages and moved to the cities, it was the service sector, not manufacturing, that absorbed the new entrants. The service sector's share of employment remained at least double that of manufacturing throughout Brazil's impressive twentieth-century industrialization. Manufacturing employment peaked at about 20 percent of total employment in the early nineties and then began to decline.[5]

China is the definitive case for the general thesis. The Korean and Brazilian cases help build the argument that the classic sequence from machine-assisted production to industrial social democracy must be seen as a historically specific possibility, not replicable in the twenty-first century. But, if China's employment trajectory looked like England from the nineteenth and twentieth centuries, the classic syllogism could be rescued. Unfortunately, China's trajectory is quite different.

If we look at the evolution of manufacturing employment in China in the latter half of the twentieth century, as shown in Figure 5.3, we are immediately struck by the *lack* of dynamic expansion. The peak share of manufacturing employment not only fails to match that in England, the United States, or Korea, but also even fails to match that of Brazil. If official statistics are to be believed, employment in Chinese manufacturing peaked in the mid-1990s at less than 15 percent and began to decline at the end of the 1990s.

Certainly there are serious flaws in the official statistical data.[6] Because persons are counted by their permanent residence, Chinese statistics persistently undercount the urban population (Pannell 2003) and hence overstate the extent of agricultural employment. However, there is no reason to believe that workers who are actually working in urban occupations while officially counted as agriculturalists are more likely to be in manufacturing rather than services. Most plausible is that uncounted rural migrants gravitate toward informal jobs at the bottom of the service sector. The fact that the official Chinese data show employment in the service sector that is dramatically lower than in most of the industrial South increases the plausibility of the assumption that most of the "missing workers" are primarily at the lower end of the urban service sector.

The main message of Figure 5.3 is that, even if industrial workers in China succeed in gaining a more equitable share of the profits derived from increased manufacturing productivity, the gains will go to a small and shrinking minority of employees. This conclusion is thoroughly reinforced by other assessments of the evolution of manufacturing employment. An independent analysis by economists at Alliance Capital Management found that between 1995 and 2002, China lost on net 15 million manufacturing jobs (Carlson 2003). Support for the declining share of manufacturing employment in the 1990s also comes from the field observations of researchers like William

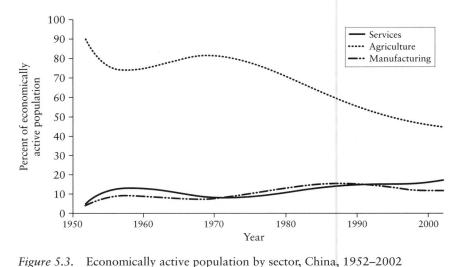

*Figure 5.3.*   Economically active population by sector, China, 1952–2002

s o u r c e s : Data for 1952–79 from State Statistical Bureau of People's Republic of China (1983–1987). Data from 1980 onward from National Bureau of Statistics of China 2006).

n o t e : Curves are smoothed representations of data trends. The percent of population in mining, construction, utilities, and "other unclassified" industries is not shown. Until 1990, these industries employed a small proportion (between 3 and 10%) of the economically active population in China. After 1990, the industrial categorization of 8 to 14% of the economically active population is not given in official statistics, hence they are not shown here. However, government statistics do provide a sectoral classification for the entire economically active population (primary, secondary, or tertiary) and these numbers reflect a much larger surge in services that is shown here. The unemployed have been excluded from the economically active population.

Hurst (2004) and C. K. Lee (1998) that emphasize the collapse of labor-absorbing state-owned manufacturing firms in the Northeast and the simultaneous expansion of technologically advanced and relatively labor-saving firms in the "greenfield sites" of the Southeast.

In interpreting these employment trends, it is important to underline the economic context. China's share of world manufactured exports has increased more than fivefold. If a fivefold increase in the share of world manufactured exports is insufficient to increase the share of manufacturing employment, is there any plausible scenario in which export-oriented industrialization is likely to result in an increasing share of manufacturing employment? It is hard to imagine one. The more likely trend—judging from the history of the East Asian tigers—would be for China to begin to shift out of the lower value-added, more labor-intensive exports (e.g., apparel) in the direction of higher value-added exports (e.g., semiconductors), improving export growth perhaps, but reducing opportunities for manufacturing employment.

Some might argue that China's huge potential internal market for manufactured goods can be the basis for future increases in manufacturing employment. This argument is flawed. Lack of new markets has not been the problem. The weak relationship between expanding markets and employment growth is driven by the same dynamics of technological change in domestic markets as in export markets. Manufacturing is simply going the way of agriculture: becoming less labor-intensive and more capital-intensive worldwide (Ghosh 2003; Reich 2003).

If we look to the future, the obvious question is: Where will the hundreds of millions of Chinese workers who currently face low incomes and declining returns to labor in agriculture go? The most likely answer is that they will head to urban areas in search of improved living standards and end up at the bottom end of the service sector. What then? What can we say about the sociopolitical implications of these employment projections?

EMPLOYMENT STRUCTURE AND INEQUALITY

It follows logically that if the manufacturing share of Chinese employment is not going to grow, then the hundreds of millions of people currently dependent for their incomes on agricultural production must either stay in agriculture or move to the service sector. Both options suggest increased inequality and a more precarious quality of life for the vast majority.

If they stay in agriculture, which seems unlikely given the intensity with which contemporary global culture promotes the allure of urban life, the Chinese peasantry is likely to face stagnating incomes. The most likely route to income growth in agriculture is through technological innovation and increased inputs of capital, both of which reduce demand for farm labor. The option of more labor-intensive, "non-traditional" agricultural strategies, such as focusing on fruits and exportable vegetables, also is unlikely to work for hundreds of millions of peasants. Thus, preservation of current levels of agrarian employment most likely will exclude a large share of the population from the returns from future growth and increase intersectoral inequality.

But what if these frustrated agriculturalists move into the service sector? The preceding discussion of empirical trends argued that expansion of the service sector is likely to produce increased inequality and precarious quality of life for the majority of the new entrants. The odds are against most ever gaining access to the lucrative slots in finance, "business services," or "symbolic analysts." Rather, given the size of the population seeking new jobs and the relatively low level of overall incomes in the urban service sector, the most likely outcome is an even more severe "bifurcation" of the service sector than in the rich countries of the North.

In short, the analysis of shifting employment trajectories turns out to be another lens for understanding one of the issues most central to all analyses of contemporary China—the question of rising inequality. Fear that China is in a process of transition from a poor but relatively egalitarian socialist past toward a richer but severely inegalitarian future that will threaten social peace and political stability appears to haunt China's leadership. The major countries of the global South that are plagued by enduring, obdurate, historically extraordinary levels of inequality are the cautionary negative models. Brazil and South Africa with Gini indices persistently hovering close to .60 are cases in point. Both are characterized by rising levels of violence that threaten governability in their major urban centers.

China's socialist heritage of an egalitarian distribution of landholdings, however, is a positive legacy that stands in contrast to the extreme maldistribution of agrarian holdings that has historically characterized Brazil and South Africa and persists to the present. Given this heritage, China might hope to replicate the evolution of Taiwan and Korea in which massive shifts out of agriculture and rapid increases in income were accomplished without corresponding increases in inequality. Yet, most analysts agree with Davis and Wang that China has not followed these East Asian tigers, but instead has experienced high growth and increased inequality.

Our analysis of employment trends reinforces existing concerns with respect to rising inequality by suggesting that the current trajectory of economic growth is likely to exacerbate inequality rather than alleviate it. If capital-intensive twenty-first–century manufacturing technology will not spread incomes to a broad cross-section of the population and service sector–dominated employment growth is likely to magnify the dispersion of incomes, then increased inequality follows logically.

Similarly, it is hard to see how contemporary patterns of economic growth can provide political foundations for the redistributive politics that are projected in the classic syllogism. Can a manufacturing labor force that consists of perhaps one worker in seven provide the political momentum necessary to propel redistributive change? It seems doubtful. At the same time, the heterogeneity of the service sector and the dispersion of service work sites make it hard to project solidarity among service workers as a catalyst for a politics of redistribution.[7] Labor organizing in the service sector is, of course, possible. The recent experience of the labor movement in the United States suggests that, given appropriate organizing models, the service sector can be fertile ground for organizing. Nonetheless, given current employment trajectories, replicating the optimistic expectations of traditional development theory is a theoretical and policy challenge.

IMPLICATIONS FOR DEVELOPMENT THEORY AND POLICY

Two variations on the classic development syllogism succeeded each other in the latter half of the twentieth century. The mid-twentieth century was the heyday of the "development project." Projects of industrialization, characteristically state-led, promised to deliver "catch-up" (Kohli 2004). Then, a generation ago, what McMichael (2005) calls the "globalization project" became hegemonic. The neoliberal globalization project deprecated the efficacy of the state, condemning state "intervention" as an almost inevitable devolution into predation and rent-seeking (Evans 1989, 1995). Markets were exalted as a universal solvent for the "inefficiencies" that kept the global South poor. While profoundly different in key respects, both projects shared the underlying logic of the classic syllogism. The "development project" championed industrialization as the engine of well-being and the globalization project promoted the specific strategy of export-oriented industrialization. Given China's successful growth, it is not surprising that it has been claimed as an exemplar of both the development project and the globalization project, even though both claims required a distorted reading of China's development trajectory.

The analysis presented here suggests a different focus for development theory, one rooted more in Amartya Sen's capability approach and less in the classic syllogism. Could China become an exemplar of this approach? The short answer would be: only as the result of a series of political and policy changes, a number of which are highly unlikely.

The policy demands of a capability-centered approach are daunting. Insufficient allocation of resources to public sector service employees is one major determinant of bifurcated service sector incomes. Correcting this requires extracting more resources from affluent owners and directing them to workers delivering public services. Increasing incomes of ordinary public sector workers also implies large investments in expanding capabilities associated with improved productivity. Both require bold public sector initiatives. Social protection in the form of a secure but efficient "safety net" makes further demands on public institutions.

China would, however, have two substantial advantages over most other countries in the global South if it should attempt to pursue a more capability-oriented strategy. First, it has the state capacity necessary to pursue such a development model. Second, it has a historical legacy of ideologically elevating questions of social protection. The active state policies implied by a capability approach to development would represent a recuperation of old socialist themes, albeit in forms necessarily different from those of the socialist era.

The most obvious barrier to the possibility of China's being able to pursue a "capability-centered" development path is the absence of the deliberative politics that Sen sees as essential to capability expansion. The growing political influence of private elites whose fortunes are derived from the continued growth of export manufacturing is likely to militate against any strategy that would shift state priorities in the direction of capability expansion. Given the historical ease with which authoritarian rule and industrial growth have coexisted (from Germany to Japan to Brazil and Mexico), it is easier to imagine the increased political influence of private elites reinforcing authoritarian tendencies within the state.

Elites cannot, of course, construct policy as they choose. Ordinary citizens are the potential beneficiaries of a development strategy aimed at countering the inegalitarian implications of the current economic trajectory. Whether they have the determination and organization necessary to provoke a shift is a question that lies well outside the purview of our analysis. What our analysis does suggest is that moving toward a more capability-expanding development strategy, in China or anywhere else in the global South, must include moving beyond the machine-based logic of the classic syllogism and recognizing the key role of conditions of employment in the service sector in determining overall levels of well-being.

## CHAPTER SIX

# Institutional Basis of Social Stratification in Transitional China

*Liu Xin*

The changing mechanisms of social stratification in China during its transition toward a market economy have been the subject of debates among numerous scholars (e.g., Nee and Matthews 1996; Bian 2002a; Liu 2003). The theoretical starting point of the debate is Iván Szelényi's (1978) institutionalist explanation of stratification that juxtaposes state socialism with welfare capitalism. Under welfare capitalism, markets dominate and are the major source of inequality, whereas state redistributive mechanisms are secondary and have equalizing effects. Under state socialism, the redistributive system of economic integration dominates and is the major source of inequality, whereas market-like transactions partially reduce the inequality created by redistribution. Redistributors in state socialism, through nonmarket trading of labor and commodities, control the surplus and create inequality by favoring "their own kind" in redistribution. Advantageous life chances are therefore linked to redistributive power (Szelényi 1978).

Applied to the stratification mechanisms of transitional China, Szelényi's explanation presents two opposing theories. Power transfer theory holds that increased reliance on markets induces a shift of distributive power to the market, creating new mechanisms of stratification and new elites (Nee 1989, 1996; Nee and Cao 2002; Szelényi and Kostello 1998). Power persistence theories, by contrast, posit that stratification mechanisms formed under the traditional redistributive economy persist even after the transition (Bian and Logan 1996; Parish and Michelson 1996; Walder 1995b, 1996, 2002; Zhou 2000b; Song 1998; Lu 2002). Empirical observations have confirmed the continuing advantageous life chances of government and CCP bureaucrats (Song 1998; Lu 2002; Sun 2002; Li Q. 2004; Liu 2005), a phenomenon that power transfer theory cannot explain. At the same time, although power persistence theories assert the continuation of power, they fail to explicate precisely the mechanisms through which power persists.

Three theoretical perspectives have been proposed to understand how the state power influences stratification continuously. The first regards state power as redistributive power that benefits redistributors. This line of explanation, however, confuses state power with redistributive power and fails to recognize how markets have already altered the institutional basis of state power. The second treats state power as bargaining power in the political market, which brings economic benefits to its possessor during the marketization (Parish and Michelson 1996). While no longer equating state power with redistributive power, this perspective does not specify in depth the institutional basis of the bargaining power and to some extent confuses politics and markets. The third, more robust, stresses the decisive changes in the property rights regime that have engendered new state power formations and argues such changes in the property rights regime preserve and even augment the power elites' economic interests (Walder 1995b). This explanation insightfully analyzes the institutional basis of power persistence. However, it lacks a systematic and rigorous account of the new power formation and the mechanisms that influence stratification.

Building on Szelényi's institutionalist theory of social inequality (Szelényi 1978; Szelényi and Manchin 1987; Szelényi and Kostello 1998), this chapter attempts to propose an alternative explanation of the mechanisms of social stratification in transitional China. The strategy of this alternative theoretical construction is to integrate the analyses of socialist domination (Djilas 1957) and of property rights regimes (Barzel 1989; North 1981, 1990; Pejovich 1995; Walder 1992; Walder and Oi 1999; Zhang 1995, 1999; Lin et al. 1999, 2002; Zhou 2002), as well as to incorporate Sørensen's concept of rent derived from property rights transactions (Sørensen 2000), to extend Szelényi's theory into a new framework.

The central thesis of this chapter is that, as the mechanism for reproduction of institutionalized inequality, the mechanism of social stratification is embedded within and explained by the fundamental institutional arrangements of a given socioeconomic system. In modern societies, the form of ownership of property rights and the relationship between state power and property rights (including property rights to human capital) are the most fundamental institutional arrangements. In China's current market economy, the administrative as well as contractual principal-agent relationship in the management of public property, combined with the market system (which is embedded within bureaucratic authority), form the institutional basis of social stratification. Such institutional arrangements maintain some redistributive state power and generate power elites with self-serving rent-seeking abilities. Thus, redistributive power, rent-seeking ability, and market capacity together constitute the motivating basis of social stratification in transitional China.

INSTITUTIONAL ARRANGEMENTS AND
DISTRIBUTION OF ECONOMIC INTERESTS

Property rights are relations among individuals that arise from the existence of scarce resources. They are "norms of behavior that individuals must observe in interaction with others or bear the costs of violation" (Pejovich 1995: 65). Every individual enjoys rights over some assets, be they capital, land, labor, or other scarce resources (Barzel 1989). Property rights regimes stipulate people's right to exclusively possess, use, and profit from scarce resources (Demsetz 1967). People's life chances are determined according to their property rights arrangements. The exercise of such exclusive rights, in turn, depends on the force of law, morals, and conventions, and hence cannot be secured without definition and protection by the state (North 1981, 1990).

The institutional basis of capitalist market economies consists of private ownership of productive resources, freedom to contract, and (limited) constitutional government, while the basis for socialist planned economies consists of state ownership of productive resources, central planning in resource distribution, and single-party monopoly of government (Pejovich 1995). I hold further that the relationship between property rights regimes and state power is the more fundamental institution, because it determines whether resources are distributed through the market or administratively. Market economies, planned economies, and transitional mixed economies all have such basic institutional arrangements to determine distribution of economic interests and hence people's social strata.

This institutional presupposition is different from that of Szelényi who takes as given the market and the redistributive systems of economic integration, but does not adequately analyze more fundamental institutional bases. The market and the redistributive system are themselves institutions arising from the relationship between property rights regimes and state power.

STRATIFICATION MECHANISMS IN
CHINA'S PLANNED ECONOMY

In traditional socialist planned economies, state power is manifested not only as the power to seek surplus in the form of rent, but also as the power to redistribute such rent. Rent arises from the lack of supply elasticity (Buchanan 1980). Lack of supply elasticity can arise from both the nature of the factors of production and governmental intervention (Sørensen 2000). The sources of rent are various, but this chapter focuses on rent arising from the intervention of state power.

At the microlevel, rent arises from property rights transactions (Barzel 1989; Sørensen 2000). In order to maximize profits in the production of goods and services, individuals use not only assets under their own control but also, through purchasing or renting, those controlled by others. The supply of others' assets may be limited due to the nature of the assets themselves or to monopoly. As a result, those who purchase or rent such assets must pay a price higher than the market price, and the suppliers gain through their monopolistic supply. Thus, rent is exceeding profits derived from preventing the profit maximization of others and depends on the ability to control asset supply (Sørensen 2000).

China's traditional planned economy was characterized by the unity of the political power of the state and public ownership of property. Such unity is formed under the absolute authority of the socialist state (Djilas 1957). If seizure of power and establishment of a socialist state—the redistributive power center (Polanyi 1944/1957; Szelényi 1978)—are through violent means, then maintenance of the authority of the newly formed state must be supported by an economic structure that answers ruling needs. In cities and towns, the state employed confiscation and joint public-private enterprise management to realize comprehensive state ownership. In rural areas, the state used cooperatives and communes to achieve collective ownership of land and the means of production (Lin et al. 2002; Dong 1999). Nationalization and collectivization can be seen as a property rights regime transformation compelled by state power. Completion of this transformation marks the metamorphosis of a regime established by force into the practical possessor of state-owned economic assets. There thus emerges a socioeconomic unity in which political, economic, and ideological powers are all in the hands of one newly formed class (Djilas 1957).

In such a centralized society, the public economy is managed through an administrative principal-agent relationship (Pejovich 1995; Zhang 1995, 1999). Public ownership stipulates that the means of production belong to the people or the collectivity. It is realized, however, through the socialist state as representative of the people, and has thus turned into a form of state ownership (Kornai 1992). The state, as an institution stipulating the exercise of public power, cannot itself exercise such power (North 1981, 1990). The power of the state is exercised by its agent, the government, which is in turn a bureaucracy composed of officials of all levels. The socialist state, as an enormous asset owner, entrusts its assets to administrative departments and lower-level governments through administrative means, and delegates its management to factory directors and managers appointed by itself (Zhang 1995, 1999; Lin et al. 1999; Lin 2000).

Within this administrative principal-agent relationship, nonmarket transactions connect the human capital of the factory director or manager to the means of production. Principal-agent relationships also exist under capitalist private ownership; however, the owner of the capital (the capitalist) relies on contracts (Zhang 1995, 1999). Within this contractual relationship, the capitalist earns the surplus through his privileged possession of capital, and the entrepreneur earns rewards through his market capacity. In socialist planned economies, on the other hand, bureaucratic appointment replaces the entrepreneur market (Zhou 2002). To prevent the business manager from encroaching on the interests of the business owner, the state then devises a series of institutional arrangements to deprive the manager of the right to seek surplus (Zhang 1995, 1999). The state thus monopolistically both possesses and redistributes the surplus, and managers receive salaries that do not reflect the market return to their entrepreneurial ability.

Within this planned economy model, nonmarket transactions also determine rewards to nonmanagerial labor. Although legally there is equal ownership of the public means of production, no individual has the power either to determine how the assets should be employed or to seek profits (Zhang 1995), and the workers who produce the goods and services are especially excluded from the exercise of property rights over public assets. Moreover, beyond administrative controls over labor (Kornai 1992; Pejovich 1995), the household registration system and the rationing systems for food, housing, and other daily necessities further limit the property rights of labor by depriving them of transactional freedom (Zhou 2002).

In such nonmarket transactions, the state administratively suppresses the price of human capital in order to maximize surplus. This surplus is different from the profit that arises from free and competitive market transactions when property ownership is independent from administrative power. It is "state rent" (Zhou 2002) or "institutional rent"[1] (Lin et al. 2002) arising from administrative pricing when the state monopolizes the means of production and property rights over human capital are severely incomplete. In traditional socialist planned economies, the state seeks surplus through rent, not profit. State power is manifested on the one hand as state rent-seeking power by virtue of the state's monopolistic possession of public assets, and on the other hand, as the state's redistributive power over reproduction and consumption. Under the principal-agent arrangement, bureaucratic officials of all levels, as redistributors, may exercise these powers. Redistributors favored themselves (Szelényi 1978) and their political loyalists (Walder 1986) in their redistribution of rent for living and consumption, and this resulted in inequalities. However, in the case of socialist China, the presence of unified state control of revenues and expenditures, the severe atrophy of the market (Lin et al. 2002),[2] and the shackles of an ascetic ideology (Walder 1986) effectively prevented the dissipation of state rent. As a result, the rent-seeking phenomenon in which the power elites seek personal gains was restrained (Lin et al. 2002).

## POSTSOCIALIST TRANSFORMATION AND
## STRATIFICATION MECHANISMS

China's reforms since the late 1970s can be seen as a triple gradual process: decentralization, profit sharing, and marketization. Decentralization of state power from central to local governments includes the division of administrative power and the division of corresponding jurisdictions of public assets (Wu 2003; Walder 1995b; Walder and Oi 1999). Profit sharing can be seen as the corresponding redistribution of the right to profit from central to local governments and enterprises. Marketization is the shift from the "planned track" to "dual-track" and eventually "market track" (Lin et al. 2002; Wu 2003; Dong 1999).

During this gradual process of reforms, the principal-agent relationship in the public economy evolved into one that is both administrative and contractual. Such a relationship is the institutional basis of the state's power to seek and redistribute surplus in the form of rent, as well as the institutional precondition for the power's evolution into the power elites' rent-seeking ability.[3] At the same time, the market that has developed under the persistence of the political structure is one embedded in the socialist bureaucratic authority structure. Such an embedded market is the institutional precondition for both returns to market capacity and for state power's evolution into the power elites' rent-seeking ability.

### Principal-Agent Relationship and the
### Persistence and Evolution of Power

Decentralization of control and profit sharing has partially eroded the extensive overlap among political power, property rights, and redistributive power. The devolution of ownership has empowered enterprise managers to rely on market transactions to allocate assets and distribute the surplus, and to set wages to reflect differential levels of human capital (Lin et al. 1999; Dong 1999).[4] However, from the early years of reform to "expand enterprise autonomy" through the recently established joint-stock systems, the state has never relinquished either ownership of public assets or the power to control surplus (Lin et al. 1999; Wu 2003). While the original intent of the reform was to grant enterprises greater managerial autonomy and right to derive profit, the political decentralization that accompanied the economic decentralization has actually transferred the property rights and profits from one level of government to another and not entirely to the enterprises (Wu 2003). Reform, therefore, has not altered basic principal-agent management of state-owned assets. The contrast to the prereform period is that the postreform principal-agent relationship is both administrative—as when the state is entrusted with the ownership of public assets—

and contractual—as when the government and the enterprises enter into contracts with each other.

Such an administrative as well as contractual principal-agent relationship is the unique link between state political power and property rights, and is thus the institutional basis of state power's persistent influence on stratification. Under this principal-agent relationship, the central government preserves its control of local governments by preserving its power to appoint or dismiss local officials and state-owned enterprise managers, whereas the local governments, managerial organs of state-owned assets, and party organizations and departments all have their own means of influencing the management of state-owned assets (Wu 2003). State political power and property rights have not been separated, nor has the government surrendered the possession of public assets and the corresponding power to seek surplus. State power can still seek surplus in the form of rent and distribute the rent in an exercise of redistributive power.

This principal-agent relationship is also the institutional basis of state power's evolution into the power elites' rent-seeking ability. It is different from the principal-agent relationship under private capitalist ownership in that the property owner is personified, that is, is a natural person. In the hierarchy of multiple principal-agent relationships in transitional China, none of the officials, or representatives appointed by these officials, is the owner of public property, although they do exercise practical control (Zhang 1995). Because owners are absent at every level of the principal-agent relationships and do not derive any profit that corresponds to their supervisory power, the principals will not actively supervise the agents as do the owners of private property. Moreover, due to the absence of the ultimate owner, the question of who should restrain the actual principals—local governments and relevant departments—also becomes problematic. Without incentive and supervision, administrative officials would be irresponsible when they, as principals, choose or supervise their agents. When choosing agents, they will entrust the state-owned assets to those who are willing to pay rent to themselves or their cliques. When supervising agents, they may conspire with them to share the rent that should enter the national treasury or local revenues.

Although the principal was also absent in the traditional socialist model, the highly centralized fiscal system of unified state control of revenues and expenditures had effectively prevented the dissipation of the rent. Under the new institutional arrangements, on the other hand, local governments have gained the actual ownership of the state-owned assets under their jurisdiction and now have strong rent-seeking powers. Institutional arrangements that separate central and local government finances promote the local governments' own fiscal irresponsibility and permit the local governments to have extra-budgetary income and "private treasuries" that dissipate state rent.

*Embedded Market and Power Evolution*

The core of the ideal market is a pricing system based on free exchange, which in turn is based on private ownership not subject to intervention by the government or any other external authority. Such a free market is, however, dependent on a series of institutional preconditions: free property, free labor force, rational law, and rational state. Under such institutional arrangements, every individual, every enterprise, and even the state can freely take advantage of market opportunities, but none can expropriate the property of others through individual power or other nonmarket means (Weber 1981). In such a market economy, the market participants—due to their different wealth, skill, and labor—possess different market capacity in the exchange competition and hence occupy different market positions, that is, different class situations (Weber 1978, Giddens 1973). Differences in market capacity determine the employer-employee division, income differences, employment insurance, promotional opportunities, and welfare benefits (Giddens 1973).[5]

China's marketization has always been advanced under the control of state power. In China's current market economy, the government still controls substantial public assets and is not external to the market. It both makes market rules and participates in market activities (Walder 1995b). The institutional basis of the socialist market economy with Chinese characteristics is far from the ideal institutional precondition envisioned by Weber or the new institutionalist economists. China's market is one embedded in the socialist bureaucratic authority structure. In such a market economy, state power is central to the emerging processes of social stratification.

First, state administrative power sets market entry rules, thus rendering the bureaucrats extensive rent-seeking space. Next, the various administrative and executive organs, especially local governments and the relevant departments, can, in accordance with certain state policies, take upon themselves the management of the private sector. When democratic supervision and rule of law are not yet well established, there are minimal restraints on the self-serving rent-seeking ability of relevant bureaucrats. Third, the nonstate sector is subject to unequal treatment in the areas of bank loans, land appropriation, taxation, and employment of labor. Non-state-owned enterprises thus pay rent to the power wielders to overcome a variety of entry barriers (Dong 1999; Wu 2003).

A market so embedded in bureaucratic state authority limits enterprises' positions as market entities with complete property rights and creates opportunities for state agents to derive substantial rent (Barzel 1989). This rent is the source for the relevant power elites' pursuit of personal gains through power. Second, the limitation on state-owned enterprises' positions as market entities also reduces autonomy to set prices. As a result, the pricing mechanism is not entirely based on the market, but is also subject to intervention from administrative authorities (Dong 1999). Distorted prices then create opportunities for the power elites to seek rent through the price differentials. During the 1980s, it was very common to seek rent through dual-track pricing (Lin et al. 2002). Third, the state-embedded market limits the role of entrepreneurship. In the public sector, administrative authority to a large extent determines the appointment and income of the enterprise managers; bureaucrats can therefore enjoy rent from the appointment of managers. Fourth, the continuing reliance on the perquisites of administrative rank limits the free flow of production factors such as capital and land, thereby creating additional opportunities for rent seeking. And finally, party-governmental power erects entry barriers by monopolizing certain industries, providing substantial rent-seeking space for the managers in such industries.

### Multidimensional Bases of Stratification and the Structure of Stratification

So far, through an analysis of the institutional basis of planned economies and market economies, I have attempted to provide a new logical interpretation of the stratification mechanisms before and after China's current market reforms.[6] I hold that mechanisms of social stratification ought to be explained by the relationship between state power and property rights that determine the characteristics of the socioeconomic formations. In China's traditional planned economy, the state monopolized the means of production and managed them through administrative principal-agent relationships. Property rights over human capital were incomplete. Such basic institutional arrangements determined that human capital could only be rewarded through nonmarket transactions, and that surplus existed in the form of state rent. State power was manifested not only as the power to seek surplus in the form of rent, but also as the redistributive power to distribute such rent. The redistributors stratified society by favoring "their own kind" or the politically loyal in the redistribution. In China's current market economy, an administrative as well as contractual principal-agent relationship combined with the market system, which is embedded within bureaucratic authority, to form the institutional bases of stratification. Redistributive power, rent-seeking ability, and market capacity constitute the multidimensional bases of stratification.

Based on these motivating factors, I propose a stratification framework consisting of ten strata to map out a holistic profile of the stratification structure of current Chinese urban society, shown in Figure 6.1.[7] At the very

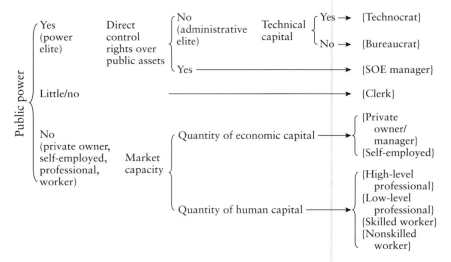

*Figure 6.1.*   A framework of class analysis in urban china

top of this stratification order are the *technocrats*, including cadres in party and governmental organizations and state-owned enterprises and nonprofit institutions who have professional titles and shoulder leadership or adminis-trative responsibilities. This stratum differs from the nontechnocratic power elites in the next stratum in that they possess not only leadership responsi-bilities, but also skilled professional ranks. Below the technocrats are the *bu-reaucrats*, including leading cadres in party and governmental organizations and institutions and party affairs workers in state-owned enterprises. These people enjoy cadre positions and shoulder some leadership or administra-tive responsibilities, but do not have skilled professional ranks. Compared to those who are not part of the power elites, they have a greater likelihood of possessing redistributive power and more rent-seeking opportunities. The third stratum among the power elites are *state-owned enterprise (SOE) di-rectors or managers*. They enjoy the rights of directly using state-owned as-sets and thus controlling the surplus. On the one hand, their power reflects entrepreneurial ability or market capacity; on the other, through the state-owned assets and employment opportunities under their control, they enjoy more rent-seeking opportunities than do staff or workers.

Among those with no public power, several strata form the rest of the stratification order. *Private enterprise owners and managers* are the owners or controllers of private property and their privilege of the possession of capital is manifested in their market capacity to obtain profits from capital in the market competition. *High-level professionals* enjoy neither redistributive power nor rent-seeking opportunities derived from state power, but they possess rich human capital, which is manifested as a market capacity greater than that of low-level professionals. *Low-level professionals* differ from high-level professionals in that their market capacity is weaker. *Clerks* are mostly ordinary staff in public departments. Compared to the leading cadres of party and government organizations or enterprises and institutions, they rarely enjoy redistributive power and their rent-seeking ability is very weak, but they may, through contact with the power elites, have more likelihood than the workers of nearing redistributive power and may even obtain limited rent-seeking opportunities.

At the bottom of the stratification order are self-employed skilled workers and unskilled workers. *Self-employed* urban Chinese have neither redistributive power nor rent-seeking opportunity but can rely only on their market capacity, consisting of limited economic and human capital, to survive in the market competition. *Skilled workers* enjoy neither state power nor economic capital, but can rely only on their market capacity, consisting of their own human capital, to survive in the market competition. They enjoy, however, more human capital than nonskilled workers. *Nonskilled workers*, like the skilled workers, are relying only on their human capital, but their human capital is less than that of skilled workers.

In constructing this theoretical framework, I have treated "rent-seeking ability" as a consequence of institutional arrangements and an internal mechanism of stratification. However, further research is needed to devise effective standards for measuring rent-seeking ability, to explicate how "rent-seeking ability" reveals a new stratification mechanism, and to test the hypothesis by empirical materials. Such research, I hope, will lead to a new and deeper understanding of the social stratification order in postsocialist China.

## CHAPTER SEVEN

# Rethinking Corporatist Bases of Stratification in Rural China

*Xueguang Zhou*

One evening in early July, 2005, the loudspeakers in Li Village transmitted the voice of village party Secretary Mr. Kang, calling for a village meeting at 9:30 p.m. that evening.[1] It was in the middle of a busy season, as villagers worked day and night, spreading insect sprays on the grapevines, mowing weeds in the fields, and irrigating draught-stricken fields. They would go to the fields before sunrise, and return home after dark—usually after 8:00 p.m. In between, they would take a long nap at noon to escape the summer heat. To call for a village meeting at this moment of the season, there must be something urgent. Village meetings, a routine practice in the collectivist era, have become a rare phenomenon in the post-Mao villages where, after the collapse of the commune, each household tends to its own fields. Li Village, however, is an exception. From time to time, Mr. Kang, the party secretary and village committee head, would gather members from among the 200 families to discuss major issues affecting the villagers' well-being.

The meeting that evening was about preparing for the visit of a township inspection team sent to assess the implementation of the government-initiated Slope Land Conversion Program (SLCP). The aim of the SLCP is to provide villagers with cash payments in exchange for returning their crop fields to natural areas of trees and wild grass. A key requirement of the SLCP prohibits the planting of any tall-stem crops (e.g., corn) in those fields that participate in the SLCP. In Li Village, many families had already planted corn in these fields. The inspection was to ensure that the participants in the program would comply with the requirements and uproot crops planted in these designated areas.

Around 10:00 p.m., representatives of the households finally gathered at the village center—a courtyard in front of the rooms housing the village and the party branch offices. After introducing the main purpose of the meeting, Mr. Kang spoke with unmistaken authority:

> As you all know, this year our village has another 600 *mu* in the SLCP in addition to the 1,323 *mu* we had in 2002.[2] Our village benefits tremendously from this program. We receive close to 300,000 yuan each year, amounting to

2,400,000 yuan in eight years. We need to make sure that we pass the inspection smoothly. The SLCP quota for our village did not come easily. I should let you know how difficult it was. At first, our village was not given any quota in this round. Why, you may want to know. As you may have heard, we had a bad relationship with Mr. Y [the head of the forestry office in the township government]. And he did not want to give us any quota. When I found out, I went directly to the township party secretary Z, and fought for our share. Secretary Z finally gave a direct order to Mr. Y that we be given the quota.

Mr. Kang's speech lasted for about an hour; after that, the meetings ended with few questions and discussion. It seems that the villagers were already accustomed to this kind of government inspection and to speeches by Mr. Kang. Nevertheless, this meeting and the associated SLCP episode offer us a glimpse into the bases of governance in rural China and how evolving patterns of interaction between state agents and peasants shape the emerging order of social stratification.

Social stratification is primarily a consequence of resource mobilization and transfer across group boundaries. To explain patterns of social inequality, therefore, we need first to identify the processes through which resources are allocated across groups, the mechanisms that govern these processes, and the bases on which group boundaries and identity are aligned and maintained. Because resource mobilization is rarely based on individual actions or choices, the core transfer occurs between and among corporate entities such as villages and townships. And the institutional dynamics of village governance affect distributional outcomes among village residents.

In earlier work on the relations between rural governance and the economy, scholars emphasized "the merger of government and economy" (Oi 1999:11) and developed a corporatist mode of governance based on stable social institutions such as kinship relations and collective legacies of the Mao era (Lin 1995; Walder 1995b). Today, however, the rapid privatization of previously collectively owned village and township enterprises (TVEs) in the late 1990s and the massive outflow of rural labor to the cities have altered key parameters of village life. The institution of elections to village committees after 1998 has also reshaped authority relations between local officials and ordinary villagers. Amid the new economic freedom, mobility, and contested elections, the party and government institutions still maintain key monopolies and officials still exercise power over state-initiated resource allocation. The main theme of this study is to understand how corporate power has been maintained or transformed after the decollectivization and privatization of the rural economy, and to identify the implications for formation and maintenance of the group boundaries within the contemporary social stratification order. As will be shown below, because resource infusion from the state plays a critical role in the rural economy, and because state resources flow to village households on the basis of the officially sanctioned egalitarian land tenure system, corporate-based resource allocation plays a critical role in equalizing opportunities and creating some "drag" on the overall pattern of increasing social inequality.

This study is based on my fieldwork in a township in North China between 2004 and 2007. During my trips to this township, I usually stayed in a dormitory room in the township government and mingled with cadres and villagers on a daily basis, and let events and information come to me in an informal, unobstructed manner. In addition to close observations of the daily operation of the township government, I also kept track of events in several villages in this township by regularly visiting these villages and chatting with village cadres and villagers. Economic and political conditions vary widely across China, from township to township and from village to village; hence, my fieldwork aims to identify theoretical issues and mechanisms at work to guide future research rather than to test particular propositions or offer definitive conclusions.

### THE SLCP PROGRAM: INFUSION OF RESOURCES FROM OUTSIDE

Located on poor farmland surrounded by mountains, Li Village historically struggled with droughts and unpredictable yields. However, the situation dramatically improved when Mr. Kang, the village party branch head, led the village to build irrigation facilities that turned cornfields into vineyards. The results were immediate and dramatic: In a few years village incomes rose dramatically, new houses filled the village lanes, and motorcycles populated the streets. But then in the early 2000s, the price of fertilizer and other agricultural supplies rose more rapidly than the price of grapes, and most households again struggled to make ends meet and pay the increasingly heavy taxes and fees levied by local governments (Chen and Chun 2004; Zhou 2005a).

Significant changes have been taking place in recent years. When I began my fieldwork in early 2004, state funds from outside the township had become significant and the abuses that had been featured in the press during earlier years were largely under control. By 2006, the agriculture tax—the most significant component of government taxation in rural areas—was completely abolished and other taxes or fees had been curbed.

For Li villagers and their neighbors in this county, 350 kilometers to the north of Beijing, the key source of government funds came from the SLCP, a central government initiative to reduce the sandstorms that assaulted the capital each spring and summer by taking hilly land out of grain cultivation in an effort to create a greenbelt outside the city. In this most ambitious program, the central government committed 337 billion yuan (US$40 billion) over eight years to subsidize peasants, who agreed to plant trees and wild grass instead of grain crops. For each *mu* of land converted, the government would annually pay twenty yuan plus the cash equivalent of 100 kilos of corn (the main crop in this area). In the township where Li Village is located, a total of 26,000 *mu* of land was taken out of cultivation between 2002 and 2004 and more than 4 million yuan went to village families. In Li Village, the 300,000 yuan per year was equal to a quarter of all household income.

The SLCP is not the only program that brings resources into the rural areas. In recent years, governments at county, regional, and provincial levels have invested in rural infrastructure. For example, of the five villages in which I gathered data, three received significant amounts of resources for new irrigation facilities that allowed considerable expansion of arable land. In one particular case, a village received close to 500,000 yuan—an astronomical figure for a village collective in this area—to irrigate new fields, pave the village streets, and renovate the village offices.

The changing role of local governance, economic opportunity, and higher-level government transfers raise several issues relevant to understanding emerging patterns of social inequality in rural China. For a long time, analysis in social stratification research in industrialized market societies has taken the individual or household as the unit of analysis, comparing changes in socioeconomic status across generations within a family or over one's life course. But when the state plays a salient role in allocating resources, the principles for resource allocation and transfer are often based on categories or sectors that are beyond the individual or family. In the case of postsocialist economies, favorable state policies affect life chances either through the direct inflow of resources, or by indirectly creating new opportunities that may lead to additional resources.

Corporatist governance and communal identities have had strong influence in the region of my research, where in everyday conversations, villagers still call themselves "commune members" (*sheyuan*), identify their village as "the brigade" (*dadui*), and occasionally refer to the township government as the "commune" (*gongshe*). Yet, beneath the seeming uniformity of structures are *interactions* among state policies, local authorities, and villagers that shape and perpetuate patterns of resource allocation. State policies create opportunities and dictate the broad strokes of resource allocation across groups, sectors, and regions, but microprocesses mobilize and redistribute resources among individuals and families, and it is those microfoundations on which observed patterns of social stratification and inequality are based.

DIVIDING THE RESOURCES: WHO GETS WHAT AND HOW?

Previous studies have scrutinized the interplay among the state, local authorities, and peasants in the top-down processes of the state extracting resources from villages. For example, Oi (1989) emphasizes the role of clientelist relations among government officials and local elites in protecting local interests. In this model of governance, the state still has its mighty presence, but local cadres and peasants adopt various strategies to resist and evade the demands from above (in the urban context, see Wank 1999). Since the late 1970s, rural China has undergone profound changes, as evidenced by the demise of the People's Commune and the privatization of collective enterprises. Nevertheless, as I observed in Li Village, resource flow from governments to rural areas can be frequent and salient. Scrutiny of how these opportunities and resources are distributed, therefore, speaks directly to the contemporary modes of corporatist action and their role in shaping the new order of stratification.

Let us take a closer look at the SLCP program. Here my analyses focus on the lowest two levels of the resource allocation, across villages within townships and between households and the village collective within villages. Following the top-down flow of resources, we first look at the link between the township government and villages and the resource flow between the two. At first glance, the implementation process for SLCP is straightforward. Each year the authorities in Beijing and at provincial government levels determine the acreage and subsidies for each county and township. Eligibility requirements are specific and detailed, and only households that meet these criteria can voluntarily participate. Moreover, in the recent past, the quota allocated to the township of my research often exceeded the demand; hence, there is minimum competition within the villages for resources in the area of SLCP program implementation.

Nevertheless, allocation across villages can be contentious. As Mr. Kang made clear at the village meeting, the SLCP quota for Li Village was partly obtained by appealing to the township authority. However, his statement is at odds with my own investigation. My interview with the township officials in charge of the SLCP revealed that there was more quota than requested by the villages; the issue was which land could be included. In almost all villages, there was land that had been cultivated outside of official statistics. This land typically was of poor quality with low yield. Because the government does not officially recognize such land, farmers cannot get SLCP subsidies by taking it out of grain production. The village and individual families would gain greatly if they could fool the higher-level government into counting these nonofficial fields as crop fields and get compensation for turning them into conservation areas. To accomplish this, the village must get acquiescence from the township government, which has the knowledge about these pieces of unqualified land. It is in this grey zone that I suspect special relationships between the village and the township government come into play.

For decades Li Village has been the showcase for the township government, and Mr. Kang, the model village leader. Government delegations are often directed to this village, because Mr. Kang had been the kind of person who can make things happen. In a recent road construction project advocated by the regional government, for example, Mr. Kang was the first to wholeheartedly embrace the government's advocacy and mobilized his village to carry out the project, while leaders elsewhere were hesitant. He and Li Village also benefited from these close ties. When Mr. Kang incurred debts in the road construction project, the head of the township government quietly channeled additional resources to him. In contrast, the township government withheld resources and diverted the flow of resource from those villages whose cadres were not cooperative. In one instance, elected cadres in a village were at odds with the township government over a series of issues. In response, the township government withheld SLCP compensation packages to this village with the aim of undermining the elected village cadres.

As one can see, corporate institutions (local governments and village governments) still play a critical role in channeling resources into villages and households. When resources flow into the township from above, the township government plays a subtle but critical role in directing these resources into different villages. When tax collection and reimbursement were present, the township government could also offer flexible assessments of accomplishments and selectively reward village elites. These observations are consistent with what Walder (1986) observed in the Mao era: Allocation of resources serves as an incentive for compliance—resources are directed into those villages that cooperate with the township government.

But there have been substantive, even fundamental, changes since the mid-1990s in the corporate bases of governance in this region in particular and in rural China overall. First, because of the recentralization of financial resources, since the mid-1990s, many township governments and village governments have fallen into debt (Oi and Zhao forthcoming; Xiang 2005). Limited financial resources have severely constrained the capacities of the township government to impose its authority by establishing and maintaining its clientelist ties with villages. Over time, we observe a pattern of gradual withdrawal of the township government in supervising everyday life and an increasingly loose coupling between the township government and villages.

Second, even when there were flows of resources through township governments, the central government has adopted a series of measures aiming to prevent local governments from tapping into these resources. For example, in the SLCP, the township government only identifies eligible villages and households but does not have direct access to the funds. Compared with its older counterpart, the People's Commune, the township government today is much weakened in its authority and capacities in resource allocation. As a result, the township government is less effective in rewarding compliance and in forming political coalitions with village elites than were commune cadres in the 1970s.

One consequence of these shifts is that township-village linkages have evolved into a symbiotic relationship distinct from the top-down administrative authority relationship of the commune era. Mr. Kang proudly told me: "In my role as the village head in the past twenty some years, I have worked with a succession of seven heads of the township government. I don't care who is in charge of the township government. I have always been doing my job well and helped the township government. So, every government head always had a good relationship with me and my village."

In brief, unlike the proactive local state of the past, today the township government is paralyzed by shrinking resources and heavy administrative constraints imposed by supervising agencies. My observation is that the township government cadres tried to avoid going to the villages as much as possible. When they have to go to villages, they only get in touch with the key cadres in the village. As one township government official put it: "If we have contact with villagers, and they raise questions, what can we do? We don't have resources or authority to solve any problem. All we do is to listen to these complaints and name calling."

We now shift attention from the relationship between the township government and villages to mechanisms of resource allocation within villages, especially the role of village government in this process. The first thing to notice is that, because there is more than enough quota to go around, in the SLCP case the allocation of quota among households appears to be in compliance with policy regulations. In my interviews and casual chats with villagers, I did not hear serious complaints of unfair treatments in the SLCP program. Another factor that contributed to this smooth allocation, as we see below, is that the criteria are transparent and accessible to all households through TV news programs and other media reports, which greatly curtailed the arbitrary power of the local cadres in this region.[3]

Within the village, the key struggle is not between households, but between households and the village. Similar to township governments, most village collectives are in heavy debt, resulting from bad loans in the collectivization era and excessive taxation. Moreover, there are mounting pressures for villages to fund collective projects, such as road construction and family planning. To launch such projects, village cadres had to borrow from local banks against their own personal credits, incurring enormous debts on their own shoulders. Take Li Village as an example. Before 2004, the village had accumulated debts of more than 200,000 yuan, and in 2004 they had to borrow another 600,000 yuan to finance a road construction project initiated by the higher-level governments.

As a result, village officials are desperate to put their hands on any resources that can be claimed for the village. But they also face mounting challenges. First, as state policies become increasingly transparent, transmitted through TV programs and other media reports, villagers on the receiving end become more and more aware of the regulations and provisions, and they form strong expectations to resist local cadres' appropriation attempts. Second, the stake for violations has increased significantly. To ensure "social stability," the central government adopted various measures to prevent local cadres from intervening in the intermediate steps. For example, in allocating the SLCP funds to village households, higher-level government offices put the funds directly into the household heads' personal accounts in the local credit union, which requires the household head to use his own photo ID to access his account so as to prevent local cadres from appropriating these funds.

Nevertheless, village cadres still develop various strategies to obtain a share of the resources flowing into the village. In SL Village next to Li Village, Mr. Song, the party secretary, kept 50 percent of the cash payment, about 50,000 yuan in total, from this fund. He told me that he made his claims on the ground that this was partial repayment for the past taxes and fees that the households owed the village and that he was doing it for the public good. In contrast, in Li Village, the village retained a far smaller share of SLCP compensation, along with clear guidelines. For each *mu* that is taken out of cultivation 5 yuan goes to the village and for any family that owes the village 300 yuan or less, the village will cancel their debt immediately with funds from their SLCP fund. For families owing more than 300 yuan, they will pay back 80 percent of their debt. These policies were recommended by the village committee and approved by the village meeting. Compared with the huge debt the village had accumulated, the amount retained by the village collective was tiny and inconsequential. I asked Mr. Kang why he did not demand more, as the neighboring SL Village had done. He sighed: "I wanted to. . . . But someone from my village reported this to the provincial government office. The higher authority sent inquiries down, and the township government intervened. So I could no longer make the move."

The episodes above revealed not only varying capacities in resource mobilization across villages but also the major shift in the basis for making legitimate claims in acquiring resources. Village cadres can no longer simply exercise their power to extract resources at will; instead, they need to justify their claims on a legitimate basis. First, the claim on these resources, in both villages, was made in the form of paying back the debts that the households owed the village collective from the past (mostly in the form of overdue agricultural tax). Second, the cadres justify their actions by claiming that the collection of these payments is used for the public good, such as road construction. Both claims are legitimate in the eyes of the villagers and thus allow village cadres to capture the resources, even in violation of government policies.

Here, we observed two distinct but interrelated mechanisms in the microallocation of resources. One is based on clientelist ties. For example, as described by Mr. Song, instead of exercising official authority, the village cadres used interpersonal relationships to persuade villagers to surrender part of their SLCP fund to the village collective. This observation is consistent with the role of social institutions in local coordination emphasized by Lin (1995). The clientelist relationships are institutionalized rather than personal. That is, the flow of resources between corporate entities (township, village) is based on their contribution to the institutional agenda of the township government rather than personal favors. Second is the importance of the basis for making legitimate claims, as embodied in the retention of portions of SLCP funds, to induce the villagers' acceptance of these behaviors of resource extraction. This is in sharp contrast to the previous use of naked coercive power in resource extraction. In both cases, the bases of corporate governance have evolved considerably from the traditional administrative authority to a process of negotiation among the different parties, the outcome of which has become contingent and uncertain.

## "US" VERSUS "THEM": THE SOCIAL CONSTRUCTION OF GROUP IDENTITIES AND BOUNDARIES

Not far from the orderly scene of Li Village—clean streets, newly installed village logo, and even one row of colorful flags to attract tourists—is the SB Village. As you enter the SB Village, it is as if you were walking through a garbage dump. Litter is everywhere: scattered on the main streets, filling in the sewage tunnels, and overflowing through cracks in the walls along the streets. Only a few years ago, this was one of the more prosperous villages in this township. Factional conflicts within the village in recent years, among other things, led to the collapse of village corporate governance in a short period of time.

The contrast between Li Village and the SB Village is not an isolated instance. Indeed, as recounted by the locals, village governance and prosperity are fragile and can unravel dramatically and quickly. In this township, there are several villages whose governance is dysfunctional and paralyzed because of infighting among factions in the village. Our discussion above illustrated how macrolevel institutional changes have greatly undermined the microfoundations of village corporatism. Central to these changes is the shift from collective land use in the Mao era to household-based land use in the reform era. The latter offers a new incentive system for villagers to seek opportunities and profits by attending to individual or family-based activities rather than corporate projects. In addition, recently instituted village elections provide competing bases of governance between top-down government sponsorship and bottom-up popular support. Finally, the exit option—migrating from rural areas to urban areas for jobs—allows able individuals to leave their village behind and seek outside opportunities. In brief, villages are no longer glued together by administrative rules as in the Mao era, and the degree of solidarity varies widely both within and across villages.

In this context, the maintenance of corporate bases and group boundaries and identities is by no means an easy task. It is not difficult to see that village cadres face a most daunting job: simultaneously to please local authorities, protect collective assets, meet the demands of the villagers, and pursue their own interests. These goals induce conflicting constraints on their behaviors. In the meantime, the very basis for their authority and legitimacy is eroding substantially. These observations invite this question: What are the mechanisms that reinforce or undermine group solidarity and boundaries?

One strategy to reinforce identity and boundaries involves the distinction between group boundaries of "us" and "them" and the reinforcement of "common consciousness" (Becker 1963; Durkheim 1984). The village meeting is such a stage and Mr. Kang's rhetoric at the meeting is a crystallization of the boundary-maintenance practice in action. So, let us return to the scene of the village meeting described at the beginning of this chapter.

Mr. Kang faced a challenging task. He had to demand that his villagers make sacrifices—to destroy their crops with their own hands. At the same time, he could not afford to alienate his fellow villagers, and he needed to keep them together—and on his side. He showed his political skills in his speech at the village meeting. He identified those "outsiders"—the authorities from higher-level governments—that developed and enforced this "unreasonable" policy. He sought to reinforce group identity and group boundaries by drawing a clear line between "us" and "them." He self-promoted by letting the villagers know how hard he had fought for the village interests on their behalf. He also persuaded by convincing the villagers why this sacrifice—the termination of high-stem crops in the fields—has better payoffs because of the larger gains of policy-based compensation packages. He displayed a variety of tactics in accomplishing these tasks: threats, pleas, persuasion, and a call for collective consciousness.

Several aspects stand out in this process. First, the most interesting observation is that boundaries were not clear-cut, nor were they static; rather, they were dynamic and shifting, in and out of focus with circumstances. And different actors were drawn into the social construction processes for different role-playing. At one point at the village meeting, Mr. Kang tried to educate his fellow villagers:

> I know none of you wants to uproot the corn planted in your field, and I know the government demand is unreasonable. But the inspectors are unsympathetic and they only follow the rules. If they find out that we have not met these requirements, all benefits from the SLCP will be withdrawn. You all should learn how to deal with the inspection teams. You have different pieces of land; some are in better compliance than others, right? When the inspectors ask you to show your designated SLCP land, you should take them to the one with better compliance. You see, this morning I was with the regional government bureau head Mr. Lin and a provincial inspection team. When the provincial inspection team looked at our land and asked why we did not comply with the regulation, Mr. Lin answered for me, telling them that this piece of land was not designated for conservation. The inspection team was fooled easily.

As one can see, high-level government authorities, such as provincial inspection teams, were portrayed as unsympathetic and zealous bureaucrats whose only purpose was to implement regulations to the letter. But, beyond this faceless villain, officials from other government agencies were at times treated as one of "us" or part of the strategic alliance. Even the regional government official was dragged into this episode to take the side of "us" to highlight the boundary between "us" and "them."

On the other hand, even local authorities much closer to the village may be treated as outsiders to rally within-group solidarity. At the meeting, Mr. Kang particularly singled out the head of the forestry office in the township government as such an outsider. As he put it:

> We should take serious steps to comply with the requirements. As you all know, the head of the township forestry office had a bad relationship with our village and he always tried to find faults with us. He may direct the inspection teams from the higher authorities to our village. So, we cannot take the risk of noncompliance that may cause the loss of SLCP resources flowing to our village.

Here, again, villains were invented to reinforce group solidarity and help reinforce compliance to government regulations. Interestingly, the actors and boundaries shifted on different occasions even in the same speech, but no one seemed to notice any irony in these imagined, contradictory alliance formations.

The shifting of boundaries is by no means confined to public rhetoric. Village leaders also construct boundaries between villages and government offices, strengthen in-group solidarity, build subtle pressures for the villagers to comply with government regulations, and firmly place local cadres on the side of their fellow villagers. In this process, actors are identified, behaviors highlighted, and episodes recounted; some state policies become the vehicle to heighten the awareness of boundaries between "us" and "them."

What are the implications of these observations for our understanding of classes, groups, and identities in the era of social transformation in the Chinese context? One implication is that the analytical categories that researchers often used for analysis—villagers, village cadres, township cadres, superior (county, regional) governments, and the state—are overlapping, intertwining, and interpenetrating in everyday practice. Along with these microdynamics, the boundaries of groups as well as mobilization for collective action may change from occasion to occasion, depending on the issues and interests affected. On the other hand, it is also obvious that corporate entities—kinship, villages, and township—still function with enough stability to pattern the mobilization and make legitimate claims. The challenge is to identify under what circumstances corporatist affiliations trump.

## DISCUSSION AND REFLECTIONS

In this study, I described and discussed a series of events associated with a government-initiated land conservation program and other related episodes in one township in Northern China to understand the complexities and local dynamics of rural transformation and evolving bases of governance. My analytical lens, as consistent with the theme of this book, is on emerging patterns of social stratification. My central argument is that corporatist bases, as conceptualized in the earlier literature, still play a significant role in determining rural life chances. However, these corporate institutions have also been undergoing profound changes in recent years. In this concluding section, I take stock of these major changes and draw implications for our knowledge about patterns and sources of social stratification in rural China. Because my arguments are mainly built on my fieldwork in villages in one township, I develop these ideas and reflections not as conclusions but as propositions or hypotheses—interpretations and speculations—to be further explored, revised, and to be empirically examined proved to be true or false.

When I began my fieldwork for this study, I carried with me an implicit baseline for comparison—the rural China of the mid-1970s when I worked as a "sent-down" youth in a village in Northern China. During that period of time, state control over the countryside reached its height in both scope and intensity: The presence of the state—through the administrative apparatus of the People's Commune, the production brigade, and the production team—was deeply entrenched. The images of struggles between the state and peasants over harvest in Oi (1989) and the "honeycomb" pattern of local resistance in Shue (1988) aptly captured the state-society relationships in the Mao era (see also Chan, Madsen, and Unger 1992; Friedman, Pickowicz, and Selden 1991; Zweig 1989).

Since then, rural China has witnessed profound institutional changes. One defining characteristic of these changes, as emphasized in the local state corporatist model, was the central role of local governments in the early economic takeoff in rural China (Oi 1999; Walder 1995b). Local governments were actively involved in resource allocation and redistribution across sectors and groups and thereby directly shaped distributional outcomes.

One key finding from my recent fieldwork is that corporate institutions of governance remain central in determining patterns of resource allocation. Their centrality is evident in the fact that various government-initiated programs—the SLCP program, the road construction program, and the "new socialist rural China" program launched by the central government in early 2006—are organized and implemented by local governments at the township and village levels. When the role of the state, central or local, increases in allocating or extracting resources in rural areas, the corporatist basis of governance is extended and strengthened. Even economic transactions taking place in the marketplace, such as price setting in the market for grapes for wine making, often involve the participation of corporate bodies, such as village governments and large wine-making companies. In so doing, they reinforce the corporate mode of governance in rural China. On this basis, my first proposition is that, *to understand patterns and sources of social inequality in rural China, we need to shift attention from individual (and extended family) basis to the corporate bases associated with regions, groups, and categories.*

My view in this regard echoes the main arguments in the local corporatist model and recent arguments on the importance of categorical inequality (Wang 2008). Central to this line of argument is the continuing role of state and local governments in allocating resources and opportunities in the reform era. Even in those areas where the government has retreated from everyday life, the legacy of collective institutions in the Mao era—the work point system, the collective infrastructure—still provides the basis for organizing shared work in collective projects such as irrigation facilities.

For example, in the SLCP program subsidies to farmers are typically based on the size of the fields that were allotted to the households in the egalitarian land tenure system of the early 1970s. The principle of land distribution was based first on household size and then on the number of adult members in the household at the time. As a result, state-initiated resource allocation based on land size reinforces such egalitarian patterns, and to some extent has slowed the increasing discrepancies among households. In recent years, programs like SLCP, coupled with increasing prices for produce, have noticeably increased returns to agricultural activities and lured some migrant peasant workers back to their farmland.

Yet, my research has also revealed significant changes over time in the corporatist bases of governance in rural China. These findings can be summarized in my second proposition as follows: *The traditional mode of corporatist governance in rural China today has become increasingly fragile, marginalized, and ineffective, and this trend accelerated after the mid-1990s.* By "traditional mode of corporatist governance," I refer to those corporatist mechanisms that are legacies of the Mao era—the role of township and village governments in their functions as agencies implementing state policies, extracting resources, and supervising everyday lives. This grand trend of change is above all reflected in the observation that in recent years the authority of township and village governments has declined significantly. Today villagers make decisions about what to grow, where to sell and at what price, and what to consume, with little interference from local governments (Zhou 2007a). Recent institutional changes, such as the abolition of the agriculture tax and the privatization of collective properties, have further loosened the institutional link between local governments and villages. Moreover, in many instances in this township under study, as large numbers of those aged between 18 and 40 leave their villages to work in cities as migrant workers, village households are increasingly detached from local politics. In other words, the role of local governments is at best marginal and occasional, if at all, in the *daily activities* of village households and of village governance.

Several ongoing institutional changes have contributed to this trend. First, shrinking resources in the township and village governments have fundamentally changed the traditional dependency relationship between villagers and governments. The lack of resources means that the township government is highly constrained in its capacities to cultivate and maintain clientelist relations with villages and in its ability to reward compliance. Second, in response to the increasing number of social protests in rural areas, the central government and provincial authorities have strengthened regulations and administrative control of local government behaviors in extrabudgetary resource seeking. In so doing, they have greatly weakened the authority of local governments. For example, in the SLCP program, the central government requires that compensation funds be directly distributed to the households through local credit unions, preventing local authorities from getting their hands on these resources. Third, village elections, although initially seen as symbolic window dressing have now become an effective bottom-up basis of legitimacy for popularly elected village cadres, a process that undermines the legitimacy of the township government in exercising its authority in villages (Zhou 2007b).

Compared with the declining effectiveness of township governments, the changing role of village governments is more complicated. Since the decollectivization of the late 1970s, village governments have experienced multiple and often conflicting forces of change: the selective and continuing intervention by the local governments, the bottom-up processes of local village election, and the presence of exit options for villagers to leave home for jobs in the cities. As institutional links between the township government and villages weaken, there is an institutional void in village governance. In this context, village cadres play an important role in filling the vacuum, shaping the relationship with external environments and the flow of resources into and out of villages. Some still follow the traditional route in cultivating a good relationship with the township government so as to get privileged access to resources; others are disillusioned about the local government and keep at best an arms-length relationship.

Along with these changes in institutions, the behavior of the township government and village cadres has evolved considerably as well. My third proposition is that *there are significant changes in the basis of legitimacy on which the power of local authorities is derived and exercised.* In the Mao era, local governments—the People's Commune and village cadres—derived their authority from political power and bureaucratic appointment from above. With the widespread village elections in recent years, and the increasing transparency of state policies through mass media, an implicit alliance between higher-level government officials and villagers increases constraints on local authorities. As a result, local cadres must engage in symbolic struggle over legitimate claims for their actions. As shown in this study, the retention of conservation funds by village governments, interactions between villages and the township government in resource allocation, and the implementation of SLCP policies within villages, all these were carried out through negotiating processes based on making legitimate claims rather than naked power. And we also observe multiple bases for making legitimate claims: some appeal for the purpose of the collective good, others resort to subtle in-group solidarity, and still others evoke the rational calculation of the peasants. Perhaps more than anything else, these subtle shifts in symbolic claims have best captured fundamental changes in authority relationships in rural China.

One important consequence of these changes is that there are significant variations across villages in their corporate bases of resource redistribution, with great consequences for life chances of village households (Davis et al.

2007). My discussions above contrasted corporate governance between Li Village and SB Village, one with a strong village government office in control, and the other with the village government paralyzed and ineffective. Even among those villages with strong governance, we observe diverse governance practices. In one village of my research, for example, the village head told me that he deliberately put any resources that flow into his village directly in the hands of the villagers with little left for the village collective, whereas in SL Village, the village head tried hard to retain as many resources as possible in the collective body. These instances demonstrate significant variations even among villages in the same region.

If the reader finds uneasy tensions and contradictions among the propositions outlined above, this is indeed the case. These propositions are drawn from observations about multiple processes of institutional change that are full of inconsistencies and contradictions. On the one hand, the increasingly resourceful central government and provincial governments are playing an active role in rural development and demanding that township and village governments take responsibility for policy implementation; on the other hand, deep suspicion of local authorities leads the central government to adopt such measures as budgetary resource control and regular personnel transfers to constrain the autonomy of local governments. Along with these changes in the political arena, the expansion of markets reduces control of government agents over household spending and decision making (Nee 1989).

As a result, we observe numerous ironies and contradictions in those processes and episodes at the local level. Indeed, to a large extent the future of rural China depends on how these ironies and contradictions are resolved in the process of institutional change. In my view, rural China is at a crossroads today. After gradual changes over many years, the earlier mode of corporatist coordination at township and village levels is in disarray, unable to respond to such profound changes in rural areas as the extensive land transfer and intensified market competition; as a result, both farmers and local authorities face high levels of uncertainty. In my view, there is a high possibility of bifurcation in rural China. On the one hand, as shown in Oi (1999), villages in coastal areas with natural endowment and trade links with the outside world are likely to continue rapid economic growth, which may induce the emergence of new institutions of governance. On the other hand, in the hinterland of China where villagers struggle on the edge of poverty, institutional involution, in the form of stagnation in institutional forms and mechanisms, may force farmers to retreat into the traditional mode of governance and reliance on kinship ties and neighborhood mutual assistance for survival. In either case, there is a distinct possibility that we are witnessing the beginning of a postcorporatist era with emerging new modes of governance that are significantly different from those of the past.

## CHAPTER EIGHT

# Creating Wealth: Land Seizure, Local Government, and Farmers

*Zhou Feizhou*

This chapter focuses on the role of local governments in creating wealth in rural China. For more than a decade, sociologists have debated how political power in the postsocialist era creates economic advantage. On one side are those who hold that in the transition from a planned economy to a market economy, old political elites are replaced by emerging economic elites (Nee 1989; Nee 1996; Nee and Cao 1999). On the other side, are those who see the political elites maintain and reproduce superior status through past and current social networks (Bian and Logan 1996; Walder 2002; Zhou 2000a). Oi and Walder (Oi 1992, 1995; Oi and Walder 1999), for example, highlight how institutions of rural governance create a context in which local political elites reap disproportionate rewards. Most studies of China's postsocialist transformations, however, have not fully specified the exact mechanism by which local governments and their agents have expanded and maintained their rent-seeking character. Moreover, existing scholarship has not yet dealt with economic and political consequences of the recent surge of land sales as the primary source of government wealth. In this chapter, I use recent examples of land sales in economically dynamic Zhejiang Province to illustrate how local government elites have used the de-collectivization of rural land to their advantage. By focusing in particular on the issues of government revenues, we speak to larger arguments about creation and distribution of financial gain in postsocialist China.

## FROM RUNNING FACTORIES TO LAND DEVELOPMENT

Advocates for fiscal decentralization argue that devolving financial management to lower levels of government not only grants greater autonomy to local governments and increases the operational efficiency but also triggers competitive mechanisms that may spur more equitable distribution of resources (Wang 1997; Qian and Weingast 1997; Litvak, Ahmad, and Bird 1998). However, decentralization that removes a government's taxing power may also weaken regulatory control, and thus result in "fiefdom economies" that both undermine state power and increase spatial/regional inequalities.

In the mid-1980s, as part of a drive to decentralize the economy, the Chinese government introduced reforms to heighten local accountability for public welfare and reduce indirect tax burdens. Over the next decade, decentralization produced many winners and few losers. In particular rural residents and local governments prospered from the exponential growth of industrial enterprises owned collectively by townships and villages (TVEs). In the process "fiefdom economies" began to form and the state's ability to collect taxes declined. Between 1979 and 1993, the ratio of revenues to GDP dropped from 28.4 percent to 12.6 percent and the ratio of central government revenues to overall revenues dropped from 46.8 percent to 31.6 percent (refer to http://www.51kj.com.cn/news/ 20051206/ n40884.shtml).

At the same time as local governments altered their relationship to the central authorities, local collective enterprises were caught in a complex relationship to local governments. On one hand, the TVEs had access to easy credit, and even when they faced serious operating losses received bailouts from local governments. On the other hand, the close ties between government and enterprises encouraged local governments to "hide their wealth in their enterprises" by using locally controlled enterprises as tax shelters and allowing enterprises to pay fees to local governments rather than taxes to higher level units (Xiang 1999). Originally, scholars had hoped that fiscal decentralization would help resolve the problem of "soft budget constraint," but over time nonbudgetary revenues actually increased at local levels.

In response to the loss of central government revenue, the central government implemented the 1994 tax-sharing system that separated tax collection from other financial affairs. Soon after, China adopted a value-added tax (VAT) as the major tax category levied on all local enterprises whereby 75 percent of the tax was remitted to the central government and 25 percent remained for local governments. Henceforth, collectively owned and privately owned enterprises would all be subject to the same tax ratio as opposed to the earlier system of fixed payments to local governments. Under the new VAT system the central government reduced its overall risk, while local governments that ran enterprises received less revenue and faced increased risk of bankruptcy. Furthermore, since value-added tax was categorized as a turnover tax, it was collected whether an enterprise turned a profit or not; as long as the enterprise had input and output, it was subject to taxes. As a result, local enterprises with low profits became a heavy burden for local governments. Moreover, VAT was collected through a national taxation system that was completely independent from local government's tax collections. Even though the central government's tax rebate policy for VAT was positive for areas making a large contribution to VAT, local government's became less enthusiastic about setting up industrial enterprises and began to turn to other sources of revenue growth. In the rich coastal provinces that were benefiting from massive foreign direct investment (FDI) for greenfield development, land sales became the primary new revenue source.

As early as 1989, the central government had established the ground rules for handling profits from sale of collective land.[1] But when land prices were low, conversion rates were modest and initially profits were of relatively little consequence.[2] In 1992, however, sale of collective land suddenly expanded and land conversion revenues reached 52.5 billion yuan. (*China Economic Times*/zhongguo jingji shibao), March 19, 2004) To encourage proactive collection of land conversion income by local governments, local governments were allowed to retain 100 percent of land conversion income revenues starting in 1994. In other words, they no longer turned over any of their profit to the central government. After 1998, land conversion income continued to grow, and in 2002 it reached 241.68 billion yuan (China Economic Times/zhongguo jingji shibao), March 19, 2004).

Legally, rural land can be converted for only three purposes: public good (e.g., facilities for transportation, water conservancy or irrigation, health care, public health), industrial use, or business development (e.g., real estate or commercial development).[3] In booming coastal areas, the demand for nonagricultural land rose sharply and these restrictions from the central government have not been rigorously enforced; indeed, they've been largely ignored. Local governments came up with all kinds of "creative" ways to develop land, such as breaking large plots (which must be dealt with at the central government level) into smaller plots for verification and approval at the local level, cross-province "occupation and compensation balance" trade-offs, and so forth. The upsurge in land development was accompanied by the overheating of infrastructure investments; as the economy grew, local governments obtained enormous revenues from land development and conversion.

## GOVERNMENT LAND REVENUE

First, we need to clearly define government "land revenue": land revenue is revenue related to land seizure or conversion and obtained by a government through tax collection, fees, or sale. In the current tax system, there is no distinct category of taxes or fees dedicated to land seizure or sale; government land revenue is scattered among a variety of taxation systems and fees. There is no comprehensive reliable statistical source on government revenues from land sales, and thus our analysis must filter out the necessary numbers from a variety of taxes collected by the government and must build on initial estimates.

Land revenue can be divided into two major categories: the first from land taxes and fees, and the second from land conversion income. Land taxes and fees are further comprised of three sources: The first source is tax revenue directly related to land, including the urban land use tax, land value-added tax ("land VAT") (both of which are collected via the local tax system); arable land occupancy tax, and title tax (both collected via the government financial system). The second source is revenue derived from taxes on the real estate industry and from sources related to land seizures. We can call these indirect land taxes: There is no strict definition of this term, but we can understand it to mean taxes that are incurred by industries that benefit from land seizures and conversion. In Eastern China, the key industries are construction and real estate development. The third source derives from departmental fees such as arable land reclamation fees or fees for new construction-use land in cities and towns, collected by the Land Bureau. These are fees directly related to land. In addition, a diverse and complex range of fees is levied by different governmental departments at various stages of land seizure, conversion, transfer, and real estate development.

The second category of land revenue derives from land conversion income. Land conversion income is not a tax, but a rental fee given to the government for conversion of land. For the sake of convenience, herein we shall use this term to indicate the total revenue derived from land conversion (calculated in accordance with the transaction land value). I will use "land conversion income net profit" to indicate the profit gained after the land conversion cost has been deducted. Thus, land conversion income means the total earnings of the local government from land conversion after the land has been sold via auction or negotiated agreement. There is no accurate number for the national land conversion income, but according to one report, seen by the author, national land conversion income exceeded 1 trillion yuan between 1992 and 2002, with the bulk of this revenue accruing between 2001 and 2003, when the national land conversion income totaled 910 billion yuan.[4] The land conversion income net profit was approximately one-fourth of this figure.

An example of land conversion income composition can be seen from the data for one of the study areas, shown in Table 8.1. The total land conversion income in J City of Zhejiang Province increased from 513 million yuan in 2001 to 1.3 billion in 2002, and to 2 billion in 2003. The local government tax revenues for this time period were approximately 1 to 1.1 billion yuan per year. Thus in 2003 the land conversion income greatly surpassed the local government tax revenues. The last column in Table 8.1 compares costs to derive the net profit for land conversion income. The four types of costs added up to approximately 84.4 percent, whereas the net profit represented approximately 15.6 percent of the land conversion income.

TABLE 8.1
*Land conversion income costs and net profit, J City, Zhejiang Province*

| | 2001 | | 2002 | | 2003 | | PERCENT OF TOTAL |
|---|---|---|---|---|---|---|---|
| | Million yuan RMB | % | Million yuan RMB | % | Million RMB | % | |
| Total land conversion income | 513.86 | 100 | 1,379.82 | 100 | 2,077.45 | 100 | 100% |
| Land tax fees | 18.58 | 3.6 | 80.78 | 5.9 | 203.72 | 9.8 | 7.6% |
| Land compensation fees | 296.58 | 57.7 | 795.43 | 57.6 | 976.90 | 47.0 | 52.1% |
| Land development fees | 66.28 | 12.9 | 330.30 | 23.9 | 504.89 | 24.3 | 22.7% |
| Land conversion business fees | 10.28 | 2.0 | 27.60 | 2.0 | 41.44 | 2.0 | 2% |
| Net profit | 122.13 | 23.8 | 145.71 | 10.6 | 350.49 | 16.9 | 15.6% |

SOURCE: Field survey.

In another of our study areas, S County, land conversion income in 2003 generated gross revenues of 1.92 billion yuan, which is far higher than the budget revenue of 1.3 billion yuan for the year 2003. In a third study area, Y City, the total revenue from land conversion income is 2 billion yuan. After deducting costs, the net revenue is approximately 400 million yuan, or 20 percent of the total land conversion income.[5]

## LAND REVENUE AND LOCAL GOVERNMENT FINANCE

It is widely believed that land revenues have become essential for the financial survival of local governments and that financial management of land has created a system external to government with its own cycle of revenue and expenditure. Local governments like to say "the first financial pillar is industry, the second is land." This popular expression demonstrates the existence of two revenue streams. Another expression, "for sustenance, rely on the first source of revenue, for construction, rely on the second," explains the way in which these two revenue streams are expended. These two expressions clearly demonstrate the significance of land finance to local governments. However, looking at the results of our survey, only one part of the above view is accurate, because not only does the "secondary financial system" rely on land revenues, but also the first formal budgetary revenues are becoming increasingly reliant on land rather than on industry.

Extrabudgetary revenue sources consist primarily of land conversion income and departmental fees. From our research we learned that land-

TABLE 8.2
*Extrabudgetary revenue in three study sites, Zhejiang Province, 2003*

|  | S COUNTY | | J CITY | | Y CITY | |
|---|---|---|---|---|---|---|
|  | Million yuan | % | Million yuan | % | Million yuan | % |
| Administrative fees | 480 | 16 | 1,360 | 39 | 500 | 20 |
| Government funds | 510 | 18 | 100 | 3 | 500 | 20 |
| Land conversion income | 1,920 | 66 | 2,000 | 58 | 1,500 | 60 |
| Total extrabudgetary revenue | 2,910 | 100 | 3,460 | 100 | 2,500 | 100 |

SOURCE: Field survey.

related revenue is the primary source of extrabudgetary revenue as shown in Table 8.2, which presents sources of extrabudgetary revenue in the three locales where we conducted our research. Since some administrative fees listed in Table 8.2 are also derived from land revenues, the total estimated land revenue makes up 60 percent to 80 percent of the total extrabudgetary revenue.

Land taxes, another source of local government revenues deriving from land conversion, are also a major driving force for the overall growth of revenues in recent years. Table 8.3 lists a few of the main taxes that have contributed to the growth of local government budget revenues. We can see that the growth of local government revenues was 7.1 percent in 2002 and 28.1 percent in 2003. However, the growth in the land taxes was 28.2 percent in 2002 and 69.6 percent in 2003, which far surpassed that of the total revenue. Land tax revenues contributed 109.9 percent of the total revenue growth in 2002 and 71.3 percent in 2003. In other words, increases in land revenue drove growth of local government revenues.

TABLE 8.3
*Land revenue's contribution to local budget revenues (S County)*

|  |  | GROWTH IN 2002 | | GROWTH IN 2003 | |
|---|---|---|---|---|---|
|  |  | Million yuan | % | Million yuan | % |
| (1) | Total local budget revenue | +70.03 | 7.1 | +303.40 | +28.1 |
| (2) | Direct land taxes | 37.82 | | 148.16 | |
| (3) | Indirect land taxes (business tax) | 82.53 | | 65.39 | |
| (4) | Indirect land taxes (income tax) | −43.39 | | 2.67 | |
| (2) + (3) + (4) | Total land taxes | 76.96 | +28.2 | 216.22 | +69.6 |
| [(2) + (3) + (4)]/(1) | Contribution rate | 109.9% | | 71.3% | |

SOURCE: Field survey.

118     *Zhou Feizhou*

EXPENDITURES FROM LAND SALES

Extrabudgetary land conversion income is primarily used in the following three areas. First it is used to pay for the costs of land development and transfer. This includes compensation for farmers and costs for providing public utilities such as road, water, electricity, and sewage. As our above analysis of land conversion income pointed out, this portion is not included in the calculation of land conversion income net profit. Net profits from land conversion income have two primary uses. The first is to cover land seizure compensation fees and other costs involved in land seizure, the second is to finance construction of local infrastructure.

Land conversion income is "easy money" in the hands of the government, not bound by budgetary constraints and not part of the formal capital expenditure system. However, not all conversions are equally profitable. Officially all rural land falls into three categories, each with its own mechanism for setting prices: land for the public good (*gongyixing yongdi*) is priced by government fiat, industrial-use land (*gongyexing yongdi*) by negotiated agreement, and for-profit-use or commercial-use land (*jingyingxing yongdi*) by auction. Because revenue derived from land converted for the public good (for public roads, waterworks, education, medical or public health facilities, etc.) often does not fully cover costs of developing the land, the government usually needs to put money into these "unprofitable" ventures. Because governments discount prices for industrial-use land, they also rarely profit from land developed for industrial purposes. Thus we can see in the comparison of prices in Table 8.4, governments primarily rely upon commercial-use land to enhance revenues via land seizure and transfer. [6]

The second major use of extrabudgetary expenditure is as initial capital for establishing development and construction companies directly under the local government. In developed areas of Eastern China, most county gov-

TABLE 8.4
*Two types of construction use—land conversion, S County, 1999–2004*
*(Units: area = mu, price = million yuan)*

|  |  | 1999 | 2000 | 2001 | 2002 | 2003 | 2004 |
|---|---|---|---|---|---|---|---|
| Industrial-use land | Area | 909 | 2597 | 1215 | 4602 | 4220 | N.A. |
|  | Land price | 0.13 | 0.15 | 0.14 | 0.12 | 0.13 | N.A. |
|  | Total price | 122.59 | 403.77 | 170.63 | 540.76 | 530.08 | N.A. |
| Commercial-use land | Area | 214 | 196 | 392 | 268 | 3170 | 633 |
|  | Land price | 0.59 | 0.74 | 0.34 | 1.82 | 0.64 | 2.39 |
|  | Total price | 125.10 | 146.15 | 136.20 | 477.19 | 1,924.54 | 1,387.70 |

SOURCE: Field survey.

ernments have several such companies. The bulk of the land conversion income goes to such entities as Urban Investment Development Corporations, Ltd., Urban Transit Investment Corporations, Ltd., Urban Waterworks Groups, Urban Residential Village District Revitalization Corporations, Ltd., and the like. These companies are usually referred to as "government companies," and are categorized as state-owned investment corporations. Most were established after the year 2000, and all have government officials serving as chairman of the board or general manager. With the exception of transit companies, most of these corporations are not-for-profit, and their primary purpose is to invest in and construct urban public infrastructure. For instance, in S County, the registered capital of Urban Investment Development Corporations was 186 million yuan, and the bulk of these funds came from government appropriations (mostly derived from the land conversion income). In 2003, 120 million yuan was appropriated, and 300 million yuan was appropriated in 2004, with all funds coming from the land conversion income controlled by the county government's fiscal system. Urban Transit Investment Corporations had a registered capital of 80 million yuan, with 50 million of this coming from the government fiscal system. The waterworks and urban village district reform companies follow the same model.

While initially it may appear that these capital funds are all used on construction of municipal public infrastructure, in fact, things are not so simple. Another major goal for establishing these funds and corporations is to garner finance from the banking sector. In other words, the government's injection of land conversion income into the companies is not directly used for construction, but to serve as capital funds for obtaining bank loans.

In land development and urban construction, the method of "using land to foster development of other land" (*yidi yangdi*) is often employed. This logic is that some of the public-good-use land that is found in good locations can be converted to business-use land through auction, and the resulting large conversion revenue can be used to subsidize the costs of construction for public good projects. For example, 200 mu of a 1,000 mu school construction project could be converted to commercial- and residential-use land for development, and the revenue from this conversion can then be used to pay for all of the costs of land seizure, development, and construction for the school. After these costs are covered, there will still be money to spare. Obtaining land collateral loans by a government-controlled company, in fact, establishes a logic of "using land to foster development of other land," except that when "good land" is used to "foster the development of other land," it is not truly used for land development, but to serve as high-value collateral in order to obtain a bank loan.

The basic logic of this process is to use collateral loans on old land reserves to carry out a new round of land seizures, then to use the revenues from land conversion to pay off collateral loans, and then use the newly seized land to borrow a new round of land collateral loans. In this way, banking sector funds serve as a "lubricant" for land seizure, development, and conversion, allowing the government to quickly expand the scope of land development and to accumulate large revenues from land conversion. Most of these land revenues, as we have seen in the analysis above, end up being injected into construction projects for urbanization. In this cyclical process, the logic of the government and the banks is very clear: Land is used as collateral for bank loans, which are generally paid back to the bank within one or two years. The loans that are guaranteed with government finance, though longer term, are guaranteed by a source that will not go bankrupt, and thus the banks do not worry when granting such loans. As long as government finance and banking sector capital continue to be injected into urban construction, the government land tax revenues, especially those collected from the construction and real estate industries, will continue to grow, and government fiscal strength will also increase. Taking the process one step further, it is a "win-win" scenario, in which the growth of government revenues promotes the further expansion of banking sector finance and land seizure.

There are, however, two potential risks. One is the financial risk for the banking sector. We can see very clearly that this "win-win" situation can only be maintained if the scope of land seizure continues to expand and the value of converted land continues to rise. If land seizures cannot continue or land conversion values drop, the government's land conversion incomes will shrink, and the government will be unable to pay back the large land collateral loans. In the short term, this kind of risk is closely linked to state policies; any tightening of land development policies or restriction on the scope of infrastructure would undoubtedly increase this risk. From the long-term perspective, it's only a matter of time until this risk becomes a reality. Although the income of the general population in Eastern China has grown rapidly, many of the new urban residents are blue-collar workers who do not create a demand for high-value commercial- and residential-use land. Thus it is not possible in the long term to maintain high land prices through continual expansion of land development.

Land development also faces a societal risk: The local governments and banking sector operate effectively together because the government can minimize the claims of individual farmers and village residents. In the 1950s, the state relied on monopoly powers to hold down grain prices to support industrialization. Today, the relationship between the government and the farmers remains the same, but "land" now substitutes for "grain," and "urbanization" for "industrialization."

## THE GOVERNMENT AND THE FARMERS

According to the current regulations of the "Land Management Law," the government must pay three kinds of fees to farmers whose land is seized: compensation fees, resettlement fees, and expropriated acreage fees. The general guideline for compensation is a sum equal to six to ten times the value of the average annual production of the seized land over the previous three years, and the resettlement fee is four to six times the value of the average annual production of the seized land over the previous three years. Furthermore, the total compensation for land and resettlement may not exceed thirty times the value of the average annual production of the land as it had been used over the previous three years. There is no unified standard for the expropriated acreage compensation fee for farmers' houses and plants that cannot be harvested.

Actual cash values for land compensation vary widely, not only across provinces and counties but also among townships within a single county (see Table 8.5). These differences primarily arise from the differences in average annual production values for the three years prior to land seizure, but they inevitably create friction between the farmers and the government.

TABLE 8.5
*Land and resettlement compensation allowance standards for each township,
S County (in yuan)*

| Name of township | Average annual production value over the preceding three years | Land compensation fee per mu | Resettlement compensation fee per mu | Expropriated acreage compensation fee per mu |
|---|---|---|---|---|
| Lanqiao | 1,560 | 12,480 | 12,850 | 25,330 |
| Qixian | 1,360 | 10,880 | 11,570 | 22,450 |
| Qianqing | 1,410 | 11,280 | 12,690 | 23,970 |
| Sunduan | 1,330 | 10,640 | 10,430 | 21,070 |
| Fuquan | 1,330 | 10,640 | 10,430 | 21,070 |
| Ma'an | 1,260 | 10,080 | 7,850 | 17,930 |
| Pingshui | 1,110 | 8,880 | 8,330 | 17,210 |
| Anchang | 1,330 | 10,640 | 11,950 | 22,590 |
| Wangtan | 980 | 7,840 | 9,160 | 17,000 |
| Huashe | 1,510 | 12,080 | 12,840 | 24,920 |
| Hutang | 1,400 | 11,200 | 11,590 | 22,790 |
| Lanting | 1,340 | 10,720 | 10,370 | 21,090 |
| Jidong | 940 | 7,520 | 12,500 | 20,020 |
| Yangxunqiao | 1,490 | 11,920 | 11,550 | 23,470 |
| Lizhu | 1,300 | 10,400 | 9,650 | 20,050 |
| Fusheng | 1,250 | 10,000 | 8,750 | 18,750 |
| Taoyan | 1,320 | 10,560 | 8,580 | 19,140 |
| Xialu | 1,160 | 9,280,993 | 13,140 | 22,420 |
| Pingjian | 1,090 | 8,720 | 11,620 | 20,340 |
| Jijiang | 1,000 | 8,000 | 9,840 | 17,840 |

SOURCE: Field survey.

Compensation standards are extremely low not only in terms of farmers' revenue, but also in comparison to revenues obtained by the government. Looking at farmers' revenues, in places like Zhejiang Province, most farmers in suburban areas grow flowers, trees, vegetables, and other cash crops, often with a net profit of over 10,000 yuan per mu per year. However, compensation standards are calculated in accordance with the production values of grain crops, and so the land compensation fees at best are equal to the net profit per mu for only two years of the cash crops actually grown on the land. Looking at government revenue, whether the government engages in a negotiated industrial conversion or an auction sale of for-profit-use land, after the farmers' land is seized, 20 percent of the seized land will become public-use land, and 60 percent of the industrial-use land will be converted at cost. However, the farmers do not know these details; what they see is that the government is giving them a compensation fee of approximately 30,000 yuan per mu, whereas industrial-use land conversion agreements convert the land at approximately 180,000 per mu, and commercial-use land compensation reaches 1 million yuan per mu. Beyond the shadow of a doubt, the compensation for farmers is excessively low.

What's more, farmers often do not even receive the fees in full. According to the current national land system, rural land is owned by the village collective rather than the individual farmers; individual farmers only possess the land use rights and a portion of the income rights. Therefore, the land compensation fee ownership rights belong to the village collective, not individual villagers, and in practice, these compensation fees generally become "village collective property." Only the resettlement compensation fee and the expropriated acreage compensation fee are directly allocated to the farmers. And in practice even resettlement compensation may not go entirely to the farmers.

The resettlement compensation fee takes into consideration the farmers' immovable property in recognition that after land has been seized, farmers need to set up a new life and to find a new source of employment. The state also requires that local governments prioritize employment and compensation for farmers who have lost land. Therefore, local governments are exploring ways to provide guarantees or safeguards for the livelihood and employment of such farmers. In our survey of S County, we found a pilot project that provides an old-age pension of 220 yuan per month to female farmers 55 or older and male farmers 60 or older who have had their land seized. Three parties—the government, village collective, and farmers—all put up capital for this pension fund. On average, 23,000 yuan must be put into the pension plan for each participant, with 16,000 yuan coming from the government (primarily from land conversion income), 3,500 yuan from the village collective (primarily from the land compensation fees), and 3,500 yuan from the individual farmers (primarily from the resettlement compensation fee). According to Table 8.5, the standard for the resettlement compensation fee is approximately 8,000 to 12,000 per mu. Since individuals hold on average 0.3–0.5 mu, nearly all of the resettlement compensation fee goes into the pension security fund. According to our on-site interviews, strict and precise calculations are not followed in the S County government's maintenance of and allocations from this fund, and a portion of the fund's capital has already been put to other uses by the government.

The above analysis shows that of the three compensation fees, only the expropriated acreage compensation fee is given directly to the farmers. It is thus no surprise that farmers faced with land seizure fraudulently "plant" houses and fields. The "planting house" scheme is one in which farmers quickly erect simply constructed buildings on their housing site before their land is seized to increase the area of residential use so that they can obtain more compensation allowance for associated structures on the land. The "planting field" scheme is one in which farmers work to falsify plantings in their fields. For instance, they may stick tree branches in the ground and pretend that they are trees.

Of course, in the process of land seizure or urbanization, farmers may receive more than just the small portion of compensatory fees listed above. In our survey of urbanized areas, we found that farmers' revenues rose rather quickly. However, this was due to rental income rather than government compensation fees. In the past decade, a huge number of migrants from Central and Western China have found industrial jobs in Eastern China. Many live in dormitories provided by the factories in which they work, but a large portion live in houses rented from local residents. Some pay higher rent for houses in better locations or houses that face the street. Interviews in Hongjian village in S County showed that renovations to the old village resulted in many farmers having one house torn down and another one given to them in compensation (*chai yi bu yi*). In general, if the majority of the land in a village is seized, the government will set aside land in the village for farmers to build houses. The land is zoned as a new residential district, and farmers hold the land ownership rights.

In general, however, land seizure bestows more power on the village collective than on the individual farmers. Not only does the collective gain possession of the land compensation fee, but also it can increase its revenue through the "set-aside land policy" (*yuliudi zhengce*). The size of the area set aside corresponds to the size of the village. Large villages (over 1,000 mu) set aside 25 mu, medium-sized villages (between 670 and 1,000 mu) set aside 20 mu, whereas small villages (under 670 mu) set aside 15 mu. The set-aside land is converted at cost, and any net profit made by the county is returned to the village. Conversion costs include seized-land compensation fees (including land compensation fees, resettlement compensation fees, expropriated acreage compensation fees, etc.), tax-reporting fees, and construction-use land offset index fund fees. Set-aside land is usually allocated all at once, in accordance with planning for development within the village boundaries, and must conform to overall plans for land use and city planning. Set-aside land serves as an important and stable economic resource at the village level, and is usually used for the village to build standard factories, office buildings, commercial-use buildings for rental, or shareholding land equity investments. As an example, when the Keqiao Street District carried out an asset inventory survey in 2004, the net for-profit assets ranged from a low of 12.7 million for Hongfeng Village to a high of 56.94 million for Shuangchuan Village. Although collective set-aside land obviously provided compensation for farmers in areas where land was seized, the compensation did not go directly to the individual farmers. In truth, the income from the collective set-aside land resulted from negotiations between the village-level collectives and the government, not the farmers and the government. Also, the way in which the revenue from the set-aside land was distributed between the village collective and the individual farmers varied greatly from village to village, depending on the power structure within each village.[7]

## CONCLUSION

Massive conversion of agricultural land is one of the most significant and conspicuous processes of wealth creation in China's postsocialist history. This chapter explains how land conversion became a primary strategy for local governments to regain income after recentralization of the tax system in 1994 and examines the evolution of this process from the perspective of families that lost land and local governments that reaped the bulk of the monetary compensation.

In terms of administrative practice, the tax-sharing reforms initiated in the mid-1990s to restore central government coffers fundamentally changed the relationship between central and local governments. However, although the local governments changed some of their specific behaviors, the new reliance on land sales exhibited strong continuities at the local level in terms of the practices of the extrabudgetary fiscal systems. Moreover not only did extrabudgetary "soft budget constraint" problems persist but they also became more hidden and egregious in light of the huge windfall profits.

The second similarity in local government behavior is their reliance on bank loans to finance their futures. Prior to reforms, the national movement to create township enterprises so that "the chimneys are smoking in every village and every household has work" (*cuncun maoyan, huhu shangban*) resulted in a large amount of bad debt; after reforms, government finance also leveraged banking capital to support large-scale land seizures and to provide input into infrastructure. But this time the capital has been used to support a high-priced real estate market rather than new jobs for local residents or payments for school and medical fees.

It is still too early to gauge the long-term level of financial risk in this new approach to local government; however, in the short term, we can see that individual farmers have paid a steep price. Prior to the tax-sharing system reforms, booming township and village enterprises provided favorable conditions for farmers to engage in nonagricultural work. The process of land conversions and the land enclosure behavior (*quandi xingwei*) of the government, in contrast, have put most farm households at a disadvantaged position in the process. Not only do they rarely receive adequate compensation for the loss of their immovable property, but also they have been unable to exercise their rights as owners of collective land. Local governments choose this path for creating wealth partly because of pressures created by recent fiscal reforms. But with no institutional safeguards to guarantee equal voice for individual farmers, a handful of local officials gain at the expense of individuals. Moreover, within the current institutional framework, the risk of social inequity and political instability is likely to become greater with the passage of time.

## CHAPTER NINE

# Resolution Mechanisms for Land Rights Disputes

*Zhang Jing*

## INTRODUCTION

Between 1987 and 2001 approximately seven million acres of farmland were transferred to nonagricultural use.[1] Assuming rural land use of 0.13 acre per capita, some estimate that as many as 60 million rural residents have lost legal claim to their land and that were this rate of transfer to continue, more than three million would be pushed off the land in each subsequent year (Song et al. 2003; Li 2004). Clearly such a massive shift in control over land has altered the distribution of relative wealth and power in rural communities. Moreover, because this transformation in property rights occurred in the context of radical departure from past socialist practices, there have been numerous disputes about how to distribute the profits among the multiple parties involved.[2] According to recent studies, in some locales, 20 percent of profits from requisitioned land are distributed to local governments, 40 percent to land developers, 25 percent to village organizations, and less than 10 percent to individual farmers (Wang H. 2004; Zhou in Chapter 8 of this volume). Not surprisingly, petitions, resistance, and conflicts related to land transactions are becoming increasingly more common. One official report claims that land-related petitions constituted 70 percent of farmers' petitions in 2003 (Wang H. 2004).

Land rights disputes, however, are not limited to conflicts over land requisition; they extend to disputes over how to adjust the allocation of land contracted among individual households within villages, terms of contracts between farmers and the state, and terms for pricing the land. Most fundamentally, these disputes revolve around the question of who has the power to decide on land-related matters; and therefore, who will define subsequent property rights. What concerns us, therefore, is not only a purely economic and legal process, but also a social and political process. Legal recognition of ownership is not equivalent to social recognition and without social legitimization, the economic process of property rights clarification cannot proceed. Even if it does proceed, it will be stopped short by sociopolitical problems. In this chapter I explain how legal and political uncertainties operate in a property regime distinct from the legal-rule-directed model of the West.

At first it may seem that conflicts arise because the law is unclear, but I propose that conflicts over competing logics of entitlement, not the formal law, are decisive as various parties search for criteria most advantageous to their own interests. The parties concerned do not steadfastly support any one legal clause, but choose different ones according to their changing needs. In Chinese land dispute cases, different claims based on multiple sources of legitimacy are often invoked. Some cite the land contract to assert that the land belongs only to those named in the contract and that the right to profit from a sale belongs solely to those listed. Others cite the collective ownership clause in the Chinese land law and assert that because all rural land is public property belonging to the village collective, profits from sale of that land should therefore be shared by all villagers. Still others cite the general idea of public ownership to assert that land is public and should therefore be disposed of by public organizations such as governments and their representative organizations, including the elected village committees. What logic, then, do they follow? What factors can influence the transactions' outcomes?

From the legalistic standpoint the cause of the conflicts is the lack of clear legal stipulation of property rights, and the solutions lie in legal actions that clarify property rights. The case materials discussed in this chapter, however, show that while sometimes land disputes in China manifest themselves as economic and legalistic problems, the deeper causes are disagreements over who can influence or participate in the making of the rules, how influence is exercised, and on what grounds consensus is achieved. In the following sections of this chapter, I will first offer a number of concrete examples of land right disputes, followed by an analysis of the mechanisms leading to different resolutions. I will conclude by highlighting the simultaneous existence of two modes of social order formation, rule-law-based order versus social-interest-based order.

## COMPLEXITIES OF PROPERTY RIGHTS: FIVE EXAMPLES

To illustrate how land dispute cases were situated within the broad institutional configurations and local conditions, I describe five different cases from recent fieldwork in Inner Mongolia and Hebei and Zhejiang Provinces.

### Case One

In 1984, an Inner Mongolian farmer SH contracted from the government of D Town H Village 492 acres of desert. It was stipulated that the farmer would be responsible for greening the desert by planting trees and that after ten years, any profits from the sale of timber would be split 20 percent to the village government and 80 percent to the farmer, SH. SH persuaded seven more farmers to join him in planting trees. They sold their family property to purchase saplings and achieved a 95 percent survival rate for the trees. At a 1985 desert treatment meeting held in Shanxi Province, SH was praised as an "advanced model." Following his initial success, SH asked to expand his contracted area for additional tree planting. The director of the town forestry department supported him and with the director's connections and encouragement, he contracted another 951 acres. Profit division was again 20:80. This time SH also mobilized 127 other farmers to join him as stockholders. At first they didn't have the proper technology and the trees' survival rate was only 10 percent in the first year and 20 percent in the second year. In the third year, the farmers consulted desert treatment experts and employed the technology of netted protection walls, which called for first steadying the sand and then planting the trees. With the plentiful rain that year, the survival rate reached 85 percent. The greening of the desert created a miracle for the town and hundreds more wanted to participate. SH then started the "Desert Treatment Joint Stock Limited Liability Company" and expanded his contracted area to 37,392 acres. Company regulations required group responsibility, stock dividends, and separate individual contracts. The contract between the company and the village government also clearly stipulated that the stock-holding households would receive 80 percent of future profits.

By 1993, trees planted in the 1980s were ready for harvest and some stock-holding farmers began to fell the trees and sell the timber. The town forestry department, however, claimed that the trees had already been incorporated into the national protective forest system and could not be felled arbitrarily. Some stockholders experiencing financial difficulties demanded that the company pay stock dividends. Citing the terms of the contracts, SH refused, but stockholders insisted on payment of stock dividends. SH could not meet their demand, and eventually had to take loans from credit unions to pay stockholders. Many farmers received no compensation for years of labor; people began to distrust the company and many quit the desert treatment effort.[3]

In this case, the contract was officially signed by the farmers and the village government, but rules for profit distribution obviously had not adequately specified exclusive authority. Because the trees on the desert were defined as part of the protective forest, policies limiting their felling terminated the profit division between the parties concerned. Although the desert, which was within the contractors' residential area, should normally be considered their collective property, the contractors' right to profit from this property was prohibited by the state. Here state power trumped the terms of the land rights contract and the rights of individual parties to the contract.

### Case Two

In Q Town in Hebei Province, chestnut trees are farmers' main source of income. During initial land adjustments after 1980, the village estimated the yield of every chestnut tree and then distributed the land based on the number of persons in each household. In 1991 land was again redistributed, but this time the contracts between the village cadres and the farmers stated that there would be no further adjustments until 2000. However, in 1995, as part of national government efforts to promote long-term investment in farmland and to enforce birth control efforts, the central government enacted a new policy stipulating that land contracts should remain unchanged for the next 30 years. At the same time, the township government issued its own directive to suit the local conditions, stipulating that villages that had already made adjustments should adhere to them or readjust according to local needs, whereas villages that had not made adjustments should follow state policy and make no significant adjustments for the next 30 years. In practice, however, different villages employed different adjustment plans. Some made no adjustment and extended the contract for 30 years in accordance with the state policy, while others made minor adjustments, allowing households whose size had changed to adjust agreements between themselves and the village. Those who had been allocated insufficient trees would receive compensation of 55 pounds of chestnuts from trees grown in the remaining public land. Yet other villages made major adjustments, abolishing the boundaries of the older production brigades and establishing new standards, allowing households to divide up the land and the chestnut trees anew (Xu 2002).

In this case the influence of local leaders trumped that of the central state. In determining the right to redistribute land, local officials exercised significant leverage and initiative and did not completely follow either state policy or town directive. If they had completely followed the state policy, the contracts should have remained unchanged for 30 years and there should not have been the various methods of adjustment. If they had completely followed the town policy, there should have been a uniform standard for whether a village should or should not adjust. But in practice, local level cadres made the rules based on conditions in their villages and reasonably reinterpreted the "needs" mentioned in the town directive. Here the function of the local cadres is to choose what plan to adopt in land distribution adjustment, and how to use remaining public land to compensate the losers in minor adjustments. Although the particular villages studied all produced commonly applicable proposals, dissent existed in all three villages. In one,

70 percent of the people were unsatisfied with the outcomes; in another, almost 100 percent of the households had complaints (Xu 2002), but neither state policy nor town directive could sway these decisions. According to one village cadre, their decision-making position was derived from their status as the "contract-issuing party." In the words of this cadre, "We village committees are the party issuing the contract and have the right to revoke it when the time comes" (cadre interview 2002). In this case we see clearly that despite clear stipulations of the state policy, local cadres, as representatives of the owner, could still dispose of collective property through flexible adaptations to local conditions.

### Case Three

Two towns in Zhejiang Province jointly requisitioned approximately 44 acres of land from Y Village for urban construction. According to the city government's stipulations, for every 0.164 acre of land taken away, the household should be compensated 60,000 yuan in cash and 25 percent of the acreage should be returned to the farmers for the villagers' residential construction or collectives use. Based on these regulations, Y Village should have received 11 acres of land, which, if distributed among 200-odd households, would provide each household new residential land equivalent to the size of one room. Because the transferred land was close to a new city planned by the city government and thus had good commercial value, many villagers looked forward to the sale and expected future gains from selling or renting houses. The village cadres, however, did not return the land to the villagers, but instead made an agreement with the town urban construction department whereby the village committee would control construction on the land, and the urban construction department would be responsible for securing construction permits and gain rental rights to a tea shop. In addition, a 1.8 acre parcel on the eastern bank of the river would be given to the town government for constructing new homes for the town cadres.

When construction began in 1998, more than one-hundred villagers assembled at the construction site on the eastern bank to block construction and demand their land. In the confrontation, the urban construction department admitted to having taken the farmers' land, but claimed that the village committee chair had agreed to this arrangement. They offered other pieces of land as substitutes, but when villagers discovered that the land intended as substitute had already been sold to developers in return for their promise to secure building permits for village committee cadres to use another piece of land to build a six-story rental building, the villagers refused the substitute land. From their perspective, villagers believed that their profits from the returned land had been expropriated by the village cadres. To retrieve their land, the villagers repeatedly appealed to higher-level governments. In 2000, part of the land was returned after town government intervention, but some villagers continued to appeal to the provincial Land Inspection Bureau. In petitions signed by more than 700 villagers, villagers stressed repeatedly that the village cadres violated the village's collective interest and finally the case reached the Central Commission for Discipline Inspection (Zhang and Song 2001). Through the villagers' collective efforts, the parties concerned promised to search for a plan to return the land.

The difference between this case and the previous one in Hebei is that here villagers mobilized their collective will. Thus, even in the absence of formal procedures, the collective action of the villagers torpedoed the village cadres' land transactions and partially annulled their contracts. By contrast villagers in the previous case were divided. They were originally passive and had no representative to draw up and negotiate the contract, and the village cadres became their representatives despite their different interests. In case number three in Zhejiang, villagers believed that local leaders had monopolized gain that should have gone to all. When they discovered that they were deprived of their share in the economic opportunity provided by the land resource, they came together and forced the cadres to acknowledge the principles of collective ownership over land and equitable distribution of economic opportunities. They did not oppose privatization or transfer of ownership. Rather they demanded their right to exert influence on how ownership and fruits of ownership would be clarified.

### Case Four

In a land adjustment several years ago, X Village in Hebei Province left more than 164 acres as public reserve land to be controlled by the village committee. Part of this land was originally a wasteland that had been contracted to households for 15 years if they agreed to improve it. Some households signed written contracts; others only reached oral agreements with the village cadres. Among the latter were several who paid their contract fees only for a year and never paid again. After membership on the village committee changed, other households in the village complained and asked the new committee members either to urge the payment of the owed contract fees or to recontract the land to someone else. During the review, some households brought out written contracts, others claimed that it was originally agreed orally that they would use the land for 15 years in exchange for planting cotton—and the village leaders had agreed that they would purchase the cotton and provide subsidies. Because the village never paid the subsidies, these households refused to pay the contract fees. Considering that such oral agreements and written contracts existed, the new village committee neither recontracted the land to someone else nor demanded payment of the owed contract fees, but instead remeasured the contracted land and signed new contracts with every contractor (villager interview 2000).

This case shows that, when village cadres change, terms of contracts may change. In some villages cadres acknowledge and continue contracts of the parties concerned whether they were written or oral; others completely renounce the old ways and follow only the new ways. However, if an individual household is weak and has no influential support, their contracts may easily be altered, as the minority (opinion) usually cannot match that of the majority (opinion).

### Case Five

In X Village in Hebei Province, Villager A purchased a piece of residential land from Villager B but actually intended to use it to run a flour mill. Because Villager A was not eligible to purchase residential land (he already had residential land) according to state policy, he should not be able to receive legal land certificates nor have electricity supplied for production. Nevertheless the two parties still agreed to a land transfer contract that explicitly clarified each party's rights and duties: "B is responsible for procuring the residential land certificate and electricity for the flour mill. The 40,000 yuan owed is not to be paid until the legal certificate is procured. Before procurement of the certificate, B is responsible for all disputes arising from the flour mill's land. After the procurement of the certificate, such disputes are not to concern B."[4]

This land transaction between the two villagers was illegal, but with the cooperation of the village cadres, the legal certificate was procured without any problem. Many land transactions can actually bypass formal procedures and develop outside state control, which shows that whereas the state can renounce the land contracts between the parties concerned, the parties can also renounce the influence of state policy. Who eventually wins out depends on the particular executors, not legal documents or policy stipulations. Relatively speaking, the power of clearly explicated regulations, clauses, laws, and contracts is actually the weakest.

#### RESOLVING CONFLICTS: LOGICS AND MECHANISMS

The five cases above show that, despite uniform policy stipulations about the rules and authority limits in land transactions, in practice guiding principles and transaction outcomes vary. State policies, village cadre decisions, collective will, and prior oral agreements between the parties concerned all exert some but not necessarily decisive influence. However, within the local variation, we can identify three decisive factors.

## Information Flow Control

In theory, state authority ranks the highest, and the state can force through changes as the desert treatment case shows. However, the state cannot be the actual executor in every land transaction, but must rely on its local representatives. The actions of local representatives—institutions and individuals with the power to examine, approve, manage, and distribute land—have meaningful consequences, because these local representatives monopolize the access to information. Town governments can reinterpret state policies according to local conditions. Village cadres, acting as the executors, can change state policies according to local circumstances, and the parties concerned can agree to land use contracts that do not necessarily follow state policies. Thus, although villagers often appear to be powerless, they can, through transactions with village cadres, prevent the upward movement of information and in this way gain flexibility.

## Legitimization of Primary Executors

Final outcomes depend on how primary executors understand and in particular legitimize their actions. This legitimization, however, has no certain principle—for example, the principle of collective ownership, market efficiency, or state supremacy. Cadres differ in their understandings of the policy, in constituents and representational bases, and in their values and interest orientations. They can enforce the principle of equal sharing, or the principle of stability (which benefits the investors), or even the principle of maximal utilization of land resources.

Which principle is used to legitimate a decision largely depends on their particular goals and interests. For example, the cadres in case five in X Village in Hebei Province supported land adjustment because they hoped to carve out a piece of land to contract and receive fees to supplement administrative expenditures. Some village cadres in case two in Q Town saw adjustment as necessary because they worried that unequal distribution might adversely affect subsequent village revenues. According to them, without adjustment, profits for sharing from land cannot be collected. A town cadre in Q Town supported stabilization of contracts, because of the long-term, legitimate need to develop the village's orchard industry: "Whoever owns the trees should also manage the land under the trees. If someone plants trees on his contracted land and grows them with hard work, how can he be expected to dedicate his hard-won and high-yielding trees to the collective without compensation? . . . The state has stipulated that the trees, especially fruit trees, should not be felled, but what can you do with these trees grown by the households themselves? To whom do these trees belong? What do you do with the people who fell them? If you fine them, who will ever grow trees in the future? If no one grows trees, the trees planted during the production brigade period will become older and older, and how then can you develop an orchard industry?" (Xu 2002)

The villagers who insisted on land adjustment, on the other hand, used a different legitimization logic. In their petition, they claimed that if land rights were to remain unchanged for 30 years, an unfair situation would arise in which some households would have many people but little land, whereas other households would have few people and much land. Households with less land, therefore, demanded a more equal redistribution of land, so that "the kids may have something to eat." The village cadres admitted that this legitimization logic created huge pressure for them to redistribute the land.

Obviously people support different ideas and use different legitimization logics according to their own interests. Then to whom should we listen? This is the basic problem in land transactions. Since there is no institutional procedure to organize the differentiated interests and values or to identify an order in which people should rank the different legitimization bases, solution to the basic problem can only depend on the choice of the particular executors. In most cases, the cadres naturally follow their own ideas, unless there is significant resistance.

### Incident Creation

Without resistance, the powerful executors have the last word; with resistance, power confrontation decides. When severe disagreement exists among villagers, numbers and power usually decide the outcome, that is, if the persons involved are numerous enough and the incident big enough, there would arise political pressure that threatens social stability. Maintenance of stability affects the primary cadres' administrative accomplishment and hence promotion. Therefore, when facing strong disagreement in land disputes, the cadres have to seek majority support in order to quell dissatisfaction, although this by no means indicates the establishment of institutional democratic processes. For example, in Q Town in Hebei Province, when agreement still could not be reached after several rounds of talks, cadres were forced to employ majority voting: "One of the villages was in chaos. There were all sorts of opinions and many petitioned. I did some one-on-one talks. Afterwards I held a meeting for village representatives who were party members. Outside was all snow and ice, but many gathered, some even stood on the windows to listen. There was still no agreement at the meeting. Eventually, I said that if there were no agreements, let every household send a representative to vote. In the end 85 percent of the people did not wish to adjust, so we decided that this village would not adjust."[5]

One of the strengths of collective will is to create public opinion and incidents. Once a huge impact is obvious, collective will may change decisions that have already been made, whether by state policy or by cadres. Pressure from the collective can also influence the persistence of agreements between the parties concerned: If an individual contract is widely accepted by villagers, it may persist; if not, it may be blocked. This shows that, in the process of choosing the rules, the legitimacy of state policies, cadre decisions, and individual decisions may be reassessed by interested parties. What rules can eventually be realized does not completely depend on either the authoritative position of the executing organization or preexisting rules, but accords with the intensity and scale of responses from the people. Such responses, signaling whether consent has been given, affect the persistence or discontinuance of established rules.

In most cases, collective responses are peaceful, although sometimes they may be violent. For example, in Q Town of Hebei Province the state issued policies in 1998 to auction off barren mountains. The village thus auctioned a chestnut field and its surrounding barren mountains, contracting them to the highest-bidding farmers for 30 years. Proceeds from the auction were shared among the villagers in W brigade, at 20 yuan per person. Later, when the township government stressed the state's land stabilization policy and prohibited significant further land adjustment in each village, the villagers of W brigade felt disadvantaged and demanded that the land be returned for their own management. But the farmers who held the contracts had already invested heavily. They had bought saplings, leveled the barren mountains, and planted new chestnut trees. They demanded that the contract be followed. If the land must be returned, the contractors demanded compensation equivalent to 30 years' projected income. The villagers of W brigade believed that since they themselves had not participated in drawing up the contract, the contract was void and they should not be held responsible for the contractors' loss. If there must be compensation, it could only be the 20 yuan that had been distributed to everyone earlier. The village leaders insisted that they had the power to dispose of collective property and the contract should therefore be valid. The township government believed that the dispute was an affair of the village and should be decided by the village. When appeals and negotiations proved ineffective, the villagers of W brigade forcefully seized the barren mountains and divided up the chestnut trees. The families appealed, but there were many villagers and only a few contractors. The township government quieted down the affair and didn't even punish the villagers for their forceful seizure of the land and breach of contract. Eventually W brigade got back the land (Xu 2002).

The collective could use violence to destroy the trees, seize the land, and divide it among themselves, and such actions could be accepted as valid because most villagers wished to revoke the land and contract it themselves. The party issuing the contract (the collective) can revoke the contract at any time because they think the land belongs to them. When land disputes arise between the individual and the collective, the two sides are not on an equal footing and the interests of the individuals are often compromised. The agreement can be easily broken because the rights of the collective always supersede the rights of the individual. As socialist values and institutions are increasingly in conflict with the pursuit of wealth under market transition, however, collective property can be sacrificed (Zhang 2002). In Q Town in Hebei Province, when some contractors realized that they had to surrender their land to participate in adjustment, they felled the chestnut trees they had planted and then burned them. Such property-destroying actions arise from the contractors' inability to accept the legitimacy of other people's enjoying the fruits without the labor. Such values indeed do not accord with the interests of the majority of the villagers and can hardly be supported as legitimate. One may conjecture that legal clarifications of such values will also be difficult.

On the whole, due to lack of a commonly accepted legal principle, different parties use their real power to fight for outcomes beneficial to their interests. Their modus operandi is to assess rules based on their interests, not the legitimacy of their interests based on rules. The final outcome is therefore decided by the power to invoke legitimacy and the ability to block information. As different parties legitimize their own interests, there arise many legitimization logics, such as collective land ownership; the legitimacy of everyone's entitlement to land, food, and authority; and the encouragement of individual labor.

## RIGHTS, CONFLICTS, AND TWO MODES OF SOCIAL ORDER FORMATION

The different mechanisms and logics emerged in resolving land rights disputes reveal different modes of social order formation. If we observe differences in social orders through different action-rule relationships, we can discover two modes. With the first mode, social order is formed when the legitimacy of actions is established by rules. With this mode, outcomes of people's actions can be predicted, because rules that serve as standards of measurement already exist. This mode can be termed the rule-based mode of social order formation. There is also a second mode of social order formation, which is guided by competition among interest groups. With this mode, outcomes of actions cannot be clearly predicted, because power configurations change continuously. This mode can be termed the interest-based mode of social order formation.

Ownership clarification is related to these two modes of social order formation. Under the rule-based mode, people's legal statuses have already been defined and structured by political and social processes, and the structure determines what laws can be enforced. Problems become quite simple once the laws are made. The transactional contract and distribution of future profits are to be determined by the parties concerned. The law's responsibility is to protect the authority of the contract. Clearly the stability of this order derives from the authority of the rules, which in turn derives from the rules' legitimization process—a structure characterized by the differentiation and organization of political and social interests that produces compromises and the consensual principles concerning power, status, value, and interest. Rules affirmed by such principles are thus accepted by society and become the basis for legitimacy claims (Zhou 2000b). This structure authoritatively confers legitimacy and provides a uniform standard for measuring actions and defining statuses. In other words, rules are the standards that measure actions and not the reverse.

In contrast, under the interest-based mode, numerous legitimacy claims exist and engage in continuous power competition. The winner occupies the dominant position and can determine the prevailing statuses, interests, powers, and values. The weaker parties cannot participate in the legitimization process on an equal footing. There thus exists no fundamental principle acknowledged by the numerous interests, statuses, powers, and values, and the authority of rules cannot be established. Although parties differ in power, each actively pursues its own interests.

Within a rule-based order, relevant legal principles and rules are uniform, relevant interpretative powers are specialized (professional), and relevant statuses are unique. Members of the society with different interests have to employ a uniform standard to express and legitimize their own interests. In terms of standards for actions, every party faces the same restrictions, because the choice of rules has already been accomplished during the inceptive period of law-making. Thus, the point of the dispute is to determine whether a certain interest is by law legitimate and ought to be protected. Within an interest-based order, on the other hand, there are constant disputes to clarify and explicate legitimate property rights. Thus, the principal obstacle in land rights transactions during the transition period is not a problem of explicating property rights, but rather of recognition. Here I use "principal obstacle," because I do not suggest that property rights should not be clearly explicated, but only that, under the interest-based mode, any clarification and explication of property rights must face the problem of gaining social recognition and legitimization. Clear explications of property rights are important, but prior to explication is social legitimization. Otherwise all explications will lose their normative authority.

Under the rule-based mode, however, balance of interests and establishment of relationship structures are accomplished within the political sphere, which is related to the legal sphere, but each has its own structure, themes, and social functions. The basic activity of the political sphere is power competition, which, during certain periods (time) and in certain areas (space), allows interest politics to enjoy full competition, mobilize social consensus, and organize interest identification, thus making certain fundamental principles become through debates the consensus and the basis for the establishment and amendment of laws. When people disagree about specific details of the rules, they judge by citing the consensual principles. Once the laws are made, execution becomes a function of the legal sphere and the above-mentioned competition is limited: It is no longer possible to continue to influence the rules through competition, for such activities should belong in the political sphere. If one is dissatisfied about a certain law, one should not interfere with its execution, but should return to the political sphere to seek support for its amendment, abolishment, or renovation.

In a differentiated institutional structure, principles measure actions, that is, actions follow established rules until they are changed by the political process. In an undifferentiated institutional structure, actions choose the principles and tend to change the rules according to the interests. Rules are uncertain as a result. The interest-based mode combines problems that should have been dealt with separately in differentiated spheres and thus produces a negative mutually detrimental relationship between them. Activities of interest competition have no standards, and rules are constantly abolished and remade.

At one level, land disputes tear communities apart because rules are not uniform, but more fundamentally, the absence of mechanisms to arbitrate among different ideals of justice and competing interests causes the problems. Consequently, we observe frequent conflicts and the triumph of the parties that control information, possess power, and perform the actual execution.

In resolution of land rights disputes, the interest-based mode is based on the logic of determination by the influential. Thus, groups or individuals who occupy weaker positions in power, information, number, and legitimization ability often have little influence over the outcomes of the disputes. At the same time, the interest-based mode reproduces interest group politics and extreme actions: If people wish to exert influence, they have to resort to such means as expanding their numbers, gathering forces, and even destroying property, all of which encourage an increase in unconstructive social actions. Moreover, this mode allows the ideas of part of the group, through confrontations, exchanges, and power struggles, to influence the rules and make choices for the entire group. Although such competition is one type of balancing mechanism, without society's acceptance, it is unstable. Because rules change with interests and powers, the resolution of one case cannot serve as reference for the resolution of similar future cases and the methods of resolution cannot become the precedent that guides future actions. Similar social conflicts will recur and resolution will have to be sought through new power confrontations. The stability of the interest-based mode depends on satisfaction by and large of all parties, but the party with greater power, positions, influence, and demands will often have opportunities to use their own dissatisfaction to influence outcomes. As a result, the opportunity structure is unbalanced and is unlikely to receive wide social acceptance. The social cost in resolving disputes remains steep.

## CHAPTER TEN

# Regional Inequality in China: Mortality and Health

*Yong Cai*

This chapter reviews the history of health improvement in contemporary China within a global context and uses census data to examine its regional variation in the postsocialist era. One of the most remarkable achievements for China over the past 50 years has been a dramatic increase in life expectancy. At the turn of the twenty-first century, a child born in China is expected to live almost twice as long as one born in 1949. The chapter focuses on two questions: How does regional mortality inequality in China compare to mortality inequality across the world? And what accounts for the current patterns? Because it is often assumed that economic growth improves life expectancy, I shall pay special attention to distinguishing the impact of macroeconomic development from the consequences of local ecology, education and cultural factors, and quality of public health programs.

## RISING LIFE EXPECTANCY AND PERSISTING REGIONAL INEQUALITY

China's mortality transition since 1949 can be subdivided into three stages: (1) the dramatic increase of life expectancy in the 1950s brought by massive public health campaigns emphasizing sanitation and inoculation; (2) the consolidation in the 1960s and 1970s brought by the expansion of a cooperative medical care network to almost every village in China; and (3) modest gains during the postsocialist decades associated with economic growth and improved health care facilities. Across these several decades, mortality outcomes varied by region; for example, urban residents enjoyed greater gains than rural residents. Nevertheless, mortality reductions during the socialist era were praised as relatively egalitarian. In the postsocialist era, however, there is concern that marketization may have reversed the relatively egalitarian outcomes in health care of the socialist era. We now look more closely at change over time.

### Rising Life Expectancy in China and Postsocialist Reforms

The success of China's mortality reduction is illustrated in Figure 10.1, in which I compare trends in female life expectancy ($e_0^f$) in China, India, and

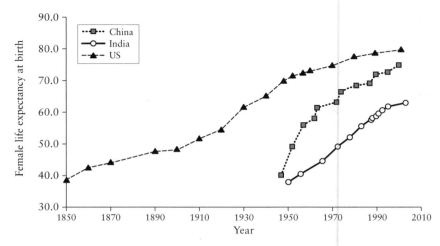

*Figure 10.1.*   Female life expectancies at birth in China, India, and the United States, selected years

SOURCES: China: Huang and Liu 1995; National Bureau of Statistics 1996, 2004a. India and United States: UN 1997, 2002. When the life expectancy is calculated for a period of time, we choose the central year to graph.

the United States. The United States represents the developed world. India is often regarded as a good comparison for China because of the similarities in size, history, and social diversity. In the United States, $e_0^f$ gradually increased from about 40 years in 1850 to about 70 years in 1950 and close to 80 years in 2000. Until 1950, $e_0^f$ for India and China stood at the level that the United States had achieved by the middle of the nineteenth century. Over the next 50 years, however, China in particular quickly closed the gap. By the year 2000, $e_0^f$ in China was a mere five years lower than that in the United States. Thus a mortality transition that took one century in the United States, occurred in China in only four decades. Similarly, it took India only four decades to increase its life expectancy from around 40 to 60 years—gains that took the United States 80 years.

With the risk of oversimplification, there are two general models of mortality decline. Mortality decline in developed countries was gradual and driven by rising standards of living, improvements in public health, and advances in medicine. By contrast, mortality decline in developing countries is often the result of aggressive public health efforts (Davis 1956; Preston 1977). Mortality rates declined more quickly in developing countries than they had in earlier decades in the developed countries due to the benefits from diffusions of knowledge and technology in health care that had already proven effective in the developed countries.

The gains at relatively low levels of per capita income make China an extreme example of the developing country model of mortality decline (Livi-Bacci 1997). Before its economic reforms in the 1980s, China was among the poorest countries in the world, but it ranked near middle-income nations in terms of population life expectancy. The key to this outcome was the government's efforts on public health featured with emphases on simple, preventative measures and broad access to primary care, which were made possible by an egalitarian ideology, a powerful hierarchical delivering system, and well-organized grass-roots campaigns (Banister 1987; Jamison et al. 1984; Johnstone and McConnan 1995; Salaff 1973).

The experience of China in recent years is also distinctive. China's health care system has undergone dramatic changes in its postsocialist era. The market reforms and resulting economic growth have provided the economic foundation and the incentives to further expand China's health care system. For example, the total expenditure on health care increased fifty-fold from 11 billion yuan (3.06 percent of GDP) in 1978 to 568 billion yuan (5.42 percent of GDP) in 2002 (MoH 2004).[1] The number of physicians per 1,000 population increased almost 60 percent from 1.08 in 1978 to 1.69 in 2001 (MoH 2004). There were also dramatic increases in hospital beds, medical equipment, and other health care facilities in the same period. In short, the market reform greatly expanded the supply of medical resources. In contrast to the economic transitions in the former Soviet Union, China's market reforms have not precipitated a decline in life expectancy. In fact, there have been moderate gains. Life expectancy at birth increased from 67.7 years in 1981 to 70.1 in 1989–1990 and to 72.3 in 2000. Infant mortality declined from 37.7/1000 births in 1981, to 27.3 in 1989–1990, and to 26.3 in 2000 (NBS 2004).

However, simultaneous with the gains in population life expectancy, we also see some major negative consequences from the reform (Lim et al. 2004; Ooi 2005), such as the deterioration of endemic disease controls in some regions, the return of many sexually transmitted diseases, and the emergence of new problems, such as HIV/AIDS, SARS, and the bird flu. Because China's postsocialist reforms have increased economic inequalities and produced new forms of poverty, a question that naturally follows is, regardless of gains for the population as a whole in terms of average mortality rates, do we also see new inequalities within these outcomes or new determinants of mortality among different segments of the population?

Most notably, the reform shifted the burden of health care from the state to individuals. The contribution from individuals to the total health expenditure increased from a little over 20 percent in the late 1970s to close to 60 percent by 2000 (MoH 2004). In urban areas, the reform repealed the universal health care coverage and replaced it with market-based health insurance programs, which covered no more than 50 percent of the urban residents. In rural areas, the reform bankrupted the cooperative medical system, which had covered about 90 percent of China's rural population. A recent report by the State Council (DRCSC 2005) named the declines in equal access to medical care and deterioration of the health care system's macroperformance as the two most prominent challenges to China's health care reform. The same state council report rated China's reform of its medical and health care system "basically unsuccessful"[2] and called for new directions for the reform. Among WHO's 191 members, China ranked 141 for its health system's overall performance, and ranked 188 in terms of "fairness of financial contribution to health systems" (WHO 2000). This was a startling reversal given China's reputation for equal health care access in its socialist years.

How does the reform affect the regional inequality of health? We would expect a (re)strengthening of the association between economic development and health conditions, as the socialist system is replaced by a market-based system. We would also expect rising regional economic inequality to contribute to regional health disparity: People in coastal areas benefited more from the economic growth than those in the hinterland, not only due to the different paces in economic development, but also due to the migration of people with skills and knowledge, such as doctors, from less-developed to more-developed areas. Economic development also leaves the most dangerous jobs in the poor regions and shifts pollution-heavy industries to less-developed areas. There is indeed a great concern and public outcry over inequality in health care access, amplified by the sensational news stories such as those about hospitals that let patients who can't afford an operation bleed to death.[3] Next, we use mortality census data to examine the hypothesis that along with economic stratification, there is a widening health gap between poor and rich regions across China.

### Persisting Regional Inequality

Mortality data from China's three most recent censuses provide a basis to assess the change of regional health inequality in the last two decades of the twentieth century. The 1982 census data represent a good approximation of conditions in prereform socialist China. The 1990 census data provide a midterm snapshot of the reforms, when market economic reforms were well established, but the dramatic health care reform had yet to be fully implemented. The 2000 census data reflect the dramatic social and economic reforms carried out in the 1980s and 1990s. Comparing regional patterns of life expectancy variation by these three census dates therefore provides strong data to assess the general trend of mortality change.

A comparison of regional life expectancy across China's provinces reveals persistent regional inequality.[4] According to the 1982 census, provincial life expectancies cover a range of 12.3 years with a high of 73.0 years for Shanghai to a low of 60.7 in Xinjiang. No data were available for Tibet. By 1990, the interprovincial range, including Tibet, increased to 14.7 years, with Shanghai at 75.5 and Tibet at 60.8. The 2000 census reports a range of 13.2 years, with Shanghai at 79.2 and Tibet at 66.0. However, such broad provincial comparisons might obscure important patterns because Chinese provinces are often as large and as diverse as many countries in terms of both population and geography.

To document the true range of geographic inequality, I now turn to county-level data.[5] There are several advantages of using the county as the primary study unit. First, counties are directly responsible for implementing social policies and thus capture variation in government efforts. Second, as the basic administrative units for more than 2,000 years, counties provide a basic social identity for Chinese. Third, county-level units in China have populations adequately large to calculate stable mortality parameters, such as infant mortality rate and life expectancy.

There are 2,378 county-level units in the 1982 census data. Excluding counties that reported no infant deaths, the reported infant mortality rates in 1982 range from as low as 6 per thousand (Langfang City in Hebei Province) to as high as 319 per thousand (Dacaidan in Qinghai Province). This wide range clearly indicates the large regional inequality across China in infant mortality. However, the extremely low infant mortality rates also signal potential data problems. For example, an infant mortality of 6 per thousand, which is roughly the level in the United States in 2005, is too low to be true for a Chinese county in 1982. Nevertheless, careful demographic examinations suggest the overall high quality of the 1982 census (Coale 1984; Banister and Hill 2004), and we therefore assume that problems in the data are mostly random.

International experience suggests that economic development, measured by GDP per capita, is one of the best predictors of mortality level. For example, there is a well-observed relationship between economic development and infant mortality (linear if both GDP per capita and infant mortality rate are log transformed). Using data published in the United Nations *Human Development Report* of 2005 from 172 countries and regions, in log scale, economic development explains about 77 percent of the variation in the infant mortality rate. In original scale, a one percent increase in per capita GDP is associated with an approximately 0.6 percent decrease in infant mortality.

However, the 1982 China data offer only limited support of such a linear relationship; the correlation between these two log-transformed measures at county level is merely −0.3: that is, logged economic development only explains about 14 percent of the variation in logged infant mortality, not 77 percent as observed with the international data. This relatively low correlation for the 1982 outcomes supports the disassociation between economic development and mortality reduction during the Mao era and suggests that the most important factor shaping differential mortality outcomes in that era was not the level of economic development.

To find out how the reform changes the landscape of regional mortality inequality in China, the same analysis as that for 1982 is repeated using data from 2000. To facilitate comparison, I exclude Tibet from the 2000 data because there were no data for Tibet in 1982. I also make the same assumption about measurement errors in infant mortality rates.

The range of reported infant mortality rates in 2000, from 0 to 245 per thousand, is smaller than what we saw in 1982, but is still a very large range: The high end of infant mortality shows that infant mortality in some counties in China was still at a predemographic transition level in 2000. This is a rather shocking reality of regional inequality in China: There are areas that have been left far behind.

What is more important is a restrengthened connection between economic development level and infant mortality. In 2000, the correlation between log transformed per capita GDP and infant mortality was −.59, that is, the economic development alone explains 35 percent of the variation in infant mortality. This relationship is still not as strong as seen in the international comparison; nevertheless, it is a dramatic increase from 1982. Moreover, the 2000 data suggests that 1 percent increase in the GDP per capita is associated with .66 percent decline in infant mortality, very similar to the value from the international comparison.

The comparison of infant mortality data at the county level between the 1982 and 2000 censuses clearly documents an important change and suggests that postsocialist reforms have indeed impacted differential mortality. During the socialist era, the association between mortality and economic development was dampened by government efforts to extend the primary health care network and strengthen infectious disease control. With the weakening of the public health system during the postsocialist era, economic development plays a more prominent role in shaping the map of regional health inequality in China.

## EXPLAINING HEALTH INEQUALITY IN 2000

To provide a comprehensive picture of local health conditions, I next examine life expectancy at birth ($e_0$), which is an age-standardized comprehensive measure of mortality of general population.

Using the population age structure and death data from the 2000 census, Cai (2005) constructed life tables for 2,367 county-level administrative units that matched with a GIS base map (NBS 2003).[6] Two more sets of life tables are constructed, one based on Brass Logit Model, which adjusts age-specific mortality estimates assuming a linear relationship in mortality across age in logit scale, and the other using empirical Bayesian estimates, which assume spatial contiguity. There is very good consistency across these three sets of estimates. The fact that these three sets of estimates are based on totally different aspects of mortality reporting but produce similar results alleviates the major concerns on data quality. We use the estimates based on Brass Logit Model, which smoothes out some irregularities in mortality reporting.

Life expectancies at birth at the county level in 2000 display larger variation than those at the provincial level. Life expectancies for Chinese county-level units in 2000 range from a low of 46.0 to a high of 80.8, roughly equivalent to the range between Niger (46.0) and Japan (81.6) (UNDP 2004): the gap between the richest, most developed parts of China and the poorest parts of China is almost as large as the gap between the richest and the poorest nations in the world.

County-level life expectancies are mapped in Figure 10.2, with darker gray indicating a higher life expectancy. Provincial boundaries are shown

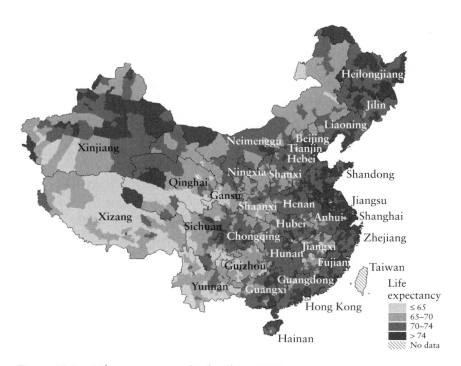

*Figure 10.2.* Life expectancy at birth, China 2000

for reference. Even with these simplified categories, one observes large variations and distinctive clusters both within and between provinces. Another major feature of regional mortality variation is the obvious division between east and west along a southwest-northeast line that runs across China through Guangxi, Hunan, Hubei, Henan, and Hebei Provinces, then turns farther northeast following largely the boundary of Inner Mongolia. East of this line, the life expectancy exceeds 70 years with the exception of a group of counties in Jiangxi province. West of this line, life expectancy is predominantly below 70 years with the exception of the Sichuan Basin and the northern half of Xinjiang.

What we see in Figure 10.2 is a startling indication of high regional health inequality generally consistent with the regional economic inequality. While coastal areas tend to have high life expectancies, the hinterland, particularly those counties in the southwest bordering areas, tend to have the lowest life expectancy in the country. The areas of high life expectancy in the hinterlands are also the cores of regional economies such as the Sichuan Basin, Weihe Valley, and the areas around Urumqi.

Health of a population is the outcome of a complex set of factors and processes. Among many, general economic development is often regarded as one of the most important, as we saw in the analysis of infant mortality. Urbanization also played an important role in the history of mortality transition (Wood 1985). Although in early stages of industrialization, urban settings were more prone to disease due to high population density and sanitation problems, over time better urban planning and environmental control provided health benefits to residents. In China, there is also a strong bias in favor of urban residents as a legacy of the harsh rural-urban divide of the socialist era.

In addition to the economic factors, specific public health efforts reduce the exposure to diseases, and cultural factors mediate a general strategy of disease management (Johansson and Mosk 1987; Caldwell 1990; Riley 2001). We have seen the importance of public health efforts in China's mortality transition. It is also well-known that education has positive effects on health and mortality reduction, particularly the effects of mother's education on their children's mortality (Caldwell 1986, 1990; Cleland and Ginneken 1988). Cultural identifiers such as ethnicity stand for a set of values and practices that may have an important effect on health but may not be otherwise directly measured (Caldwell 1986, 1990). For example, Chinese and Malays have rather different mortality patterns during infancy (in Malaysia: DaVanzo, Butz, and Habicht 1983) and in old age (in Singapore: Goldman 1980). Lee and Wang (1999) argue that a proactive mortality-control culture is one factor that contributed to the quick mortality reduction in China.

As China completes its epidemiological transition, moving from infectious diseases to degenerative diseases (He et al. 2005), how does this range of factors explain the regional mortality variations identified above? To answer this question, I use regression models. Because counties neighboring each other are likely to be correlated, I use a spatial regression model that provides control for spatial correlation structure (Haining 1990). Fourteen explanatory variables are grouped into four categories: (1) ecological variables, (2) general economic development indictors, (3) education and cultural factors, and (4) public health–related indicators. I include four ecological variables to control for possible large-scale effects, as suggested by the map of life expectancy in Figure 10.2.[7] Three general economic measures are GDP per capita, percentage of urban population, and percentage of population age 15 and above employed at the time of the census. Log transformed is used to capture GDP per capita's curve-linear effects on mortality. Also included in the model is a variable measuring population's sex composition to control for the well-known gap between male and female life expectancy. The two education and cultural variables are the average years of school and ethnicity. Public health–related variables include the proportion of people working in the health care industry, and percentages of households having lavatory, tap water, and bath facilities.

Definitions and descriptive statistics of these variables are presented in Table 10.1. Please note that the mean and standard deviation of each vari-

TABLE 10.1
*Variable definition and summary statistics*

| Variable Name | Definition | Mean | Std |
|---|---|---|---|
| Life expectancy | life expectancy at birth of both male and female | 71.5 | 3.8 |
| Latitude | latitude of county centroid | 33.0 | 6.6 |
| Longitude | longitude of county centroid | 111.2 | 9.5 |
| Elevation | average elevation | 853.1 | 1,098.6 |
| Terrain | standard deviation of elevation | 200.2 | 210.8 |
| Sex composition | percentage of male population | 51.7 | 1.1 |
| GDP | GDP per capita (1,000 Yuan, log transformed) | 1.5 | 0.7 |
| Urbanization | percentage of urban population | 28.9 | 23.5 |
| Employment | percentage employed (age 15 and above) | 24.1 | 8.9 |
| Education | average years of school | 7.1 | 1.4 |
| Ethnicity | percentage of non-Han minorities | 18.6 | 31.1 |
| Health care | health care workers (per 1000 population) | 5.4 | 2.9 |
| Water | percentage of households having tapwater | 40.1 | 28.2 |
| Lavatory | percentage of households having lavatory | 65.5 | 28.4 |
| Bath facility | percentage of households having bath facility | 19.3 | 19.9 |

SOURCES: Census data are from the *2000 China County Population and Socioeconomic Indicators with County Maps*, distributed by University of Michigan China Data Center. Geographic variables are based on the U.S. Geological Survey's digital elevation model.

able are calculated using the county-level unit as the unit of analysis, thus those numbers are not the same as the reported national statistics (weighted by population size). Bivariate analysis (not shown here) between life expectancy and these 14 predictors reveal the generally expected correlations. Most of these predictors have a moderate to strong positive relationship with life expectancy.

I now turn to multivariate regression to further examine the relationship between these variables and life expectancy. The variables are added sequentially to the regression models by block. Model summary statistics (AIC, BIC, and Pseudo $R^2$) suggest that more complicated models fit the data better.[8] The modeling results are presented in Tables 10.2 and 10.3.

In Model 1, three out of four geographic measures are significant. This confirms what we have observed in Figure 10.2. In Model 2, the *Sex Composition* variable confirms the known gender gap in life expectancy, and all three economic variables are highly significant. However, the effects of *Latitude* and *Longitude* now become insignificant, which suggests that the geographic pattern we saw in Figure 10.2 is largely due to socioeconomic factors. In Model 3, we see *Education* has a significant positive effect on life expectancy. Ethnic minority populations are worse off than the Han majority, as shown by the significant negative effect of the percent of minority in the county on life expectancy. Adding the *Education* and *Ethnicity* variables also changes the effects of geographic variables, as well as reducing the predicting power

TABLE 10.2

*Spatial conditional autoregressive models predicting life expectancy at birth, Models 1–3 (N = 2,367)*

|  | MODEL 1 | | MODEL 2 | | MODEL 3 | |
|---|---|---|---|---|---|---|
| Predictor | coefficient | s.e. | coefficient | s.e. | coefficient | s.e. |
| (Intercept) | 65.4912 | 1.9640*** | 80.8323 | 3.1722*** | 79.1363 | 3.0612*** |
| Latitude | 0.0565 | 0.0179** | 0.0254 | 0.0161 | −0.0267 | 0.0156+ |
| Longitude | 0.0535 | 0.0177** | 0.0142 | 0.0158 | 0.0186 | 0.0152 |
| Elevation | −0.0018 | 0.0001*** | −0.0015 | 0.0001*** | −0.0003 | 0.0001* |
| Terrain | −0.0006 | 0.0004 | 0.0001 | 0.0003 | −0.0009 | 0.0003** |
| Sex composition | | | −0.2140 | 0.0498*** | −0.3016 | 0.0474*** |
| GDP | | | 1.1419 | 0.1128*** | 0.8133 | 0.1083*** |
| Urbanization | | | 0.0211 | 0.0034*** | −0.0008 | 0.0037 |
| Employment | | | 0.0356 | 0.0091*** | 0.0183 | 0.0087* |
| Education | | | | | 1.1069 | 0.0867*** |
| Ethnicity | | | | | −0.0236 | 0.0029*** |
| Log likelihood | −11264.1 | | −10969.0 | | −10831.7 | |
| AIC | 22538.2 | | 21956.0 | | 21685.4 | |
| BIC | 22567.1 | | 22008.0 | | 21748.9 | |
| Pseudo $R^2$ | 0.18 | | 0.36 | | 0.43 | |

+$p < .1$; *$p < .05$; **$p < .01$; ***$p < .001$.

TABLE 10.3

*Spatial conditional autoregressive model predicting life expectancy at birth, Model 4 (N = 2,367)*

| Predictor | MODEL 4 | | MODEL 4 (STANDARDIZED) | |
|---|---|---|---|---|
| | *coefficient* | *s.e.* | *coefficient* | *s.e.* |
| (Intercept) | 76.7907 | 3.0818*** | | |
| Latitude | −0.0130 | 0.0173 | −0.0223 | 0.0296 |
| Longitude | 0.0176 | 0.0151 | 0.0439 | 0.0377 |
| Elevation | −0.0002 | 0.0001 | −0.0615 | 0.0395 |
| Terrain | −0.0009 | 0.0003** | −0.0512 | 0.0183** |
| Sex composition | −0.2702 | 0.0475*** | −0.0809 | 0.0142*** |
| GDP | 0.7436 | 0.1118*** | 0.1363 | 0.0205*** |
| Urbanization | −0.0007 | 0.0041 | −0.0043 | 0.0252 |
| Employment | 0.0228 | 0.0089* | 0.0529 | 0.0207* |
| Education | 1.0621 | 0.0924*** | 0.3763 | 0.0327*** |
| Ethnicity | −0.0228 | 0.0029*** | −0.1853 | 0.0235*** |
| Health care | −0.0513 | 0.0275+ | −0.0389 | 0.0209+ |
| Water | 0.0030 | 0.0026 | 0.0219 | 0.0191 |
| Lavatory | 0.0058 | 0.0022** | 0.0433 | 0.0160** |
| Bath facility | 0.0125 | 0.0042** | 0.0649 | 0.0217** |
| Log likelihood | | −10817.44 | | |
| AIC | | 21662.88 | | |
| BIC | | 21743.65 | | |
| Pseudo $R^2$ | | 0.44 | | |

$^+p < .1$; $^*p < .05$; $^{**}p < .01$; $^{***}p < .001$.

of the socioeconomic variables in Model 2. For example, the coefficient of *GDP* declined from 1.14 to .81 and urbanization becomes insignificant.

To facilitate between-variable comparisons, I place the standardized version of Model 4 side by side with the unstandardized one in Table 10.3. Two of four public health related measures—water supply and bath facility have significant positive effects on life expectancy. One big surprise is that the availability of health care, measured by number of health workers per 1,000 people, has a negative effect on life expectancy, although it is only significant at the $\alpha = .1$ level. This may be interpreted as an indicator of the "unsuccessful" health care reform and the low efficiency of China's health care system. Given the cross-sectional nature of the data, we need to be cautious about making such a conclusion.

The standardized version makes it possible to compare the relative strength of each predictor on life expectancy in terms of standard deviation. Among all 14 variables, *Education* has the most powerful effect: Change in education level by one standard deviation is associated with an increase of life expectancy by .38 standard deviations, which is equivalent of 1.4 years. A similar change in *GDP* (log transformed) would result in an increase in life expectancy of .5 year, and a drop of 0.72 year with similar change in *Ethnicity*.

The relative strength of each variable's contribution to life expectancy highlights three important aspects in Chinese mortality and health. First, as Figure 10.2 suggests, a correlation between regional mortality inequality and the regional socioeconomic inequality, the multivariate analysis indicates that while economic development explains some proportion of regional mortality variation, it is not the most important factor. It is education rather than economic development that is most decisive. According to the regression models, increasing average schooling level by one year produces an increase of more than one year in life expectancy, net of all other socioeconomic development effects. This has a very important policy implication. Education, as the most important factor of social stratification, demonstrably has a central role in policies to foster social equality. Second, although we only have a rudimentary measure of ethnic diversity across China, the message from the analysis is unequivocal: Non-Han minorities have a considerable health disadvantage compared to the Han majority, even after controlling for general socioeconomic development variables. This conclusion certainly does not apply to every ethnic group—for example, the Hui (Chinese Muslim) have a life expectancy comparable to that of the Han, and the Man (Manchu) have a life expectancy higher than that of the Han according to the 1990 census.[9] Third, this analysis indicates that the prevalence of sanitation facilities, such as lavatory and bath facilities, still has a visible effect on mortality, suggesting that promotion of public and personal sanitation is likely to continue showing positive results on health.[10]

CONCLUSIONS AND DISCUSSIONS

Postsocialist China has not only ushered in a new economic and social stratification system, but also a new institutional context affecting the life chances of the population. Health condition is one such life chance that has been directly affected by recent reforms. Following the remarkable increase in life expectancy in the last 50 years through public health campaigns and economic development, some parts of China today still have very low life expectancy and the gap between the most developed counties and the least developed counties approaches the range of life expectancy across the world at the national level. Moreover, comparisons between 1982 and 2000 suggest that local economic conditions play an increasingly prominent role in shaping the regional map of health inequality. While similar to the current world stratification system and not an unexpected result given the uneven power of market forces in postsocialist China, it is still striking given that China is under a unified social and political system.

Could the regional inequality pattern diminish if China stays on the fast track of economic growth for another decade? The recent experience in the last 20 years seems to suggest the opposite. As market force became increasingly dominant, it did not equalize the country; rather it greatly increased economic disparity among different regions. Thus, we cannot expect the market to reduce regional health inequalities in the near term. In fact, it is possible that the poor health conditions in some regions will curb future growth as much as current economic poverty is increasingly decisive in predicting mortality outcomes (Bloom and Canning 2000). In addition, less than ideal local economic conditions may motivate selective out-migration as a form of human resource drainage, which places the less-developed areas in an even more unfavorable position economically and thus causes further deterioration in both the local economic and local health situations, and enlarges the regional inequality.

The unsuccessful reform of China's health care system and the emergence of new epidemiological threats such as SARS, the bird flu, and HIV/AIDS have pushed the Chinese government to reconsider earlier policies to marketize health care (Kaufman 2005). In a speech of 2005, President Hu emphasized the increasingly important role that his government must play in providing health care as the country seeks to narrow the gap in health care coverage for rich and poor: "We must uphold the public welfare character of public health care, deepen reform of the medical system, strengthen government responsibility, and have strict oversight and control."[11] However, it is yet to be seen how this new state intervention would change the regional pattern of health conditions. Unlike the political institutions in the United States, which have a constitutional protection in favor of rural and sparsely population areas, the Chinese political system has a strong bias in favor of its urban parts. It thus remains unclear how the poor and those concentrated in poor regions will reduce their current health "deficits."

## CHAPTER ELEVEN

# Beyond Cost:
# Rural Perspectives on Barriers to Education

*Emily Hannum and Jennifer Adams*

In postsocialist China, educational attainment is more closely tied to adult earnings than in the Mao years (Yang 2005; Zhang et al. 2005). During the first 15 years of market reforms, economic returns to education in urban China increased, but between 1992 and 2003 they nearly tripled, rising from 4.0 to 11.4 percent (Zhang and Zhao 2007). In rural areas, returns to education also rose. By the year 2000, an additional year of education increased wages by 6.4 percent among those engaged in wage employment, and education was becoming the dominant factor in determining whether rural laborers succeeded in finding more lucrative off-farm jobs (de Brauw et al. 2002; de Brauw and Rozelle 2007; Zhao 1997). Given the rising role of education as a determinant of economic status, those who lack access to schooling are at high risk for a life of poverty.

Fortunately, access to basic education has improved significantly since 1980. Recent surveys document rising enrollment rates through the 1990s, and near parity between enrollment of girls and boys (Hannum and Liu 2005). By the year 2000, entry into primary school among rural youth between 10 and 18 years of age had reached 99 percent for China as a whole (Connelly and Zheng 2007), and by 2003, five-year retention rates in primary school increased to 99 percent (Hannum, Wang, and Adams 2008). Yet, studies through the 1990s and the early twenty-first century have revealed substantial enrollment disadvantages associated with rural residence and with both household and community poverty (Adams and Hannum 2005; Brown and Park 2002; Connelly and Zheng 2003; Hannum 1999, 2003; Hannum and Liu 2005). Children at greatest disadvantage come from the poorest rural households and from communities with the fewest resources to provide social welfare. When these children do enter school, they face weak infrastructures and less-qualified teachers than do their counterparts in wealthier areas. The curriculum is often foreign to their lived experiences and teachers use a vernacular not spoken at home. Many children quickly surpass their parents' level of schooling, and thus lack guidance at home when they face academic difficulty or become discouraged.

This chapter offers a perspective on rural educational problems that differs from earlier work by focusing on issues identified by impoverished rural children and their parents themselves as the most significant constraints to educational access. We present an analysis of a survey of 2,000 children, families, and schools in rural Gansu Province in 2000 and 2004. We supplement survey data analysis with evidence from in-depth interviews conducted among students and their mothers in three villages in Gansu in 2002. We begin by providing an overview of educational policies under market reforms that have shaped access to schooling for rural children.

## EDUCATION POLICY AND RURAL ACCESS IN THE REFORM ERA

From the perspective of educational access, two of the most important initiatives have been the 1985 Decision on the Reform of the Education Structure (hereafter the 1985 Decision), and the 1986 Law of Compulsory Education. The 1985 Decision was issued as a part of public finance reforms developed to ease the transition to a market economy. The 1985 Decision included many initiatives, such as nine years of compulsory education, the expansion of vocational education, and the strengthening of educational leadership. It also mandated financial decentralization (Cheng 1994). A major objective of finance reform in education was to diversify school financing by mobilizing new resources for education, and the 1985 reform specified that multiple methods of financing should be sought (Hawkins 2000; Tsang 1996, 2000).

Several months later, in early 1986, the National People's Congress passed the Law on Compulsory Education, mandating six years of primary and three years of lower secondary school education (Ministry of Education 1986). In recognition of uneven starting points, the government varied the deadlines for each region to reach the targets. However, because the law did not guarantee the funding for education, many schools, particularly those in poor rural areas, were forced to increase direct charges to parents. Thus, even as the national leadership mobilized resources, decentralization created new barriers to access for the poorest children.

Through the reform period, the Chinese government has responded to problems of access with a series of equity-oriented policy proclamations. For example, the Education Law of 1995 affirmed the government's commitment to equality of educational opportunity regardless of nationality, race, sex, occupation, property conditions, or religious belief (Ministry of Education 1995, Article 9). It also specified that the state should support educational development in minority nationality regions, remote border areas, and poverty-stricken areas (Article 10). The central government launched a massive education project for children living in poor areas between 1995 and 2000 with a total investment of 1.2 billion dollars, the most intensive allocation of educational funding in the last 50 years (Ross 2005, p. 39). The 1999 Action Plan for Revitalizing Education in the twenty-first century confirmed a commitment to implementing compulsory education across the country (Ministry of Education 1999).

These efforts continued into the twenty-first century. In 2003, the State Council held the first national working conference since 1949 to formulate plans for the development of rural education, with a focus on protecting access to and improving the quality of compulsory education in rural areas (Postiglione 2007). Among the ideas to emerge from the conference were plans to establish an effective system of sponsorship for poor students receiving compulsory education, exempting poor students from all miscellaneous fees and textbook charges, and offering poor students lodging allowances by the year 2007.

In March of 2004, the State Council approved and circulated the 2003–2007 Action Plan for Revitalizing Education, called the New Action Plan (State Council 2004). One of the strategic priorities of the New Action Plan was the implementation of compulsory education in rural areas. In 2005, it was announced that the government would spend 218 billion yuan to help improve education in rural areas in the subsequent five years (CERNET 2005a). A mechanism would be established to guarantee the wages of rural middle and elementary school teachers, and by 2007, the government committed to eliminating educational tuition and fees and providing free textbooks and subsidies for needy rural students in compulsory education (CERNET 2005a; see CERNET 2005b for a different timeline for eliminating fees). More recently, during the 10th National People's Congress, Chinese Premier Wen Jiabao pledged to "eliminate all charges on rural students receiving 9-year compulsory education before the end of 2007" (*People's Daily*, March 5, 2006).[1] Nearly four months later, in June 2006, the Standing Committee of the National People's Congress approved the Amendment to the Compulsory Education Law, which was slated to come into effect September 1, 2006 (Xinhua June 29, 2006).[2] Considered a strategic part of the nation's plan to develop a "new socialist countryside," this law aims to give rural children the same educational opportunities as their urban counterparts—nine years of free compulsory education (Pan 2006). Costs are to be jointly shouldered by the central government and provincial governments, which will be required to place expenditures for compulsory education in their budgets (*People's Daily*, February 25, 2006; Xinhua June 29, 2006a). To improve educational quality in rural schools, the amendment also requires teachers in urban schools who want to receive the senior professional title or are newly employed to teach in rural schools for a period of time (*People's Daily*, February 25, 2006).

The goal of improving quality has also motivated curricular reforms. In 1999, following the Third National Working Conference on Education, the State Council issued a proclamation entitled "Deepening Education Reform and Advancing Essential Qualities-Oriented Education in an All-Round Way" (Central Committee of the Communist Party and State Council 1999). 'Essential qualities-oriented education,' *suzhi jiaoyu*, is also translated as quality education or all-round education. The *suzhi jiaoyu* initiative sought to develop the diverse skills of the whole child, not just promote test-taking skills, and to stimulate critical thinking (Sargent 2008).

These goals were reinforced in the official curriculum reforms launched in 2001, in a circular entitled "Guidelines for Curriculum Reform of Basic Education" (Ministry of Education 2001). The document called for an end to the overemphasis on imparting "book knowledge" and allowed for more of curriculum content to be locally determined (Zhu 2007, pp. 224, 228). The new curriculum was intended to advance curricular links among society, science, and technology, and to enhance the relevance of the curriculum to students' lives. The policy initiatives described here underscore the overwhelming problem of economic barriers to access in rural areas. They also bring to the fore an emerging concern with improving the educational experience of children, including those in rural areas.

STUDY SITE AND DATA SOURCE

This case study focuses on rural areas of Gansu, an interior province in northwestern China where 76 percent of the population resides in rural areas (UNESCAP 2005). Gansu Province provides a useful environment for exploring barriers to education confronted by the rural poor. In China, poverty remains heavily concentrated in rural areas and disproportionately affects the interior and western regions. Gansu is one of China's poorest provinces. In 2001, Gansu was ranked second-to-last among provinces in per capita GDP, with a figure that was only 55 percent of China's national average (Woo and Bao 2003). By China's official poverty estimates for the same year, the rate of poverty in Gansu was three times the national average, and Gansu was home to 6.64 percent of China's poor rural population (Wang 2004).

Focusing on the educational disadvantage of children who reside in severely resource-constrained areas is an important task. Many studies have examined educational access using nationally representative data and revealed significant, enduring rural-urban disparities. However, these studies have been unable to consider the obstacles beyond costs that constrain children's ability to attend school and to flourish in school in China's poorest communities.

To address this limitation, we draw on survey data and qualitative interviews from the Gansu Survey of Children and Families (GSCF), Waves 1 and 2 (2000 and 2004). The GSCF is an interdisciplinary, longitudinal study of 2,000 children ages 9 to 12 in the year 2000, along with their families, teachers, principals, and communities. The overarching goal of the project is to shed light on factors that matter for the welfare of impoverished rural children, with welfare defined broadly to include educational experiences, physical health and psychological well-being, and subsequent economic outcomes. The GSCF sample was drawn using a multistage approach, selecting counties,[3] townships, villages, and then children from birth registries.[4] Three minority autonomous counties were excluded from the sampling frame due to travel restrictions to these areas, language barriers, limited transportation, and sparse and dispersed populations. Unfortunately, the sample does not contain sufficient numbers of minority children for meaningful analysis. With this caveat, the GSCF is representative of children in rural areas of Gansu, and includes wealthier and poorer rural counties.

We supplement our main analysis with findings from in-depth interviews conducted in 2002 with a purposive sample of primary-school aged children, mothers, and teachers in three villages in two counties. Respondents were recruited with the help of school principals. Principals were asked to recommend students with a variety of backgrounds and achievement levels. A team of researchers that included the authors and other GSCF researchers conducted the interviews, with graduate students from Northwest Normal University leading most interviews. Interviews were conducted in Mandarin or, when possible, in the local dialects. All interviews were taped and transcribed for analysis. Quotes in this chapter are identified by interview identification number.

BARRIERS TO SCHOOLING IN RURAL GANSU

Because we are interested in looking at risk factors for school-leaving, we focus here on children who were in school in 2000 when they were 9 to 12 years old. Four years later, in 2004, 88 percent of the children who were in school in 2000 remained in school at ages 13 to 16. In the surveys, we asked different versions of questions about factors that contributed to school-leaving to children, mothers, fathers, and village leaders, and found

TABLE 11.1
*Respondent reports of factors contributing to non-enrollment, 2004 (N = 1,817)*

| | Village leaders | Mothers | Out-of-school children |
|---|---|---|---|
| School is too far away from home | 12.5% | 10.1% | 13.7% |
| Poor school or teacher quality | 8.3% | 5.1% | 5.1% |
| Not worth the money | — | 7.8% | 8.1% |
| Poor student performance | 67.7% | 31.7% | 46.7% |
| Tuition high / family cannot afford school costs | 51.0% | 41.3% | 36.0% |
| Child needed at home | 26.0% | 11.9% | 23.9% |
| Child did not want to go | 58.3% | 50.5% | 46.2% |
| Child had health problem | — | 8.3% | 6.1% |
| Child violated school rules | — | 2.8% | 5.1% |
| Observations | 96 | 218 | 197 |

SOURCE: GSCF-2 (2004).

strikingly consistent responses. Table 11.1 presents a subset of responses from children, mothers, and village leaders. Because multiple factors often cluster together to contribute to the school-leaving decision, we asked respondents to say whether each of several items in a list was a contributing factor. Respondents could cite as many factors as they thought relevant.

In 2004, the top three categories cited by village leaders, mothers, and children were poor student performance, child unwillingness to attend school, and unaffordable costs. For example, among out-of-school children themselves, 46.7 percent cited poor performance as a contributing factor to their status; 46.2 percent cited unwillingness to attend school; and 36.0 percent cited inability to afford costs. Interestingly, around one-fourth of village leaders and one-fourth of children themselves said that they were needed at home, suggesting that the opportunity costs of children's school attendance remains an issue. However, only 11.9 percent of mothers of out-of-school children indicated that they were needed at home.

These results show that economics, performance, and engagement are key issues reported by rural residents as barriers to continuation in school. These findings are consistent with themes that emerged in the qualitative interviews. Many children and mothers mention poverty explicitly as a source of educational problems. First and foremost, children in many families are aware that fees are a burden. One child explained an older sister's dropping out with "The tuition fees were too high, and we couldn't borrow enough" (Dang02c). Mothers interviewed also commented frequently on both the high tuition and numerous fees (e.g., Cai01m). One mother complained, "They charge a fee every other day, the class fee, and the cleaning fee for the class . . . last winter, they asked for heating costs" (Dang03m). The same mother, whose oldest daughter had dropped out of school, lamented, "We'd have to provide tuition for all three of them . . . it is around six to seven hundred yuan. Just letting two [children] attend school is a huge stress on our financial situation."

Impoverished parents make visible sacrifices for their children in these settings. For example, one child knew that her parents treated her well because they often gave the good food available to the children to eat, while reducing their own consumption (Dang05c). Another child, living on her own with an elderly grandmother, was asked about how her family could change to support her education. She said, "Our family is the largest family in the village. My older sister and my aunt have left to work, and my father and mother are also working at home to support us to go to school. For a year now our food is all from my parents, using money gotten by their sweat and blood to buy some noodles for us to eat. That is, [our area] has been very dry, right? For a year now, four seasons, it hasn't rained, and the wheat hasn't grown tall, so we have had to buy things to eat all along, so our family is also very poor" (Wang04c). Children in these circumstances are brutally aware of the struggles of their parents to raise them and to support their enrollment in school.

Economic constraints can also hinder learning for children once actually in school. One child responded to the question "What do you think is the biggest difficulty you've encountered in your studies?" with "Just that I don't have any money to buy school supplies." The interviewer then asked, "Normally, do you have a lot of the necessary school supplies?" to which the child responded, "Not a lot." It came out that when the child needed school supplies, the parents would borrow money from other families, so that the child's normal approach was just to try to borrow supplies from others (Dang06c). Much later in the interview, when asked a general question about problems, the child again responded, "What upsets me the most is that I don't have school supplies at school, and when I ask for them from my parents, they don't have the money. This is what upsets me the most." A mother commented, "Another thing that we don't have is money. We cannot buy our child's composition book" (Cai02m). When asked, some children noted their minimal access to books besides those required for school, and a few mentioned that school libraries did not allow them to borrow books.

Children in poor families are often also hindered by a dearth of effective parental educational support, despite most parents' strong desires to help their children. Most parents have low levels of education, and many work long hours to make ends meet. As a result, after the early grades, children have little access to help at home with navigating the school system. Many parents lamented that they could not solve the majority of their children's homework problems, and that, as one mother explained, "The kids are suffering from our lack of education" (Cai03m). Children echoed this frustration. One child, living in what appeared to be much better material conditions than other children interviewed, stated, "My mom had schooling till grade three," and went on to say that her mother tutored her during grades one, two, and three. Her mother was unable to help her beyond those grades, and her father was away running a factory in another town (Wang01c). Another child said, "My father did not learn to read and was not able to teach me. My father wanted me to correct my homework when I left school. So my father and mother did the household duties [to free up my time to study]." In this case, even had the father the ability to help with homework, he was extremely busy due to deaths of two of the child's uncles in the preceding year, which meant that he had to help with farm work and housework for two other households. The child explained, "When I am at home doing my schoolwork, if I can't do a problem, there is no one there to ask for help" (Cai03c).

Many parents and children have dreams of high educational attainment, but these dreams are curtailed by economic realities that necessitate hard choices about educational investments. Many mothers and children explained that children would continue to receive financial support for schooling as long as they performed well. For example, in describing which one of her children would be allowed to continue in school, one mother stated, "We will provide education for whoever studies better" (Dang03m). Another mother reasoned that if her daughter had studied well, then they would have let her continue in school, but she didn't do well, so she quit. "She cannot learn anything, and the tuition was high, and so, she quit," the mother explained (Dang02m). Children understood the financial burdens on their parents and accepted the need to perform well as a condition to remain in school. One child said, "[My parents] want me to study well; [they say] 'If you pass entrance exams, even if we have to sell our house and vehicle, we will, in order to support your schooling'"(Dang01c). Another child had won a certificate of merit, and stated: "Even though they don't say anything, I just know that they're very happy; each year they pay the school fees, all [with money] borrowed from others, so I think that when I get a certificate of merit, they're definitely happy" (Dang06c).

Not all children, however, share their parents' desire for them to stay in school, and children's reluctance to study can be decisive. One mother commented that "it is both painful and complicated to make children go to school" (Cai02m). Another mother explained, "In this village, if you do not study, you are in for a hard life . . . but if your child refuses to learn, we, as parents, really cannot do anything." She described trying to persuade her son to return to school by telling him, "If you do not have an education, you will have a very difficult life" (Cai03m). One of the better-off children in the qualitative sample reported a similar story. Her brother stopped school after junior high because he didn't want to continue, despite his mother wanting him to do so (Wang01c).

Parents and students linked the quality of schools to desires for school continuation. For example, one mother explained that the school in their village did not have good teachers, so children had a hard time raising their grades (Cai03m). As another mother assessed the quality of the local school, she said, "Teachers [here] do not teach well—the teaching is pretty poor. After the students graduate, they are not able to test into college" (Dang04m). Both mothers believed that their children would have better chances for the future if they could attend a school with better teachers.

Another key dimension of school quality—and one that is much harder to quantify—is social climate. Children and mothers characterized climates in their schools and classrooms in terms that ranged from welcoming and nurturing, to competitive, strict, and, sometimes, even violent. Some children praised teachers for their empathy toward students, for their high standards, and for their strictness. Many children reported experiences with corporal punishment at school, though they did not always view physical punishment in a negative light. Some did report fearing teachers and principals, and some reported experiences with violence or bullying from peers. Educational quality—whether defined conventionally in academic terms, or more broadly to include school and classroom social climate—is likely to shape students' and parents' desires for school continuation.

ANALYSIS OF SCHOOL PERSISTENCE

Guided by the views expressed by rural residents themselves, we next consider the extent to which household wealth, student performance, and student engagement in the year 2000 are linked to school persistence—continued school enrollment four years later. We also consider the impact of current educational costs on enrollment, with costs measured as the average educational costs experienced by families in the child's village in 2004.

Table 11.2 shows enrollment in 2004 for children who had been enrolled in 2000 tabulated by household wealth, village average educational costs, mathematics achievement quintiles, and student aspirations. These associations offer evidence about early signals of risk for school-leaving. It is clear that poverty is associated with subsequent non-enrollment. Children in the poorest quintile of household wealth were twice as likely to be out of school (16 percent) as children in the wealthiest quintile (8 percent). Regarding costs, nearly 17 percent of sample children who were in villages with the highest educational costs—in the top quintile of average village costs experienced by families for education—were out of school, compared to 9 to

TABLE 11.2
*Enrollment rates in 2004 by hypothesized barriers to enrollment (N = 1,817)*

|  | % enrolled | % not enrolled |
|---|---|---|
| Wealth quintiles 2000 | | |
| Wealth quintile 1 (poorest) | 84.1 | 15.9 |
| Wealth quintile 2 | 87.4 | 12.6 |
| Wealth quintile 3 | 87.9 | 12.1 |
| Wealth quintile 4 | 89.8 | 10.2 |
| Wealth quintile 5 (wealthiest) | 92.3 | 7.7 |
| $X^2 (4) = 13.08^*$ | | |
| Village average educational costs quintiles 2004 | | |
| Cost quintile 1 (lowest) | 89.7 | 10.3 |
| Cost quintile 2 | 87.0 | 13.0 |
| Cost quintile 3 | 90.6 | 9.4 |
| Cost quintile 4 | 90.6 | 9.4 |
| Cost quintile 5 (highest) | 83.4 | 16.6 |
| $X^2 (4) = 13.08^*$ | | |
| Math achievement quintiles 2000 | | |
| Math quintile 1 (lowest) | 82.9 | 17.1 |
| Math quintile 2 | 86.7 | 13.3 |
| Math quintile 3 | 88.3 | 11.7 |
| Math quintile 4 | 93.4 | 6.6 |
| Math quintile 5 (highest) | 92.2 | 7.8 |
| $X^2 (4) = 23.08^{***}$ | | |
| Child aspirations 2000 | | |
| 6 years | 77.4 | 22.6 |
| 9 years | 80.2 | 19.8 |
| 11 years | 89.8 | 10.1 |
| 12 years | 86.0 | 14.0 |
| 14 years | 88.2 | 11.8 |
| 16 years | 91.4 | 8.6 |
| $X^2 (5) = 30.72^{***}$ | | |

SOURCE: GSCF-1 (2000), GSCF-2 (2004).

$^*p < .05; ^{**}p < .01; ^{***}p < .001.$

13 percent for children in other cost quintiles. The true effect of cost might be somewhat masked by the fact that children in villages where families are spending more on education probably experience higher costs, but may also be wealthier.

Performance quintiles are also strongly associated with continued enrollment. Approximately 17 percent of children in the poorest math achievement quintile in 2000 were out of school in 2004, compared to 7 to 8 percent of the children in the highest math achievement quintiles. Finally, differences by child's earlier engagement—measured as educational aspirations—are also striking: less than 10 percent of children who in 2000 aspired to tertiary-level education were out of school in 2004, in contrast to over 20 percent of those who had only aspired to complete primary school.

It is likely that these early aspirations are informed by children's awareness of their own performance, their perceptions of the usefulness of what they are learning, and the degree of hardship that their parents might face in continuing to support them in school.

Because we anticipate that enrollment is affected by a range of individual, household, and village characteristics, we next present a multivariate analysis of enrollment in 2004 (see Table 11.3). Model 1 controls for child background characteristics only; Model 2 adds child performance; Model 3

TABLE 11.3

*Parameters estimates, robust standard errors, and goodness-of-fit statistics for a taxonomy of fitted logit models of enrollment*

|  | MODEL 1 | MODEL 2 | MODEL 3 | MODEL 4 | MODEL 5 |
|---|---|---|---|---|---|
|  | Control | Poor performance | Family finances | Local educational costs | Child aspirations |
| Child gender | 0.451** | 0.475** | 0.466** | 0.475** | 0.440** |
| (0 = female, 1 = male) | (0.157) | (0.159) | (0.160) | (0.161) | (0.162) |
| Child age |  |  |  |  |  |
| 14 years-old | −1.370** | −1.335** | −1.383** | −1.395** | −1.436** |
|  | (0.489) | (0.491) | (0.489) | (0.489) | (0.494) |
| 15 years-old | −2.566** | −2.521** | −2.571** | −2.596** | −2.633** |
|  | (0.466) | (0.469) | (0.466) | (0.465) | (0.471) |
| 16 years-old | −3.147** | −3.144** | −3.204** | −3.211** | −3.243** |
|  | (0.464) | (0.468) | (0.464) | (0.463) | (0.471) |
| Mother's years of | 0.107** | 0.096** | 0.077** | 0.097** | 0.098** |
| completed schooling | (0.023) | (0.024) | (0.024) | (0.025) | (0.025) |
| Number of children in | 0.116 | 0.133 | 0.154 | 0.127 | 0.140 |
| the household | (0.112) | (0.112) | (0.114) | (0.115) | (0.115) |
| Child math |  | 0.020** | 0.019** | 0.021** | 0.017** |
| performance 2000 |  | (0.005) | (0.005) | (0.005) | (0.006) |
| Log family wealth 2000 |  |  | 0.274** | 0.350** | 0.333** |
|  |  |  | (0.088) | (0.089) | (0.089) |
| Log village average |  |  |  | −0.717** | −0.724** |
| educational costs 2004 |  |  |  | (0.209) | (0.210) |
| Child aspirations 2000 |  |  |  |  | 0.090** |
| (years of schooling) |  |  |  |  | (0.026) |
| Constant | 3.374** | 1.867** | −0.442 | 2.618* | 1.940 |
|  | (0.543) | (0.637) | (0.972) | (1.313) | (1.335) |
| Pseudo R² | 0.128 | 0.141 | 0.149 | 0.160 | 0.169 |
| −2 Log likelihood | 1144.582 | 1128.639 | 1118.219 | 1103.522 | 1091.608 |
| Observations | 1817 | 1817 | 1817 | 1817 | 1817 |

SOURCE: GSCF-1 (2000), GSCF-2 (2004).

*p < .05; **p < .01.

adds family wealth; Model 4 adds average village average educational costs experienced by families; and Model 5 adds child aspirations. Overall, we find that on average, boys, children of educated mothers, and younger children are significantly more likely to be in school. Adding to this baseline set of characteristics, math performance, family wealth, average village costs, [5] and child aspirations all exert significant net impacts on continued enrollment in the expected directions.

Because of the long-standing policy attention to the negative impact of household poverty and high direct costs and the assumption that parents, more than children, are the key decision makers, it may surprise readers to learn that children's attitudes and experiences matter. However, our statistical findings confirm the views expressed in the in-depth interviews about the key role of the children themselves. For example, the coefficients in Model 4 show that, net of all else, each additional point in math performance increases the odds of enrollment four years later by about 2 percent. Findings from Model 5 suggest that the odds of enrollment in 2004 increase by 9 percent for every year more of educational aspirations in the year 2000, after accounting for performance, wealth, costs, and other factors in the model.

DISCUSSION

Rural residents' expressed views and our statistical analysis point to a common set of barriers to education, namely economic resource constraints, performance, and aspirations. It is important to note that none of these are necessarily fixed attributes of children: impoverishment, achievement, and engagement are dynamic statuses, and are likely affected by the institutions in which children function.

Poverty, of course, can be a long-term and fixed characteristic. Chronic household poverty is linked to low human capital of adults and to characteristics of the local community that retard economic growth—conditions that are relatively difficult to modify in rural China (Jalan and Ravallion 2000). But descent into poverty can also be precipitous and the pathways to destitution have been changing in rural China as a direct result of social welfare policy decisions. In particular, the decisions to privatize and decentralize health care have dramatically raised direct costs to patients and their families. Consequently, catastrophic medical spending is an increasingly important precipitant of poverty in rural areas (Kaufman 2005; Liu and Hsiao 2001; Wang, Zhang, and Hsiao 2005). One recent estimate suggests that 20 percent of China's poor blame health care costs for their financial straits (Lim 2006). Moreover, there are clear implications for the education of children: analyses of a 2002 survey of households in six townships in Guizhou and Shanxi Provinces showed that, compared to households without hospitalization, households with hospitalization had a reduction in educational expenditures of 26 percent (Wang, Zhang, and Hsiao 2005).

In rural Gansu, poor parental health is strongly associated with poverty. In qualitative interviews, parents expressed frustration that their health problems and medical expenses had delayed their children's studies. In the 2004 GSCF survey, children in the poorest quintile were more than twice as likely to have a father who reported poor health as were children in the wealthiest (about 14 percent versus about 6 percent) (Hannum, Sargent, and Yu 2005). Parents who reported poor health were also more likely to report borrowing money for their children's education, and 77 percent of children whose fathers reported poor health were enrolled as compared to 88 percent of those whose fathers reported average or good health. These examples illustrate that social sector policies of the reform era have changed both the mechanisms of poverty creation and the transmission of poverty across generations in rural Gansu.

Just as poverty is conditioned by structures and institutions beyond the individual, so are performance and engagement with education. Other research using the Gansu data shows that children with better-paid teachers have significantly higher math scores. Mother's education, mother's aspirations, and the presence of children's books are also associated with better math performance in school. Moreover, the effect of family wealth on performance dissipates with inclusion of measures of a supportive home environment for learning, such as mother's educational expectations for the child and books in the home (Hannum and Park 2007).

Educational aspirations were also significantly related to mother's educational expectations, which, in turn, were shaped by family economic circumstances (Hannum and Park 2007; Zhang, Kao, and Hannum 2007).[6] While few teacher characteristics could be systematically linked to engagement, student subjective experiences at school are closely linked to their aspirations: In 2000, students who reported that teachers care for students, treat students fairly, and encourage questions had significantly higher aspirations in multivariate analyses, and students who reported that teachers assign lots of homework and always lecture in class had lower aspirations (An, Hannum, and Sargent 2007; Hannum and Park 2007).

Not surprisingly, aspirations are also related to performance. For students enrolled in 2004, math performance in 2000 significantly predicted current aspirations (Hannum and Adams 2007). Aspirations also appear to be linked to the support children receive earlier in the educational process. For example, the higher the mother's and teacher's educational expectations for the child in 2000, the higher the child's aspirations in 2004, net of socioeconomic background, teacher characteristics, and student performance (Hannum and Adams 2007). Moreover, a year more of expectations on the part of mothers or teachers was about as beneficial as a year more of mother's education.

Collectively, these findings highlight several points. First, economic barriers to schooling were still important in 2004, and to some extent these barriers are the outcome of policies during the 1980s and 1990s that raised direct charges for social services. Families may have reacted to the need to pay high fees for services, and to the potential for catastrophic costs, by being less willing to spend precious savings on schooling for children for whom additional years in school will have marginal economic impact. Children themselves can be unwilling to subject their parents to the hardship of continued educational fees if they see little value in continuing their education. In these circumstances, children may take decisions into their own hands.

Second, beyond economic factors, children's performance and attachment to school significantly predict continued enrollment. These attributes of children may affect their own willingness to stay in school, and their parents' willingness to invest in them. This finding is particularly important in light of new policies in the twenty-first century aimed at eliminating the financial burden of compulsory education for rural children. As private costs for basic education are removed, the school-related determinants of performance, engagement, and persistence will be of great consequence in ensuring universal access to education. Moreover, performance and engagement with schooling both shape and are shaped by parental expectations for children.

Furthermore, the institutional factors that affect performance and engagement are not yet well established. The new curriculum is intended to improve the quality of schooling experienced by children, and especially their motivation. In rural Gansu, certain student experiences in the classroom do appear to be closely tied to their aspirations. If China is successful in its new efforts to minimize cost barriers to education, understanding the motivation of students will become even more important in the study of educational stratification.

CONCLUSIONS

For decades, China and other developing nations have grappled with the formidable challenge of creating an educational system that can enhance the lives of future rural citizens while also serving as a stepping stone to social mobility outside of rural areas—the dream of many rural children and parents. China is now in the fortunate position of having unprecedented resources at hand with which to engage this challenge. Moreover, government concerns about gaping economic inequalities in the twenty-first century have created a favorable political climate in which the task of addressing educational deficits in poor rural communities has taken on new urgency, as part of the "new socialist countryside" agenda (e.g., Pan 2006).

In this chapter, rural residents' assessments of the barriers to schooling in one of China's poorest interior provinces offer a window into the implications of past policy decisions for rural education, and into the likely implications of current policy initiatives. We have suggested that decentralization policies begun in the mid-1980s, which had the effect of raising costs to individuals for social services, created a situation in which inability to pay school fees became a serious barrier to compulsory education in poor regions, even as average incomes rose under market reforms. Rural residents themselves cited costs as a barrier, and analyses show that children from poorer families and those in villages where average educational costs experienced by families were higher were significantly less likely to remain enrolled in school. Families may simply lack access to cash or credit to pay fees; they may have been pushed into poverty by costs of social services; and they may have become conservative about investing in marginal students in a context where future expenses for education and health care for all family members needed to be anticipated.

Beyond costs, rural residents cite children's performance in school and attitude toward school as significant issues, and these factors emerge as predictors of continued enrollment in multivariate analyses that control for wealth and costs. Other research has shown that linking attributes of teachers to student performance and engagement is difficult. It is clear, however, that when poor rural children do enter school, they face weak infrastructures and less-qualified teachers than do their counterparts in wealthier areas. Many quickly surpass their parents' level of schooling and thus lack experienced guidance when they face academic difficulty and social problems. They often lack the resources for basic educational supplies, much less enrichment materials. Many also witness bitter struggles and sacrifices made by parents in support of their education, and these experiences may detract from children's desire to continue. They may also face a curriculum that is foreign to their lived experiences, and offered in an unfamiliar dialect. Our findings reveal a complicated portrait of demand-side barriers to education related to school quality.

Policies of the early twenty-first century seek to grant equal educational rights to rural and urban children, eliminate student fees, set aside funds for rural schools, and ask urban teachers to teach in rural areas for a fixed term. Curriculum reforms aim to provide a more interactive, engaging, and locally relevant curriculum. These government initiatives have sought to alleviate financial burdens on rural parents; they have also addressed some of the issues of quality that loom large in the concerns of rural parents. Success in these initiatives would address many pressing problems in rural education.[7]

Designing feasible strategies that might address additional consequences of poverty—such as the constraints on enrichment and learning that go far beyond the direct barriers of school costs, and the difficult school environments that often emerge in impoverished communities—will require additional creativity and a high degree of political will.

# Urban Occupational Mobility and Employment Institutions: Hierarchy, Market, and Networks in a Mixed System

*Yanjie Bian*

Occupational mobility provides an ideal yardstick to capture the dynamics and social consequences of the postsocialist institutional transformation of Chinese society. In the prereform employment system characterized by a high degree of labor immobility, the rigidities of state planning bound wage earners to the workplaces to which they were assigned in the places of birth (Whyte and Parish 1984; Walder 1986; Davis 1990; Lin and Bian 1991). While full employment was a design of the plan, labor markets were eliminated, individuals given no freedom to seek or move between workplaces, and personal connections mobilized to obtain favors from authorities for a desirable assignment or reallocation (Bian 1994, 1997). Since 1980, the return of labor markets has gradually eroded these institutional foundations of bureaucratic control over labor, ending state assignments and generalizing the experiences of job hunting and job change. Millions of peasants have left their villages to work and live in towns and cities (Keister and Nee 2000; Ma 2001), massive layoffs and organized transfers by state-owned enterprises have pushed millions of urbanites into a booming private sector (Solinger 1999b, 2000), and social networks actively facilitate employment processes (Bian 1999, 2002b; Bian and Zhang 2001).

In this chapter I assess these changing patterns of occupational mobility in Chinese cities by focusing on three interrelated issues. The first is the frequency in job shifts between employers since 1980. The second is a comparison of the roles of three employment institutions—hierarchy, market, and network—that allocate jobs in both the pre- and postreform eras. And the third is the effect of these institutions on upward and downward occupational mobility. Hierarchy, market, and network have coexisted in the entire reform era, but their roles have been distinctive. Hierarchy, in essence, represents the coercive nature of the Communist party-state as it rejects an individual's rights over his or her labor force and work choices. Market, on the other hand, recognizes these rights, and in doing so motivates individuals to choose jobs within the constraints of personal and nonpersonal factors. And network functions in the extent to which institutions of hierarchy and market are embedded in and constrained by ongoing social relationships in the employment process. Thus, the changing roles of these three institutions in shaping occupational mobility provide an excellent yardstick to assess China's paths of transition away from the traditional model of state socialism.

I ground my assessment with data from the 2003 Chinese General Social Survey (CGSS), a nationally representative sample of 5,894 urban households in which 5,094 respondents had ever worked on a paid civilian job. Whether retired or working by 2003, these respondents were requested to provide information about their job histories, channels through which they obtained their last jobs, and their personal attributes at the time of job acquisition. Table 12.1 describes the 2003 CGSS sample. With these data, I evaluate the ways in which hierarchy, market, and network interact to pattern the urban opportunity structure distinctively for individuals with different attributes and in different occupational strata.

TABLE 12.1

*Descriptive information of the 2003 CGSS sample: Relevant variables*

| | | | |
|---|---|---|---|
| N for the total sample | 5,894 | Current occupation** | |
| N for the analysis* | 5,094 | Managerial/administrative | 9.3% |
| Sex: % male | 51.3 | Professional | 15.2% |
| | | Clerical | 9.6% |
| Age | | Skilled manual | 27.5% |
| Mean | 43.38 | Unskilled manual | 38.4% |
| Standard deviation | 13.11 | Prior occupation | |
| Party membership: % CCP | 18.3 | Managerial/administrative | 3.6% |
| Years of schooling | | Professional | 6.9% |
| Mean | 10.66 | Clerical | 3.3% |
| Standard deviation | 3.36 | Skilled manual | 12.9% |
| | | Unskilled manual | 16.6% |
| Period of job entry | | None (still in first job) | 51.4% |
| 1956–1979 | 29.8% | Missing | 5.3% |
| 1980–92 | 34.8% | Current sector** | |
| 1993–99 | 20.6% | Government/public org. | 20.4% |
| 2000–03 | 14.9% | State-owned enterprise | 43.0% |
| City of residence | | Nonstate | 36.7% |
| Beijing-Tianjin-Shanghai | 20.4% | Prior sector | |
| Eastern | 25.9% | Government/public org. | 8.1% |
| Central | 35.9% | State-owned enterprise | 16.0% |
| Western | 17.8% | Nonstate | 24.5% |
| | | None (still in first job) | 51.4% |

*Our criterion for the inclusion of respondents into analysis is that the respondent either held a paid job at the time of the survey or had had a paid job before retirement. Excluded from the analysis are housewives (340), students (149), and, those who entered into last job before 1956 (68), those whose job information was incomplete or missing (103), and those who did not hold a civilian urban job at the time of survey or before retirement (140).

**Retirees' preretirement jobs and sectors are counted in these variables.

RATES OF JOB TURNOVER

*Past and Present*

Systematic data on job changes before 1985 are unavailable. Scattered observations and ethnographic reports suggest that in the years before marketization, an urban Chinese worker's first workplace was often his/her last workplace (Wolf 1985). Such an impression, however, probably overstated the degree of immobility. In the prereform era, besides organized transfers (Walder 1986: 69–70), urban enterprises did permit job shifts for personal reasons, with the leading reason being "getting closer to home" (Davis 1990). Exploring work histories of over 1,000 individuals in 200 families in Shanghai and Wuhan through 1988, Davis (1992) found that while resistance to individually initiated job changes curbed mobility, more than 50 percent of the middle-aged or recently retired parents had changed employers at least once before the early 1980s and that fathers had an average of 2.28 employers and mothers 1.99 in their lifetimes.

A 1985 Tianjin survey, reported in Lin and Bian (1991), is probably the earliest representative sample of a major industrial city. Of the 752 respondents who held a job in 1985, 40 percent had changed jobs at least once since they first entered the work force, leaving 60 percent who remained in their first jobs by the survey year. When we applied this crude measure of "lifetime job change" to the 2003 CGSS, we found that 59 percent of the Tianjin respondents had changed jobs, showing a significant 19 percent growth in "lifetime job changes" from the earlier estimates for 1985. Other cities in the CGSS sample average "lifetime job change" rates of approximately 60 percent; with Shanghai being the lowest at 52 percent in 2003.

A more standard measure of job change than lifetime rates is the annual rate of job change, calculated as the percentage of workers who change jobs within a year over the year's total workers who are at risk of changing jobs. Job changes can occur within employers and between employers. From a 17-city Chinese sample in 1994, Zhou et al. (1997) reported annual rates of job change between employers of 5.5 percent, 4.2 percent, and 2.6 percent for the periods of 1949–1965, 1966–1979, and 1980–1993, respectively. In comparison, based on annual surveys of Russia, Gerber (2002) reports increasing rates of job change from 4.6 percent in 1991 to 6.7 percent in 1997, a period of dramatic regime change due to a shock-therapy design of market reforms. Within only six years, Russia's shifts between employers rose from 3.9 percent to 5.5 percent, job changes within employers rose from 0.7 percent to 1.1 percent.

*Findings from the 2003 CGSS*

The 2003 CGSS provides respondents' job histories from which annual rates of job change can be calculated. The sample's age criterion of respondents was 18–69, and respondents were randomly selected from all eligible household members by using the Kish grid, a standard procedure of random selection. To recognize an official retirement age of 60 for men and to deal with a few missing cases for technical reasons (see an interpretation in the next paragraph), the remaining 5,094 respondents worked on paid jobs and were at risk to change jobs from the year of job entry until the year of retirement. This is the working sample from which annual rates of job change are calculated, as displayed in Table 12.2.

Four technical notes are necessary before discussing the results presented in Table 12.2. First, although we have a complete job history of each working respondent, and some of these respondents entered the labor force even before 1949, I am interested only in post-1978 rates of job change. Second, the working sample from 1978 to 2002 is divided into three age groups of 18–30, 31–45, and 46–60; annual rates of job change for both the total sample and the age groups are calculated, and gender-specific rates are

TABLE 12.2

*Rates of job change and age structure by year, 2003 CGSS (urban), percentages*

| Age group | OVERALL JOB CHANGE | | | | | JOB CHANGE BETWEEN EMPLOYERS | | | | |
|---|---|---|---|---|---|---|---|---|---|---|
| | Total | 18–30 | 31–45 | 46–60 | | Total | 18–30 | 31–45 | 46–60 | |
| Year | | | | Men | Women | | | | Men | Women |
| 1978 | 5.0 | 4.6 | 5.4 | — | — | 3.0 | 2.8 | 3.3 | — | — |
| 1979 | 4.9 | 4.9 | 4.9 | — | — | 2.9 | 3.2 | 2.5 | — | — |
| 1980 | 6.2 | 6.1 | 6.4 | 5.1 | 3.2 | 3.4 | 3.3 | 3.7 | 2.6 | 0.0 |
| 1981 | 3.9 | 4.5 | 3.4 | 2.1 | 2.0 | 2.4 | 2.7 | 2.0 | 2.1 | 2.0 |
| 1982 | 4.8 | 5.3 | 4.3 | 4.5 | 2.6 | 2.9 | 3.4 | 2.3 | 3.0 | 1.3 |
| 1983 | 4.7 | 5.1 | 4.5 | 3.9 | 2.0 | 2.9 | 3.2 | 2.7 | 1.7 | 2.0 |
| 1984 | 5.8 | 5.8 | 5.8 | 8.6 | 0.0 | 3.2 | 3.8 | 2.8 | 3.3 | 0.0 |
| 1985 | 5.3 | 5.8 | 4.8 | 5.0 | 5.1 | 3.2 | 4.2 | 2.5 | 2.1 | 1.3 |
| 1986 | 5.3 | 6.0 | 5.2 | 4.3 | 2.3 | 3.1 | 3.4 | 3.2 | 1.8 | 1.7 |
| 1987 | 4.7 | 5.2 | 4.7 | 2.8 | 3.1 | 3.1 | 3.7 | 2.8 | 2.2 | 1.5 |
| 1988 | 4.8 | 5.5 | 4.6 | 3.4 | 2.9 | 2.5 | 3.8 | 1.9 | 0.3 | 1.5 |
| 1989 | 4.8 | 6.6 | 4.0 | 2.9 | 2.2 | 2.9 | 4.5 | 2.2 | 1.3 | 0.4 |
| 1990 | 5.5 | 7.0 | 4.8 | 6.1 | 0.8 | 3.5 | 4.9 | 2.7 | 3.4 | 0.0 |
| 1991 | 4.4 | 5.5 | 3.8 | 3.3 | 3.9 | 2.8 | 3.7 | 2.7 | 1.1 | 1.2 |
| 1992 | 5.4 | 6.7 | 5.1 | 3.4 | 2.7 | 3.2 | 4.3 | 3.0 | 1.2 | 1.2 |
| 1993 | 5.5 | 7.7 | 4.5 | 3.7 | 2.7 | 3.6 | 5.4 | 2.8 | 1.6 | 1.6 |
| 1994 | 4.8 | 8.3 | 3.2 | 2.7 | 2.6 | 3.0 | 5.4 | 2.0 | 1.4 | 1.3 |
| 1995 | 5.8 | 8.6 | 5.1 | 3.4 | 2.7 | 3.7 | 5.9 | 3.1 | 1.9 | 1.2 |
| 1996 | 4.8 | 6.6 | 4.3 | 3.7 | 2.3 | 2.8 | 4.4 | 2.5 | 1.7 | 0.0 |
| 1997 | 5.5 | 9.6 | 4.1 | 2.7 | 3.0 | 3.6 | 6.8 | 2.6 | 1.3 | 1.9 |
| 1998 | 6.4 | 11.3 | 4.7 | 3.4 | 2.6 | 4.6 | 9.1 | 2.9 | 2.9 | 1.5 |
| 1999 | 6.3 | 9.9 | 5.9 | 3.4 | 1.8 | 4.3 | 7.1 | 4.1 | 1.6 | 1.1 |
| 2000 | 6.9 | 11.1 | 5.9 | 4.1 | 4.3 | 5.0 | 9.1 | 4.0 | 1.9 | 3.5 |
| 2001 | 7.1 | 10.8 | 6.6 | 4.2 | 4.2 | 4.6 | 6.8 | 4.5 | 2.6 | 3.1 |
| 2002 | 7.6 | 12.5 | 6.7 | 4.9 | 4.5 | 5.8 | 10.3 | 4.7 | 3.6 | 4.5 |

calculated for the 46–60 age group in order to set off the effects of differential age criteria of retirement for men (60) and women (50 or 55). Third, the return of sent-down youths to the cities after 1978 and the organized transfers from the military into the civilian labor force in the first half of the 1980s were beyond a normal definition of job shifts and therefore are treated as the entry into the urban labor force. Peasants taking nonagricultural jobs in the cities, however, are defined as job shifts in all years. Fourth, the CGSS was conducted in October to December of 2003. Because the year of 2003 was unfinished, the 2003 annual rate was not calculated.

As shown in Table 12.2, first section, annual rates of total job change increased from 5.0 percent in 1978 to 7.6 percent in 2002, with an increase margin of 2.6 percent over a 25-year span. Meanwhile, the rate of job change between employers increased from 3.0 percent in 1978 to 5.8 percent in 2002, with an increase margin of 2.8 percent. Older age groups have had substantially lower rates of job change, however. For the 46–60 age group, while males seemed more mobile than females in each year, their rates of overall job change and job turnovers between employers do not significantly increase across the years even as the system has become more marketized over time. To examine the effects of marketization on rates of job change, we must pay special attention to the younger 18–30 group whose members are least affected by changing retirement ages and who were least embedded in the socialist era enterprises.

The younger group has large numbers of eligible workers each year (from 1,193 in 1978 to 726 in 2002) and its annual rates are therefore reliable. For this most mobile group, the overall job change rates increased from 4.6 percent in 1978 to 12.5 percent in 2002, with a large increase margin of 7.9 percent. Meanwhile, job changes between employers increased substantially also, from 2.8 percent to 10.3 percent, producing an increase margin of 7.5 percent over the 25 years. Although annual rates of job change fluctuate from year to year, the increasing trend from 1978 to 2002 is impressive and clear. This trend is repeated by a moderate degree in the middle and older age groups.

Zhou et al. (1997) argue that state policy shifts have tremendous impact on life chances under state socialism. When market reforms are anchored by a durable Communist state, this impact also can be felt in the changing rates of job change in reform-era China. Around 1984 to 1986, the government began allowing professionals and technicians to change employers through a new arrangement of "talent centers" (*ren cai zhong xin*) (Davis 1990). As shown in the 2003 CGSS data, 5.8 percent of the 18–30 age group changed jobs in 1984, of which 3.8 percent moved to a different employer. However, it is after Deng Xiaoping's South China Tour in 1992 and the Fifteenth CCP

Congress in 1993, that we see more noticeable increases. Millions of urbanites "plunged into the sea" and a larger number of peasants moved to towns and cities for nonagricultural work after 1992 (Ma 2001). In 1998, the Zhu Rongji administration launched another new wave of state-owned enterprise reforms, precipitating large numbers of layoffs, job shifts, and job hunting in the booming private sector. In each year after 1998 except for 1999, overall job change among those between 18 and 30 never fell below 10 percent and job changes between employers remained in the range of 7 to 10 percent.

Although China's prereform system of employment was not as immobile as is often assumed, the growth since 1978 has been significant and sustained. By 1998, the annual rate of job change was 6.4 percent, of which 4.6 percent was between employers, and by 2002 these two rates reached the historical height of 7.6 percent and 5.8 percent, respectively. Behind these rates are a great number of job changes. In the 10 years from 1993 to 2002, for example, the accumulated rates of total job change and job change between employers are 60.7 percent and 41.0 percent, respectively, and these reveal 2,253 total job changes of which 1,520 involve job shifts between employers. How did these job shifts occur? Through what channels did people locate the jobs to which they moved? And more generally, what employment institutions facilitated occupational mobility in the pre- and postreform periods?

## CHANGING ROLES OF EMPLOYMENT INSTITUTIONS

In postrevolutionary China, 1956 marks the beginning of a socialist economic system, in which the state consolidated strategic economic resources and controlled and assigned urban jobs in the state and collective sectors. As the system matured, urban labor markets effectively disappeared and a job control system—able to dispatch almost 20 million urban youths to the countryside (1968–1976)—dominated urban employment. Starting in 1980 labor markets gradually reemerged in the cities, while at the same time state assignments continued in the allocation of college and technical school graduates to job slots in the state sector, creating what has been known as a dual-track system in which hierarchy and market coexist as employment institutions. After 1992, labor markets expanded more quickly and layoffs in the state sectors became routine by the end of the decade. Meanwhile the private sector grew tremendously, becoming the main source of jobs for both the new cohorts and the laid-off workers from the state sector. By 2000 markets were the dominant mode of job allocation. To capture the importance of historical shifts, Table 12.3 summarizes job search channels across four periods: 1956–1979, 1980–1992, 1993–1999, and 2000–2003.

TABLE 12.3
*Search channel by period, 2003 CGSS (urban)*

|  | Total | PERIOD | | | |
|---|---|---|---|---|---|
|  |  | 1956–1979 | 1980–1992 | 1993–1999 | 2000–2003 |
| Total N | 5,094 | 1,516 | 1,772 | 1,048 | 758 |
| Search channel |  |  |  |  |  |
| Hierarchy | 57.4% | 77.7% | 63.8% | 40.1% | 26.0% |
| Market | 35.3% | 21.7% | 30.2% | 47.7% | 57.5% |
| Networks | 32.2% | 15.7% | 31.0% | 43.9% | 51.6% |
| Users of multiple channels | 23.5% | 14.4% | 23.5% | 29.2% | 33.0% |
| Market and hierarchy | 1.9% | 2.5% | 1.8% | 1.5% | 1.5% |
| Networks in hierarchy | 6.7% | 6.5% | 8.5% | 6.0% | 3.7% |
| Networks in market | 13.3% | 4.7% | 11.7% | 19.2% | 25.7% |
| Networks in hierarchy |  |  |  |  |  |
| and market | 1.6% | 0.7% | 1.5% | 2.5% | 2.1% |
| N of network users | 1,638 | 238 | 549 | 460 | 391 |
| Network resources gained |  |  |  |  |  |
| Information | 91.4% | 88.2% | 90.5% | 92.2% | 93.6% |
| Influence | 73.8% | 63.4% | 72.1% | 76.7% | 79.0% |
| Both | 65.2% | 51.7% | 62.7% | 68.9% | 72.6% |
| Ties with contacts |  |  |  |  |  |
| Weak | 49.2% | 52.1% | 63.0% | 43.9% | 49.1% |
| Quite strong | 13.8% | 13.0% | 13.6% | 13.9% | 18.2% |
| Very strong | 37.0% | 34.9% | 25.4% | 42.2% | 33.7% |

Hierarchy, market, and network are three distinct institutions through which to allocate jobs. I define hierarchy as any form of job assignments by the state or organizational authority. These include "state assignments" (*guojia fenpei*), in which a school graduate received an assignment; "organized transfers" (*zuozhi diaodong*), in which a job holder is reallocated by the authorities for career or noncareer reasons; "internal recruitments" (*nei zhao*), in which employees' children or relatives are hired into vacated job slots within the organization of the employees; and "retirement replacements" (*ding ti*), in which a child gets his/her parent's job upon the parent's retirement. In contrast to the coercive nature of a hierarchical channel, a market channel permits free will. Here, individuals search for jobs on their own, whether through direct application to employers or the use of employment services. Some become self-employed. A network channel, finally, is one in which an individual uses his/her social contacts to find or secure a job. This can be done in three ways: to use a contact to secure a job that is assigned through a hierarchical channel; to increase the chances of getting a job that is available from a market channel; or to receive a job directly from a social contact who controls and distributes it. In this last practice, the job seeker does not have to go through either a hierarchical or a market channel; a job "comes" through a network tie to the person who wants it.

As shown in Table 12.3, 57.4 percent of the respondents arrived at their last jobs through a hierarchical channel and 35.3 percent through a market channel. These two channels had their respective historical momentums. The hierarchical channel was the dominant mode in the 1956–1979 period, allocating 77.7 percent of the jobs. It declined to 63.8 percent in the 1980–1992 period in which labor markets began to emerge in the cities, to 40.1 percent in the 1993–1999 period in which labor markets expanded, and sharply down to 26.0 percent in the 2000–2003 period in which labor markets finally became the dominant mode of job allocation nationally. Meanwhile, jobs allocated through market channels increased from 21.7 percent in the first period to 57.5 percent in the last.

The shift from hierarchy to market is an incomplete story without putting network channels into the picture. On a general level, researchers offer no definite position about the fate of social networks in reform-era China. Under the assumption that market economies are an efficient system that rewards rational behaviors, and because Chinese *guanxi* networks are thought to be irrational, unethical, and antimarket, Guthrie (1998, 2002) proposes that the significance of social networks in the economic sphere, including labor markets, will decline with marketization. An alternative position is that social networks will continue to play a significant role in China's emerging labor markets for several reasons (Bian 2002b). Emerging market institutions are rooted in the family and kinship networks (Lin 1995; Whyte 1995b; Peng 2004); market information circulates within social networks (Boisot and Child 1996); and market activities, whether in public or private sectors, are never divorced from the influence of government bureaucracies and state officials (Oi 1999; Wank 1999). The results from the 2003 CGSS support this alternative view.

As shown in Table 12.3, networks were persistent search channels in all historical periods, and they grew as labor markets expanded in the most recent periods. While network channels perform independently for some job seekers (roughly 32.2 percent – 23.5 percent = 8.7 percent), primarily they supplement the deficiencies of other search channels (23.5 percent – 1.9 percent = 21.6 percent). With the growth of labor markets, an increasing number of jobs were allocated through the combination of market and network channels, or more specifically, from 11.7 percent in the initial reform period (1980–1992) to 25.7 percent in the most recent (2000–2003). Because labor markets are less rigid and more uncertain than are state assignments, job seekers thus became more rational by using multiple search channels to boost job opportunities. Users of multiple search channels, mostly coupled with network channels, more than doubled from the 1956–1979 period (14.4 percent) to the 2000–2003 period (33.0 percent).

## NETWORK CHANNELS AS JOB ALLOCATION INSTITUTION

How to understand the increasing role of social networks in occupational mobility? Sociologists have offered two different arguments. One argument, which is tied to market economies, points to weak ties of infrequent interaction and low intimacy for channeling nonredundant information about job openings that are not immediately available to job seekers (Granovetter 1973, 1995). This argument implies that information networks of weak ties optimize labor markets by allocating jobs to those who are probably the best-qualified candidates (Fernandez and Castilla 2001). The other argument, tied to state redistributive economies, contends that strong ties of trust and obligation relay influence from authorities to individuals whose jobs are assigned through a hierarchy of government offices and state-run employers (Bian 1997). In this situation, because jobs are favors that are secretly given to the connected others whose qualifications may be irrelevant or inadequate, there is a probability that influence networks of strong ties distort or de-optimize job allocation in a market or nonmarket economy (Bian 1999).

While information and influence are two distinctive network resources mobilized by job seekers, it is extremely difficult to distinguish them in a questionnaire survey. To culturally sensitive Chinese individuals, helping someone get a job requires much more than merely informing them about job openings. On the other hand, substantial intervention or influence from kin, friends, or acquaintances is usually of a secretive nature, and therefore, the information is not supposed to be disclosed. Does a survey respondent easily tell an interviewer that he/she got a job because his/her uncle used his power to influence the hiring authority? Very rarely. It would require interviewing skills to have the information "slip" out and in a highly structured questionnaire survey to a nationally representative sample of individuals of unknown backgrounds like CGSS, paid interviewers are not allowed to make up conversations with respondents at their discretion.

The 2003 CGSS used four different questions to help differentiate the information and influence resources that are mobilized by job seekers from their social ties. (1) From a given list, respondents were requested to identify all sources they used during their job searches. (2) They were then asked how many people helped them with job searches by "getting job information, doing the communication, or providing any other help." Then, the respondents were asked to confirm (3) whether any of these people provided information about specific jobs, and (4) whether any of these people provided any other kind of help. A positive response to the last question indicated the degree of influence that the respondent received from his or her contacts on the prospective employers.

Contrary to the belief that the role of Chinese *guanxi* networks is mainly to provide influence rather than information (Bian 1997), more than 91.4 percent of network users gained job information from their social ties, much higher than the 73.8 percent who gained some kind of influence (see Table 12.3). A great majority (65.2 percent) of the network users actually gained both information and influence from social ties; to these dual-resource receivers, information might be just a by-product of the influence gained, an argument that has been put forward previously for explaining the role of *guanxi* networks during the years of state assignments (Bian 1997, 1999). But still, pure information receivers (26.2 percent) outnumbered pure influence receivers (8.6 percent), and this is true across all periods even for the period of 1956–1979 in which state assignments dominated. Moreover, the shift from hierarchical channels to market channels in the post-1980 periods did not stop network users from obtaining influence from social ties. On the contrary, respondents reported increased use of influence as market reforms deepened. One lesson from capitalist societies is that as competition and uncertainty increase, social networks become an important channel through which to allocate jobs (Granovetter 1995; Erickson 2001). Thus, it is not surprising that as more and more urban jobs were allocated via markets, job seekers increasingly became dual-network-resource receivers, obtaining both information and influence from social ties to secure work opportunities.

In order to ascertain if weak ties are predominately to flow information while strong ties relay influence, we compare the strengths of ties to information and influence providers. Roughly 30 percent of the network users used multiple ties. Given the nature of CGSS as a general survey, we simply cannot measure the strength of each pair of these ties. Instead, we asked all respondents to identify a "key" contact. Of the 1,638 network users, 973 identified a key contact and ranked the tie from "very familiar" to "not so familiar," and 675 failed to identify any key contact; most of this latter group were only indirectly associated with the helpers. From these responses, I construct three tie strength categories by treating "very familiar" as "strong," "quite familiar" as "quite strong," and all others as "weak." The results are displayed in the last section of Table 12.3.

On the whole, weak ties account for half of the ties between the respondents and their job helpers. Keep in mind that the weak ties are predominantly indirect ties which, according to a 1988 Tianjin survey (Bian 1997), are likely to be within a strong-tie chain in which the job seeker is strongly connected to an intermediary, who is strongly connected to the final helper even though the job seeker and the final helper have only a weak tie. The 2003 CGSS data was unable to track these intermediary links, although we may assume that the growth of market channels and the decline of hierarchical channels have not dramatically affected the logic of how indirect ties work for employment purposes.

From the pre-1979 to the post-2000 period, hierarchical channels in job allocation declined from 77.7 percent to 26.0 percent, market channels increased from 21.7 percent to 57.5 percent, and network channels increased from 15.7 percent to 51.6 percent. Interestingly, network channels tend to be used in conjunction with hierarchical and market channels. This finding supports the view that networks are informal institutions that supplement the deficiencies of formal institutions of employment (Bian 2002b; Sato 2003). Unlike widely-known hypotheses that information channels through weak ties and influence through strong ties (Granovetter 1973; Bian 1997), we found that both information and influence are channeled through ties of varying strengths. What are the relative efficacies of hierarchy, market, and networks in delivering a job to the job seeker? How did the relative importance of each channel change across the four historical periods?

IMPACT OF EMPLOYMENT INSTITUTIONS

A job seeker can try multiple channels to search for work. The question is Which channel ultimately delivers a job? Because a job seeker can simultaneously use hierarchy, market, and network, our statistical analysis in Table 12.4 uses logistic regression, rather than multinomial regression, which assumes the exclusive use of one channel. My interpretation of the results focuses on a comparison of relative effects of specific predictors on the three channels.

As shown in Table 12.4, hierarchical channels sharply declined after the 1956–1979 period. If a hierarchical channel delivered a job by a probability of 100 percent in the 1956–1979 period (as a point of comparison), its probability was as low as −.95 percent (that is, Exp B − 1 = 0.050 − 1 = .95%) in the most recent period after 2000. Meanwhile, the probabilities of job delivery through market and network channels all increased considerably in an incremental manner across the periods. As we see in the large magnitudes of their coefficients, the increasing effects of network channels are most impressive, as their job-delivery capacities increased more than four and eleven times during the 1993–1999 period (Exp B − 1 = 5.574 − 1 = 4.574) and the 2000–2003 period (Exp B − 1 = 12.229 − 1 = 11.229), respectively. Such increases were felt most strongly in the three big cities of Beijing, Tianjin, and Shanghai (Exp B = 2.880).

Economic sector and occupation of one's prior work affect one's searching for jobs through these channels. Prior work in the state increases one's probability of using hierarchical channels (Exp B of 2.974 and 2.393) more than market channels (0.410 and 0.505), but it does not affect one's use of network channels (.932 and .938), making it explicit that social networks

TABLE 12.4
*Logistic regression on the use of search channel that delivers a job*

| | HIERARCHY | MARKET | NETWORK |
|---|---|---|---|
| | *Exp(B)* | *Exp(B)* | *Exp(B)* |
| Period (1956–1979 = ref) | | | |
| 1980–92 | 0.441*** | 1.862*** | 2.973*** |
| 1993–99 | 0.150*** | 1.485*** | 5.574*** |
| 2000–03 | 0.050*** | 3.638*** | 12.229*** |
| City (western region = ref) | | | |
| Beijing-Tianjin-Shanghai | 1.064 | 0.796* | 2.880*** |
| Eastern | 0.853 | 0.933 | 1.872*** |
| Central | 0.915 | 0.963 | 2.003*** |
| Prior sector (nonstate = ref) | | | |
| Government / public organization | 2.974*** | 0.410*** | 0.932 |
| State-owned enterprise | 2.393*** | 0.505*** | 0.938 |
| Prior position (no job = ref) | | | |
| Managerial/administrative | 0.718 | 1.185 | 1.359 |
| Professional | 0.395*** | 2.102*** | 1.574** |
| Clerical | 0.559* | 1.479 | 1.505* |
| Manual worker | 0.442*** | 1.529*** | 1.627*** |
| Individual attributes | | | |
| Sex (male = 1) | 1.365*** | 1.012 | 0.825** |
| Party (CCP = 1) | 2.582*** | 0.502*** | 0.736* |
| Year of schooling | 1.130*** | 0.927*** | 0.946*** |
| Age | 1.057* | 1.003 | 0.920*** |
| Age squared/100 | 0.974 | 0.950 | 1.092* |
| Age interactions with periods | | | |
| 1980–92 | — | — | — |
| 1993–99 | 0.963*** | 1.040*** | — |
| 2000–03 | — | 1.025* | 0.958** |
| Constant | 0.357** | 0.757 | 0.605 |
| Cox and Snell R$^2$ | 0.218 | 0.114 | 0.111 |
| N | 4,824 | 4,824 | 4,824 |

*$p. < .05$; **$p. < .01$; ***$p. < .001$.

are a persistent informal mechanism that exists under any job allocation institution, hierarchy or market. Managers and administrators do not seem to favor a particular channel, whereas others are nearly equally likely to use market and network channels (Exp B of greater than 1) to search for jobs, leaving hierarchical channels the least useful (Exp B of less than 1).

Individual attributes shape choices among search channels. Although both men and women are equally likely to use market channels, men are 36.5 percent more likely than women to use hierarchical channels and 17.5 percent (.825 − 1) less likely to use networks. Party membership has even greater effect. Given a 100 percent probability for non-Party members, Party members' probabilities are 258.2 percent for hierarchy, 50.2 percent for market, and 73.6 percent for network channels. To a lesser extent, the same pattern is true for people with different levels of education: one year of schooling increases the probability by 13 percent for using hierarchical channels and decreases the probabilities by 7.3 percent (.927 − 1) and 5.4 percent (.946 − 1) for using market and network channels, respectively. These results seem to suggest that men, party members, and the highly educated are the socially and politically advantageous groups that are favored by the party and state hierarchies.

Age effects are also significant. While older persons are generally more likely to use hierarchical channels than younger persons by a margin of 5.7 percent, such an age effect became nil during the 1993–1999 period (.963 + .057 = an insignificant 1.020). On the other hand, people of all ages seem equally likely to use market channels, but significant positive age effects (1.040 and 1.025) emerged in the 1993–1999 and 2000–2003 periods, in which many middle-aged employees were forced out of the state sector due to large-scale layoffs. Finally, younger persons are significantly more likely to use network channels than are older persons, by a rough estimate of 8 percent (.920 − 1 for the Exp B of age), but the differential margin enlarges in the 2000–2003 period to an additional 4.2 percent (.958 − 1 for the Exp B of age interaction with period). The significant Exp B of 1.092 for the term of age square indicates a curve linear effect, with the largest being around age 40. The middle-aged workers, when many of whom were laid off from the state sector in the post-1993 periods, actively tried both market and network channels for a reemployment opportunity.

Job changes can be horizontal providing no change in class status or they can produce either upward or downward mobility. While the most recent research on China's social stratification has suggested several ways of classifying occupations into positions of class distinction (Davis et al. 2005), the fundamental class boundaries are property ownership, authority on the job, and level of skills that bestow bargaining power in the labor markets (Wright 1997). In the analysis of the 2003 CGSS I use the last two class boundaries, authority and skill, to assess the relative efficacies of different employment institutions on occupational mobility, constructing three categories of job position: (1) nonmanual, which comparably has authority and professional and technical skill; (2) skilled manual, which generally has no authority but a higher level of technical skill than the unskilled manual group; and (3) unskilled manual, which has no authority but a low level of technical skill. These constructs assume that cross-boundary mobility can be a one-boundary crossing (from unskilled manual to skilled manual, and from skilled manual to nonmanual) or a two-boundary crossing (from unskilled manual to nonmanual). A two-boundary crossing move is more difficult than a one-boundary crossing move.

Using these three categories in a descending order of authority and skill, we then categorize the respondents' job changes between their prior job types and their current job types. As a result, among the 2,206 respondents who changed employers, 54.9 percent changed jobs within a job position (although across employers). These are the "within boundary movers" and shall be used as a reference group to compare with "cross-boundary movers" of upward or downward mobility in regression analysis that will follow shortly. In addition, 24.1 percent experienced upward mobility; 175 moves were from skilled manual to nonmanual, 177 from unskilled to skilled, and 178 from unskilled to nonmanual. Finally, 21.0 percent experienced downward mobility; 60 moved from nonmanual to skilled manual, 98 from nonmanual to unskilled, and 204 from skilled manual to unskilled manual.

What search channels promote upward mobility and prevent downward mobility? Results from the multinomial regression, as displayed in Table 12.5, are suggestive. In each of the three left-side models for downward mobility, the estimated probabilities indicate the likelihood of moving into a lower position as compared to maintaining the same position. While market and network channels certainly facilitate more and more job changes as jobs increasingly are out of the hands of state bureaucrats, they do not prevent downward mobility. Quite to the contrary. As compared to hierarchical channels, both market and network channels increase downward moves from a nonmanual to an unskilled manual position (Exp B of 3.292 through market, and Exp B of 2.571 through network). For downward moves from nonmanual to skilled manual, and from skilled manual to unskilled manual, however, the estimated exponentials vary in size but do not pass the significance test, implying that the three search channels are equally effective in these two types of downward mobility.

On upward mobility, the results in the three right-side columns of Table 12.5 show that hierarchy, rather than market or network, lifts someone into a higher position. More specifically, if an upward move through hierarchy is given a probability of 100 percent, then the probability through market is 59.8 percent to move from a skilled manual position to a nonmanual position, 36.3 percent to move from an unskilled manual position to a nonmanual position (note that this is breaking two class boundaries of skill and professionalism), and 47.6 percent to move from an unskilled manual position to a skilled manual position. Network channels, on the other hand, do much better than market channels, since the probabilities of upward mobility through networks are not significantly different from those through hierarchy for one-boundary-crossing movements, that is, from skilled manual to nonmanual, and from unskilled manual to skilled manual (Exp B of 1.218 and .982 are statistically insignificant). However, for a two-boundary-crossing movement, networks are only about half as

TABLE 12.5

*Multinomial regression on the effects of search channels and network resources on up/downward mobility (Exp B presented)*

| Predictors | DOWNWARD MOBILITY[1] | | | UPWARD MOBILITY[1] | | |
|---|---|---|---|---|---|---|
| | *3 to 2* | *3 to 1* | *2 to 1* | *2 to 3* | *1 to 3* | *1 to 2* |
| Search channel (Hierarchy = ref) | | | | | | |
| Market | 1.329 | 3.292*** | 1.096 | 0.598+ | 0.363*** | 0.476** |
| Network | 2.160 | 2.571+ | 0.626 | 1.218 | 0.475+ | 0.982 |
| Network resources (no = ref) | | | | | | |
| Information | 0.854 | 0.396* | 1.208 | 0.566 | 1.147 | 0.858 |
| Influence | 0.965 | 1.672 | 1.201 | 1.429 | 1.422 | 1.138 |
| Tie with key contact (Weak = ref) | | | | | | |
| No contact / no mention[2] | 0.510 | 0.267 | 1.330 | 0.860 | 0.270* | 0.249* |
| Quite strong | 0.290 | 0.174 | 0.756 | 0.411 | 0.244* | 0.114** |
| Very strong | 0.356 | 0.199 | 0.488 | 0.486 | 0.147** | 0.236* |
| Period (1956–1979 = reference) | | | | | | |
| 1980–92 | 0.772 | 1.611 | 1.764* | 0.808 | 0.641+ | 1.082 |
| 1993–99 | 0.696 | 1.776 | 2.262* | 0.923 | 0.328*** | 0.430* |
| 2000–03 | 0.660 | 1.569 | 1.563 | 0.980 | 0.346** | 0.675 |
| City (western = 1) | | | | | | |
| Beijing-Tianjin-Shanghai | 2.903* | 1.842 | 1.248 | 0.753 | 0.813 | 1.866* |
| Eastern | 0.675 | 1.259 | 0.996 | 0.368** | 0.607+ | 0.848 |
| Central | 0.973 | 1.698 | 1.014 | 0.634+ | 0.653 | 1.005 |
| Prior sector (nonstate = ref) | | | | | | |
| Government / public organization | 0.436* | 0.364** | 0.940 | 0.963 | 1.440 | 1.000 |
| State-owned enterprise | 1.130 | 0.709 | 0.721 | 0.750 | 0.882 | 1.272 |
| Individual attributes | | | | | | |
| Age | 0.867 | 1.072 | 0.971 | 1.036 | 1.031 | 0.861* |
| Age squared/100 | 1.094 | 0.870 | 1.049 | 0.953 | 0.964 | 1.179 |
| Sex (male = 1) | 1.106 | 1.123 | 1.235 | 0.762 | 0.933 | 0.929 |
| Party (CCP = 1) | 0.476+ | 0.375** | 0.601 | 2.843*** | 3.406*** | 1.313 |
| Years of schooling | 0.789*** | 0.694*** | 0.932* | 1.291*** | 1.368*** | 1.034 |
| Cox and Snell pseudo  $R^2$ | | | .540 | | | |
| N | | | 2,136 | | | |

[1] 1 = unskilled manual; 2 = skilled manual; 3 = nonmanual.

[2] No contact (1,418) and no mention (307) are used as a control.

+$p < .10$; *$p < .05$; **$p < .01$; ***$p < .001$.

good as hierarchy (Exp B of .475) in moving someone from unskilled manual to nonmanual. These results indicate that hierarchy is comparatively a stronger channel than market and network to prevent downward mobility and promote upward mobility in job changes.

On the individual level, those who have greater network, institutional/ political, and human resources are better able to move upwardly. Information, not influence, that is learned from network ties lowers the probability of moving from a nonmanual position to an unskilled manual position, and weak ties, as compared to strong ties, help to boost one's chances of upward mobility in all categories through market and especially hierarchical channels. Prior employment in a government or public organization reduces the chances of downward mobility, and Party members are less likely to move downwardly and more likely to move upwardly than are nonmembers. Finally, education prevents downward mobility and promotes upward mobility; one year of schooling would lower the probability of downward mobility by 7–30 percent and increase the probability of upward mobility by about 30 percent. While hierarchical channels are paths for upward mobility, individuals with network, institutional/political, and human resources are better able to move through the paths in a transitional Chinese society.[2]

As of 2003, China remains a mixed system of employment institutions. Hierarchy, while delivering fewer jobs over time, remains visible and significant in China's urban labor markets: it delivers a quarter of the jobs in the post-2000 period, and the jobs that are delivered through hierarchy are more likely to imply upward rather than downward mobility. Market and network channels, on the other hand, are more effective among the working classes; while markets offer a lot of opportunities for skilled and unskilled jobs, networks are important in upward mobility into nonmanual jobs of authority or high skill. Finally, higher education, party membership, and institutional affiliations with the state hierarchies prevent downward mobility and promote upward mobility significantly.

CONCLUSION AND DISCUSSION

The 2003 CGSS offers a decisive answer to the three interrelated questions raised at the beginning of the chapter about occupational mobility in urban China. First, the rise of labor markets during the reform-era increased job changes within, and especially between, places of employment. China's rate of overall job change in 1998, 6.4 percent, was comparable to Russia's 1997 level, and by 2002 the rate reached the historical height of 7.6 percent, with 5.8 percent for turnovers between employers. Second, on the changing roles of three employment institutions, the 2003 CGSS shows a significant decline of reliance on hierarchical channels from 77.7 percent before 1979 to 26.0 percent after 2000. Meanwhile, market and network channels increased and expanded, each surpassing hierarchy around 1993 to account for more than 40 percent of the jobs and by 2000 reaching levels similar to those found in capitalist economies in the West. Third, hierarchy, while delivering fewer jobs, remains a viable path for upward mobility; market and network channels offer many opportunities for skilled and unskilled jobs, but networks, especially those with weak ties, also are key channels for upward mobility into nonmanual jobs of authority or high skill.

Below, I discuss some of the theoretical and empirical implications of these findings. First, however marketized and globalized, China remains a durable Communist party-state, and the implications are not just political but also go into the work life of individuals, elite and nonelite. Government and public organizations are a significant source of jobs of skill, authority, good income, health insurance, and employment security. More than 160 of the largest enterprises are still under the jurisdiction of the central government and offer employment in high-profit sectors to which access is not yet open to nonstate firms. In addition, millions of local firms are in one way or another under the influence, through formal and informal arrangements, of local state officials. These are the labor market bases for explaining why hierarchical channels still deliver a quarter of the jobs in the first years of the twenty-first century and why these jobs offer many opportunities for upward mobility. After 25 years of economic reform, the path to some of the most desirable jobs in the country are still controlled and monopolized by the government hierarchy. This, I argue, will remain true as long as the Communist Party is the ruling party of China.

The significance of hierarchy is also evident at the individual level. Although hierarchical channels deliver fewer and fewer jobs, they are selectively used by advantageous groups in society. From Table 12.4, we learn that men, Communist Party members, and the highly educated are more likely than their counterparts to use hierarchical channels for job change purposes, and these groups also tend to prefer hierarchy over market and network as a channel to search for new opportunities of employment. The reason is obvious: The paths to many good positions are controlled by state hierarchy, and these advantageous groups rationally choose the hierarchical channels in order to get on the path.

Among those who support the market transition theories, it is assumed that as markets increase, political power will decline and then become insignificant after the "tipping point" when half of the Chinese economy is privatized (Nee and Cao 2002). These findings from the 2003 GCSS, by contrast, support the power-persistence explanation of recent patterns of inequality (Bian and Logan 1996; Parish and Michelson 1996; Zhou 2000b). In short, as long as the Communist Party is in state power, party-sponsored mobility into elite jobs, as argued and found by Walder, Li, and Treiman (2000), will continue in transitional China.

Second, market channels expanded rather quickly during the reform era, accounting for about 58 percent of the jobs obtained by the 2003 CGSS respondents in the 2000–2003 period. While labor markets operate in all regions, they are more active and frequently used in nonstate sectors than in state sectors; obviously many state jobs are still channeled through hierarchical arrangements. Except for managers and administrators, all other occupational groups frequently use market channels to search for new jobs to which to move, and movers with a lower level of education and without a party membership are more frequent users of market channels. As compared to hierarchy and networks, markets are likely to facilitate mobility into manual jobs of low skill, rather than nonmanual jobs of authority or high skill.

These findings offer an image of labor markets for the working classes. Manual jobs require relatively lower qualifications on the part of job seekers, and demand less information about their education, work attitudes, and traits of reliability, a set of merits that are generally required of nonmanual jobs. Instead, short-term training on the job and high turnover rates are usually coupled with manual workers. For managerial and professional hires, in-school training, skill qualification, and certification of work experience would need assistance from insider contacts, available through social networks or hierarchical channels. In an advanced labor market system, such as Hong Kong, this assistance can be secured from such formal mechanisms as head hunter companies (Bian 2004). Occupational labor markets for managerial and professional skills take time to develop in Chinese cities.

Third, the findings from the 2003 CGSS refute the thesis that market economies reduce the significance of personal networks (Guthrie 1998, 2002). First, jobs that are obtained through the assistance of social networks grew from one-sixth before 1979 to more than one-half after 2000. Second, the roles of social networks during the reform era are both to relate information about job openings and to channel noninformational resources to influence hiring authorities. Third, network channels are persistent in all economic sectors, not just state sectors but also private sectors. And finally, network ties, especially weak ties, are useful not just for delivering a job to the job seeker, but they also are particularly useful to the upward mobility from a lower position to a higher position of authority and skill.

How do we understand the growing roles of social networks in a transitional economy, in China or elsewhere? First, we see that in both pre- and postreform eras, social networks do not act independently. Rather, in most instances networks serve to minimize the deficiencies of hierarchical and market channels in helping job seekers secure opportunities, and they are especially useful where hierarchy has been on the decline and market on the rise. As of the 2000–2003 period, about 26 percent of the CGSS respondents combine network and market channels to secure a job opportunity, but only about 4 percent try the joint effect of networks and hierarchy. While the rigidity of hierarchy might have made it hard for network ties to play a role in a redistributive economy, the "you are on your own" feature of labor markets opens up all kinds of opportunities for individuals to pursue work opportunities through interpersonal networks in the growing market system.

A standard interpretation from institutional economics is that all labor markets lack sufficient, reliable, accurate, and symmetrical information about jobs and job seekers. To minimize these information deficiencies, social networks, and especially weak ties, are mobilized (Granovetter 1973, 1995). Post-Communist economies in transition are thought to be even more problematic, as information is largely "uncoded," not readily available in markets, but circulated through ties of kinship, intimacy, and friendship, and it is in this sense that China has been described as experiencing "network capitalism" (Boisot and Child 1996). Other versions about the growing roles of social networks in China emphasize the persistent role of kinship and family (Whyte 1995a; Peng 2004), patron-client relations between local officials and entrepreneurs (Wank 1999), and the relational nature of private property (Zhou X. 2005b).

In earlier publications I have interpreted the growing roles of social networks as examples of "institutional holes" created by the incompatibility and gaps between conflicting institutions that coexist in a mixed economy (Bian 2002b). These holes appear because the rapid decline of hierarchical institutions and the slow growth of market institutions undermine the efficacy of formal channels in transmitting information, building trust, and binding obligations between job seekers and prospective employers. Social networks, therefore, provide the informal mechanisms to fill these holes. In contrast, both advanced capitalist systems and traditional redistributive systems have fewer such problems and therefore, social networks are less active than in transitional economies. Evidence is gained from a tentative test of this argument with a comparison of Chinese cities: on a continuum of market maturity, a city's "social networking space" is the greatest in the middle of the continuum and the lowest on the two extremes, when cities' market maturity is the highest (Hong Kong) and lowest (Changchun) (Bian 2004).

The coexistence of hierarchy, market, and network as institutions of economic coordination is common in any society. The lesson from this chapter is that the coexistence of these institutions may not be a transitional phenomenon in China. There, the growing market sector provides an ever-greater share of urban jobs, but the shrinking hierarchy maintains its sizable share in the labor markets and, more importantly, continues to channel ample opportunities of upward mobility into positions of great desirability. Social networks, which helped break hierarchical rigidities before labor markets emerged, are now highly active to make up institutional deficiencies or "holes" of hierarchy and market. Both institutions, after all, are designed and played out by human actors living in a relational society.

## CHAPTER THIRTEEN

# The Social Contours of Distributive Injustice Feelings in Contemporary China

*Chunping Han and Martin King Whyte*

The dismantling of centrally planned socialism and the transformation of China into a market-based economy after 1978 have fundamentally altered that society's social order. In many respects China's reforms have been extraordinarily successful, with sustained high rates of economic growth, rising income levels, growing integration of China into the global economy, massive inflows of foreign investment, and sharp reductions in poverty. However, this transformation from a socialist to a market-based society has also had a number of more divisive consequences. Older Chinese who had learned how to survive by playing by the rules of Mao-era socialism had to adapt to a fundamentally changed distribution system in which there were plenty of losers alongside the many winners. Chinese society changed from being a society with relatively modest income disparities to one with large gaps between the rich and the poor. Many who felt they should have been honored for their contributions to building socialism found themselves unemployed, while suspicion was rife that many of China's new millionaires were the beneficiaries of corruption and official favoritism. In recent years China has been rocked by a rising tide of public protests by peasants, workers, and others who denounce the current social order as unjust.

The implications of these complex trends for popular attitudes of Chinese citizens toward current patterns of inequality have been the subject of sharp debate, both within China and among foreign observers. Some analysts contend that China's robust economic growth, improved living standards, and ample new opportunities promote general optimism, acceptance of current inequality levels, and little nostalgia for the bygone socialist era. According to this view, although some individuals and groups who experience unemployment, downward mobility, and abject poverty may be angry and feel that the current social order is unjust, for the bulk of the population the benefits produced by market reforms far outweigh the disadvantages and promote broad acceptance of the current system as at least relatively just. This broad acceptance of China's market system helps prevent local grievances and social protests from escalating into general challenges to the system. So according to this view, China today might best be characterized as enjoying "rocky stability" (see Shambaugh 2000).

The contrary view is that rising income gaps and popular beliefs that current inequalities are unjust are threatening to turn China into a "social volcano," with China's social and political stability threatened. Perhaps stimulated by apparent sharp increases in recent years in local social protest incidents, the social volcano scenario has gained wide currency both in China and in the West.[1] For example, a poll of senior officials conducted by the Central Party School in 2004 concluded that the income gap was China's most serious social problem, far ahead of crime and corruption, which were ranked two and three (*Xinhua* 2004). On a similar note, a summary of the 2005 "Blue Book" published by the Chinese Academy of Social Sciences (an annual assessment of the state of Chinese society) stated, "The Gini coefficient, an indicator of income disparities, reached 0.53 last year, far higher than a dangerous level of 0.4" (Ma 2005). Reports in the Western media echo these themes, particularly regarding rural protest activity. A recent edition of the *Economist* declares: "A spectre is haunting China—the spectre of rural unrest" (*Economist* 2006), while *Time Magazine*'s Asian edition tells us, "Violent local protests . . . are convulsing the Chinese countryside with ever more frequency," and continues its report with phrases such as "seeds of fury" and "the pitchfork anger of peasants" (*Time Asia* 2006).

China's current leaders have responded to fears that rising inequality and the discontent of peasants and other disadvantaged groups will threaten political stability by adopting a number of major reforms, such as announcing the abolition of rural taxes and fees and a planned waiving of school tuitions for rural students. Chinese Communist Party leader Hu Jintao and Premier Wen Jiabao claim they want to shift China from an emphasis on "growth at all costs" to "growth with equity" and to develop China into a "harmonious society."

The research we report here is designed to weigh in on this debate. Is China today enjoying "rocky stability," or is it a "social volcano" about to erupt? In late 2004 we participated in a collaborative survey project that for the first time collected systematic data on popular attitudes toward inequality and distributive justice issues from a representative national sample of Chinese adults.[2] What do we learn from our survey about how Chinese citizens view the fairness or unfairness of current patterns of inequality? There are two primary research questions of concern. The first is a comparative question: How relatively fair or unfair does the average Chinese citizen feel current patterns of inequality are, compared to citizens of other societies (particularly other postsocialist transition societies in Eastern Europe)? Analyses reported in earlier papers suggest that in many respects Chinese citizens are on average more accepting of and less angry about current patterns of inequality than citizens of several other postsocialist societies (Whyte 2002; Whyte and Han 2003, 2005).[3] This chapter presents some evidence related to this comparative question by showing the greater prevalence of positive rather than negative responses to many questions about current patterns of inequality. However, our primary focus here is on a second question: Which groups and locales in China harbor the strongest feelings that current patterns of inequality are unjust?

Most previous analyses of Chinese popular attitudes adopt a straightforward approach in speculating about this second question, an approach based on the distinction between "winners" and "losers" in the reform process. Certain groups and locales are seen as objective beneficiaries of recent economic and stratification trends and, as a consequence, as being more likely than others to view the current social order as basically fair. A list of "winners" typically includes those with high incomes and the well-educated; white-collar workers (particularly intellectuals, managers, and professionals); members of the Chinese Communist Party (hereafter CCP); private entrepreneurs; urban residents in general; residents of coastal provinces; perhaps men and young people; and anyone whose standard of living has been improving. On the other hand, those with low status or who have experienced downward social mobility are assumed to be more likely to feel that the current social order is unjust. A listing of "losers" in the reform process typically includes rural residents in general, perhaps particularly those still mainly engaged in agriculture; rural migrants living in cities; those with low incomes and little schooling; the unemployed; factory workers; those still employed by financially troubled state-owned enterprises; non-Party members; residents of China's interior (particularly Western provinces); perhaps women and those middle-aged and older; and anyone whose standard of living is threatened or has fallen. In the pages that follow, we examine whether this conventional approach is a good way to understand the social contours of feelings about distributive injustice in China today.

## MEASURING DISTRIBUTIVE INJUSTICE ATTITUDES AND THEIR PREDICTORS

How does one measure popular attitudes toward distributive injustice in a questionnaire-based survey? Our questionnaire contained a very large number of questions probing respondent attitudes toward issues regarding inequality and distributive injustice, and no single question or scale computed from several questions could summarize views on all aspects of distributive injustice. We focus our attention here on four measures designed to reflect a perception that current patterns of inequality are unfair (versus fair) and a variety of possible reactions to such a perception.

First and most central to our investigation of views on distributive injustice, we asked respondents to give their assessments of why some people in China today are poor, and why some others are rich. The list of possible reasons included such factors as ability, effort, luck, personal character, discrimination, dishonesty, personal connections, unequal opportunities, and system deficiencies. Respondents were asked to rate whether each trait mentioned had a very large importance, large importance, some importance, small importance, or no importance at all in explaining why some people are poor, or why some people are rich. Within this larger set of questions, we constructed a scale designed to assess the perceived importance of structural (i.e., not based on individual merit) explanations for why some people are rich while others are poor (seven items: discrimination, lack of equal opportunity, defects in the economic structure as explanations of poverty, dishonesty, unequal opportunities, personal connections, and unfairness of the economic structure as explanations of wealth).[4] We refer to this as our "Unfair Inequality" scale. The presumption is that individuals who score high on Unfair Inequality feel that external features (such as dishonesty, unequal opportunities, and discrimination) rather than individual merit are the main sources of current inequalities in China, which are therefore seen as unjust.[5]

Second, we include a measure of feelings of pessimism (versus optimism) about chances for getting ahead in Chinese society today, feelings we assume will be affected by how fair or unfair respondents perceive current inequalities are. For that purpose we rely on a single, global question: "Based on the current situation in the country, the opportunities for someone like you to raise their standard of living are still great," with the five response categories provided ranging from strongly agree to strongly disagree. A high score thus indicates pessimism about ordinary people being able to improve their standard of living, and we refer to this as a measure of perceived "Lack of Opportunity."

If individuals feel that current inequalities are unfair and mobility opportunities are scarce and unequal, they may feel that the government should be taking active steps to limit income gaps and level the playing field of economic opportunities. The third measure we use is a summary scale derived from three questions about what role respondents think the government should (or should not) play in reducing inequalities in Chinese society. Each interviewee was asked to say whether they strongly agreed, agreed, were neutral, disagreed, or strongly disagreed with the following statements: "The government should assure that every person is able to maintain a minimum standard of living"; "The government should provide an opportunity to work for every person willing to work"; and "The government has the responsibility to shrink the gap between high and low incomes." These items were then reversed, so that a high score means support for an active role of the government in promoting social equality, and then the resulting scale is a common factor score computed from the three item scores. We refer to this as our "Government Leveling" scale. The presumption is that those who score high on this measure think that more active measures should be taken to reduce current inequalities (since none of these three things are currently being done much) and are willing to entrust the government with this role.

Another possible response to perceived unfairness of the social order is to react with fatalism and despair and to assume nothing can be done to improve things. A fourth and final scale is designed to tap such feelings of hopelessness about injustice. Three questions were used, again with respondents asked to give responses ranging from strongly agree to strongly disagree to each statement: "Since we are unable to change the status quo, discussing social justice is meaningless"; "Looking at things as they are now, it is very difficult to say what is just and what is unjust"; and "Government officials don't care what common people like me think." Again we reversed these items, so that high scores indicate feelings of hopelessness and injustice, and then our scale is a common factor score computed from the three item scores. We refer to this as our "Feelings of Injustice" scale.[6] These four measures (Unfair Inequality, Lack of Opportunity, preferences for Government Leveling, and Feelings of Injustice) constitute the attitude domains we focus on in this chapter.

In the remainder of the chapter we investigate which social background traits are related to agreement versus disagreement with these four distributive injustice attitude measures. As we examine how attitudes in these four realms vary across the face of Chinese society, we start with a rather simpleminded set of expectations. Other things being equal, we expect that survey respondents who feel the current system is unjust will score high on all four distributive injustice attitude measures, while those who are comfortable operating in the current system and don't have strong feelings of distributive injustice will score low on all four measures.[7] In the analysis that follows, can we identify respondents with particular social backgrounds, or who live in particular locales, who fit these patterns, and thus are particularly aggrieved and pessimistic (versus satisfied and optimistic) about current Chinese patterns of inequality and social mobility opportunities?

In order to answer this question, we examine how scores on these four aspects of distributive injustice attitudes vary in relation to a range of social and geographical background characteristics of our 3,267 survey respondents. Our social background "predictors" of distributive injustice attitudes are of several types: categories of occupational and household registration status, measures of other objective demographic and status characteristics, measures of subjective social status and experiences, and indicators of location within China's overall geographic and economic space. We measure the background predictors used in the present analyses as follows.

### Occupational/Household Registration Status Groups

Many observers agree that the most important social cleavage in China today is based on that society's distinctive system of household registration (*hukou*), which divides China socially into three status categories: rural residents, rural migrants residing in urban areas, and urban residents with urban *hukou* (see, for example, Wang 2005). This division overlaps with, but does not fully correspond with, another important basis of social status: occupation. For example, almost all farmers are rural residents, but many rural residents are engaged in other, nonfarming occupations. In order to capture this complexity, we rely on questions in our survey about place of residence, *hukou* status, and occupation to classify our respondents into the following nine occupational/household registration status categories:

1.  farmers—current or retired farmers regardless of their *hukou* status
2.  rural migrants—migrants from rural to urban areas regardless of their current employment or occupational status
3.  rural nonfarming—agricultural *hukou* holders having a nonfarming job currently or before retirement
4.  rural others—agricultural *hukou* holders who do not belong to categories 1–3
5.  urban workers—current or retired workers with nonagricultural *hukou*
6.  urban white collar—current or retired white-collar workers (e.g., professionals, managers, officials, clerks) with nonagricultural *hukou*
7.  urban private—current or retired urban private business owners or the self-employed with nonagricultural *hukou*
8.  urban unemployed—urban *hukou* holders who are currently not working and have been looking for a job over the past month
9.  urban others—other nonagricultural *hukou* holders who do not belong to categories 5–8

### Other Objective Demographic and Status Characteristics

We include the following other objective demographic and socioeconomic characteristics as additional predictors of distributive injustice attitudes: gender, age, educational attainment, marital status, ethnicity, household income, Chinese Communist Party membership, and experience of working in a state-owned enterprise.[8] Together with our occupational/household registration status measure, these characteristics allow us to examine the influence of a range of objective social status and demographic background characteristics on our four indicators of distributive injustice attitudes.

*Indicators of Subjective Social Status and Experience*

Research in other countries has shown that subjective perceptions of personal and family status and of changes in social position over time often have about as much influence on distributive justice attitudes as objective indicators of current social status (e.g., Kluegel 1988; Kluegel, Mason, and Wegener 1995; Kreidl 2000). Therefore we include three measures of subjective social status and experiences. One is the response to a single question about how the respondent's family is doing economically compared to five years previously (ranging from 1 = much worse to 5 = much better), which we term "5 year standard of living (SOL) trend." Second, we created a summary scale of inequality-related bad personal or family experiences during the last three years, and we refer to the summary score of such experiences as a measure of "bad experiences."[9] Finally, our third measure, which we call "relative social status," is based on four questions asking respondents to compare their current living standards with that of their relatives, their former classmates, their co-workers, and their neighbors.[10] We expect that respondents who perceive they have been downwardly mobile, who have had many inequality-related bad experiences, and who feel they have low relative social status will have strong feelings of distributive injustice, no matter how they rank in terms of objective measures of current social status.

*Location in Geographic and Economic Space*

It is logical to assume that the views respondents have about distributive injustice will be influenced not only by their personal characteristics and social status, but also by where they work and live. For example, we noted earlier the common perception that people residing in coastal provinces of China have benefited disproportionately from the reform era and will thus support the status quo, while residents of inland provinces have seen few benefits trickling down to them (despite recent government efforts to "develop the West") and are likely to feel aggrieved. However, some coastal provinces (such as Guangdong) have benefited much more from market reforms than others (such as Liaoning), while within any province some people live in globally connected major cities while others live in isolated and poor villages. (See the critique of traditional groupings of provinces into regions presented in Skinner 2005.)

In order to try to capture the complexity of such location influences, we use three different measures here. First, we use the conventional division of China into Eastern, Central, and Western provinces as defined by China's National Statistics Bureau and classify each respondent by their current residential location. Second, we classify the distance to the nearest prefecture or higher-level city of the current de facto residence of each respondent.[11] Finally, we utilize research conducted by scholars in China (Fan and Wang 2004) to incorporate a composite estimate of the relative degree of market transformation of each province included in our sample, with the values ranging from 3.61 for Ningxia to 9.74 for Guangdong (out of a possible 10).[12]

### Unfair Inequality Attitudes as an Intervening Variable

In our conceptualization of distributive injustice, as discussed earlier, we see the Unfair Inequality scale as a basic measure of the perceived unfairness (versus fairness) of actual patterns of inequality in China currently and our three other attitude measures as responses to such perceived fairness or unfairness—feelings of pessimism about getting ahead, a desire for the government to intervene to limit inequality, and despair about the chances for injustices to be corrected. In order to reflect this conceptualization, in addition to the variety of objective and subjective background "predictors" discussed above, when we examine variations in attitudes toward Lack of Opportunity, Government Leveling, and Feelings of Injustice, we use scores on the Unfair Inequality scale as a final "predictor" variable.

### THE SOCIAL CONTOURS OF DISTRIBUTIVE INJUSTICE ATTITUDES

Before focusing on the question of which social groups and locales have the strongest feelings that current inequalities are unfair, we want to briefly assess the general mood of Chinese citizens toward distributive justice issues. The weighted frequency distributions of responses of our entire sample to the questions included in our four distributive injustice measures are displayed in Table 13.1 (in panels 3–6), as well as responses to additional questions about current inequalities (in panels 1–2), which are included in the table to provide a broader context.

As suggested earlier, the pattern of responses shown in Table 13.1 does not suggest a dominant mood of anger at current patterns of inequality or pervasive feelings of distributive injustice. For example, while a large majority of respondents feel that national income disparities are too large (71.7 percent), much smaller proportions think that income differences within their own work organization or in their neighborhood are too large (39.6 percent and 31.8 percent), with the most common response being that such local inequalities are reasonable. Also, generally respondents rate individual merit factors, such as ability and hard work, as more important than external and unfair factors, such as dishonesty and unequal opportunity, in explaining why some people are rich while others are poor (compare panels 2 and 3), many more respondents are optimistic than pessimistic about

TABLE 13.1
*Responses to selected inequality and distributive justice questions*
*(weighted distribution, row percentages)*

| | Strongly disagree | Somewhat disagree | Neutral | Somewhat agree | Strongly agree | N |
|---|---|---|---|---|---|---|
| **1. Views on income gaps** | | | | | | |
| Inequality too large (national)* | 1.4 | 4.4 | 22.5 | 31.6 | 40.1 | 3,254 |
| Inequality too large (work unit)* | 1.6 | 8.9 | 49.9 | 27.1 | 12.5 | 2,107 |
| Inequality too large (neighbors)* | 1.9 | 10.2 | 56.1 | 26.6 | 5.2 | 3,264 |
| **2. Merit-based inequality** | | | | | | |
| Ability affects poverty** | 2.2 | 4.5 | 32.0 | 43.5 | 17.8 | 3,265 |
| Effort affects poverty** | 3.2 | 7.2 | 35.6 | 43.9 | 10.1 | 3,257 |
| Education affects poverty** | 3.0 | 8.6 | 34.0 | 37.8 | 16.6 | 3,239 |
| Ability affects wealth** | 1.8 | 3.8 | 25.0 | 46.3 | 23.2 | 3,265 |
| Effort affects wealth** | 1.5 | 5.7 | 31.1 | 49.5 | 12.3 | 3,261 |
| Education affects wealth** | 2.3 | 6.2 | 30.9 | 39.5 | 21.1 | 3,240 |
| **3. Unfair inequality** | | | | | | |
| Discrimination affects poverty** | 7.2 | 18.8 | 52.8 | 16.9 | 4.3 | 3,261 |
| Opportunity affects poverty** | 4.3 | 15.2 | 53.1 | 22.3 | 5.2 | 3,261 |
| System defects affect poverty** | 5.4 | 11.8 | 61.8 | 16.1 | 4.9 | 3,258 |
| Dishonesty affects wealth** | 13.3 | 26.7 | 42.6 | 12.8 | 4.6 | 3,259 |
| Connections affect wealth** | 1.4 | 6.3 | 32.3 | 41.0 | 19.0 | 3,261 |
| Opportunity affects wealth** | 1.9 | 8.5 | 44.4 | 34.9 | 10.4 | 3,262 |
| Unfair structure affects wealth** | 3.6 | 14.4 | 56.0 | 19.5 | 6.5 | 3,258 |
| **4. Lack of opportunity** | | | | | | |
| Lack of opportunity to get ahead | 9.6 | 47.2 | 23.5 | 15.3 | 4.3 | 3,262 |
| **5. Preference for government leveling** | | | | | | |
| Ensure min. standard of living | .5 | 2.7 | 16.1 | 39.4 | 41.4 | 3,263 |
| Provide job for everyone | .5 | 3.9 | 20.0 | 45.6 | 30.1 | 3,261 |
| Reduce income gap | 1.8 | 10.3 | 30.6 | 34.2 | 23.1 | 3,260 |
| **6. Feelings of injustice** | | | | | | |
| Meaningless to discuss justice | 6.1 | 23.0 | 36.5 | 27.5 | 6.9 | 3,261 |
| Don't know what justice is | 6.0 | 20.2 | 35.7 | 28.5 | 9.6 | 3,261 |
| Officials don't care | 4.5 | 16.5 | 28.9 | 31.2 | 18.9 | 3,260 |

SOURCE: 2004 China Inequality and Distributive Justice Survey, N = 3,267.

NOTE: Only questions in panels 3–6 were used in the distributive injustice attitude measures for this chapter. For full wording of the questions, see text.

*Actual questions asked respondents to evaluate these inequalities, with the response categories "too small," "a bit small," "appropriate," "a bit large," and "too large."

**Response category wording was actually "no influence at all," "little influence," "some influence," "large influence," and "very large influence."

the chances for ordinary people to get ahead currently, and there is some agreement but also considerable disagreement with our Feelings of Injustice questions (see panel 6). The one clear departure from this pattern of more acceptance than rejection of current patterns of inequality is in regard to Government Leveling (see panel 5). Very large majorities of Chinese respondents would like the government to take measures to alleviate poverty and reduce inequality. Apparently it is not necessary to harbor strong feelings that current patterns of inequality are unjust in order to favor government efforts to alleviate poverty and reduce overall inequality.[13]

We now proceed to the main focus of this chapter, examining how various social background "predictors" are related to scores on our four measures of distributive injustice attitudes. These results are displayed in Table 13.2, which shows the patterning of both correlations and regression coefficients that reveal the associations between the four measures of distributive injustice attitudes and the background predictors described earlier. (The bivariate correlation coefficients indicate the association between a particular injustice measure and the background variable indicated before controlling for any other predictors; the corresponding unstandardized regression coefficients displayed in the table tell us the strength of that same association while other predictors are all controlled statistically—in other words, the contribution of the background trait in question to explaining variation in the inequality scale in question, net of the other background traits.) Given the complexity of our statistical analyses, involving more than twenty predictor variables and four distributive injustice scales whose scores we are trying to predict, it is important to look for overall patterns, rather than to scrutinize each individual statistical coefficient. The search for general patterns necessarily involves a complex process of scanning results up and down the rows as well as across the columns within the table. As noted earlier, we are particularly interested in which social background characteristics are associated with the strongest feelings of distributive injustice, and whether the resulting patterns can be interpreted as the product of having a disadvantaged rather than an advantaged status in Chinese society today.

### The Role of Occupational/Household Registration Status Group Membership

In examining the statistical associations between occupational/household registration status group membership and distributive injustice attitudes (panel 1 in Table 13.2), it is immediately obvious that objective status within contemporary China is a poor guide to distributive injustice attitudes. By any reckoning, rural people in China, and those engaged in farming in particular, are at or near the bottom of the social order. However, rather than harboring

TABLE 13.2

*Predictors of distributive injustice feelings (bivariate correlations and unstandardized regression coefficients)*

| | UNFAIR INEQUALITY | | LACK OF OPPORTUNITY | | GOVERNMENT LEVELING | | FEELINGS OF INJUSTICE | |
|---|---|---|---|---|---|---|---|---|
| | Correlation | Regression | Correlation | Regression | Correlation | Regression | Correlation | Regression |
| Farmer | -.205*** | -.193*** | -.007 | -.264*** | -.170*** | -.152*** | -.118*** | -.249*** |
| Migrant | .005 | -.106+ | -.007 | -.086 | .028 | -.033 | .053** | -.028 |
| Rural nonfarming | -.018 | -.134* | -.060** | -.242** | -.056** | -.211*** | -.037+ | -.160* |
| Rural others | -.010 | -.109+ | -.024 | -.293** | -.172*** | -.372*** | -.013 | -.166* |
| Urban workers | .147*** | — | .106*** | — | .138*** | — | .099*** | — |
| Urban white-collar | .113*** | .022 | -.068*** | -.287*** | .154*** | .008 | -.029 | -.110* |
| Urban private | .037+ | -.069 | -.024 | -.113 | .044* | -.037 | .016 | -.086 |
| Urban unemployed | .055** | -.060 | .074*** | .121 | .083** | .091 | .074** | -.007 |
| Urban others | .025 | -.136* | .012 | -.063 | .056** | -.005 | .070** | .046 |
| Female | .009 | .024 | .020 | .035 | -.094** | -.066** | -.020 | -.058* |
| Age | -.008 | .011+ | .199*** | .005 | -.013 | .005 | .071** | .019** |
| Age2 | -.013 | -.000* | .197*** | .000 | -.022 | -.000 | .058** | -.000* |
| Education | .156*** | .024* | -.113*** | -.009 | .234*** | .040*** | -.023 | -.013 |
| Married | -.057** | -.071* | .020 | -.045 | .012 | .053+ | .044* | .088* |
| Han ethnicity | .060** | .009 | -.023 | -.064 | .172*** | .100** | .033 | -.006 |
| Logged HH income | .123*** | .055+ | -.159*** | -.172*** | .141*** | .005 | -.090** | -.212*** |
| Party member | -.004 | -.117** | -.001 | .052 | .104** | .084* | -.065** | -.147** |
| SOE | .132*** | .037 | .096*** | .241*** | .137*** | .025 | .026 | -.071 |
| 5 year SOL trend | -.123*** | -.042** | -.254*** | -.168*** | -.023 | .028* | -.142*** | -.020 |
| Bad experiences | .058** | .033* | .168*** | .027* | .021 | .018** | .141*** | .026** |
| Relative social status | -.047* | -.040* | -.228*** | -.146** | -.059* | -.080** | -.105*** | .015 |
| East | .085*** | — | -.066*** | — | .071** | — | .020 | — |
| Central | .000 | -.053 | .039* | .206*** | .089*** | .103** | .014 | .097* |
| West | -.124*** | -.164** | .044* | .300** | -.217*** | -.093+ | -.050* | .246*** |
| Distance to city | -.213*** | -.024* | -.011 | .003 | -.242*** | .004 | -.177*** | -.054** |
| Marketization | .043* | -.026* | -.020 | .045* | .093*** | .026* | .048* | .040** |
| Unfair Inequality | — | — | .142*** | .213*** | .292*** | .195*** | .327*** | .361*** |
| Tucker-Lewis Index | — | .985 | — | .985 | — | .986 | — | .987 |
| RMSEA | — | .041 | — | .041 | — | .039 | — | .037 |
| R2 | — | .105 | — | .160 | — | .215 | — | .194 |

+.05 < p ≤ .10; *.01 < p ≤ .05; **.001< p ≤ .01; ***p ≤ .001.

strong feelings of distributive injustice, rural people in general, and farmers in particular, are less likely than the comparison group of urban workers to see the difference between wealth and poverty as due to unfair causes, more optimistic about chances for ordinary people to get ahead, less likely to favor government leveling to reduce inequality, and less likely to harbor strong feelings of injustice. The one rural group that is least distinctive (compared to urban workers) is rural migrants working in cities. Despite the indignities that many migrants experience on a regular basis, the tendency to harbor feelings of injustice seen at the bivariate level (in column 7) disappears when controls for other background traits are applied, and the only net distinctiveness of migrants compared to urban workers is a weak tendency to be *less* likely to see current inequalities as unfair (see column 2).

The most advantaged occupational groups in our categorization are urban white-collar workers and urban private entrepreneurs and the self-employed. However, in most respects these two groups do not differ that much from the comparison group of urban workers, once other background factors are controlled for, although there are modest but statistically significant net tendencies for urban white-collar workers to be less pessimistic about getting ahead than urban (blue-collar) workers and to harbor fewer feelings of injustice. At the bivariate level the most disadvantaged urban group, the urban unemployed, seems generally aggrieved about distributive issues (see columns 1, 3, 5, and 7), but when age, education, and other background factors are taken into account, the urban unemployed do not differ significantly from urban workers on any of our attitude measures.

To sum up, we propose a tentative generalization about how occupation/registration status groups in China vary in their views on distributive issues. Other things being equal, the strongest feelings of distributive injustice appear to be held by urban workers, perhaps followed by the urban unemployed, those in the urban private sector, and rural migrants. Somewhat more favorable views on distributive issues are held by urban white-collar workers. Finally, and surprisingly, the most positive attitudes about the fairness of current patterns of inequality are held by China's rural residents in general, including farmers. In viewing a national sample, we see here few signs of the "pitchfork anger" of the peasants alluded to in recent press accounts. We will have more to say about the role of occupation/registration status groups once we have discussed the remainder of our findings.

### The Role of Other Objective Demographic and Status Characteristics

Some, although not all, of the associations with other objective background traits (panel 2) also contradict the idea that having high status translates into viewing the current system as relatively fair. At the bivariate level, both those with high incomes and those with high levels of education are *more*, rather than less, likely to emphasize external and unfair explanations of why some people are rich while others are poor, and these associations are weakened but still statistically significant when we control for other predictors in our models (compare columns 1 and 2). Membership in the Chinese Communist Party has been found in many studies to be associated with advantages in income, housing space, and other benefits, but CCP membership here is associated only with a weak tendency not to see unfairness in current inequality (in column 2) and to have slightly weaker feelings of injustice (in column 8), but also with being slightly *more* likely to favor government leveling (in column 6).

The most striking patterns found among the set of predictors in panel 2 of Table 13.2 concern age, not social status. The association appears to be curvilinear, net of the effect of other background characteristics of respondents.[14] Those now in middle age express stronger feelings that current inequalities are unfair (in column 2) and stronger Feelings of Injustice (in column 8) than do their younger and older counterparts. This striking pattern, even though not repeated in our other two attitude scales, may indicate the profound importance in China even today of the disruption of people's lives and mobility opportunities caused by the Cultural Revolution of 1966–76. One of the distinctive features of social mobility patterns in post-1949 China is the extent to which adjacent birth cohorts often had dramatically different social mobility opportunities, due to the volcanic shifts caused by Mao-era political campaigns. Those who came of age during the Cultural Revolution experienced particularly severe disruptions of their schooling and careers (Davis-Friedmann 1985; Whyte 1985; Xie, Yang, and Greenman 2006). Those who came of age at that time are, of course, now middle aged. The strong curvilinear associations between respondent age and both perceptions of Unfair Inequality and Feelings of Injustice may reflect the acute feelings of resentment over lost opportunities held by many members of China's "lost generation." The associations between distributive injustice attitudes and other objective background measures (shown in panel 2) are generally weaker and less consistent.[15]

## The Role of Subjective Social Status and Experiences

When we examine the associations with our three measures of subjective social status and experiences (in panel 3 of Table 13.2), we see that in general how people *perceive* their status and trends in their standards of living is more closely and consistently related with distributive injustice attitudes than are most *objective* status indicators in panels 1 and 2. With some exceptions, the associations with these subjective status measures also fit more closely with the conventional wisdom that "winners" see little injustice in society, while "losers" feel aggrieved. Those who rate their relative status highly compared to their peers and those who perceive that their family's living standard has improved compared to five years earlier tend to see current patterns of inequality as less unfair than others (in column 2) while being less pessimistic about chances to get ahead in China today (in column 4). Those who in the last three years had more bad experiences than the average respondent show the opposite tendency and see current inequalities as unfair and chances of getting ahead as relatively low.

The patterns in regard to Government Leveling and Feelings of Injustice are less consistent. At the bivariate level, those who perceive they have high relative status and who report their family living standard has improved are less likely than others to have strong feelings of injustice, while those with bad experiences are more likely to have such feelings. However, once other predictors are controlled for, only the tendency for those who have had bad experiences in the last three years to express feelings of injustice remains statistically significant (in column 8). In regard to government redistribution, in the regression models we see the expected pattern of those who report high relative status being less in favor of government leveling, while those who have had bad experiences are more likely to favor such a government role. However, unexpectedly, those who perceive their family living standard has improved are slightly *more* likely than others to favor government leveling. With some qualifications, in general these patterns provide some support for the notion that being a winner versus a loser in society has an impact on distributive injustice attitudes. However, what is important is whether individuals subjectively *perceive* that they have been winners or losers, rather than whether objectively or to the outside observer we classify them as belonging to groups that have been winners or losers.

### Location in Geographic and Economic Space

In panel 4 of Table 13.2 are displayed the associations between distributive injustice attitude measures and our three indicators of geographic/economic location—region, distance to a prefectural or larger city, and degree of marketization of the province. From the figures in these tables, it appears that locational factors matter, but in complex ways that are not that easy to summarize or interpret. In column 4 we see an expected pattern of those living in Central and Western provinces of China perceiving fewer chances to get ahead than residents in the East. Also, once other predictors are controlled for statistically, residents of Central and Western provinces do express stronger feelings of injustice than residents of Eastern provinces (see column 8). However, residents of favored Eastern provinces are more likely to see current inequalities as *unfair*, while those in Western provinces and living far from cities are *less* likely to share this view (see columns 1–2).

The locational predictors of attitudes toward Government Leveling also are somewhat unexpected (see columns 5–6). We anticipate that support for government leveling should be stronger in disadvantaged locales, but that appears to be the case here only in regard to those residing in the Central region. Residents in the least-favored Western region are significantly *less* likely to favor government redistribution, with views of residents of the most-advantaged Eastern region falling in the middle on the issue of government leveling. On balance it appears that being located in relatively disadvantageous places is associated with *more* opposition to, rather than support for, government leveling. Perhaps relative lack of trust in the government among those who live in China's periphery explains these unexpected patterns. We speculate that people living in disadvantaged locales might prefer a more equal society but do not trust the government to redress current gaps. China's leaders may declare their intent to "develop the West," but those living in the West may not expect much improvement to come from such proclamations.

Distance from prefectural or larger cities does not make a significant difference in perceived Lack of Opportunity (see columns 3–4 in Table 13.2). However, distance to the city shows similarly unexpected associations with the other three measures. Net of other factors, those who live far from cities are *less* likely to view current inequalities as unfair (see column 2), they demonstrate *less* support than others for Government Leveling (although the association is no longer statistically significant and turns slightly positive once other predictors are controlled for—compare columns 5 and 6), and they express *weaker* Feelings of Injustice than others (see columns 7 and 8). In some ways these patterns echo those seen earlier in regard to the occupational status groups in panel 1, with a sense of distributive injustice more associated with urban places and occupations than with distant rural ones and farmers.[16] However, it is not the case that these findings regarding residential location are explained by the "positive" views of farmers who reside in locales distant from cities. With the exception of the Government Leveling scale, these coefficients remain statistically significant even when occupational status groups and other predictors are controlled for statistically. Thus there is a net tendency of those living far from urban places to have weaker feelings of distributive injustice than those closer to or residing in cities, no matter what they do for a living.

Finally, our measure of living in a highly marketized province shows inconsistent patterns of association with the four injustice measures. The bivariate tendency of those living in highly marketized provinces to see current inequalities as unfair is reversed once other predictors are controlled for statistically, revealing a weak, predicted tendency for those in highly marketized provinces to be *less* likely to perceive current inequalities as unfair (see column 2). However, those residing in highly marketized provinces are quite unexpectedly *more* pessimistic than others about opportunities to get ahead, once other predictors are taken into account (see column 4), and they express stronger support for Government Leveling (see column 6) and stronger Feelings of Injustice (column 8). So in regard to the level of transformation to a market economy as well as in regard to distance to the city and regional location, living in a favored locale at the forefront of transformation to a market economy seems more often associated with *stronger* feelings of distributive injustice rather than the more favorable attitudes one might expect.

### The Role of Perceptions of Unfair Inequality

Finally, in the last row of Table 13.2 we show the associations between scores on the Unfair Inequality scale and the other three distributive injustice measures. Here we find few surprises. Those who perceive the difference between who is rich and who is poor as attributable particularly to external and unfair sources are, as expected, significantly more likely than others to perceive a Lack of Opportunities to get ahead, to favor Government Leveling, and to express strong Feelings of Injustice. Even when other predictors are controlled for statistically, these associations remain strong and statistically significant.

The figures at the bottom of each table show what proportion of the variance in the distributive injustice attitude in question we are able to explain with the set of predictors we employ. We have only modest success in explaining variations in whether current inequalities are perceived as fair or unfair (r-squared =.105). However, once we take into account scores on that scale as well as all the other predictors, we are more successful and quite respectable in explaining variations in the other three distributive injustice attitude scales (r-squared = .160, .215, and .194, respectively).[17]

CONCLUSIONS: INTERPRETING THE SOCIAL
CONTOURS OF DISTRIBUTIVE INJUSTICE FEELINGS

The findings from our 2004 nationally representative sample survey of Chinese popular attitudes about inequality and distributive justice issues challenge two widely held views. The first is that anger about growing inequality and social injustice is the dominant popular mood. Although this is not the primary focus of this paper, our survey respondents express more acceptance than rejection of the status quo (see again Table 13.1). The dominant mood might be characterized as "acceptance tinged by criticism." Large proportions of survey respondents think there is too much inequality nationally and would prefer that the government take more active measures to help the poor and thereby reduce income gaps. However, most don't attribute the inequality they see in Chinese society today mainly to unfairness in the system, but are instead more likely to explain who is rich and who is poor in terms of variations in individual efforts and talents. Also, the dominant mood is optimism rather than pessimism about the chances for ordinary people to get ahead, while fatalism and despair about social justice issues is a minority view. Overall we don't find much support in our survey data for the "social volcano" scenario, and the alternative "rocky stability" characterization of contemporary Chinese society seems more appropriate.

The second challenge to conventional wisdom from our national survey results is equally pointed—the strongest feelings of distributive injustice in China are not to be found among those social groups, and in those locations, that are objectively the most disadvantaged, such as among farmers, rural migrants, and those living in remote interior locales. The social contours of feelings of distributive injustice are not well mapped by assuming that low status and disadvantage automatically produce anger and discontent.

How can we explain the counterintuitive pattern that on balance disadvantaged groups and locales are less critical of current inequalities than are more advantaged ones? Is it simply the case that the most disadvantaged groups in China are so isolated and ignorant that they do not realize how bad off they are and how unfairly society treats them? We don't think this is a plausible explanation, and in fact our results point to other, more persuasive explanations. Although objective status is a poor guide to perceptions of current inequalities as unjust, *subjective* measures of relative status and mobility experiences are a much better guide (revisit panel 3 in Table 13.2). The consistent and expected patterns of association between our subjective social status measures and perceptions of current inequalities as unfair resonate with research cited earlier from other societies (e.g., Kluegel 1988; Kluegel, Mason, and Wegener, 1995; Kreidl 2000). Distributive injustice attitudes in any society are influenced not simply by current objective status positions, but also and sometimes even more powerfully by subjective factors, such as perceptions of one's relative social status, past experiences with upward or downward mobility, relative aspirations, the reference groups used to judge one's own success or failure, the fates of relatives and significant others, and the climate of anxiety versus optimism about economic opportunities and family security that prevails within one's local community.

With these influences in mind, we might say that farmers and individuals living in isolated villages in China's interior display a Chinese version of the "Lake Wobegon effect" (pace Garrison Keillor), with adult respondents (rather than children) all above average. For such individuals what is happening to millionaires and the unemployed in distant cities is peripheral to their assessments of how fair or unfair current inequalities are perceived, with those perceptions shaped much more by what they see around them in their local communities and by their own recent experiences and those of significant others in their lives. As we saw in Table 13.1, in general, respondents are not particularly likely to feel that such *local* inequalities are excessive, even though most feel that national inequalities are. When they look at rich and poor people in their immediate environment, it is plausible that they might find explanations of such differences based on corruption, unequal opportunities, and other external factors *less* persuasive than would people living in larger and more complex communities. We also speculate that rural people in general, who were for the most part locked into permanent subordination and isolation by the commune system and *hukou* restrictions imposed during the Mao era (Wang 2005), may feel that the loosening of those restrictions after 1978 and improved opportunities to leave farming and migrate to the cities *increase* the fairness of current inequalities, even if opportunities for upward mobility remain far from equal. Given how villagers were treated in the Mao era, in some sense their status and opportunities had nowhere to go but up. Perhaps the recent reductions in rural taxes and fees experienced by most farmers also contribute to improved feelings about the current system.[18]

Similar considerations lead us to conclude that the more negative views about current patterns of inequality held by urbanites in general and some relatively advantaged urban groups in particular are not so counterintuitive either. Objectively, Chinese urbanites have many more advantages over rural residents and migrants than is the case in most other societies (Khan and Riskin 2005; Whyte 1996). However, for the most part urban residents don't draw conclusions about the fairness or unfairness of the current system by comparing themselves with farmers. Rather, most likely they consider what has been happening to themselves and people they know in recent years, and they compare these fates with the rich and poor people they see in the much wider and more complex stratification systems (compared to those of villagers) in which they live. So urban workers and members of China's middle-aged "lost generation" will be confronted on a daily basis with images of the lavish and privileged existence of the newly rich and the powerful, and as a result they may have a sense of their own insecure status and lost opportunities powerfully reinforced. Unlike villagers, urbanites face not only the potential rewards of upward mobility, but also the hazards of downward mobility into unemployment and poverty. Those with high levels of education and high incomes should have a lot to celebrate, but if they compare themselves mainly with their richest and most successful neighbors, rather than with the "masses," they may also come to emphasize the unfairness of current inequalities.

Does the fact that we find relatively weak sentiments of distributive injustice in our national survey, and that such sentiments are not concentrated in the groups that are objectively the most disadvantaged, mean that

China's leaders can now take comfort in our findings and relax, and that they don't have to worry that political stability will be threatened if they do not take vigorous steps to make their society less unequal and more just? In our view such a complacent attitude would be misguided. Our study has focused only on distributive injustice issues, and there are many other kinds of injustice that can generate comparable or even stronger popular discontent. For example, individuals who feel they have lost their jobs through no fault of their own, who have had land confiscated for development without fair compensation, or who have contracted AIDS through tainted blood transfusions may legitimately be furious, even if these are not primarily distributive justice issues. By the same token, convincing Chinese citizens that the current social order is fair may depend more on such measures as improving the legal system and giving ordinary citizens increased voice in influencing the people and policies that govern their lives than it does on government redistributions from the rich to the poor.

Even in the distributive realm, the popular perception that China's leaders are concerned about excessive and unfair inequalities probably helps dampen feelings of distributive injustice among the population, feelings that could flare up if Chinese citizens saw their leaders becoming complacent about the problems of disadvantaged citizens. Furthermore, maintaining popular optimism about chances for people to improve their standards of living is probably only possible when a large proportion of citizens say they are doing better than they were earlier and feel this is the case also for many if not most of the people they know. Such feelings clearly characterized our survey respondents in 2004,[19] but a major economic downturn in China could undermine such confidence. As we noted earlier, the explanation of how distributive justice attitudes are formed that is suggested by our results also leads us to suspect that these attitudes may be somewhat volatile and subject to change in response to altered personal and family experiences and circumstances. In short, there is nothing in our survey results that says that the current "acceptance tinged by criticism" dominant popular view about current inequalities is guaranteed and permanent, or that China's political stability could not be threatened by a broader sharing of feelings of injustice, distributive and otherwise, in the future.

One final cautionary lesson can be drawn from our survey results. Our data suggest that some of the measures the Chinese government is taking to counteract feelings of distributive injustice may not be aimed at the most appropriate groups and locales. We do not advocate that reforms designed to improve the lives of China's farmers and people living in interior provinces should be abandoned because the average farmer or resident of the West is less angry about current inequalities than the average urban worker, migrant, or unemployed person. However, those concerned with China's future

212 Chunping Han and Martin King Whyte

social and political stability would be well advised to reject the assumption that objective status can be automatically equated with attitudes toward current inequalities. Assuming that feelings of injustice are an important source of potential instability, assessments of China's prospects could be more confidently made by directly asking citizens probing questions on a regular basis about how just or unjust they feel the social order is rather than by computing and monitoring Gini inequality coefficients.

# From Inequality to Inequity: Popular Conceptions of Social (In)justice in Beijing

*Ching Kwan Lee*

A quarter century of market reform in China has exacerbated durable structures of social inequality formed under state socialism. Based on longitudinal national survey data, two leading economists on inequality observed that by 1995, China had changed from being one of the most equal countries in the developing world to one of the more unequal in its region. By the turn of the millennium, inequality in China is substantially above that of other Asian countries and approaching the very high levels found in Latin America.[1] Sociologists interested in China as a case of postsocialist transition have accumulated valuable survey data on patterns of income inequality across regions, class, and gender divisions (Bian 1994; Nee 1991; Xie and Hannum 1996; Zhou 2004). As the wealth gap widens, Chinese academics, policy makers, and the international and domestic media have expressed grave concerns about social instability and the erosion of regime legitimacy.[2] Indeed, popular protests and riots have markedly increased in recent years, confirmed by statistics released by the Chinese government. The Public Security Minister reported a staggering total of 74,000 mass demonstrations and riots in 2004, a high point in a decade-long surge of social unrest.[3]

## FROM INEQUALITY TO INSTABILITY?

However, the link between wealth gaps and social instability cannot be taken for granted. In the face of inequality and hardship, the aggrieved population more often than not tightens their belts further, or puts up with inequality as if it were bad weather, part of the natural order of the universe. As the political sociologist Barrington Moore remarks in his classic study *Injustice: the Social Bases of Obedience and Revolt*, "Without strong moral feelings and indignation, human beings will not act against the social order. The history of every major political struggle reflects the clash of passion, convictions and systems of belief." (1978: 469). This system of beliefs and its expression in popular discourses is the subject of this chapter. Specifically, I ask: How do ordinary Chinese make sense of inequality as state socialism gives way to state capitalism? What moral visions and repertoire of rhetoric inform popular perceptions of inequality and inequity? What "moral boundaries" do people draw and redraw between themselves and other social groups with regard to social inequities in a transition society? What are the implications of these patterns of popular consciousness for collective action and regime legitimacy? Answering these questions will provide the necessary, albeit not sufficient, connections between inequality, inequity, and instability.

Sociological and philosophical theories of justice can provide some initial parameters to map the empirical patterns of notions of justice found in China. American sociologists have mostly been concerned with distributive or economic justice, the normative counterpart to the central sociological questions of inequality and stratification. Distributive justice has variously been defined by political philosophers as "fairness," "entitlement," "equality," and "impartiality" (Barry 1989; Campbell 2001; Nozick 1975; Rawls 1971). The development economist Amartya Sen (1999) supplements the important concept of equality in human "capabilities." In this light, justice is not just about material (re)distribution of welfare but also individual dignity and the power and right to participate in the community. Another dimension of justice analyzed by sociologists is legal justice, which stems from the Weberian theory on institutional and bureaucratic authority. The literature often wrestles with the dilemma between procedural justice, or the need for neutral administration of the law, and substantive justice, or the need for flexibility in weighing justice ethics in individual cases. Finally, critical perspectives on justice can be found among Marxist and feminist scholars who define injustice from the perspective of structural oppression and domination (Arts and van der Veen 1992; Young 1990). They argue that the scope of justice should be much wider than material distribution and should include politics in the broadest sense, especially the social structural conditions for or against popular expressions of needs and decision making. Of course, no one expects ordinary Chinese to contemplate in the manner of political philosophers and social scientists. Nor is the present inquiry merely a taxonomical exercise of mapping popular consciousness against these scholarly conceptions. Rather, I will use these scholarly conceptions as a heuristic template to locate the various popular articulations of justice. My central interest is in probing the sources and consequences of these standards of justice, asking if and how they inspire collective action and therefore social change.

COLLECTING NARRATIVES OF SOCIAL (IN)JUSTICE

This chapter reports preliminary findings from Beijing where I interviewed 40 individuals in 2 communities: an old working-class neighborhood in the west side of the city and an upscale neighborhood of luxury condominiums in the east side. In-depth interviews of one to two hours were conducted in the homes of respondents. Residential committees and homeowners' associations in the respective locales assisted in identifying respondents from different age groups, occupational and educational backgrounds, and income levels. To supplement this general sample of residents, I include a subset of ten respondents who had been victims of injustice and/or who pursued personal or collective action for redress. These aggrieved respondents were involved in disputes about property rights, labor rights, and relocation in the cities. Comparison between this theoretically significant sample and the general sample is key to generating hypotheses about the link between standards of justice and activism for justice.

In the rest of the chapter, I will report on (1) the key dimensions of social (in)justice that respondents feel most strongly about when we ask them if and why they think Chinese society is "just" (*gongping*) or "unjust" (*bu gongping*); (2) the principles, rhetoric, and claims that inform their evaluation; (3) the broad patterns of justice perceptions, i.e., those that tend to articulate particular views; and (4) the link between justice discourse and justice politics, or the behavioral implications based on their perceptions of (in)justice. I then conclude with some conjectures on the effects of justice consciousness for regime legitimacy and social change.

## SALIENT DIMENSIONS OF SOCIAL INJUSTICE

Most respondents started by voicing concerns about *distributive* justice, or characterizing income and economic disparity as the primary indicator of inequality, although they quickly point out that inequality is not the same as inequity. "Inequality" as used by them and in this chapter refers to the objective uneven distribution of material resources whereas "inequity" is the unequal distribution deemed unfair or unjust. According to my respondents, inequity had less to do with income gaps per se than with who was amassing wealth and by what means. Cadres, their incomes, wealth, and privileges, were most often singled out as morally suspect and the most salient embodiments of distributive injustice. In other words, equal right to Sen's notion of capability building, or what I call "*redistributive* justice," was a core definition of social justice among Beijing residents in this study. Besides market-allocated and state-redistributed resources, *legal and procedural* justice was most often mentioned by people who had engaged the legal system, either as professional legal representatives or as plaintiffs in lawsuits. Finally, respondents almost always returned to a *structural* critique of the unbridled official abuse of power as the root cause of injustice. As will be clear from the quotations cited in the following pages, Beijing residents invoked moral rhetoric and standards drawn from Maoism, socialism, and liberal legalism. Also, a global awareness was evident among both the younger and the older generations as they made savvy references to experiences and practices of other developed and developing countries, in addition to those found in China's own past and present.

### Distributive Justice

I have always begun the interviews with a general and open question of "Do you think this society is becoming unequal?" and asked them what comes to their mind when they hear the word "inequality"? Most working-class respondents mentioned income (wages or pensions) while middle-class professionals saw inequality in the uneven distribution of property, life-style, and status. The chairman of the homeowners' association in the upscale neighborhood owned a million-yuan penthouse and referred to his exclusive neighborhood as an indicator of social inequality because most people cannot afford it. But he immediately pointed to the even more expensive villas across the street, saying that people there made him feel inferior and unequal too.

What then are the principles of just and unjust inequality, or "distributive justice"? Overall, people subscribed to the meritocratic principle that people should be treated differently in accordance with their deserts. Inequality in material wealth was considered just when it was based on individual merit, capability, and contribution. The market was widely accepted as an institution for allocating rewards but ordinary people also believed that undue advantages accrued to political elites, and that this seriously compromised the inherent fairness of the market.[4] Our middle-class interviewees saw their economic status as rewards for their hard work and higher educational qualification. A female lawyer recalled at length how much discipline was required when studying for her bar exams in the early morning hours during the long and bitterly cold winters in her hometown Harbin to get to where she was now. The chairman of the homeowners' association emphasized his daring move to leave a state-owned work unit and become a travel guide and writer at the beginning of the reform period. His wealth was a reward for his willingness to take risk.

Perhaps more unexpected was the widespread acceptance among our working-class respondents of the merit-deserts principle. A former factory worker who was working for the residential committee found merit-based inequality fair and encouraged her son to do well at school so he could have a good life.

> We high school graduates can only earn five or six hundred yuan; but others with college education earn a thousand or more. That's why I tell my son to

work hard at school. A college degree is a must; there is no hope for those without a college degree. I do not feel this is unjust. I am very balanced, because I do not have the qualification. (B15)

Across class backgrounds respondents justified inequality because it brought aggregate efficiency and it was therefore necessary for economic development. A young accountant said, "Inequality motivates people to improve themselves. A society that is too equal lacks vigor and energy. And no society is totally fair and equal. You can see that after several hundred years of development, even developed countries find it difficult to achieve equality" (B17). In similar veins, others commented that, "Equal distribution means lack of energy and progress," or "Competition and inequality are needed for the country to move forward and develop."

Popular acceptance of inequality coexisted with an adamant awareness and critique of distributive injustice in society. First, many questioned the notions of "merit" and "capability," objecting to what they considered unreasonably high return to entertainers and movie stars.

Another critique of the meritocratic justification for inequality concerned the difficulty with defining and measuring "contribution." Retirees in particular often questioned whether or not there could be a fair way to assess and reward their past contributions to modernizing the country, contributions that allowed it to prosper today but are largely ignored. One retired worker asked,

> What is ability? . . . I was a skilled worker. I did technical work. How come my wage never went up in the past? My specialty was making big boilers and truck engines. How can you say I am not capable and therefore my retirement wage is a pittance? Who built this apartment? Of course you need architects and engineers, but bricks and tiles are put together piece by piece by workers. The wealth we created in the past brought up a whole generation. In those days, our work was much harder. (B13)

The third general critique targeted gaps that they believed had become "excessively large" and unacceptable. Almost always this view was couched in terms of the gaps between cadres and ordinary people. In other words, in respondents' minds, the gap between the rich and the poor was at bottom a gap between officials and citizens.[5] The terms used to distinguish these two groups are on the one hand, *dang guan de* (people with official positions), *gongwuyuan* (civil servants), *ganbu* (cadres), and on the other, *laobaixing* (ordinary people).

Echoing a perspective typical of an older generation, this 58-year-old former welder and union cadre in a heavy machinery factory said,

> We workers were the big brothers in the past but we are now the bottom stratum in society. I get 1,200 yuan a month as a retiree, but this is miniscule

compared to the pensions for civil servants. Our society has two poles, most are either rich or poor, with very few people in the middle. Our government should impose some unified standards. For instance, at least among retirees, pensions should all be the same because we all stay home now. You cannot give me 1,200 and another retiree 3,500. (B18)

He went on to report how popular outrage about inequity had spawned destructive behavior in his neighborhood,

Last June, there was a minor riot in our neighborhood. All the luxury sedans were vandalized. Why? Because some people could not bear seeing other people getting rich. They become unbalanced . . . and rebellious. If I cannot get it, I'm not going to let you have it either. . . . People in the bottom stratum, those working-class people live in a state of outrage, because the reward for labor is so uneven. This produces a strong rebel psychology. In the past Chairman Mao promoted the slogan that everyone should have enough rice to eat (*ren ren you kou fan zhi*). That's based on the need of our country. I am not against layoffs to increase efficiency, but if you care more about letting everyone eat a bit of rice, society will not be unstable. (B18)

Such criticism about the gap between officials and ordinary citizens can also be found among the young and educated. A 29-year-old college-educated junior bank manager voiced the same discontent with what he called the "privileged classes" (*tequanjieji*). As an insider to a state bank, he expressed misgivings about how loans had been extended mostly on the basis of personal ties. Over and over again, people were at pains to make the distinction between competition-based inequality, of which they approved, and official rent-seeking, which they condemned as immoral. Moral boundaries are drawn between the rich whose wealth results from honest hard work and qualification and those who become rich by dint of rent-seeking and abuse of official positions.

My initial hypothesis was that the moral visions articulated by elderly Chinese would be "backward-looking," invoking the days of state socialism and especially the Mao era, and the language of "workers are the masters," while the younger generations would look to the advanced West for reference. Although I have found cases that fall into this generational pattern, the overall results thus far are more mixed. Younger interviewees sometimes used their parents' downward mobility as a reference to think about social injustice, while older people emphasized the need to "modernize their views" in this new economic era. A college-educated young mother assailed the government for doing nothing to redress social injustice inflicted on her mother's generation. She espoused the view that entitlement should be differentiated along generational or political cohort lines. Whereas it was fair to distribute unequal rewards based on merit and competition among the young, equal entitlements should be the principle of distributive justice for the generation that had come of age under socialism. Her view echoed that of many elderly or middle-aged interviewees.

> I always think our government is not fair to people in their 40s and 50s. . . . My mother has been a laid-off worker for six or seven years, no income, just a lump sum of 20,000 yuan (as severance payment), and she has to pay her own social insurance from now until she retires. On the contrary, those civil servants go to work leisurely in the office, read some newspapers and drink some tea, but take home 3–4,000 yuan. My mother worked tirelessly, and in the end could only get a 1,000 yuan stipend each month. This is a huge gap inequity. Do you think this is fair? These middle-aged laid-off employees experienced ten years of Cultural Revolution. Then they were sent down to the countryside. They had no capital of any kind; they had no choice; totally unlike the childhood of those in their 20s today. Therefore these (older) people are very disadvantaged. But now, like us, higher education brings higher income. This kind of inequality is acceptable. . . . I am putting all my money and hope into my child. I teach him drawing and playing piano, and I want him to go to college and then graduate school. How much will this investment be? Probably 300,000 yuan. . . . If people like him earn more, that's fair. This kind of inequality is different from the previous kind of inequality.(B37)

Also, elderly interviewees were not necessarily confined to their own personal experience but would draw on the media and younger family members' knowledge of and travel experience in other countries to define the parameters of fair social arrangements (more below). Overall, both old and young, middle- and working-classes tended to accept a certain degree of inequality, but both agreed that the wealth gaps caused by the abuse of official power were repugnant and unjust, because the abuse distorts the market as a fair institution assigning differential rewards to people making variable efforts and demonstrating different abilities.

*Redistributive justice*

Besides unequal distribution of income and wealth, respondents across social classes and generations focused on unfair provision of such public goods as access to schooling and medical services. I call this concern a desire for redistributive justice. Interviews revealed that in popular belief, a just society should provide all individuals, regardless of backgrounds, the opportunity to develop their capabilities and then compete freely for unequal rewards. Instead of merit and deserts, our subjects propounded a need-based principle regarding redistributive justice. A 38-year-old college-educated personnel manager expressed a view typical among our middle-class interviewees. Even though she was not under any financial pressure to provide for her one-year-old daughter's education, she complained at length about the arbitrary and soaring tuition fees that primary and high schools have been allowed to charge.

A college-educated manager of a joint venture company emphasized the role of education in fostering a meritocratic society different from the pre-reform Chinese society and used India as a reference to criticize the unequal access to quality education in China today.

> In the past, your fate was determined by your family origin. If you had a bad background, you'd be denied the chance to attend university. And you had to report to your superior in order to get married. . . . I have been to India. It's a poor country and there is not even a decent road connecting the airport to the cities. But why is India so strong today? Because their government takes free universal education very seriously. You don't have to pay. People's quality is high. Thirty-five percent of physicians in the United States are Indians, and forty percent of their software engineers are Indians. Most Chinese there only open restaurants. How do you compare these two peoples? . . . I think our education system has serious troubles. It must be reformed so that poor people and rich people can have equal educational opportunity, whether it is nine-year compulsory education or higher education. Money should not be the yardstick in education. (B44)

My respondents reported many stories of parents paying high "sponsorship fees," ranging from a thousand yuan for one semester of high school to a one-time payment of 10,000–20,000 yuan to get their children into schools not in their school district. One 26-year-old stay-at-home mother complained about the 8,000 yuan monthly tuition fee that some bilingual kindergartens charged, and the class composition that a status- and fee-based school system and culture produced.

Interviewees who grew up under the old socialist education system often invoked the nominal fee they paid before the reform as a standard to criticize the present, in addition to referencing the experience of foreign countries like the United States and South Korea.

> In the past, most families had five or six children, and they could afford to feed and send them to school. Now, the two of us find it difficult to even raise a single child. How much did we pay for our school? I went to primary school in 1972, and tuition was 2.5 yuan. Nowadays, you ask every family and they will all tell you that education expenses are the heaviest burden in the family . . . . I really think our government should invest more in education. It's true that we cannot compare with advanced countries like the United States. They started development much earlier than us, but at least we should look at South Korea, which is not particularly advanced, but they have a better education system than China. My husband's company sent him to visit Korea and everyone has access to free education. If our country does not make that investment, we will continue to be poor and undeveloped. (B15)

Impediments to a fairer educational system were not confined to economic disparity among parents. Status distinctions defined by the rural-urban hierarchy and the household registration system were criticized for producing inequity. A 68-year-old retired technician in the geology bureau of the Heber government lamented the educational injustice perpetrated by the *hukou* system.

> I think the biggest mistake the reform leadership has made is in education. University admissions should provide an equal platform for all to compete. But the current practice is that if you were a Hunan local, you'd have to attain higher scores than a Beijing-born student if you wanted to enter universities in Beijing. This incestuous practice is the latent crisis for China. (B27)

Since I have not started interviews in the countryside, I cannot compare how rural and urban residents may hold different views about the hierarchy in life chances imposed by the *hukou* system. Yet, among our Beijing respondents, the most trenchant critique about *hukou* flowed from the system's discriminatory consequence for educational opportunity. A 41-year-old female lawyer hailed from Shenyang who now lived and worked in Beijing with her husband and her child offered an impassioned indictment of the *hukou* system. Whereas most people thought about economic inequality at the very beginning of our conversation, when we asked for her general view about social injustice, she went straight into the household registration system.

> The first inequality is *hukou*. It creates a lot of inequity: Beijing *hukou*, Shenzhen *hukou*, Guangzhou *hukou*, all determine your entitlement to social security. A woman who is not a Beijing *hukou* cannot buy maternity insurance. Is she a Chinese? Why can't she enjoy maternity insurance? *Hukou* was originally designed to manage the mobile population, and the government should not expand it to cover social insurance and education, creating too much injustice. . . . We talk about "human rights" these days. All Chinese citizens should have equal rights because they are all Chinese nationals. Our country's *hukou* system divides people into three, six, and nine ranks. From birth you are made to compete on different tracks. . . . I feel very deeply about this because I personally suffer from this system. . . . My son will have to return to Shenyang to take the college entrance examination and has to get higher scores than Beijing *hukou* students in order to get admitted in universities here. He has been going to school here since primary school. Why does the system demand more of him than his Beijing classmates? The minimum qualifying score for Beijing local students is 100–200 points lower than for nonlocals. If you gave special favor to students from impoverished places, we'll have no complaint. But Beijing students already have the best schools and yet they need lower scores to enter colleges. All because of the *hukou* divisions. This is the biggest inequality. Today, *laobaixing* are just too weak to resist. But this conflict will sooner or later explode and you will see if this leads to social instability. (B45)

If middle-aged parents had immediate concerns with unequal educational opportunity based on class or *hukou* status, elderly interviewees focused on health care in expressing their views on redistributive justice. The most common principle respondents enunciated was one of need-based allocation. No one advocated a return to a totally free-for-all medical care system, which was considered unfair and economically unviable. A retired female worker whose husband had been suffering from diabetes, high blood pressure, and pancreatic cancer discussed at length their financial woes incurred by the collapse of the work unit medical care system and the high cost of medication today. It is noteworthy that her repertoire of moral standards included a critical reflection on both Chinese socialist and foreign practices and values.

> My son-in-law was sent to work in Germany for three years. At one point, he had to have an emergency appendectomy. My daughter said it was all paid for by the German government. Then I told my husband how I wish our country could be the same, given all his chronic illnesses as an old man. . . . Frankly, putting our two pensions together only comes to about 20,000 yuan each year and we spend about 12,000 yuan on medicine alone. If our daughter did not give us some extra money, we'd be begging on the street like those old peasant women. . . . In the past, it was 100 percent reimbursement. Only one fee: the 5 cent or 10 cent registration fee. We were young then and never used the benefit. Now, it is economic society, we have to follow the tide of change and cannot always stick to the old way. But low-income people with chronic illness have no way of paying for medicine these days. The state should have special policies for people with serious health care needs. (Is it just to have free medical care for all?) I think it is unjust to give everyone free medical care. Those who earn several hundred thousand a year are also getting it for free, like *laobaixing* earning several thousand a year? I don't think it is just. (B13)

The articulation of a schism between normative principle and material constraint was quite common; they would juxtapose "all should be treated equally as Chinese citizens" and "our country is too big and poor to make everyone equal."

Finally, beyond concerns with educational and medical welfare, some interviewees aired the grievance about the lack of opportunity to express their views or participate in deciding how these services should be provided. Such comments gesture a broadened parameter of social justice beyond distribution and redistribution to include what Sen (1999) has called the freedom to participate as a worthy member of a community in deciding a valued way of life. At the end of an interview, a retired couple recalled going to a neighborhood consultation meeting in a local hospital. They went into the meeting with enthusiastic anticipation that they eventually were able to voice their opposition against sky-rocketing medication fees, arbitrary procedures, and inadequate medical insurance coverage. The administrator at the meeting was embarrassed by their questions and told them that the consultation meeting was not intended for soliciting such kinds of feedback but just for informing citizens about the services available at the hospital. Having their appetite for consultation whetted and frustrated, the old couple went away feeling deprived of some fundamental right of expression and of the opportunity to influence government policy on something as important as health services. The format and the rhetoric of consultation had apparently awakened new demands not just for getting certain public goods but also for participation in local decision making. The couple spontaneously told me the relief they felt at the end of our two-hour interview—they finally found someone who was willing to listen to them, and they made their voice heard.

### Legal Justice: Procedural and Substantive

Legal injustice was a salient component of popular conceptions of social injustice about which interviewees held impassioned opinions. Academic analyses often make the distinction between two competing dimensions of legal justice, between the need for certainty and predictability achieved by interpersonal neutrality of institutions, and the need for flexibility in order to treat cases differently and in proportion to the ethically significant differences between them. Respondents in this study admonished legal injustice in the administration of the law as well as the lack of substantive justice in the contents of certain laws and regulations. Both procedural and substantive injustice were considered to be caused by abusive cadres colluding with powerful commercial interests and a general state of powerlessness of the ordinary people.

Middle-class, professional subjects who tended to justify their privileged income by referring to capability and merit, and had fewer misgivings about distributive injustice were vocal critics of legal injustice. They tended to have more direct and personal experiences with the legal system as legal professionals or as plaintiffs than working-class respondents. For instance, a corporate lawyer told me how frustrated she was representing clients against those with strong backgrounds and connections to the local government and who often won cases regardless of the evidence. She saw judges dined and wined by clients and could do nothing about an occupational culture steeped in gift giving and networking between judges, lawyers, and powerful clients. Another respondent with a law degree and who worked as a labor arbitrator was adamant about the systemic lack of accountability and endemic corruption between employers and labor supervisors.

> There is no institutional supervision on labor arbitration. There are many intricate personality ties between labor arbitrators and labor bureau officials. Many

> people get transferred from one side to the other . . . and enterprises often bribe labor supervisors . . . so you have enterprises, government and labor bureaus basically sharing the same interests. There is absolutely no oversight mechanism of the labor arbitration commissions, which are in general very corrupt. And this is very unjust . . . because arbitration is a prerequisite of litigation. A negative arbitral award usually becomes a great hurdle for aggrieved workers to launch a lawsuit because the court tends to follow the decision of the arbitration commission. . . . I have seen too many of these instances in my own work. That's why I am particularly upset when I talk about these. (B45)

Most of the respondents in this study have not engaged the law or the legal system directly. Still I found expressions of distrust, not so much of the laws on the books but of the way they are enforced.

The most eloquent articulations about legal justice and its violations were offered by a group of property owners who were fighting a collective legal battle (a "10,000-person lawsuit") against the Beijing city government and its district governments for violating the State Council regulations, promulgated by Premier Li Peng in 1991, on demolition and compensation of old urban homes. In the process of claiming their property rights, these homeowners studied the law, collected original legal documents, compared the various Constitutions for their provisions on property and land rights, and excavated fine-print details in local government regulations that contradicted central edicts. According to their investigation, the local district governments in Beijing arbitrarily altered the regulations imposed by the central government regarding the procedure of compensation and relocation. The Beijing city government conspired with the subordinate officials to prohibit the local courts from accepting administrative lawsuits involving demolition and relocation. After their case was rejected by the Western District government and the Beijing city government, representatives of these homeowners decided to appeal to the Central Discipline Inspection Commission.

One of the representatives was a 50-year-old technician in a state-owned enterprise who owned an old-style *hutong* house in the western part of Beijing, a property his family bought in 1946. The Western District government evicted his entire family together with many local homeowners in 1999 to make way for what is now the sleek and glossy "Financial Street" just inside the second ring road. No compensation was given, although he had the original title paper. His critique of legal injustice pointed to the unbridled official power and corruption as the cause of procedural and substantive injustice.

> [After we filed a lawsuit charging the district government of violating our land use right] the Judge in the Intermediate People's Court in Beijing invited me to a chat in his office and told me that "since the 1982 Constitution, all urban land belongs to the State, and therefore you will not get any compensation as

a property owner. I recommended that you move out as soon as possible. You can never win this lawsuit, because you are suing the government. You will win only if the Communist Party collapses." I immediately retorted, "I don't believe you. Show me the law, the regulations that say I don't have the land use right, that say all my rights now go to developers. You are law specialists. If you cannot cite me any law, I will never be convinced." (B51)

On the day of the demolition, he refused to leave, resulting in a public stand-off between his family and the authorities, a scene that has become common in cities across China, and which provoked popular outrage, and sometimes ended in violence (Cai 2004). His recollection of that eventful day provided a glimpse into the meanings of legal rights in popular consciousness. It was a mix of legalistic and moral claims, based as much on the law as in loyalty to the regime.

> Developers, demolition bureau officials, public security, ambulance, police cars, and many demolition workers all surrounded my house. I wrote on the walls of my house the big characters "The Communist Party and the Eighth Route Army didn't take away a single pin or a penny from ordinary people"; "Equality to all before the law"; "Ordinary people's homes cannot be vio-lated". . . . In the end everything was torn down and removed, and they even wanted me to sign a confession letter, forcing me to admit that I obstructed the execution of official duty. My 12-year-old son and I refused to sign, and they detained us for 10 days. . . . I am a Chinese citizen (*gongmin*), I responded to Chairman Mao's call to construct the Third Front to move to Qinghai, and stayed there for 24 years. My two brothers are soldiers serving the Party and protect our country. Ironically, I cannot even protect our own family home. We are so oppressed. I thought, is this country ruled by the Communists? How come the government has become like the Nationalists? Are these leaders Communist or Nationalists? (B51)

Besides homeowners, some laid-off workers also questioned the substantive rationality of the law that undermined the interests of the socially disadvan-taged groups. For these former workers, the law gave employers the right to dismiss workers when enterprises changed hands but they argued that legality was not the same as justice. Some suggested that it was unjust to prioritize aggregate economic development over the livelihood security of workers and environmental safety of peasants. An articulate laid-off worker, now a temporary employee in a realty company, made many astute com-ments about inequities that were technically legal.

> Under Mao, it was a closed society, and the economy grew slowly. Yet, ordi-nary people's lives were guaranteed. Today, you cannot even secure people's basic livelihood. How can you say our country has developed? . . . Why does the new regulation only allow a maximum of two representatives for each col-lective petition? Because there are too many petitions these days, and it hurts

the image of the government. The rapid growth of the national economy is built on sacrificing the interests of the ordinary people. That's why so many people petition. How can you say this Petition Regulation is fair? . . . Or, take a look at Beijing Hyundai. It used to be Beijing Light Truck Manufacturing Company. Hyundai bought it and dismissed all workers, paying them a one-time payment and ignoring their medical care and pensions. Many workers were crying at the factory gate, as their 20- or 30-year job tenure disappeared, and they were only a few years away from retirement. Can you say this is fair? Some people say the joint venture is more profitable and productive than its state-owned predecessor. But several thousand employees' livelihood is at stake, subject to one man's (the boss's) arbitrary will. Is this justice? (B25)

In short, middle-class professionals among our respondents related many instances from their daily work about corrupt judges and government inter-ference in the judicial process. Our working-class respondents on the other hand have their own personal experiences as victims of legal injustice, par-ticularly on issues of relocation and property rights disputes. Whether or not injustice was perceived as the product of willful human agency or by some seemingly agent-less forces, respondents were making structural critiques of domination by the powerful. For the dispossessed, those who were deprived either of property or employment, there was a sense that inequity in politi-cal power was the crux of a system of legal injustice, in both the procedural and substantive senses.

## JUSTICE DISCOURSE AND JUSTICE POLITICS

A striking aspect of these Beijing respondents was their shared and mul-tidimensional conception of "justice." Whereas Han and Whyte focus on distributive justice, for my respondents distributive justice is only one com-ponent of a more complex repertoire of social justice discourse. There is almost universal perception that social injustice is ubiquitous, a view that is not restricted to the lower classes who have lost out in the reform process. Ordinary Chinese of different generational, educational, and occupational backgrounds offer extensive and passionate indictments against different manifestations of injustice. There is wide consensus that competition and in-equality in income and life chances are acceptable, if competition is fair, and if officials are not abusing their power to amass disproportionate wealth. Even elderly and working-class interviewees who have experienced down-ward social mobility subscribe to the principles of merit-desert–based dis-tributive justice and need-based redistributive justice in providing education and medical care. Structural inequity is seen by many as rooted in the *hukou* system and the extreme imbalance of political power between officialdom and ordinary people.

Second, even the upwardly mobile professional and middle classes, the "winners" in the reform process, do not always find a just society. Expressing discontent about inequity in the legal system, they point to corruption and subordination of the court to the government, and usurpation of central government regulations and laws by local government. Therefore, contrary to official, journalistic, or academic discussions, the common denominator in popular conceptions of injustice is not income inequality per se. Rather, people see structures of oppression as the core of social injustice. These political and social structures compromise the merit, desert, and needs-based principles of distributive and redistributive justice as well as the procedural and substantive justice provided by the law. That is to say Chinese citizens are concerned with *liberal* notions of distributive and procedural justice, but they are most vocal in their *structural* critique of oppression. Such structural critique of injustice is especially prominent and explicit among victims of dispossession—unemployed workers whose entitlement to severance payment, pensions, and jobs is violated, or propertied owners who saw their property rights trammeled and were being forced to relocate.

These findings have implications for our understanding of the basis of regime legitimacy. Some scholars have maintained that the legitimacy of the Chinese Communist regime in the reform era has been transformed from one based on ideology to one based on a mixture of economic performance, maintenance of political stability, benevolence, or moral righteousness. In his analysis of the divergent perceptions of state legitimacy on the eve of the Tiananmen Incident in 1989, Dingxin Zhao (2001: 238) argued that Beijing residents evaluated the state mainly for its economic and moral performance, while the elite officials still believed in the ideological legitimacy of the regime. Taking a *longue duree* perspective, Vivienne Shue (2004) analyzed the Falungong dissent as a case of symbolic politics that challenges three constitutive elements in the logics of state legitimation that have persisted from Imperial to Communist China: truth (true knowledge of the universe and ethical goodness), benevolence (showing compassionate care to the subjects and taking responsibility for people's welfare), and glory (glorifying the Sinic civilization or enhancement of China's international prestige). The challenge of popular religion today as in the past lies in its questioning of all three aspects of state legitimacy and hence the severe response by the state. What this study adds to these arguments is that ordinary citizens are not satisfied with either economic growth (distributive justice) per se or state benevolence in the form of charitable relief (redistributive justice). Their views about social justice suggest a more complex constellation of values and standards by which to judge state legitimacy. Social rights to education and medical care on the one hand, and legal rights, both procedural and substantive on the other, seem to be the two most salient popular expectations that have emerged in recent times. I have found very strong popular demands for the state to abide by the laws it has promulgated, as well as for the state to protect rights accorded to citizens in state decrees.[6] State legitimacy arguably depends on how well the state delivers and realizes these two citizenship rights.

Also notable is the expanding repertoire of moral standards and justice claims. People invoke Maoism, state socialism, and liberal legalism as standards to measure the present; they look at China's own experience and that of other advanced and developing countries. As China makes the transition from socialism to market economy, popular consciousness does not mechanically substitute socialist values of social equality and need-based allocation with the market ideology of competition and unequal distribution. Rather, there has been a process of layering, mixing, and multiplying moral standards and justice claims. But if there is such widely shared sense of injustice, it does not mean that Chinese society is on the verge of explosion and mass rebellion. Two countervailing tendencies emerge in these interviews that may limit destabilizing implications of popular discontents about social injustice.

First, condemnation of injustice coexists with the belief that inequality is inevitable or historically necessary. Many interviewees expressed in the same breath their anger about distributive and redistributive inequality and the sense of its inevitability, saying "It's no use talking about inequality and inequity. They are inevitable. Talking about it does not change anything." I often had to ask them to put aside the issue of inevitability, or their political or practical capacity to effect change, to get back to the discussions of their normative views.[7] Interviews suggest that one source of this feeling of unavoidable inequity is people's own experience with socialism and capitalism. Having lived through these two systems, they know firsthand that inequality exists in both and therefore see it as universal and unavoidable. Even people who appealed to Mao's days to criticize the present related to me stories of gross inequity in the past with little naïve romanticization of that era. The following examples, one given by an enterprising author who owned an upscale penthouse apartment in the exclusive residential area and the other by a retired female worker in the old working-class neighborhood, are telling. One spoke of economic inequality and the other of personal control by cadre under socialism.

> Our education since childhood told us that this is the greatest country on earth, that our life was the best possible and we had to liberate the whole world. But the reality I saw was totally opposite to this teaching. I saw power abuse, slavery, inequality. . . . For instance, if I came from a working-class family, I had no hope of moving ahead because everything was arranged by

the government. If you were a peasant, you'll be a peasant for life. Can you say this is fair and just? When I was allocated my first job as a server in Beijing Hotel, I was able to see for the first time the kind of life that was beyond the imagination and knowledge of the ordinary masses. I saw foreigners and officials' lives. We were taught that American imperialists were all bad, but the Americans I saw were nice, polite, and generous. Why did they cheat us? They were not spies, rapists, or murders. It was around 1977; I was only 17 years old. I was baffled but I began thinking. I worked there for three years for 17.08 yuan a month, not enough to eat a breakfast in Beijing Hotel. I asked why one month's work cannot buy one breakfast. Why my manager had the power to supervise me? Why my fate was in his hands? I did not have any hope, I thought I should escape to either the United States or Hong Kong. But none of this happened. I resigned. The first case in the history of Beijing Hotel. In the past the media was not developed so ordinary people did not know the life of privileged people. When you did not see it, you thought it did not exist. So, there was inequality in the past. (B5)

I have 31 years of job tenure but I felt wronged. That's injustice. I joined my work unit at 16 right after high school. I was a progressive worker year after year, with numerous award certificates. At that time, there was no material reward, only symbolic ones, like a flag or a diary. I even gave up my rest days to do volunteer labor. I was so progressive and very eager to join the Party. But the problem was I was too honest and did not know how to lie or cajole my superior. He only liked those with sweet words. . . . I applied persistently for Party membership ten times in ten years. No, they always refused me. All because I did not want to lie. (B13)

Besides the realization that inequality is a fact of life that only takes on different forms in different societies, there is a deep ambivalence among the respondents about the Communist regime. Although many pointed to unrestrained state power in the form of official corruption as the cause of injustice, at the same time, surprisingly, they also see the state as the solution. For instance, respondents who were critical of economic injustice and excessive income of cadres saw the solution to these problems in a state-imposed equal pension. People told us that the solution to curb corruption was for the state and the Party to redirect anticorruption propaganda at their own cadres rather than the masses. In many areas of discontent, be it the reduction of income gaps, the creation of employment opportunities for the bottom strata, or the health care needs of the sick and poor, state responsibility and policies were considered the solutions. Most tellingly, the aggrieved victims of injustice saw the solution to legal injustice in appealing through the same court system they thought was biased in favor of officials and the rich.

Underlying this staunch state orientation is a prevalent hierarchical and fragmented political imagination, which has two dimensions. First, this popular imagination sees real power to change as residing in the state machinery and neither in the market nor in the horizontal solidarity forged out of associations among citizens. In interviews, our respondents always alluded to what the central state should do and rarely mentioned the potentials of collective action to alleviate the different kinds of unjust social conditions. Second, there is a bifurcation between the central government, which is perceived as the protector of society, and local government officials, which have tremendous personal and parochial interests and real political power to sabotage the laws and regulations of the central authorities. Mining the interview narratives, one finds many references to the distinction between "central" and "local" states. Ordinary citizens invest an impressive amount of moral trust and expectation in the former, although they invariably question the integrity and competence of the latter. In many cases, trust in the center results from a lack of alternatives. A major representative of the 10,000 homeowners' lawsuit explained that if they did not believe in the righteousness and integrity of the center and its law, they would have no institutional power to even put up a fight.

Of course, in the long run, if the superior authorities failed to right the wrongs of the local cadres, this bifurcated legitimacy structure may eventually collapse and people would come to see the *entire* system as corrupt, immoral, and unjust. My research does not indicate that we have come to this point yet. What my data have shown is that this popular hierarchal political imagination that privileges state power over social associational forces to bring about social justice is not permanent or immune to change. Once inspired, people's dogged commitment to the principle of legal justice (as in the case for property rights) and the actual involvement in the process of collective struggle may transcend the feeling of powerlessness and dependence on the integrity of the central authorities. The *idea* of legal rights under a system that does not guarantee them may motivate action that results in transforming the unjust system.

Looking at these grassroots struggles for justice, my conjecture is that on the one hand, popular pressure may steer the regime's "rule by law" toward a "rule of law" system. On the other hand, if people become too disenchanted with the local government and the judiciary, they might be prompted to try something else outside the legal institutions, and become keen on developing social solidarity instead of relying on the imagined benevolence of the central government. As my own research (Lee, 2007) on labor protests documents, workers disillusioned by a legal system that promises but does not deliver legal justice brought their grievance to the street, with occasional albeit unpredictable political effectiveness. Where this wellspring of popular discontent about social injustice will go, and how this conflict between the central authorities' concern for regime legitimacy and local state's tendency toward accumulation by dispossession, will resolve will be the subject of another study. For now, for a regime that came to power through a revolution built on mass discontent and suffering of social injustice half a century ago, the palpable and wide presence of critical and rebellious sentiment caused by inequity today is disquieting enough.

## CHAPTER FIFTEEN

# Social Stratification:
# The Legacy of the Late Imperial Past

*R. Bin Wong*

Changes in social stratification remain one of the most useful arenas in which to search for indicators of larger patterns of social change as economic developments of one kind or another occur. In the 1950s and 1960s, scholars approached social stratification within a larger set of understandings about modernization. Agrarian social systems composed of lords and peasants typical of sedentary societies were increasingly displaced in the nineteenth and twentieth centuries by urban-based social systems at the top of which sat industrial and professional elites and beneath whom were the working classes. Social structures became increasingly complex. Economic differentiation meant additional occupations; social changes included the development of new forms of popular culture and the transformation of elite cultures, which created new markers of social status. Politically, the formation of modern states created new positions of authority. Power was expressed through new kinds of economic, social, and political capacities.

As the simple and confident explanations of large-scale historical change have fallen on hard times, analysts have often continued with their empirical studies without larger claims about what the phenomena represent in terms of broader patterns of change. Alternatively the broader patterns of change become so general as to encompass all manner of variations within them without necessarily having any account for the sources of variation among diverse cases. This volume has introduced new data and analyses to the study of shifting patterns of social stratification in China amidst the rapid economic development of the past quarter century. Many particular findings resemble elements of change found for other parts of the world, yet the overall picture also contains features that reflect the history behind contemporary China.

This chapter briefly considers some of the broad features of social change attending economic development in China over the past quarter century and puts these into the historical perspective of Chinese political economy at three historical moments beginning in the mid-eighteenth, mid-nineteenth, and mid-twentieth centuries. China enjoyed a vibrant agrarian commercial economy in the eighteenth century, which the state made considerable efforts to support and complement with policies designed to protect material prosperity for poorer people in wealthier areas and extend material prosperity to populations living in peripheral regions. Between the mid-nineteenth and mid-twentieth centuries, connections to an expanding capitalist economy created new problems and possibilities for people in some parts of the empire, while those in other areas came to have fewer effective political or economic ties to other regions within the empire. Foreign businessmen and diplomats enjoyed protection and privileges under their own self-rule in a growing number of treaty ports. From these bases, Western economic and cultural influences spread across China, especially in major urban centers. By the 1930s, there were increasing gaps between cities and countryside as well as starker contrasts among regions. The People's Republic established in 1949 moved swiftly to achieve a unitary state ruling a unified country in which economic development followed a Soviet-style industrialization strategy combined with varied efforts to organize and control the countryside. Central state ministries planned the construction of heavy industry and by the mid-1950s nationalized previously private, industrial consumer industries. Redistribution of agricultural land in land reform campaigns was followed in the 1950s by collectivization of agricultural production. Farming households were given work assignments by local authorities who responded to directives from higher levels of government.

The economic reforms launched in the early 1980s typically are conceived as a radical break with a planned economy in which close governmental control gave way to market-based exchange and new hierarchies of wealth, status, and power. If, however, we view economic and social changes of the past 25 years not simply in terms of post-1949 conditions, but also with respect to dynamics at work in the two centuries preceding the mid-twentieth century, we can discern some broader and deeper patterns to social and economic changes that can inform our sense of future possibilities.

## THE EIGHTEENTH-CENTURY POLITICAL ECONOMY OF AGRARIAN EMPIRE

Between the sixteenth and eighteenth centuries, the Chinese economy became increasingly commercialized. Millions of peasants produced for the market and many commodities, including daily necessities such as grain and cotton textiles, traveled long distances. In addition to a small merchant elite, there was a substantial class of small-scale traders and shopkeepers who accumulated substantial capital. Commodification of land also was extensive, but, as best as we can judge based on early twentieth-century data, only a fraction of land was controlled by large landlords; most households relied on tilling their own fields or renting use-rights of relatively small parcels (Lavely and Wong 1992). In contrast to England, however, sharp class divisions did not accompany commercialization of agrarian production in China. Instead, the continuation of rural social relations in China amidst commercialization was more similar to the experience of France and of German-speaking areas on the continent (Aston and Philpin 1985). Just as in Europe, especially parts of eastern and central Europe, China included areas untouched by markets and specialized production for long-distance trade. But overall, commercial economic expansion was as significant a phenomenon in eighteenth-century China as it was in eighteenth-century Europe. For present purposes, a simple awareness of these similarities helps us understand that the range of Chinese experiences of economic growth in the preindustrial era were broadly comparable to those found in Europe.

Peasants in the richer parts of the late imperial empire often specialized in crops and crafts for the market. The eighteenth-century agrarian economy grew through a combination of intensified use of resources and the extension of agricultural production to lands devastated by the mid-seventeenth century dynastic transition or previously uncultivated. Long-distance migrations of millions of people made possible some of the extension of cultivation across the empire, while improvements in agricultural technologies raised levels of productivity on richer lands. Chinese and Japanese scholars have led the way in documenting the expansion and transformation of agrarian economic activities between the sixteenth and eighteenth centuries. The best-studied examples are not surprisingly the best documented in original sources; they concern the development of textile handicrafts and changes in cropping in the lower Yangzi or Jiangnan region, around present-day Shanghai (Zheng 1989). Other commercially dynamic regions, such as the Pearl River delta in Guangdong and coastal Fujian, have also received attention (Marks 1998; Rawski 1972). In addition, poorer and more peripheral areas experienced additional clearance of land and the production of commercial crops. Southern Shaanxi, for example, first recovered from the fighting taking place with the fall of the Ming dynasty and establishment of the Qing dynasty in the 1640s, and then extended hill land food cropping with corn and sweet potatoes to help feed workers engaged in the timber trade, paper making, and iron production (Wong 1997:19). In both richer areas with considerable market town and city growth as well as poorer areas with limited urban sites, rural inhabitants became increasingly connected to markets and in the process often became linked to people and products in distant parts of the empire and even overseas. In richer areas like Jiangnan or the Pearl River delta, people living in villages typically went to market towns on a regular basis because physical distances were modest and the economic and social reasons for going to a market town frequent, be these to arrange a marriage, discuss a land transaction, or conduct some kind of commercial business. The lives of many villagers, therefore, were not fundamentally cut off from those of people living in towns and cities. In poorer areas where peasants might be less likely to go a larger city, there were also fewer large urban centers. As a consequence, the urban-rural divide for common people was socially more muted than it was in many parts of Europe in the same time period.

Within rural areas, late imperial Chinese economic growth seems rarely to have produced the kinds of social differentiation that took place in parts of Europe. The development of factor markets that facilitated the commodification of land, labor, and capital did not lead to the kinds of class differentiation that Marx famously found basic to the development of English capitalism. For many years, Marxist-inspired historians, both in China and beyond, looked hard for evidence that commercialization heightened social differentiation. But there was little evidence of strong connections between commercialization and increased social differentiation. Unlike villagers in Europe, some of whom became rural proletarians before moving into cities to work, Chinese households usually combined craft and crop activities, and market developments contributed to the abilities of village households to maintain, or even increase, their incomes despite rising populations. Similar economic processes, in particular the expansion of the rural textile and craft industries, did not generally lead to the European experience of a stratum of rural proletarians, working both as landless labor and in rural industries, who married and reproduced themselves before they moved to cities (Tilly 1984). In China, craft activities remained anchored in agrarian, farming households, and there was little social differentiation between people working in rural industries and those working the land (Wong 1997:33–52). Moreover, landless laborers in China rarely married, and thus they did not reproduce themselves. Rather the ranks of the landless were replenished by those who had lost or sold their small holdings. The equal division of property among males in every generation tended to reduce per capita land holding over the generations, but individuals continued to rise and fall in their fortunes beyond what happened through land partibility alone. The hardworking and lucky accumulated land or began small businesses, while the unfortunate and less diligent could lose land and even livelihood without the general distribution of household types changing.[1]

During the late imperial era, China's social and economic elite gained status from education and passing civil service exams, wealth from land and commerce, and power from government positions and leadership roles within local communities. They formed large and complex families that had interests in land and commerce and maintained residences for extended families simultaneously in villages and towns or cities. At the heart of the elite reproduction were scholars who after passing the civil service exams staffed the world's largest state bureaucracy for most of the millennium since 1000 CE. Families producing scholars often had gained wealth from land ownership, commerce, or some combination of both. But in contrast to the societies of early modern Europe or Tokugawa Japan (1603–1867), the imperial Chinese elites had far fewer institutional distinctions. Europeans distinguished among urban elites, aristocracies, and religious elites, each of whom had their own distinct institutions through which they could express their power and authority. Japanese samurai and urban elites did not enjoy the same kinds of power and authority typically found in European societies, but they were institutionally distinct from each other. The social separation of elites in European and Japanese societies was by no means consistent, let alone complete, but compared to late imperial China, the former societies had sharper breaks and more distinct concentrations of separate elites than China, where there existed a social continuum for elites between town and countryside rather than sharply distinct urban and rural elites.[2] When we look at the conditions of both elites and nonelites in eighteenth-century China and compare their social structures to those of societies in Europe and Japan, China has a structurally less complex form with fewer rigid and sharply defined divisions. Yet commercial expansion and economic change unfolded in broadly similar ways across these diverse social structures. The social changes generated by economic growth were contingent upon the character of social relations in each society. The Chinese evidence is particularly difficult to assess because it ranges over such a diverse set of conditions; it is at times problematic and occasionally even foolish to compare social and economic conditions in China with those in any European country since the spatial scales are so fundamentally different.

Eighteenth-century Chinese officials were attentive to regional differences in economic well-being as well as differences among rich and poor in a particular area (Wong 1997:19–27). Complicating their assessments and our understanding as well were the possibilities of stark differences between rich and poor in some small part of a larger poor region in which many locales lacked any rich people to speak of; in such conditions, officials typically worried more about general and absolute poverty than relative income inequalities. In richer parts of the empire, eighteenth-century officials continued to voice concerns heard for many centuries concerning inequalities of land ownership. Behind these concerns was a desire to assure that all households possessed the means to secure at least their subsistence if not a more ample prosperity. Officials continued to assume that a materially solvent society was the basis for social stability and political order. To achieve these goals, eighteenth-century officials developed a range of policies to promote agrarian production in poorer areas, including promoting migration of people and the movement of technologies and resources from richer areas to the peripheries. In addition, officials intervened in both richer and poorer areas when famine conditions threatened to cause social disruptions. Peripheral areas remained poorer than economic cores, but the movements of people and resources to these areas allowed for extensive economic expansion. These developments complemented economic growth in more prosperous areas created by division of labor and specialization for market production. Indeed, without these changes in peripheral areas, the prosperity of core areas would likely have been more limited as larger populations would have remained to put pressure on resources.

The eighteenth-century political economy of Chinese agrarian empire supported commercial growth that was the key to levels of material prosperity equal to or even exceeding those achieved over similarly large territories in Europe. Since scholars of Europe typically focus on very limited parts of northwestern Europe when looking at early modern economic growth, they largely ignore the far poorer peripheries within Europe. When these are brought into our comparative picture and scholars are able to assemble reasonable estimates of productivity and standards of living for both them and Chinese peripheries, we'll likely confirm that both China and Europe had similar ranges of economic productivity and standards of living before the Industrial Revolution. For present purposes, it especially matters that China lacked the kinds of institutionalized social stratification found across Europe before the nineteenth century at the same time as it was able through a largely different mix of institutional devices to create widespread commercial expansion.

During the nineteenth century, industrial societies were created in several European countries and by the turn of the twentieth century they were also established in North America and in East Asia, most visibly in Japan but not in China. In the nineteenth century some of the Chinese areas that had become more densely settled in the eighteenth century exhausted their resource bases or became sites of more fierce competition over scarce land. The state proved unable to affect the kinds of resource transfers it made during the eighteenth century to promote material security. The disruption of midcentury rebellions and uprisings that affected most all of the empire was, in fact, quelled but at very high costs. The strength of different eighteenth-century forms of economic and political integration were seriously weakened over the nineteenth century. Distinct and separate regional economies, which were politically and economically less integrated, took shape (Wong 2004: 27–32). The political integration of the empire thus became more vulnerable to social and economic changes that tended to enhance separation and differences among various regions of the empire.

A few eighteenth-century towns and cities grew due to their positions as trade entrepots. Many continued to prosper during much of the nineteenth century, their growth usually enhanced by trade opportunities with the West. Though Western influences are often assumed crucial, economic dynamism predated the nineteenth-century opening of China by Europeans. Moreover, as William Rowe has argued at length based on the Yangzi River port of Hankow, nineteenth-century Chinese cities developed organizational capacities for rule and public order prior to and independently of Western influences. Merchants thus were important not only economically but for their social and political leadership (Rowe 1984, 1989).

At the same time as merchants increased their economic and social importance in larger towns and cities, and at least some peasants in the hinterlands of these cities were prospering in the nineteenth century, there were many people in more peripheral areas who were doing far less well. Indeed, it seems very likely that some of them were doing less well than the previous two or three generations of people in the same areas. Exhaustion of resources, declines of trade, and mounting subsistence uncertainties produced increasing threats of Malthusian crises. Famines attacked many parts of north China in the mid-1870s. Far more widespread than famines in the eighteenth century, late nineteenth-century agrarian difficulties reflect a combination of ecological crisis and economic uncertainties. Absolute poverty may well have become more common in the late nineteenth century at the same time as peasants in other regions were doing better than people of earlier generations. The more prosperous parts of the empire became increasingly connected to international markets and prosperity spread among both new commercial elites and farming households producing for new markets. Even without industrialization, some late nineteenth-century Chinese appear to be doing better economically because of international trade.

The collapse of the dynasty in 1911 ushered in nearly four decades of political uncertainty marked by widespread conflict and violence—ranging from banditry and small-scale protests within cities and across the countryside to large-scale fighting among warlord armies in the 1920s, by Chinese armies against Japanese invaders after 1937, and between Communist and Nationalist armies between 1945 and 1949. Amidst the political turmoil of the first half of the twentieth century, the social and economic separation between poor peripheral parts of the former empire and the richer urban cores became reinforced politically by the absence of effective rule spanning the many regions of the country.

Many peasants in the interior countryside were subject to growing economic uncertainties. These peaked in the early 1930s with the Great Depression for those who had previously benefited from their connections to worldwide markets; others more isolated from international markets often faced grinding poverty that led to crisis quite separately from global trade. Economic uncertainties in some rural areas combined with structural poverty in others made for difficult conditions over much of the Chinese countryside in the 1930s, conditions only exacerbated by the Japanese invasion after 1937. Some of those who could escape left the countryside for cities.

Cities became home in the 1920s and 1930s to growing numbers of poor people, some of whom found jobs in service industries or peddling goods. But a handful of cities also housed the new commercial and industrial elites, as well as a kind of professional class. Nascent working and professional classes emerged amidst the presence of foreign elites. Urbanization and industrialization created patterns of production and consumption similar to and connected with those found elsewhere in the world. New kinds of voluntary associations and groups brought people together for economic, social, and political purposes. Focusing solely on cities, we could say that forms of social stratification associated with other modern societies were taking place in Republican-era China. We might expect that if the Communists had not come to power, one of two possibilities might have obtained. Both counterfactuals start with the assumption that urban development would have continued. They differ in their projected endpoints. One would lead to the eventual demise of rural society, which is the hallmark of social stratification in typical modern societies. The other would posit a society bifurcated between a modern urban economic sector and a traditional rural one, each sector with its own associated social system and between which a variety of gaps, barriers, and problems would be found. What is missing from both counterfactuals is any sense that the previous relationships within and between urban and rural portions of Chinese society could potentially matter to later dynamics of social change. Before suggesting that such possibilities deserve consideration in our evaluations of contemporary China, we need to consider how the high socialist interlude of some three decades might matter to present-day dynamics of social stratification and economic change.

## SOCIALIST SIMPLIFICATIONS AND THEIR AFTERMATH

From the perspective of economic and political integration between urban and rural sections of China over the previous century and a half, the Communist system of rule represented a distinctive kind of development. The Communists made administratively explicit the division between urban and rural China and controlled the links that connected them. Through the work unit and household registration system, the Chinese party state managed virtually all aspects of urban production and distribution (Bian 2002a: 92–93). Through varied forms of local administration, the party state aimed to be the one defining force beyond the village that shaped people's lives. A common Communist ideology was preached across urban and rural China. Economically, limited goods made their way from urban factories to the countryside, while considerable resources were mobilized by the government to form the capital needed for state-led industrialization.

More significant for our common purpose of examining changing forms of social stratification was the radical simplification of social life imposed on both urban and rural China during the 1950s and 1960s. A party elite spanned cities and villages to the exclusion of any other kind of elite. Even more than the late imperial Confucian elite, the Communist party state elite actively subordinated other potential economic and social sources of elite formation to their ideology and institutions. Cities were stripped of virtually all forms of social associations and political groups; those left were put under various kinds of state control and surveillance. Rural China was deprived of the market connections that created broadly horizontal links spanning economic and social purposes. These changes hardly represented a return to pre-twentieth-century forms of urban and rural social life. Native place and kinship ties were rarely visible socially or economically.

The state controlled society through a process of aggressive simplification, more radical indeed than the kinds of state simplification James Scott has suggested in his *Seeing Like a State* to be a general trait of high modernist projects of twentieth-century states. Whether considered from the vantage point of classes in which the interests of different large sections of society compete with each other or from the perspective of "civil society" organized in numerous voluntary associations—each able to pursue competing or complementary economic, social, or political agendas—industrialized or industrializing societies typically have structures that promote some degree of social autonomy from government intervention. Post-1949 China lacked both the social stratification of a capitalist society and the organizational nuclei of a strong civil society. Instead, status distinctions were labels defined politically. Those attached to one's "class background" were difficult to avoid. Individuals could, however, achieve those depending on zealous participation in political life. Such labels were a feature of political campaigns and movements through which the Chinese Communist party state was able to mobilize large segments of society. Were society organized and stratified according to the conventions more common among industrial and industrializing societies, it may well have been more difficult for the party state to achieve the kinds of political mobilizations they repeatedly made in the 1950s and 1960s. Chinese society subject to radical social simplification by the state, became, by the standards of other nonprimitive societies, weakly stratified and underorganized.

Social simplification in the countryside began with land reform and progressed under collectivization. First, major differences in land-based wealth were reduced dramatically by locale. Then, by the late 1950s, rural incomes were largely determined by the value associated with different kinds of labor.

While socialist agriculture was planned and therefore in some ways cumbersome and inefficient, the social structure it promoted was far simpler than what would have obtained under a market-based capitalist system. Similarly in cities, the state achieved direct control over production in the second half of the 1950s. The vast majority of the urban population were workers in state-managed offices and factories. The urban elite, like the rural elite, derived status, power, and wealth from their party membership and roles they played through their party positions and connections.

Eighteenth-century rural stratification had been fluid. Some locales had one or two dominant landlord families but far more places were stratified more gradually between rich and poor peasants. After 1949, there were no major differences in rural household wealth. Moreover, the main factors that promoted social mobility two centuries before—partible inheritance, which reduced average landholding over generations, and market opportunities, which raised incomes for some households—were absent after 1949. In some senses at least, post-1949 rural Chinese society was socially stable in ways more reminiscent of nineteenth- and twentieth-century Western images of rural stagnation in Asian societies than the realities of eighteenth-century agrarian life.

Urban social structures were more sharply different. Those of the eighteenth century were dominated by associational forms developed within society and with which officials attempted to gain some effective relationship. Much of the social order within Chinese cities depended on the people themselves; officials played a secondary and supporting role, in contrast to the dominant role that officials enjoyed in the three decades after 1949. Amidst these changes, a Communist elite has replaced a Confucian elite at the top of society. Absent in eighteenth-century Chinese society were the sharp corporate divisions among urban, aristocratic, military, and clerical elites that could be found across much of Europe and in Japan. A Confucian-centered Chinese elite pursued wealth, power, and scholarship without the social differentiation typical in many other parts of Eurasia. Post-1949 Chinese elite status was defined principally by party membership and position in ways more strict and narrow than those present two centuries earlier. Once again, there are certainly changes in the bases of elite formation but these hardly conform to our general expectations about social change from agrarian to industrial societies.

The shift from Confucian-centered to Communist-dominated elite structures was mediated by more than a century of social change in which multiple new elites emerged in Chinese cities based on new kinds of economic, professional, social, and political roles. Chinese cities by the early twentieth century were increasingly connected to international markets for commodities, technologies, ideas, and institutions. These ties tended to overshadow and in

242    R. Bin Wong

some cases even replace connections to the countryside. Chinese coastal cities and towns, heavily influenced by foreign agents of change, enjoyed new forms of consumption and developed new cultural sensibilities. At the same time, many rural residents in the agrarian interior faced chronic subsistence insecurities as they produced crops and crafts more similar to those of their ancestors than they were to the many new goods in Chinese urban settings. These two conditions bring us to the counterfactual for China of what would have happened in the absence of the Japanese invasion and subsequent Chinese Communist victory? Would there have been the spatial and social patterns of urban centers with strong global ties but weak economic, social, and political connections to their domestic agrarian sectors?

## REFORM ERA SOCIAL AND ECONOMIC CHANGES IN HISTORICAL PERSPECTIVES

In the three decades before the 1980s, party cadres formed the political and economic elite. Economic reforms have changed their positions in different ways. In cities, nonparty elites have emerged as well as an economic middle class quite separate from the Communist Party. In the countryside, party cadres, however, have often occupied a salient place in economic reforms because they controlled access to resources and information necessary for expanding rural industries, a key component of economic growth in the 1980s and 1990s. Not surprisingly, economic and social changes in cities and countryside differ.

Sociologists within and without China have begun to assemble increasing amounts of data and make many fascinating analyses of social change in Chinese cities. The formation of new kinds of elites who can be identified both by occupation and consumption patterns as well as the persistent presence of those who have not benefited greatly, if at all, from a quarter century of economic reforms have been studied. The general arc of change seems pretty clear—Chinese patterns of urban social stratification are generally moving toward practices we can recognize in other industrialized and industrializing societies. Previous forms of social organization under state administrative control basically get left behind as new forms of association and new kinds of networks are formed. New urban economic elites achieve their wealth through new occupations tied to an industrializing economy and the kinds of goods and services such an economy generates. Their status claims, however, may differ from the status hierarchies that have emerged in Western European and North American societies, since economic changes do not entirely drive changes in social prestige and cultural values.

The situation outside Chinese cities is less clear. The rise in per capita rural incomes has depended on a combination of labor migration to the cities and the increased employment of the remaining people in small-scale industries. The development of township and village enterprises in the 1980s and 1990s allowed new forms of production that used factor proportions far more efficiently than before. In two very different kinds of places, cadres played a very large role. First, in extremely poor and peripheral areas, officials played, and continue to play, a large role in organizing the local economy, for many of the same reasons that they were relatively more important in such areas in the eighteenth century—the paucity of private wealth to be invested in production and exchange. These areas continue to require state subventions in order to entertain any possibilities for economic development; indeed, the challenges today are far greater than those of two or three hundred years ago. In the eighteenth century the technological possibilities for production were far more limited; it was far easier to imagine transferring textile and agricultural techniques than the much more involved industrial technologies of today. Second, and unlike the situation in the eighteenth century, officials are important in particular core areas, including those in which they played a far more modest role in the political economy of eighteenth-century agrarian empire. The so-called Sunan model of the early 1990s—predicated on the involvement of cadre as entrepreneur—formed the basis for what Jean Oi has called "local corporatism" and even after most rural industry was privatized, state agents still play a critical role.

The formation of township and village enterprises, which in practice included a wide range of ownership and management forms, and their subsequent evolutions, represented a pattern of industrialization quite distinct from experience in Europe and North America where farm labor migrated to urban factories. In China, initial emphasis on heavy industry and ideological preference for an urban proletariat as the leading class of the revolution created a model of industrialization that institutionalized a sharp urban-rural divide and blocked mobility from villages to cities. The reform-era Chinese pattern of rural industrialization emerges, at least partially it seems to me, as a path-dependent outcome from earlier forms of rural production, including both late-imperial-era craft production and small-scale industrial production begun during the Great Leap Forward.

These economic connections between past and present are complemented by political parallels. The kind of political authority found in rural areas today, of course, differs from those of the eighteenth and nineteenth centuries. Yet in contrast to Europe where political authority never reached deeply into the countryside in earlier centuries and remained urban-focused in more recent times, in China the political authority that reached into rural communities during late imperial era penetrated even deeper after 1949. The reform-era opportunities for rural households to succeed economically and socially quite independently of local political authorities create complex situations with at least some social differentiation more similar to stratification possibilities under the market conditions of earlier centuries than the largely nonmarket conditions of the 30 years preceding socialist reforms. But local party leaders have often continued to enjoy advantages owing to their political connections, which have allowed them to prosper in ways that some people have sometimes found illegitimate. The most egregious cases have been identified as forms of corruption by the government and subject to severe punishments.

When we leave the countryside specifically and look at elites across both urban and rural society, Communist Party elites no longer enjoy a monopoly on most sources of status, wealth, and power. Before the 1980s party membership was the key conduit to status, wealth, and power. The limited number of alternative discrete sources of status, wealth, and power provides another indication of the relatively restricted possibilities for social stratification available, at least when compared to other developing societies or advanced industrial ones. In the reform era, the sources of status, wealth, and power have multiplied. Wealth and power remain connected, but there are many different threads of each that can be woven in more varied ways. Social status markers have become more diverse even as they are hardly divorced from wealth and power. Education, which had been so important to the status of Confucian elites in late imperial times, matters in new ways today.

Confucian elites had been at the top of the late imperial status hierarchy even if merchants were wealthier and officials were more powerful. Merchants often wanted Confucian educations for their sons and certainly hoped some family members might become officials. Confucian education was crucial to being a member of either the intellectual or political elites. Distinct from, but related to, both the changing economic and political elites of the country are the new knowledge elites whose status and wealth depend on their familiarity with science and technology. Within the new knowledge elites are people whose technical skills are used directly in production as well as those whose abilities are in finance or business organization. The latter forms of knowledge relate to broader forms of social science knowledge practiced within academia and thus bring us to issues of how intellectuals as a diverse elite figure into contemporary Chinese social structure.

There are at least three different ways in which education matters to social stratification in China. First, there are the human capital issues similar to those in other industrializing or industrialized societies; levels of education affect the kinds of jobs and therefore the kinds of income people can have. Second, education matters for both general reasons and those more particular to the Chinese situation. As elite positions become more diverse through economic development, the sources of status become more varied;

higher education will create both technocratic and critical elites with evolving relations to political elites. Third, education of different kinds also creates tastes of particular kinds that can be distinct from those of mass market consumerism. People with particular kinds of social tastes also form their own networks; Pierre Bourdieu's *Distinction* comes to mind as a relevant comparative point of departure.

All societies combine different kinds of mechanisms and processes to create social strata and economic hierarchies. The relative importance of the economist's "human capital" and the sociologist's or political scientist's "social capital" does, however, vary among societies. One can consider the importance of informal networks that cut across and through bureaucratically organized social and political space to have been especially crucial given the radical social simplifications of the bureaucratic socialist era. But networks utilizing social capital can also be built in other situations. If one thinks of the role of education in the United States today, the features distinguishing an Ivy League education from that available at other first-tier research universities and distinguished liberal arts colleges are less likely to be the substantive content that can be translated into human capital and more likely to be the social relations and networks available through the contacts only available at, or at least largely restricted to, the Ivy League. At the same time as we look in the future at how human and social capital both develop and affect Chinese social stratification, we should also be mindful of the persistence of old networks beyond those within occupations. Consider, for instance, the persistent role of native place ties to explain employment on the passenger ships working the Yangzi River; whether maid, cook, cabin boy, or ship's officer, all seem to be tied through their Chongqing connections. This is perhaps a variation of Arthur Stinchcombe's classic observations about social organization and social structure, namely that an organization takes on features reflecting the social structure of the era in which it was formed (Stinchcombe 1965).

There are two final aspects of social stratification that deserve attention and remind us of how China's future will grow simultaneously out of its past and through its connections with the larger world. Both affirm the importance of analyzing different kinds of social space. One concerns the continuing creation of new small-scale urban centers out of what were previously rural social settings. The second involves migration to larger metropolitan areas. The urbanizing social structures of areas that were formerly agrarian is a process distinct from the formation of ever-larger metropolises, but how much these processes will subsequently share and how closely they will ultimately be connected remains to be seen.

Looking more closely at social settings in the countryside in different parts of China, only some are becoming more urban, usually when they are

already close to larger cities. What will characterize the larger range of possibilities that includes rural areas farther away from existing urban centers?
Much of what are today poor peripheries were settled in the Qing dynasty
and the political economy of that era created the material possibilities of
these regions. As I previously mentioned, the state today faces a far greater
challenge in transferring technologies to these areas than the Qing state confronted. How will social stratification change in these less-developed areas
as the state continues to promote a variety of development policies for the
so-called western region? In particular, how will urban-rural social relations
evolve across the country and how will we analyze these as basic features
of changing social stratification? Since standard models posit a shift from
rural to urban as basic to modern society, the persistence of a rural sector
that is itself modern can expand the framing of social stratification issues in
the developing world. The intense concern that policy makers are currently
spending on urban-rural relations suggests that China will not necessarily be
transformed into a largely urban society at any point in the near future (Qiu
2006; Fang 2007). At the same time our understanding of contemporary
Chinese social stratification and economic change promises to illuminate
more general issues, it will benefit from being anchored in an understanding of earlier forms of political economy and social stratification, especially
those regarding urban-rural relations across the spatial scale of the former
Qing empire. The chapters of this volume offer some useful signposts for
marking the paths of social change taking place in contemporary China.
The socialist upheavals of three decades have now been followed by three
more remarkable and very different decades of social change. What will we
be writing about Chinese society 30 years from now?

REFERENCE MATTER

## Chapter One

1. This estimate of China's GDP is from CIA (2007). A World Bank report in late 2007 stated that such a GDP was inflated for China and a downward adjustment was called for. Even after the adjustment, however, China still stands as the second largest economy in the world.

2. Its annual utilized foreign direct investment increased from 2.26 billion in 1983 to 73.5 billion USD in 2006 (National Bureau of Statistics 2007, 186).

3. Chinadaily.com.cn, August 9, 2007.

4. CIA reports in 2007 listed a Gini of 0.44 for China in 2002, 0.45 for the United States in 2002, 34.8 for Indonesia in 2004, and 32.5 for India in 2000.

5. http://money.cnn.com/magazines/fortune/fortune500/.

6. In 2005, of the 2.47 million new members, 30 percent were college students; only 20 percent farmers and 9 percent workers (Xinhua 2006a).

7. In the late 1970s when GDP per capita in PPP dollars was merely $674, industry already contributed 44 percent of GDP (Naughton 2007, 9).

8. Whereas the exact Gini estimates for any one year vary and do not fully capture the full value of household incomes, numerous surveys and case studies consistently document rising inequality within rural areas, within urban areas, and nationally between 1978 and 1995. See Chapter 2 by Gao and Riskin in this volume for full discussion)

9. Moreover, when poverty is defined by per capita consumption rather than the dollar-a-day income metric, and when the monetary definition of poverty is adjusted for the local cost of living, economists estimate that 25 percent not 9 percent of rural residents and that 12 percent not 1 percent of urban residents were living in poverty at the turn of the last century (Khan 2005).

10. Between 1995 and 1999, wealth increased by 166 percent among the top decile of the surveyed households, but only by 34 percent among those in the bottom decile. Between 1999 and 2002, wealth of those in the top grew by 346 percent, for those in the bottom 111 percent (Meng 2007).

11. In January 1979 the Ministry of Public Security announced that it would remove the "hats" of landlords, rich peasants, counter-revolutionaries, and bad elements and enforce an explicit policy of non-discrimination for their children.

## Chapter Two

1. According to the official CPI, in urban areas, 100 yuan in 2002 is equivalent to 39.7 yuan in 1988 and 90.4 yuan in 1995, whereas in rural areas, 100 yuan in 2002 is equivalent to 42.0 yuan in 1988 and 92.4 yuan in 1995 (National Bureau of Statistics 2004b, 88).

2. The values of health benefits were not directly asked in the 1988 urban survey and thus are imputed using administrative data on provincial per capita public expenditure on employee health care. The administrative data differentiate public health expenditures on employees and retirees, respectively, by three types of employers—state (including public institutions), collective, and other enterprises. Provincial per capita health expenditures on current or retired employees are obtained by dividing provincial total health spending by number of employees or retirees according to employer type. The administrative data are then imputed to individuals according to their employment status and type. Data from National Bureau of Statistics and Ministry of Labor 1989; China Labour Yearbook Editorial Office 1991.

3. The formula is: $\Sigma q_i C_i = G$

    where $q_i$ = the share of income source i in total income

        $C_i$ = the concentration ratio of income source i, and

        $G$ = the Gini ratio for total income

4. These percentages add up to more than 100 because taxes, a negative item, are included in income.

5. Incomes from farm and nonfarm activities in 1988 cannot be differentiated, because the 1988 survey question lumped together the production inputs for the two types of activities.

6. It should be kept in mind that all the figures in this paragraph are per capita averages over the entire rural sample, not average amounts received by beneficiaries, which would of course be larger.

## Chapter Three

1. With gender equality as one of the political goals of the prereform Chinese Communist Party, the socialist state promoted an ideology of gender equality and also pursued policies toward this goal (for example, forbidding prostitution, allowing freedom in mate choice, and guaranteeing equal inheritance between men and women) (Croll 1983). The state also pursued universal employment for both men and women and a policy of "equal work, equal pay." As a result, women's labor-force participation in China was among the highest and wage gaps among the smallest in the world. Clearly, however, gender equality was not achieved, as many critics have demonstrated (e.g., Andors 1983; Honig and Hershatter 1988; Stacey 1983; Whyte and Parish 1984), and women remained disadvantaged in the areas of educational and occupational attainment (Bauer et al. 1992; Bian et al. 2000; Entwisle and Henderson 2000).

2. Migrant laborers of rural origin, who represent an increasing share of China's urban population but do not possess an urban household registration status, are not included.

3. The numbers in Figure 3.1 are obtained by using Ordinary Least Squared regression analyses with the natural log of yearly income as the dependent variable and the following as control variables: length of employment (both linear and squared terms), educational attainment, occupation, industry, ownership type of the work organization, and city of employment. The exponential of the regression

coefficient for being a female is then the percentage of income difference compared with males, adjusted or controlling for other factors included in the equation.

4. The magnitude in gender income difference prior to the mid-1990s from these data agrees in general with that revealed in other studies of urban Chinese employees (Bian and Logan 1996; Bian, Logan, and Shu 2000; Shu and Bian 2003; Zhou 2000b). This is in particular the case with the results based on a retrospective study by Zhou, conducted in 1994. For the period of 1978 to 1993, female employees' wages in Zhou's study were 14 to 19 percent lower than those for males.

5. The 10 percent difference in income estimated from the urban employee sample of the three provinces corresponds to Bian, Logan, and Shu's result for the city of Tianjin in 1993 (2000:127), but is substantially smaller than the differences reported for samples from other surveys, such as Zhou (2000b:1158). This could be due to differences in samples as well as different controls. For instance, the categories of education and occupations could vary; furthermore, the analysis here includes industry as a control variable.

6. The description that follows is based on the years 1992 to 2000, for which we have consistent detailed data. Detailed tables are available from the authors.

7. We note that our measure of FDI is only for the previous year, which may not be ideal, as presumably the effect of foreign investment is cumulative, with capital flows from earlier years contributing to the nature of local development. We also constructed a market employment variable, as used by Shu and Bian (2003:1116): the share of nonstate and collective workers in each city. This variable did not produce significant results and did not add to the explanatory power of the models. We then combined it with logged FDI per capita, with which it is correlated ($r = .36$, $p < .05$), to make a marketization index with two of the three variables used by Shu and Bian (2003). This variable (made from the average of the two variables' $z$-scores) also was not significant and did not add to the power of the models. Therefore, we left GDP and FDI in the models and dropped the marketization variable.

8. In addition, HLM calculates level-1 random effects with empirical Bayes estimators, which adjust less reliable estimates (e.g., those from smaller cities) in the direction of the overall effects. Formally, the models take the following form. The level-1 (worker-level) equation is:

$$Y_{ij} = \beta_{0j} + \beta_{1j}(\text{Female})_{ij} + E\beta_{jk}X_{ijk} + r_{ij}$$

where $Y_{ij}$ is the natural log of income for worker $i$ in city $j$; $\beta_{0j}$ is the level-1 intercept (men's income); $\beta_{1j}$ is the effect of being female on income; $\beta_{jk}X$ are the slopes for $k$ control variables $X$ (centered at their grand means); and $r_{ij}$ is the level-1 error term (assumed to be normally distributed with zero mean and constant variance, $\sigma_2$). With the level-1 control variables centered, the intercept is the predicted income for a male worker with average characteristics, and the effect of gender is predicted for a woman with the same characteristics. These two coefficients become dependent variables at the second level of the model, estimated simultaneously.

The complete city-level model is:

$$\beta_{0j} = \gamma_{00} + \gamma_{01}(\text{GDP}_j) + \gamma_{02}(\text{FDI}_j) + \gamma_{03}(\text{GDP growth}_j) + \gamma_{04}(\text{Pop}_j) + U_{0j}$$
$$\beta_{1j} = \gamma_{10} + \gamma_{11}(\text{GDP}_j) + \gamma_{12}(\text{FDI}_j) + \gamma_{13}(\text{GDP growth}_j) + \gamma_{14}(\text{Pop}_j) + U_{1j}$$
$$\beta_{jk} = \gamma_k$$

where $\gamma_{00}$ is the intercept for the city-level model of income; $\gamma_{01}$ is the effect of gross domestic product per capita on average income; $\gamma_{02}$ is the effect of logged foreign direct investment per capita on average income. Both of these variables are measured for 1998 and expressed as natural logs in the models. Next, $\gamma_{03}$ is the effect on the intercept of the proportion change in the size of GDP from 1992 to 1998, intended to capture recent economic growth; and $\gamma_{04}$ is the effect of the natural log of population size. The coefficients $\gamma_{11}$ through $\gamma_{14}$ are the effects of these city-level variables on the gender gap in income, in other words cross-level interactions. These coefficients allow us to test how these city variables are associated with gender inequality net of individual characteristics. Finally, the U terms are the city-level error terms, assumed to be normally distributed with mean 0 and constant variance $\tau_0$. The individual-level variables in the HLM analysis are as used in the OLS regressions above. HLM results are presented in Table 3.4, which shows a series of models that include the gender effect, with or without other individual controls and city variables. These permit analysis of the coefficients and variance components as variables are added to the model.

9. The HLM software computes chi$^2$- and $p$-values for the variance components, which are less than .001 in this model.

10. Shenzhen, another special economic zone, is clearly an outlier with regard to both GDP per capita and the gender gap (80 percent). After examination of the population data, we decided to drop Shenzhen from the analysis because, without a reliable population estimate we could not calculate reliable per capita GDP.

11. Although we do not see a decrease in women's share of the labor force, our data do not permit more nuanced analysis of hours worked or time taken off from careers with effects on income over the life course.

## Chapter Four

1. In 1999 the service sector created 5.71 million new jobs, representing almost 70 percent of new urban employment (Luo 2001:20). In the city selected for this study, Beijing, the tertiary sector employs 64 percent of the population and accounts for almost 60 percent of GDP (China Labor Statistics Yearbook 2001:53, 487).

2. I gained access to the hotel by offering my unremunerated services as an English teacher, living outside the hotel in a small apartment. Beginning in October 1999, I interviewed a variety of employees including waitresses, bellmen, security staff, housekeepers, hostesses, doormen, butlers, and custodial workers as well as middle and executive managers. I also shadowed the work of employees, attended multiple training meetings, and participated in activities including a family planning seminar, a Chinese New Year Party, a single's party, birthday parties and other outings. In addition, I observed 19 managerial evaluations of staff members.

3. This is a pseudonym, as are all names used in this paper.

4. This alternative reckoning of ability and worth is reminiscent of the "lads" of Willis's (1982) study of working-class boys in England, who distinguished themselves from the more bookish (middle-class) types by extensive socializing.

5. Front desk receptionists, who are college-educated and enjoyed more mobility opportunities than other workers, are not included in this analysis.

6. The family-planning policy focused on female workers. Female managers were assigned to implement the policy so that they could comfortably speak to female workers about birth control. In other words, it was part of their job to

control women's reproductive activity. Male managers might have talked to male workers about their sex lives in passing, but they were not required to do so.

7. While contract workers are referred to as staff (*renyuan*) or associates, which connotes a partner-like relationship, the temp workers are referred to as "*dagognzhe*," laborers, denoting work in exchange for cash.

## Chapter Five

1. "Bit-based" growth is a term derived from Nicholas Negroponte's (1996) famous distinction between economic value generated by manipulating "atoms" (i.e., the physical transformation of tangible goods) and value generated by the manipulation of "bits" (i.e., information). The idea of "bit-based" growth implies both that the most valuable production inputs in a modern economy are knowledge and ideas and that an increasing share of the value of the goods consumed are accounted for by their intangible characteristics—images, ideas, and cultural attributes like brand names.

2. Morris and Western (1999) find that among OECD countries, service wages are highly unequal. Tilly et al. (1986) and Bernard and Jensen (1998) have also shown that the increased reliance on services that follows from "deindustrialization" increases income inequality in other contexts.

3. For data on the United States 1870–1970, see Tables D1-10, D11-25, & D127-141 in *Historical Statistics for the United States, Colonial Times through 1970* (U.S. Department of Commerce, 1975).

4. It is possible that the apparent decline in Korean manufacturing employment is simply a function of the 1997–1998 East Asian financial crisis, but since even the Great Depression produced only a flattening of the growth of manufacturing employment, not a decline, this hypothesis must be treated with some skepticism.

5. Data on the evolution of Brazil's employment structure are available from the ILO Yearbook of Labor Statistics (1960–2005).

6. See Holz (2004) for a discussion of problems with official Chinese statistical data. We are particularly grateful to Holz for his willingness to review these data problems with us, but would underline that he is in no way implicated in either our sectoral estimates or the interpretations of them that we offer here.

7. Eileen Otis's analysis (this volume) suggests further that service sector employment may be more corrosive of solidarity among workers because it magnifies divisions based on gender.

## Chapter Six

This chapter is an adaptation of "Dangqian zhongguo shehui jieceng fenhua de zhidujichu" (the institutional foundations of social stratification in contemporary China), published in *Shehuixue yanjiu* (Sociological Research) No. 5, 2005.

1. Since a nationwide free market did not exist at the time, it is difficult for us to estimate the size of the rent arising from administrative pricing. However, if we take the price indices from local marketplaces to represent market prices, we get that, for the period from the late 1950s when planned economy was established to the eve before the reform, the commodity prices listed by the state were only equivalent to about 40 to 60 percent of market prices (Lin et al. 2002: 43). We can therefore imagine how sizable the state rent had been.

2. It may also be seen as great monopolization of the market, for the state monopolistically possesses almost all the means of production.

3. In the socialist public economy, rent-seeking ability refers to the power elites' ability to use state power to seek personal gains or prevent the profit maximization of others. The greater the rent-seeking ability, the more opportunities for acquiring rent. According to the estimates of some Chinese economists, from the late 1980s to the early 1990s, rent arising from price differentials due to the Chinese economy's "dual-track" system exceeded 600 billion *yuan*, comprising more than 16 percent of GDP (Hu 2001). Of people's income differences, 13 to 23 percent was due to illegal income, but the major part was income from rent (Chen and Zhou 2001).

4. The research on human capital's contribution to income by Walder (1995a), Xie and Hannum (1996), Bian and Logan (1996), Zhou (2000b), Zhao and Zhou (2002), Wu and Xie (2003) all attest to this.

5. The market capacity that Weber and neo-Weberians refer to is based on private ownership. In my opinion, basing the concept of market capacity on property rights that can be separately possessed or used can better explain the stratification mechanisms of socialist market economies with a substantial public economy component. Market capacity can be defined as people's ability to exchange their property rights, which is what Weber calls the possibility of becoming a commodity of exchange (Weber 1978). Such a concept of market capacity is suitable for analyzing the separate use of bundles of property rights under both private and public ownership.

6. Many scholars (e.g., Walder 1992, 1995b; Bian and Logan 1996; Li and Wang 1999) have considered institutional factors' influence on China's stratification through studies of institutions such as the work unit (*danwei*) system, the household registration system, and the personnel system, which are derivatives of basic state institutions. My difference from them is that I have explored in depth the institutional basis of these derivatives. The *danwei* system is simply the logical consequence of the basic institutions and the household registration system and personnel system that can be seen as the state's restraints on property rights over human capital. Using basic institutional arrangements to analyze stratification mechanisms not only simplifies the analytical dimensions, but also helps us come to new theoretical insights about the essence of stratification in socialist states and the interest relationship between the various strata. It is, however, a topic worthy of further research to explore the relationship between basic institutional arrangements and the derivatives and to clarify the mechanisms through which the derivatives influence stratification.

7. The ten strata that form my mapping of social stratification in contemporary China differ significantly from the stratification map summarized in the study by the research group based in Chinese Academy of Social Sciences (Lu 2002: 9). In contrast to their mapping, which aggregates occupations into ten strata according to individuals' possession of organizational, economic, and cultural resources and their industrial sectors, my profile does not follow such an order. Rather, the position of each social stratum is based on its public power and market capacity, the two sources of stratification elaborated in this chapter.

## Chapter Seven

The research reported in this study is supported by a fund from Hong Kong University of Science & Technology (HIA 03/04.BM01), and CEAS and Hewlett faculty research funds at Stanford University. In the research process, I benefited from discussions with He Cai, Yuan Shen, Shukai Zhao, and Xiaoye Zhe. An earlier version of this paper was presented at the workshop on "Creating Wealth and Property in Contemporary China" at Yale University, January 6–8, 2006. I thank the participants at the workshop, especially Deborah Davis, C. K. Lee, John Logan, Wang Feng, and Marty Whyte for their comments. Please direct communication to xgzhou@stanford.edu.

1. All names of villages and persons in this article are altered to protect their anonymity.

2. 1 *mu* ≈ 0.165 acre.

3. There are also numerous media reports of abuse and unfair implementation in other regions. Clearly, there are significant regional variations in the implementation process.

## Chapter Eight

1. PRC Provisional Regulations on the Conversion and Transfer of Urban Land Use. These regulations stipulate that the departments in charge of land conversion can collect 2 percent to 5 percent of land conversion income as a land conversion business fee. Upon collection of the business fee, the local government retains 20 percent as the urban land development construction fee; from the remaining portion, 40 percent is submitted to the central government, and 60 percent is retained at the local government level. At both levels of government, the revenue generated by this fee is used solely for land development and construction of urban infrastructure (http://www.lawyee.net/Act/Act_Display.asp? ChannelID=1010100& ItemID=0&RID=28216).

2. 1.05 billion RMB in 1990 and 1.13 billion RMB in 1991 (China Economic Times/zhongguo jingji shibao), Mar. 19, 2004).

3. Relevant national laws stipulate that land seizure must be approved by the People's Government at the provincial level and higher. They also stipulate that State Council approval is necessary for seizure of capital farmland and arable land not categorized as capital farmland that exceeds 35 hectares, or other types of seized land exceeding 70 hectares. (Land Administration Law of the People's Republic of China).

4. "Yunnan Daily," June 25, 2004. Please refer to http://news.sina.com. cn/c/2004-06-25/12212906924s.shtml.

5. If we add together the four types of land revenue (direct taxes, indirect taxes, fees and the net profit on land conversion income), we can see the full scope of government land revenues. According to our rough estimates, this number reached 1.4 billion RMB in S County, one of the three study areas, in 2003. This figure happens to equal S County's 2003 local government revenue. This number is calculated in accordance with the net profit of the land conversion income. If it were calculated in accordance with the total land conversion income, then the land revenue would reach 2.7 billion RMB, which is two times the size of the local government revenue. In the other two areas the number should be roughly the same. The above analysis of the four components of government land revenues gives us an initial estimate of the scope and scale of each of the four components. Of course, it must be said that these numbers are derived from a study on only three areas of Zhejiang province, and that the numbers in other parts of China may be very different.

6. The area of land converted to industrial use and commercial use grew rapidly, but the price of land converted for industrial use did not change much. By contrast, the price of land converted for commercial use reached over 1.82 million yuan per mu in 2002 and 2.39 million yuan per mu in 2004. Before 2003, the total conversion value was essentially the same for the two types of land use, but in 2003 the conversion value for commercial-use land reached 1.92 billion yuan, and in 2004 it reached 1.39 billion yuan, whereas the conversion price for industrial-use land totaled only 530 million in 2003. In sum, the conversion price for industrial-use land is usually about the same as the cost, whereas commercial land prices are much higher than the cost; thus, a portion of the land conversion income net profit from commercial-use land can be used to subsidize the cost of land seized for public use.

7. If the land of a village is seized in its entirety, then the character of this village naturally changes because the land now belongs to the state rather than the collective. This change is accompanied by a "village conversion to neighborhood committee (*juweihui*)"—that is, a village turns into a urban neighborhood (*cun gai ju*). If all of the land of a township is seized, then the township is changed into a residential street district. Our survey of the Keqiao Street District began when its status was changed from a township to a residential street district in 2001. From 1991 to the end of 2003, 12,812 mu of land was seized piece by piece, leaving only 80 mu of land from all 17 villages within this township. In 2001, Keqiao Town was changed into two urban districts: Keqiao Street District and Keyan Street District. The change from village to neighborhood district(s) usually goes through the following stages: the village performs assessment and quantification of its assets using the formula "total assets—resource assets—non-for-profit assets—assets retained for welfare." The remaining portion is distributed to individuals based on the population (60 percent), and on the number of years individuals have spent working in agriculture (40 percent). In this town, the best village net assets were valued at 40 to 50 million yuan, the poorest village had over 20 million yuan yuan in village net assets. When the villages are converted to neighborhoods, usually these assets become subscribed capital, ranging from 5,000 yuan per person to 26,000 yuan per person in stock shares, for an average of 14,000 yuan per person. So far, urbanization has caused farmers to lose their land, become urban residents, and become "stockholders" for the assets of the former village collective.

## Chapter Nine

1. According to statistics from the Ministry of Land and Resources, between 1987 to 2001, nonagricultural land use reached 33.946 million mu (5.56 million acres), of which 70 percent were "legally" requisitioned through administrative means. If we account for the proportion of illegal land requisition (20–30 percent), the actual land requisition in this 14-year period is estimated to be 40.80–44.20 million mu (6.69 to 7.24 million acres).

2. For the first six months of 2004, the Ministry of Construction received 4,026 petitions, of which 905 were from collectives representing 13,223 individuals and 3,121 were from family units representing 5,397 persons. This number exceeded the total for the entire year of 2003 (*Xin Jing Bao* 2004.07.05).

3. Source: Compiled from June 2002 CCTV series "SH's Problem."

4. Source: August 27, 1998 land transfer contract of a villager in X Village.

5. Source: Recording of July 2002 speech by a Legal Affairs Committee cadre in Q Town, Hebei Province.

*Chapter Ten*

1. The costs have been adjusted for inflation.

2. This is the literal translation of the Chinese term used in the DRCSC report by the *China Daily* in its reporting. Many news agencies, in China or internationally, put it as "the medical reform was basically a failure."

3. For example, the Xinhua News Agency featured an article on Sept 18, 2006 with a title "Male patient died in the hospital because he had no money." Similar stories have appeared in other media and draw heated discussion on social justice and inequality in China's health care system.

4. 1982 and 1990 provincial-level life expectancies are from Huang and Liu 1995; those for 2000 were calculated by the author from the published 2000 census data.

5. County-level units include counties, county-level cities, urban districts, and autonomous counties and banners. County-level infant mortality data for 1982 are from *China Historical County Population Census Data with GIS Maps* (NBS 2005), distributed by the University of Michigan China Data Center. County level infant mortality data are derived from *The Complete Collection of County/District Population Census Data Assembly*, electronic version (NBS 2003), distributed by University of Michigan China Data Center.

6. There were a total of 2,870 county-level administrative units at the time of the 2000 census. The base map has merged some urban districts together.

7. Latitude and longitude refer to GIS-based county centroid, which is not necessarily a socioeconomic or population center of the county. The mean and standard deviation of elevation is created from the USGS Digital Elevation Model (DEM).

8. I use an implantation provided in S+ SpatialStats (Kaluzny et al. 1998) to fit four conditional spatial autoregressive models by sequentially adding covariates in blocks. Pseudo $R^2$ (Cox and Snell 1989), log likelihood, AIC, and BIC statistics are provided for model comparison.

9. It is important to understand why minorities in China have a lower life expectancy: Is it because of some unique characteristics in their cultures, such as attitude toward medical technology, or because most of them live in a particularly harsh environment, or because of differential social policies? Improving health conditions and promoting socioeconomic development for minorities and in minority-concentrated areas are critical for China to be able to build the "harmonious society" heralded by Chinese leaders.

10. Considerable variations in life expectancy across China remain after controlling for the 14 predicting variables. The analysis of residuals from regression models suggests that certain local clusters deviate significantly from the development-driven mortality pattern. These local clusters call for special studies. The areas where its life expectancy is above the model prediction could serve as model areas with lessons for developmental policy. Meanwhile, the areas where life expectancy is well below the model prediction should be investigated for specific epidemiological patterns and targeted for intervention.

11. *China Daily*, October 25, 2006.

*Chapter Eleven*

1. Reports on the timeline for eliminating tuition charges vary (see *People's Daily*, March 5, 2006 and CERNET 2005c).

2.  At this time, clauses in the law still remain to be approved by the State Council.

3.  These three minority autonomous counties were Subei Mongolian autonomous county, Akesai Kazak autonomous county, and Sunan Yugur autonomous county.

4.  Using a stratified, fixed interval, systematic sampling strategy, 2,000 children, aged 9–12 years old, were sampled from across rural Gansu, China. First, a systematic sample of 20 counties was selected from the total of 83 eligible counties in Gansu (see note 4). All counties in Gansu were listed in descending order according to the per capita income level in each county. Beginning from a randomly selected county, every fourth county was selected into the county sample pool. Next, a random start, systematic sample of 42 townships was selected from a list of all of the townships, which were listed in geographic order, in each county in the sample. The number of townships selected from each county was determined by the rural population in each selected county. Then, a random start, systematic sampling strategy was used to sample 100 villages from the 42 townships in sample pool. Again, the total number of villages selected from each township was decided according to the rural population in each township. Finally, a random sample of 20 children was selected from a listing of all 9–12 year olds in each village in the sample.

5.  We found no evidence of an interaction between wealth and average educational costs.

6.  However, clearly, causal relationships run both ways between maternal aspirations and performance: Mothers hopes may be raised by promising students, and student performance and certainly aspirations are enhanced by high maternal expectations.

7.  It is important to note that the costs of postcompulsory education will continue to preclude many rural children from seeking upper-secondary and tertiary education.

## Chapter Twelve

The Chinese General Social Survey (CGSS) project was a collaboration between Hong Kong University of Science and Technology and Renmin University of China. Both institutions provided funds along with a grant from Hong Kong SAR's Research Grants Committee (CA03/04.HSS01) to finance the project. I'm grateful to Li Lulu for collaboration on the CGSS project, to Deborah Davis, Bonnie Erickson, John Logan, and Wang Feng for helpful comments on earlier drafts, and to Li Yu and Zhang Lijuan for research assistance.

1.  To test the possibilities that search channels might have had differential impacts on individuals of varying characteristics for rates of upward and downward mobility, terms of interaction between search channels and individual attributes were included in an initial analysis. However, none of these interactions was significant and all were removed from the final models reported in Table 12.5.

## Chapter Thirteen

1.  Official statistics reported by China's Ministry of Public Security claim that the number of "mass incidents" nationally increased from 8,700 in 1993 to 87,000 in 2005 (Tanner 2006; Chung, Lai, and Xia 2006).

2.  Our China Inequality and Distributive Justice survey project resulted in completed interviews with a representative sample of 3,267 Chinese adults between

the ages of 18 and 70 who were selected through spatial probability sampling methods based on de facto residence, rather than on the basis of their household registrations (see Landry and Shen 2005). Because our survey included an over-sampling of urban residents, sampling weights are used where appropriate in the analyses that follow to compute figures representative of all Chinese adults. The sample included cases in 23 of China's 31 provincial units—all except Jilin, Inner Mongolia, Tianjin, Sichuan, Chongqing, Tibet, Qinghai, and Gansu. Martin Whyte serves as Principal Investigator (PI) for the project, which also involves Albert Park (formerly at the University of Michigan, now at Oxford University), Wang Feng at the University of California-Irvine, Jieming Chen at Texas A&M University-Kingsville, Pierre Landry at Yale University, and Shen Mingming at Peking University, with Chunping Han joining the project as a research assistant in 2003. Primary funding for the survey came from a grant to the PI from the Smith Richardson Foundation, with supplementary funding provided by Harvard's Weatherhead Center for International Affairs, the University of California at Irvine, and Peking University.

3. The comparisons reported in these earlier papers were made possible by the fact that we replicated many questions from the International Social Justice Project (hereafter ISJP), which was designed to explore popular perceptions and attitudes toward inequality issues in other countries, particularly in Eastern Europe. The ISJP researchers carried out two rounds of comparative surveys in several East European transitional societies, in 1991 and in 1996 (Kluegel, Mason, and Wegener 1995; Mason and Kluegel 2000). No comparative data will be presented in this chapter.

4. The items were reversed in creating the scale, so that a high score indicates that respondents felt that the traits listed had a very important influence on whether people were rich or poor. The resulting scale is then estimated by a score of the common factor the constituent items share, a procedure also used in creating our other distributive injustice scales. (Factors scores were used in preference to a simple mean of each item because they allow items that are closer to the common factor to influence the final scale score more than items that are not quite as close to the common factor they all share.) We attempted to create a second scale from this set of items to tap views on the importance of individual merit explanations for why some people are rich while others are poor—factors such as hard work, ability, and education. However, the resulting scale, while internally consistent, did not have external validity, in the sense of consistent and interpretable associations with other measures used in our study, so we dropped this scale from our analysis. (However, the pattern of responses to several of these "merit attribution of inequality" questions is displayed later, in Table 13.1, panel 2.)

5. This logic is explicitly stated in a *New York Times* report from China (Kahn 2006): "Because many people believe that wealth flows from access to power more than it does from talent or risk-taking, the wealth gap has incited outrage and is viewed as at least partly responsible for tens of thousands of mass protests around the country in recent years."

6. Note that none of these three questions specifically refers to distributive injustice. However, we presume that the focus in our questionnaire generally on inequality and distributive justice issues would predispose most respondents to answer these questions with distributive issues in mind.

7. Note that the pattern of correlations among our four attitude scales for the most part supports the idea that these distributive injustice attitudes are organized

in the fashion described in the text, the only exception being the essentially zero correlation between Lack of Opportunity and Government Leveling:

*Correlations among the four distributive injustice attitude measures*

|  | Unfair inequality | Lack of opportunity | Government leveling | Feelings of injustice |
|---|---|---|---|---|
| Unfair inequality | 1 |  |  |  |
| Lack of opportunity | .142* | 1 |  |  |
| Government leveling | .292* | −.001 | 1 |  |
| Feelings of injustice | .327* | .150* | .247* | 1 |

*$p \leq .001$

8. For statistical purposes in Table 13.2, females are coded as 1 and males as 0; age is simply years, but we also include age-squared to detect any curvilinear associations with age; educational attainment is classified in seven levels ranging from 0 = less than primary to 6 = MA or higher and treated as a continuous variable; married individuals are coded as 1 and all others as 0; members of the dominant Han Chinese ethnic group are coded as 1 and all others as 0; household income is entered as the logarithm of income; and both Chinese Communist Party membership and experience of working in a state-owned enterprise are coded as 1 = yes and 0 = no. It should be noted, however, that our most complete family income data come from a categorical measure involving 26 income categories, rather than from our open-ended questions about total family income. For the purpose of analysis we use the midpoint of each income range (e.g., 55,000 for the 50,000–59,999 yuan per year category) of this categorical measure and compute the log of this number and treat the resulting values as a continuous variable.

9. In our survey, we asked respondents whether they or members of their families had had the following negative experiences over the past three years: being seriously ill, suffering physical injury or economic loss due to natural or artificial disasters, being laid-off or becoming unemployed, having difficulty paying for medical care, dropping out of school because of inability to pay the tuition, having to borrow money to cover basic expenses, and being treated unfairly by local officials. For each item, we assigned 1 to those who replied they had had that experience and 0 otherwise. Then we created a scale of negative experiences by summing the values for those seven items. The higher the value of the scale, the more bad experiences a respondent's family had suffered recently.

10. Reponses to each question ranged from 1 = much worse to 5 = much better, and we computed the mean of these four questions to construct the relative social status scale.

11. Prefectural cities are cities intermediate in the administrative hierarchy between counties and the provincial capital. This measure has eight categories ranging from 0 = resides in prefectural or higher-level city to 7 = 200 km or more distant from the nearest such city and is treated as a continuous variable.

12. Fan and Wang utilize 23 separate indicators of degree of marketization of each province, with each measure ranging from 0 to 10, and then the summary marketization scale is simply the mean of the 23 separate indicators. The marketization measure is based upon 2002 economic statistics, two years prior to our survey, since this was the most recent set of figures available.

13. In the United States and other mature capitalist societies, large portions of the population also voice support for government efforts to provide jobs and mini-

mum income guarantees to the poor, although less support for government efforts to reduce overall income gaps (see Kluegel and Smith 1986).

14. The strong positive coefficients for the associations with age, and strong negative coefficients with age-squared, indicate that these injustice sentiments tend to rise with increasing age, but then decline again among the oldest individuals in our sample, thus following roughly a parabolic curve. The apparent zero coefficients for the age-squared regression coefficients for Unfair Inequality and Feelings of Injustice are somewhat misleading. Since unstandardized regression coefficients tell us how much change occurs in the injustice measure in question for each unit change in the predictor, these zero coefficients simply tell us that one more year in age squared (e.g., for a 50 year old, from 2,500 to 2,501) is associated with only a tiny change in the injustice measure in question. However, differences between the injustice scores of groups spanning large age ranges—the young, the middle-aged, and the old—are nonetheless substantial and statistically significant.

15. Women differ from men only in expressing weaker support for government redistribution and being slightly less likely to have Feelings of Injustice. Those who are married differ from those in other marital statuses mainly in being less likely to perceive current inequalities as unfair (in column 2), but curiously they also express stronger Feelings of Injustice (in column 8) and slightly more support for Government Leveling (in column 6). Finally, at the bivariate level, those who work or have worked in state-owned enterprises appear to have stronger negative attitudes on three out of four injustice measures, but once other predictors are controlled for, the only association that remains statistically significant is a net tendency of those affiliated with SOEs to be more pessimistic about getting ahead (see column 4).

16. One puzzle about these findings is that a substantial amount of research on rural governance in China indicates that many villagers feel and express a great deal of anger and discontent in regard to local (township in particular) officials. Insofar as this is the case, one would expect that respondents in our survey living in distant rural locales would strongly agree with one of the statements used in constructing our Feelings of Injustice scale: "Government officials don't care what ordinary people like me think." However, past research also indicates that rural people have much greater trust in higher level officials, and particularly in the central government, as a possible source of relief from oppression by local officials (see, for example, Li 2004). If that is the case, then our findings may indicate that our use in this question of the phrase "government officials" may be taken by respondents to refer to officials above the level of the local cadres that many villagers actively despise.

17. The Tucker-Lewis Index and RMSEA statistic are two other measures (besides R-squared) of how good a fit to the data the multivariate statistical model is. Generally to be judged a good statistical model the Tucker-Lewis Index should be above .95 and the RMSEA statistic should be under .06. By these standards all four of our regression models in Table 13.2 are a fairly good fit to the underlying data on injustice attitudes.

18. During the 1990s, the growing burden of taxes and fees provoked discontent and protests in many parts of rural China (see Bernstein and Lu 2003). After many years of temporizing and of repeated unsuccessful attempts to limit rural taxes and fees, China's leadership instituted tax reforms and other measures early in the new millennium that appear to have been successful in lightening the

rural "burden problem." In response to a question included in our survey, 70.3 percent of rural respondents said that the taxes and fees paid by their families had decreased compared to three years earlier (i.e., 2001), 14.2 percent said they had remained about the same, and only 15.2 percent said their taxes and fees had increased.

19. Converting the "5 year standard of living trend" measure used in Table 13.2 into proportional terms, nearly ⅔ of survey respondents said that their families were "somewhat better" or "much better" off now than they were five years earlier.

## Chapter Fourteen

Funding for this stage of the research has been provided by the e-Institute at Shanghai University. I thank Xia Xue at Tsinghua University for her research assistance, and Deborah Davis and Wang Feng for their comments.

1. The Gini coefficient for China as whole in 2004 was 0.53, compared to 0.4 in the United States, 0.46 in Costa Rica, and 0.57 in Chile (Khan and Riskin 2001, p. 49, 2005).

2. For instance, the Ministry of Labor and Social Security warned that China's growing income gap is likely to trigger social instability after 2010 if the government finds no effective solution to end the disparity. See "Warning of Unrest Over Income Gap," *South China Morning Post*, August 23, 2005. A newly released report by the Chinese Academy of Social Science states that "The rich-poor disparity has led to the intensification of social disputes, mass protests, and criminal cases," Josephine Ma, "Wealth Gap Fueling Instability, Study Warns," *South China Morning Post*, December 22, 2005.

3. Nationwide, the Ministry of Public Security recorded 8,700 collective disturbances in 1993, rising to 11,000 and 32,000 in 1995 and 1999 respectively. In 2003, three million people were involved in 58,000 incidents (Pei 2003; French 2005).

4. For an elaboration of a similar concept of "economic justice," see Daniel Little (2003, Chapter Four).

5. A People's University survey conducted in 2003 also reported that "officials versus ordinary citizens" was the most salient category (41.5 percent) that people used to think about the haves and have-nots and their conflictual relationships. It was even more popular than the category "the rich and the poor" (32.8 percent). (Feng 2005).

6. It has been argued that Chinese conception of "rights" is different from the Anglo-American notion derived from Locke and Mill in that Chinese perceive rights as flowing from state decrees rather than as entitlements by virtue of their being as ends in themselves (e.g., Diamant, Lubman, and O'Brien 2005). While I did find that respondents referred to the law as the basis of their rights, and that they saw limits of their rights as defined by the law, they also articulated comments about the fundamental rights of being treated equally as human beings when they talked about educational opportunities and the injustice of differentiating people into rural and urban residents. This important issue will be taken up in later interviews.

7. This sense of futility is not unique to China. In his surveys of eight post-Communist countries with varying degrees of democratization in the early 1990s, David Mason (1995) found that more than a third think it was futile to argue

about social justice because things will not change. He interpreted that as a reflection of people's distrust and disaffection in post-Communist states.

## Chapter Fifteen

1. Crop and craft production for the market was basic to the livelihoods of rural households in China's most economically advanced areas in which eighteenth-century-standards of living appear broadly comparable to those in England. The relative paucity of data has allowed considerable debate on this point. I made some basic assertions about the similarities of expansion and standards of living in Wong 1997, pp. 22–31; Kenneth Pomeranz subsequently led the way in establishing the comparable levels of agricultural productivity and standards of living in Pomeranz 2001. For some of the debate and discussion this work has generated, see the contributions to the *Journal of Asian Studies* 61.2 (May 2002): 501–662 and to *Itinerario* 3/4 (2000), pp. 7–134. My comment on the debate is published on the Association for Asian Studies website at http://www.aasianst.org/catalog/wong.pdf.

2. For overviews of China, see Rowe 2003; for Japan, Wakita 1991: 121–125; for Europe, Doyle 1992.

REFERENCES

Adams, Jennifer, and Emily Hannum. 2005. Children's Social Welfare in China, 1989–1997: Access to Health Insurance and Education. *The China Quarterly* 181:100–121.

An, Xyehui, Hannum, E. and Sargent T. 2007. Teacher Qualifications, Teaching Quality and Student Educational Outcomes. *China: An International Journal* 5(2):309–334.

Andors, Phyllis. 1983. *The Unfinished Liberation of Chinese Women, 1949–1980*. Bloomington, IN: Indiana University Press.

Arts, Wil, and Romke van der Veen. 1992. Sociological Approaches to Distributive and Procedural Justice. In *Justice: Interdisciplinary Perspectives*, ed. K. Scherer. Cambridge: Cambridge University Press.

Aston, T. H., and C. H. E. Philpin, eds. 1985. *The Brenner Debate: Agrarian Class Structure and Economic Development in Pre-industrial Europe*. Cambridge: Cambridge University Press.

Atkinson, Anthony B. (2003). "Income Inequality in OECD Countries: Data and Explanations" CESifo Working Paper Series No. 881. Available at Social Science Research Network (SSRN): http://ssrn.com/abstract=386761.

Banister, Judith. 1987. *China's Changing Population*. Stanford, CA: Stanford University Press.

Banister, Judith, and Kenneth Hill. 2004. Mortality in China 1964–2000. *Population Studies* 58(1):55–75.

Barry, Brian. 1989. *A Treatise on Social Justice* Vol. 1: *Theories of Justice*. Emel Hempstead: Harvester-Wheatsheaf.

Barzel, Yoram. 1989. *Economic Analysis of Property Right*. New York: Cambridge University Press.

Bauer, John, Wang Feng, Nancy Riley, and Zhao Xiaohua. 1992. Gender Inequality in Urban China: Education and Employment. *Modern China* 18:333–370.

Baum, Carol. 2003. So Who's Stealing China's Manufacturing Jobs? *Bloomberg News,* October 14.

Becker, Howard. 1963. *Outsiders: Studies in the Sociology of Deviance*. New York: Free Press.

265

Bernard, Andrew B., and J. Bradford Jensen. 1998. "Understanding Increasing and Decreasing Wage Inequality." National Bureau of Economic Research Working Paper 6571. Cambridge, MA.

Bernstein,Thomas, and Xiaobo Lü. 2003. *Taxation without Representation in Contemporary Rural China*. Cambridge: Cambridge University Press.

Bian, Yanjie. 1994. *Work and Inequality in Urban China*. Albany, NY: SUNY Press.

———. 1997. Bringing Strong Ties Back In: Indirect Ties, Network Bridges, and Job Searches in China. *American Sociological Review* 63:266–285.

———. 1999. Getting a Job through a Web of *Guanxi* in Urban China. In *Networks in the Global Village*, ed. Barry Wellman, 255–277. Boulder, CO: Westview.

———. 2002a. Chinese Social Stratification and Social Mobility. *Annual Review of Sociology* 28:91–116.

———. 2002b. Institutional Holes and Job Mobility Processes in the PRC: Guanxi Mechanisms in Emergent Labor Markets. In *Social Connections in China: Institutions, Culture, and the Changing Nature of Guanxi*, eds. Thomas Gold, Doug Guthrie, and David Wank, 117–136. New York: Cambridge University Press.

———. 2004. The Social-Network Space in the Domain of Occupational Mobility: A Hong Kong–China Comparison. *Hong Kong Journal of Sociology* 5:103–117.

Bian, Yanjie, and John W. Logan. 1996. Market Transition and the Persistence of Power: The Changing Stratification System in Urban China. *American Sociological Review* 61:739–758.

Bian, Yanjie, John Logan, and Xiaoling Shu. 2000. Wages and Job Inequalities in the Working Lives of Men and Women in Tianjin. In *Re-Drawing Boundaries: Work, Households, and Gender in China*, eds. Barbara Entwisle and Gail Henderson, 111–133. Berkeley, CA: University of California Press.

Bian, Yanjie, Xiaoling Shu, and John R. Logan. 2001. Communist Party Membership and Regime Dynamics in China. *Social Forces* 79:805–842.

Bian, Yanjie, and W. Zhang. 2001. Economic Regime, Social Networks, and Occupational Mobility. (Jingji tizhi, shehui wang luo, yu zhiye liudong). *Journal of Chinese Social Sciences* (*Zhongguo shehui kexue*) 128(2):70–89.

Bloom, David E. and David Canning. 2000. Public Health: The Health and Wealth of Nations. *Science* 287(5456):1207–1209.

Boisot, Max, and John Child. 1996. From Fiefs to Clans and Network Capitalism: Explaining China's Emerging Economic Order. *Administrative Science Quarterly* 41(4):600–628.

Bourdieu, Pierre, and Löic J. D. Wacquant. 1992. *An Invitation to Reflexive Sociology*. Chicago: Chicago University Press.

Brown, Philip H., and Albert Park. 2002. Education and Poverty in Rural China. *Economics of Education Review* 21(6):523–541.

Buchanan, James M. 1980. Rent Seeking and Profit Seeking. In *Toward a Theory of the Rent-Seeking Society*, eds. J. Buchanan, R. Tollison, and G. Tullock, 3–5. Texas: Texas A and M University Press.

Cai, Yong. 2005. "The National, Provincial, Prefectural and County Life Tables for China Based on the 2000 Census." *CSDE Working Paper 05-03*. Center for Studies in Demography and Ecology, University of Washington. http://csde .washington.edu/downloads/05-03.pdf.

Cai, Yongshun, 2004. Civil Resistance and Rule of Law: the Case of Home Owners' Rights Defense. Paper presented at the Conference on Grassroots Political Reform, Harvard University, October 30–31.

Caldwell, John C. 1986. Routes to Low Mortality in Poor Countries. *Population and Development Review* 12(2):171–220.

———. 1990. Cultural and Social Factors Influencing Mortality Levels in Developing Countries. *The Annals of the American Academy of Political and Social Science*, Vol. 510(1):44–59.

Campbell, Tom. 2001. *Justice*. New York: St. Martin's Press.

Carlson, Joseph. 2003. Manufacturing Payrolls Declining Globally: The Untold Story. October 20. http://www.axaonline.com/axa/ public_articles/ 10202003Maufacturing_Payrolls_Declining.html.

Central Committee of the Communist Party and State Council. 1999. *Zhonggong zhongyang guowuyuan guanyu shenhua jiaoyu gaige quanmian tuijin sushi jiaoyu de jueding* [Decisions of the Central Committee of the Communist Party of China and the State Council on Deepening Education Reform and Advancing Essential-Qualities-Oriented Education in an All-Round Way]. Beijing: People's Press.

Central Intelligence Agency (CIA). 2007. *The World Factbook*. https://www.cia .gov/cia/publications/factbook/index.html.

CERNET (China Education and Research Network). 2002. Ethnic Education Improving in Gansu. Retrieved July 7, 2006. http://www.edu.cn/ 20020107/3016576.shtml.

———. 2005a. China to Spend 218 Bln Yuan Promoting Rural Education. Retrieved July 7, 2006. http://www.edu.cn/20051227/3167788.shtml.

———. 2005b. Rich-Poor Education Gap to Be Addressed. Retrieved July 7, 2006. http://www.edu.cn/20051130/3163495.shtml.

Chan, Anita, Richard Madsen, and Jonathan Unger. 1992. *Chen Village under Mao and Deng*. Berkeley, CA: University of California Press.

Charles, Maria, and David Grusky. 2004. *Occupational Ghettos, the Worldwide Segregation of Women and Men*. Stanford, CA: Stanford University Press.

Chen Guikang and Chun Tao. 2004. *Zhongguo nongmin diaocha* (China Peasant Survey). Beijing: Zuojia Chubanshe.

Chen, Shaohua, and Martin Ravallion. 2004. *How Have the World's Poorest Fared Since the Early 1980s?* Washington, DC: The World Bank, available

online at http://www.worldbank.org/research/povmonitor/MartinPapers/How_
have_the_poorest_fared_since_the_early_1980s.pdf.

Chen, Zhongsheng, and Yunbo Zhou. 2001, "Feifa fei zhengchang shouru dui
jumin shouru chabie de yingxiang jiqi jingjixue jieshi" (The Role of Illegal and
Abnormal Income in Income Differentials and Its Economic Explanations).
*Jingji yanjiu* (Economic Research) No. 4.

Cheng, Kaiming. 1994. Education, Decentralization, and Regional Disparity in
China. In *Social Change and Educational Development: Mainland, China,
Taiwan, and Hong Kong*, eds. G. Postiglione and W. O. Lee, 53–56. Hong
Kong: Hong Kong Centre for Asian Studies, University of Hong Kong.

China Economic Times, March 19, 2005. (Newspaper, Beijing, China).

*China Labor Statistics Yearbook*. 2001. Beijing: China Statistics Press.

China Labor Yearbook Editorial Office. 1991. *China Labor Yearbook 1988–1989*.
Beijing: China Labor Press.

Chung, Jae Ho, Hongyi Lai, and Ming Xia. 2006. Mounting Challenges to Governance in China: Surveying Collective Protestors, Religious Sects, and Criminal
Organizations, *The China Journal*, 56:1–31.

Cleland, John G., and Jerome K. Van Ginneken. 1988. Maternal Education and
Child Survival in Developing Countries: The Search for Pathways of Influence.
*Social Science Medicine* 27(12):1357–1368.

Coale, Ansley. 1984. *Rapid Population Changes in China, 1952–1982*. Washington, DC: National Academy Press.

Cohen, Philip N., and Matt L. Huffman. 2003. Individuals, Jobs, and Labor
Markets: The Devaluation of Women's Work. *American Sociological Review*
68(3):443–463.

Connelly, Rachel, and Zhenzhen Zheng. 2003. Determinants of School Enrollment
and Completion of 10 to 18 Year Olds in China. *Economics of Education Review* 22(4):379–388.

Connelly, Rachel, and Zhenzhen Zheng. 2007. Educational Access for China's
Post-Cultural Revolution Generation: Patterns of School Enrollment in China
in 1990. In *Education and Reform in China*, eds. E. Hannum and A. Park,
64–80. London: Routledge.

Cox, David Roxbee, and Eleanor Snell. 1989. *The Analysis of Binary Data*, Second
Edition. London: Chapman and Hall.

Croll, Elisabeth J. 1983. *Chinese Women since Mao*. London: Armonk, NY: Zed
Books/M.E. Sharpe.

Davanzo, Julie, William Butz, and Jean-Pierre Habicht. 1983. How Biological and
Behavioural Influences on Mortality in Malaysia Vary during the First Years of
Life. *Population Studies* 37(3):381–402.

Davis, Deborah. 1990. Urban Job Mobility. In *Chinese Society on the Eve of Tiananmen*, eds. Deborah Davis and EzraVogel, 85–108. Cambridge, MA: Harvard University Press.

————. 1992. Job Mobility in Post-Mao Cities: Increases on the Margins. *The China Quarterly* 48:1062–1085.

————. 1995. Inequality and Stratification in the Nineties. In *China Review,* eds. L. C. Kin, S. Pepper, and T. K. Yuen, 11:1–11:25. Hong Kong: Chinese University of Hong Kong.

————. 2000. Social Class Transformation in Urban China: Training, Hiring, and Promoting Urban Professionals and Managers after 1949. *Modern China* 26:251–275.

————. 2003. From Welfare Benefit to Capitalized Asset. In *Chinese Urban Housing Reform*, eds. R. Forrest and J. Lee, 183–196. London: Routledge.

————. 2005. Urban Consumer Culture. *The China Quarterly* No. 183:677–694.

Davis, Deborah, Yanjie Bian, and Shaoguang Wang. 2005. Material Rewards to Multiple Capitals under Market Socialism. *Social Transformation in Chinese Societies* 1:31–58.

Davis, Deborah, Pierre Landry, Yusheng Peng, and Jin Xiao. 2007. Gendered Pathways to Rural Schooling, *The China Quarterly* No. 189:60–82.

Davis, Kingsley. 1956. "The Amazing Decline of Mortality in Underdeveloped Areas." *American Economic Review*, 46(2):305–318.

Davis-Friedmann, Deborah. 1985. Intergenerational Inequalities and the Chinese Revolution. *Modern China* 11:176–201.

de Brauw, Alan, Jikun Huang, Scott Rozelle, Linxiu Zhang, and Yigang Zhang. 2002. The Evolution of China's Rural Labor Markets during the Reforms. *Journal of Comparative Economics* 30(2):329–353.

de Brauw, Alan, and Scott Rozelle. 2007. Returns to Education in Rural China. In *Education and Reform in China,* eds. E. Hannum and A. Park, 207–223. London: Routledge.

Deane, Phyllis, and William Alan Cole. 1967. *British Economic Growth, 1688–1959: Trends and Structure.* London: Cambridge University Press.

Demsetz, Harold. 1967. Toward a Theory of Property Rights. *The American Economic Review* 57(2):347–359.

Development Research Center of the State Council (DRCSC). 2005. An Evaluation of and Recommendations on the Reforms of the Health System in China. *China Development Review* 7(supplement 1):1–158.

Diamant, Neil, Stanley Lubman, and Kevin O'Brien. 2005. Law and Society in the People's Republic of China. In *Engaging the Law in China: State, Society, and Possibilities for Justice,* eds. N. Diamant, S. Lubman, and K. O'Brien, 3–27. Stanford, CA: Stanford University Press.

Djilas, Milovan. 1957. *The New Class.* New York: Praeger.

Domański, Henryk. 2002. Is the East European Underclass Feminized? *Communist Post-Communist Studies* 35:383–394.

Dong Fureng. 1999. *Zhonghua renmin gongheguo jingjishi* (An Economic History of the People's Republic of China) (vol. 1 & 2). Beijing: Jingji Kexue Chubanshe.

Doyle, William. 1992. *The Old European Order 1660–1880*. Oxford: Oxford University Press.

Durkheim, Emile. 1984. *The Division of Labor in Society*. New York: Free Press.

Economist. 2006. How the Other 800m Live. *The Economist*, March 22:12.

Eichen, Marc, and Zhang Ming. 1993. Annex: The 1988 Household Sample Survey—Data Description and Availability. In *The Distribution of Income in China*, eds. Keith Griffin and Zhao Renwei. New York: St. Martin's Press.

England, Paula.1992. *Comparable Worth: Theories and Evidence*. New York: Aldine de Gruyter.

Entwisle, Barbara, and Gail E. Henderson, eds. 2000. *Re-Drawing Boundaries: Work, Households, and Gender in China*. Berkeley, CA: University of California Press.

Erickson, Bonnie H. 2001. Good Networks and Good Jobs: The Value of Social Capital to Employers and Employees. In *Social Capital: Theory and Research*, eds. N. Lin, K. Cook, and R. Burt, 127–158. New York: Aldine de Gruyter.

Evans, Peter B. 1989. Predatory, Developmental and Other Apparatuses: A Comparative Political Economy Perspective on the Third World State. *Sociological Forum* 4(4):561–587.

———.1995. *Embedded Autonomy: States and Industrial Transformation*. Princeton, NJ: Princeton University Press.

Fan Gang and Xiaolu Wang. 2004. *Zhongguo shichanghua zhishu—Gediqu shichanghua xiangdui jincheng 2004 niandu baogao* (Marketization Indexes for China: Report on Relative Progress toward Marketization in Various Localities in 2004). Beijing: Economic Science Press.

Fang Chuanglin. 2007. *Quyu guihua yu kongjian guanzhilun* (Regional Planning and the Management of Space). Beijing: Shangwu Yinshuguan.

Fei, John C. H., Gustav Ranis, and Shirley W. Y. Kuo. 1979. *Growth with Equity: The Taiwan Case*. New York: Oxford University Press.

Feng, Shezheng. 2005. "Urban Residents" Status Consciousness and Social Identification. In *Research Reports on China Social Development, 2005*. Beijing: Zhongguo Renmin Daxue Chubanshe.

Fernández, Roberto M., and Emilio J. Castilla. 2001. How Much Is That Network Worth? Social Capital in Employee Referral Networks. In *Social Capital: Theory and Research*, eds. N. Lin, K. Cook, and R. Burt, 85–104. New York: Aldine de Gruyter.

French, Howard. 2005. Land of 74,000 Protests (But Little Is Ever Fixed). *New York Times*, August 24.

Friedman, Edward, Paul Pickowicz, and Mark Selden. 1991. *Chinese Village, Socialist State*. New Haven, CT: Yale University Press.

Friedman, Edward, Paul Pickowicz, and Mark Selden. 2005. *Revolution, Resistance and Reform in Village China*. New Haven, CT: Yale University Press.

Gao, Qin. 2006. The Social Benefit System in Urban China: Reforms and Trends from 1988 to 2002. *Journal of East Asian Studies* 6(1):31–67.

Gao, Qin. 2008. Social Benefits in Urban China: Determinants and Impact on Income Inequality in 1988 and 2002. In *Understanding Inequality and Poverty in China: Methods and Applications*, ed. G. Wan, 173–217. New York: Palgrave Macmillan.

Gerber, Theodore. 2002. Structural Change and Post-Socialist Stratification: Labor Market Transitions in Contemporary Russia. *American Sociological Review* 67, 629–659.

———. 2006. Getting Paid: Wage Arrears and Stratification in Russia. *American Journal of Sociology* 111:1816–1870.

Gerber, Theodore, and Michael Hout.1998. More Shock Than Therapy. *American Journal of Sociology* 104:1–50.

Ghosh, Jayati. 2003. Exporting Jobs or Watching Them Disappear? In *Work and Well-Being in the Age of Finance*, eds. J. Ghosh and C. P. Chandrasekhar, 99–119. New Delhi: Tulika.

Giddens, Anthony. 1973. *The Class Structure of the Advanced Society*. London: Hutchinson.

Glenn, Evelyn Nakano. 1999. The Social Construction and Institutionalization of Gender and Race: An Integrative Framework. In *Revisioning Gender*, eds. M. Marx Ferree, Judith Lorber, and Beth Hess, 3–35. Thousand Oaks, CA: Sage.

Goldman, Noreen. 1980. Far Eastern Patterns of Mortality. *Population Studies* 34(1):5–19.

Granovetter, Mark. 1973. The Strength of Weak Ties. *American Journal of Sociology* 78:1360–1380.

———. 1995. Afterword to *Getting a Job* (2nd ed.), 139–182. Chicago: University of Chicago Press.

Guthrie, Doug. 1998. The Declining Significance of *Guanxi* in China's Economic Transition. *The China Quarterly* 154:254–282.

———. 2002. Information Asymmetries and the Problem of Perception: The Significance of Structural Position in Accessing the Importance of *Guanxi* in China. In *Social Connections in China: Institutions, Culture, and the Changing Nature of Guanxi*, eds. T. Gold, D. Guthrie, and D. Wank, 37–56. New York: Cambridge University Press.

Haining, Robert. 1990. *Spatial Data Analysis in the Social and Environmental Sciences*. Cambridge: Cambridge University Press.

Hamilton, Gary. 2006. *Commerce and Capitalism in Chinese Societies*. Oxford: Routledge.

Hannum, Emily. 1999. Political Change and the Urban-Rural Gap in Basic Education in China, 1949–1990. *Comparative Education Review* 43(2):193–211.

———. 2003. Poverty and Basic Education in Rural China: Villages, Households, and Girls' and Boys' Enrollment. *Comparative Education Review* 47(2):141.

Hannum, Emily, and Jennifer Adams. 2007. Choices, Hopes, and Expectations: Does Gender Still Shape Access to Basic Education in Rural Northwest China? In *Social Exclusion, Gender and Education: Case Studies from the Developing World*, eds. M. Lewis and M. Lockheed. Washington DC: Brookings.

Hannum, Emily, and Jihong Liu. 2005. Adolescent Transitions to Adulthood in China. In *Studies on the Transition to Adulthood in Developing Countries*, eds. Jere Behrman, Cynthia Lloyd, Nellie Stromquist, and Barney Cohen. Washington, DC: National Academy of Science Press.

Hannum, Emily, and Albert Park. 2007. Academic Achievement and Engagement in Rural China. In *Education and Reform in China*, eds. E. Hannum and A. Park, 154–172. London: Routledge.

Hannum, Emily, Tanja Sargent, and Shengchao Yu. 2005. *Poverty, Family Health Problems and Children's Access to Schooling: Case Studies from China, India, and Indonesia*. Montreal: UNESCO Institute for Statistics.

Hannum, Emily, Meiyan Wang, and Jennifer Adams. 2008. Urban-Rural Disparities in Access to Primary and Secondary Education. Forthcoming in *One Country, Two Societies? Rural-Urban Inequality in Contemporary China*, ed. M. K. Whyte (accepted for publication, Harvard University Press).

Hawkins, J. N. 2000. Centralization, Decentralization, Recentralization: Educational Reform in China. *Journal of Educational Administration* 38:442–455.

He, Jiang, Dongfeng Gu, Xigui Wu, Kristi Reynolds, Xiufang Duan, Chonghua Yao, Jialiang Wang, Chung-Shiuan Chen, Jing Chen, Rachel P. Wildman, Michael J. Klag, and Paul K. Whelton. 2005. Major Causes of Death Among Men and Women in China. *The New England Journal of Medicine* 353(11):1124–1134.

Heyns, Barbara. 2005. Emerging Inequalities in Central and Eastern Europe. *Annual Review of Sociology* 31:163–197.

Holz, Carsten. 2004. China's Statistical System in Transition: Challenges, Data Problems, and Institutional Innovations. *Review of Income and Wealth* 50:381–409.

Honig, Emily, and Gail Hershatter. 1988. *Personal Voices: Chinese Women in the 1980's*. Stanford, CA: Stanford University Press.

Hu Angang. 2001, *Zhongguo tiaozhan fubai* (China Challenges Corruption). Hangzhou: Zhejiang Renmin Chubanshe.

Huang, Rongqing, and Yan Liu. 1995. *Mortality Data of China*. Beijing: China Population Publishing House.

Hurst, William. 2004. Understanding Contentious Collective Action by Chinese Laid-Off Workers: The Importance of Regional Political Economy. *Studies in Comparative International Development* 39:94–120.

Hussain, Athar. 2003. *Urban Poverty in China: Measurement, Patterns and Policies*. Geneva: International Labour Office, 2003.

Hyde, Sandra T. 2001. Sex Tourism Practices on the Periphery: Eroticizing Ethnicity and Pathologizing Sex on the Lancang. In *China Urban: Ethnographies of Contemporary Culture*, eds. Nancy N. Chen, Constance D. Clark, Suzanne Z. Gottschang, and Lyn Jeffery 143–164. Durham: Duke University Press.

International Labour Organization. 1960–2005. *Yearbook of Labor Statistics*. Geneva: International Labour Office.

Iversen, Torben. 1999. *Contested Economic Institutions: The Politics of Macroeconomics and Wage Bargaining in Advanced Democracies.* New York: Cambridge University Press.

Jalan, Jyotsna, and Martin Ravallion. 2000. Is Transient Poverty Different? Evidence from Rural China. *The Journal of Development Studies* 36(6):82–99.

Jackson, Robert M. 1998. *Destined for Equality: The Inevitable Rise of Women's Status.* Cambridge, MA: Harvard University Press.

Jamison, Dean, John Evens, and Timothy King. 1984. *China, the Health Sector.* World Bank Country Study, Washington DC (WA 540 JC6 C536 1984).

Johansson, Ryan, and Carl Mosk. 1987. Exposure, Resistance and Life Expectancy: Disease and Death during the Economic Development of Japan, 1900–1960. *Population Studies* 41(2):207–235.

Johnstone, Paul, and Isobel McConnan. 1995. Primary Health Care Led NHS: Learning from Developing Countries. *British Medical Journal* 311(7010):891–892.

Kahn, Joseph. 2006. China Makes Commitment to Social Harmony, *The New York Times*, October 12.

Kaluzny, Stephen, Silvia Vega, Tamre Cardoso, and Alice Shelly. 1998. *S+ Spatial-Stats—User's Manual for Windows and Unix.* New York: Springer-Verlag.

Kaufman, Joan. 2005. China: The Intersections between Poverty, Health Inequality, Reproductive Health and HIV/AIDS. *Development* 48(4):113–119.

Keister, Lisa, and Victor Nee. 2000. The Rational Peasant in China: Flexible Adaptation, Risk Diversification and Opportunity. *Rationality & Society* 13:33–69.

Khan, Azizur Rahman. 2005. An Evaluation of World Bank Assistance to China for Poverty Reduction in the 1990s. World Bank Operations Evaluation Department (OED paper no. 32904).

Khan, Azizur, and Carl Riskin.1998. Income and Inequality in China: Composition, Distribution and Growth of Household Income, 1988 to 1995. *The China Quarterly*, 154:221–253.

———. 2001. *Inequality and Poverty in China in the Age of Globalization.* Oxford: Oxford University Press.

———. 2005. China's Household Income Distribution, 1995 and 2002. *The China Quarterly* 182:356–384.

Killingsworth, Mark R. 1983. *Labor Supply.* New York: Cambridge University Press.

Kislitsyna, Olga. 2003. "Income Inequality in Russia during Transition: How Can It Be Explained?" Economic Research Network, Russia and CIS, Working Paper Series ISSN 1561-2422:03/08.

Kluegel, James. 1988. Economic Problems and Socioeconomic Beliefs and Attitudes. *Research on Social Stratification and Mobility* 7:273–302.

Kluegel, James, David Mason, and Bernd Wegener, eds. 1995. *Social Justice and Political Change.* New York: Aldine de Gruyter.

Kluegel, James, and Eliot Smith. 1986. *Beliefs about Inequality: Americans' Views of What Is and What Ought to Be.* New York: Aldine de Gruyter.

Knight, John, and Lina Song. 1999. *Rural Urban Divide: Economic Disparity and Interactions in China.* Oxford: Oxford University Press.

Kohli, Atul. 2004. *State-Directed Development: Political Power and Industrialization in the Global Periphery.* New York: Cambridge University Press.

Kornai, Janos. 1992. *Socialist System: The Political Economy of Communism.* Princeton, NJ: Princeton University Press.

Kreidl, Martin. 2000. Perceptions of Poverty and Wealth in Western and Post-Communist Countries. *Social Justice Research* 13:151–176.

Lamont, Michèle. 2000. *The Dignity of Working Men: Morality and the Boundaries of Race, Class, and Immigration.* New York: Russell Sage Foundation.

Landry, Pierre, and Mingming Shen. 2005. Reaching Migrants in Survey Research: The Use of the Global Positioning System to Reduce Coverage Bias in China. *Political Analysis* 13:1–22.

Lavely, William, and R. Bin Wong. 1992. Family Division and Mobility in North China. *Comparative Studies in Society and History* 34:439–463

Lee, Ching Kwan. 1998. The Labor Politics of Market Socialism: Collective Inaction and Class Experience among State Workers in Guangzhou. *Modern China* 24:3–33.

———. 2002. From the Specter of Mao to the Spirit of the Law. *Theory and Society* 31(2):189–228.

———. 2007. *Against the Law: Labor Protests in China's Rustbelt and Sunbelt.* Berkeley: University of California Press.

Lee, James, and Wang Feng. 1999. *One Quarter of Humanity.* Cambridge, MA: Harvard University Press.

Leidner, Robin. 1993. *Fast Food, Fast Talk.* Berkeley: University of California Press.

Li Lulu and Fenyu Wang. 1999. *Dangqian zhongguo xiandaihua jinchengzhong de shehui jiegou jiqi biange (Social Structure and Its Change in China's Process of Modernization).* Hangzhou: Zhejiang Renmin Chubanshe.

Li Qiang. 2004. Zhongguo shehui fenceng jiegou de xinbianhua (New Changes in Social Stratification in China). In *Zhongguo shehui fenceng (Social Stratification in China)*, eds. Li Peilin et al., 16–41. Beijing: Shehui Kexue Wenxian Chubanshe.

Li, Shi. 2003. *New Trends in Income Distribution in China and Related Policy Changes.* Beijing: Institute of Economics, China Academy of Social Science.

Li Yahua. 2004. Jiejue shidi nongmin baozhang wenti de jidiansikao (Thoughts on Solving the Problem of Social Protection for Farmers Losing Their Land). *Wuhan daxue xuebao* (Annals of Wuhan University), 57.3.

Lian, Xinzhen. 2005. Redistributing Wealth through Income Tax. *Beijing Review* Oct. 13:18–22.

Liang, Zai. 2001. The Age of Migration in China. *Population and Development Review* 27(3):499–524.

Liang, Zai, and Zhongdong Ma. 2004. China's Floating Population: New Evidence from the 2000 Census. *Population and Development Review* 30(3):467–488.

Lim, Louisa. 2006. The High Price of Illness in China. *BBC News* Thursday, 2 March 2006, 06:27 GMT. http://news.bbc.co.uk/2/hi/asia-pacific/4763312.stm.

Lim, Meng-Kin, Hui Yang, Tuohong Zhang, Wen Feng, and Zijun Zhou. 2004. Public Perceptions of Private Health Care in Socialist China: China's Burgeoning Private Health Care Sector Holds Both Promises and Perils. *Health Affairs* 26(3):222–234.

Lin, Nan. 1995. Local Market Socialism: Local Corporatism in Action in Rural China. *Theory and Society* 24:301–354.

Lin, Nan, and Yanjie Bian. 1991. Getting Ahead in Urban China. *American Journal of Sociology* 97:657–688.

Lin Yifu. 2000. *Zailun zhidu, jishu yu zhongguo nongye fazhan (On Institution, Technology, and Agricultural Development in China)*. Beijing: Beijing Daxue Shudian Chubanshe.

Lin Yifu, Fang Cai, and Zhou Li. 1999. *Zhongguo guoyou qiye gaige (Reform of China's State-Owned Enterprises)*. Hong Kong: Hong Kong Chinese University Press of Hong Kong.

———. 2002. *Zhongguo de qiji: fazhanzhanlue yu jingji gaige (China's Miracle: Developmental Strategy and Economic Reforms)*. Shanghai: Sanlian Shudian Chubanshe.

Little, Daniel. 2003. *The Paradox of Wealth and Poverty*. Boulder, CO: Westview Press.

Litvack, J., J. Ahmad, and R. Bird. 1998. *Rethinking Decentralization*. Washington, DC: World Bank.

Liu Xin. 2003. Shichang zhuanxing yu shehui fenceng: lilun zhengbian de jiaodian he youdai tantao de wenti. (Market Transition and Social Stratification: Theoretical Debates and Unresolved Issues). *Zhongguo shehui kexue (Social Sciences of China)* 5.

———. 2005. Dangqian zhongguo shehui jieceng fenhua de duoyuan quanli jichu: yi zhong quanyi yansheng lun de jieshi (The Multiple Sources of Social Stratification in China: A Power Generation Explanation). *Zhongguo shehui kexue (Social Sciences in China)* 4.

Liu, Y., and W. C. Hsiao. 2001. China's Poor and Poor Policies. *Conference on Financial Sector Reform in China*. Cambridge, MA: Harvard School of Public Health.

Livi-Bacci, Massimo. 1997. *A Concise History of World Population*. Malden, MA: Blackwell.

Lu Xueyi, ed. 2002. *Dangdai zhongguo shehui jieceng yanjiu baogao (Report on Social Stratification in China)*. Beijing: Shehui Kexue Wenxian Chubanshe.

Lucas, Robert. E. 1993. Making a Miracle. *Econometrica* 61:251–272.

Luo, Yadong. 2001. *China's Service Sector: A New Battlefield for International Corporations*. Copenhagen: Copenhagen Business School Press.

Ma, Zhongdong. 2001. Urban Labor-Force Experience as a Determinant of Rural Occupation Change: Evidence from Recent Urban-Rural Return Migration in China. *Environment and Planning A* 33:237–255.

Ma, Josephine. 2005. Wealth Gap Fueling Instability, Studies Warn. *South China Morning Post*, December 22.

Macdonald, Cameron Lynne, and Carmen Sirianni. 1996. The Service Society and the Changing Experience of Work. In *Working in the Service Society*, eds. C. Macdonald and C. Sirianni, 1–26. Philadelphia: Temple University Press.

Marks, Robert B. 1998, *Tigers, Rice, Silk and Silt: Environment and Economy in Late Imperial South China*. New York: Cambridge University Press.

Mason, David. 1995. Justice, Socialism, and Participation in the Post-Communist States. In *Social Justice and Political Change: Public Opinion in Capitalist and Post-Communist States,* ed. J. Kluegel, 49–80. New York: Aldine de Gruyter.

Mason, David, and James Kluegel. 2000. *Marketing Democracy: Changing Opinion about Inequality and Politics in East Central Europe*. London: Rowman and Littlefield.

McMichael, Philip. 2005. Globalization. In *The Handbook of Political Sociology: States, Civil Societies, and Globalization*, ed. T. Janoski, 587–606. New York: Cambridge University Press.

Meng, Xin. 2007. Wealth Accumulation and Distribution in Urban China. Institute for the Study of Labor Working Paper, IZA DP No. 2553.

Meng, Xin, Robert Gregory, and Guanghua Wan. 2007. Urban Poverty in China and Its Contributing Factors. *Review of Income and Wealth* 53(1):167–189.

Ministry of Health China (MoH). 2004. *China Health Statistics Yearbook 2004*. http://www.moh.gov.cn/public/open.aspx?n_id=9963&seq=0.

Ministry of Education. 1986. People's Republic of China Law on Compulsory Education. Beijing: Ministry of Education. (Electronic translation available from http://www.womenofchina.com.cn/policies_laws/law_reg/1469.jsp.)

———. People's Republic of China Education Law. (Electronic version posted to http://www.moe.edu.cn/edoas/website18/info1432.htm.)

———. 1999. Action Plan for Revitalizing Education for the 21st Century. (Electronic version posted to http://www.moe.edu.cn/.)

———. 2001. Guidelines for Curriculum Reform of Basic Education. (Electronic version posted to http://www.moe.edu.cn/.)

Mitra, Pradeep, and Ruslan Yemtsov. 2006. Inequality and Growth in Transition: Does China's Rising Inequality Portend Russia's Future? *Annual Bank Conference on Development Economics (ABCDE), Beyond Transition*: St. Petersburg, Russia.

Moore, Barrington Jr. 1978. *Injustice: the Social Bases of Obedience and Revolt*. White Plains: M. E. Sharpe.

Morris, Martina, and Bruce Western. 1999. Inequality in Earnings at the Close of the Twentieth Century. *Annual Review of Sociology* 25:623–657.

Naquin, Susan, and Evelyn Rawski. 1987. *Chinese Society in the Eighteenth Century*. New Haven: Yale University Press.

National Bureau of Statistics of China (NBS). 1991–2004. *China Population Statistical Yearbook*. Beijing: China Statistics Press.

———. 2003. *2000 China County Population and Socioeconomic Indicators with County Maps*. All China Marketing Research Co. Ltd. CDC-S-2003-136.

———. 2004a. *China Statistical Yearbook 2004*. Beijing: China Statistics Press.

———. 2004b. *China Statistical Abstract*. Beijing: China Statistic Press.

———. 2005a. *China Historical County Population Census Data with GIS Maps*. All China Marketing Research Co. Ltd. CDC-S-2005-129.

———. 2005b. *China Statistical Yearbook 2005*. Online. http://stats.gov.cn. Accessed December 20, 2005.

———. 2006. *China Statistical Yearbook 2006*. Beijing: China Statistic Press.

———. 2007. *China Statistical Abstract*. Beijing: Ching Statistic Press.

National Bureau of Statistics and Ministry of Labor. 1989. *China Labor and Wage Statistical Yearbook 1989*. Beijing: Labor and Personnel Press.

Naughton, Barry. 1995. *Growing Out of the Plan*. Cambridge: Cambridge University Press.

———. 1997. Danwei: The Economic Foundations of a Unique Institution. In *Danwei, the Changing Chinese Workplace in Historical and Comparative Perspective*, eds. Xiaobo Lü and Elizabeth J. Perry, 169–194. Armonk, NY: M. E. Sharpe.

———. 2007. *The Chinese Economy: Transitions and Growth*. Cambridge, MA: MIT Press.

Nee, Victor. 1989. A Theory of Market Transition: from Redistribution to Markets in State Socialism. *American Sociological Review* 54:663–681.

———. 1991. Social Inequality in Reforming State Socialism: Between Redistribution and Markets in State Socialism. *American Sociological Review* 54:663–681.

———. 1996. The Emergence of a Market Society: Changing Mechanisms of Stratification in China. *American Journal of Sociology* 101:908–949.

Nee, Victor, and Rebecca Matthews. 1996. Market Transition and Societal Transformation in Reforming State Socialism. *Annual Review of Sociology*. 22.

Nee, Victor, and Yang Cao. 1999. Path Dependent Societal Transformation: Stratification in Hybrid Mixed Economies. *Theory and Society* 28.

———. 2002. Post-Socialist Inequalities: The Causes of Continuity and Discontinuity. *Research on Stratification and Mobility* 19: 3–40.

Negroponte, Nicholas. 1996. *Being Digital.* New York: Vintage Books.

North, Douglas C. 1981. *Structure and Change in Economic History.* New York: Norton.

———. 1990, *Institutions, Institutional Change and Economic Performance.* Cambridge: Cambridge University Press.

Nozick, Robert. 1975. *Anarchy, State and Utopia.* New York: Basic Books.

Oi, Jean C. 1989. *State and Peasant in Contemporary China.* Berkeley, CA: University of California Press.

———. 1992. Fiscal Reform and the Economic Foundations of Local State Corporatism. *World Politics,* 45(1) (October 1992): 99–126.

———. 1999. *Rural China Takes Off: Institutional Foundations of Economic Reform.* Berkeley, CA: University of California Press.

Oi, Jean, and Andrew G. Walder. 1999. *Property Rights and Economic Reform in China.* Stanford: Stanford University Press.

Oi, Jean, and Shukai Zhao. Forthcoming. Fiscal Crisis in China's Townships: Causes and Consequences. In *Grassroots Political Reform,* eds. M. Goldman and E. Perry. Cambridge, MA: Harvard University Press.

Ooi, Elaine Wee-Ling. 2005. *The World Bank's Assistance to China's Health Sector.* http://www.worldbank.org.

Pan, L. T. 2006. Key Points of the 11th Five-Year Plan. Gov.Cn: The Chinese Government's Official Web Portal (Tuesday, March 7, 2006). (Retrieved 11/13/2007 from http://english.gov.cn/2006-03/07/content_246929.htm.)

Pannell, Clifton W. 2003. China's Demographic and Urban Trends for the 21st Century. *Eurasian Geography and Economics* 44:479–496.

Parish, William. 1984. Destratification in China. In *Class and Social Stratification in Post-Revolution China,* ed. J. Watson, 84–120. Cambridge: Cambridge University Press.

Parish, William L., and Ethan Michelson. 1996. Politics and Markets: Dual Transformations. *American Journal of Sociology* 101:1042–1059.

Park, Albert, John Giles, and Fang Cai. 2006. How Has Economic Restructuring Affected China's Urban Workers. *The China Quarterly*: 61–95.

Park, Albert, and Sangui Wang. 2001. China's Poverty Statistics. *China Economic Review* 12(4):384–398.

Pearson, Margaret M. 1992. *Joint Ventures in the People's Republic of China: The Control of Foreign Direct Investment under Socialism.* Princeton, NJ: Princeton University Press.

Pei, Minxin. 2003. Rights and Resistance. In *Chinese Society: Change, Conflict and Resistance.* 2nd ed., eds. E. Perry and M. Selden, 23–43. London and New York: Routledge Curzon.

Pejovich, Svetozar. 1995. *The Economic Analysis of Institutions and Systems.* Boston: Kluwer Academic Publishers.

Peng, Yusheng. 2004. Kinship Networks and Entrepreneurs in China's Transitional Economy. *American Journal of Sociology* 109:1045–1074.

People's Daily. 2006. Draft Amendment to Compulsory Education Law Under 1st Review of China's Legislature. People's Daily Online 2006 (February 25).

———. 2006. China Pledges Elimination of Rural Compulsory Education Charges in Two Years. People's Daily Online 2006 (March 5).

Polanyi, Karl. 1944/1957. *The Great Transformation: The Political and Economic Origins of Our Time.* Boston, MA: Beacon Press.

Pomeranz, Kenneth. 2000. *The Great Divergence: China, Europe, and the Making of the Modern World Economy.* Princeton, NJ: Princeton University Press.

Postiglione, Gerard. 2007. School Access and Equity in Rural Tibet. In *Education and Reform in China,* eds. E. Hannum and A. Park, 93–116. London: Routledge.

Preston, Samuel H. 1977. Mortality Trends. *Annual Review of Sociology* 3:163–178.

Qian, Yingyi, and Barry R. Weingast. Federalism as a Commitment to Preserving Market Incentives. *Journal of Economic Perspectives.* Fall 1997, 11(4):83–92. http://www.blsq.com/xiangcun/View.asp?ViewID=26

Qiu Baoxing. 2006. *Hexie yu chuangxin (Harmony and Innovation).* Beijing: Zhongguo Jianchu Gongye Chubanshe.

Raudenbush, Stephen W., and Anthony S. Bryk. 2002. *Hierarchical Linear Models: Applications and Data Analysis Methods.* Thousand Oaks, CA: Sage.

Ravallion, Martin, and Shaohua Chen. 2004. China's (Uneven) Progress against Poverty. World Bank Policy Research Working Paper 3408. Washington, DC: The World Bank.

Rawls, John. 1971. *A Theory of Justice.* Cambridge, MA: Harvard University Press.

Rawski, Evelyn. 1972. *Agricultural Change and the Peasant Economy of South China.* Cambridge, MA: Harvard University Press.

Reddy, Sanjay, and Camelia Minoiu. 2006. Has World Poverty Really Fallen during the 1990s? Available at SSRN: http://ssrn.com/abstract=800130.

Reich, Robert. 1991. What Is a Nation? *Political Science Quarterly* 106:193–209.

———. 2003. Nice Work if You Can Get It. *The Wall Street Journal,* December 26:A10.

Research Group for Social Structure in Contemporary China. 2005. *Social Mobility in Contemporary China.* Montreal: American Quantum Media.

Riley, James. 2001. *Rising Life Expectancy.* Cambridge: Cambridge University Press.

Riskin, Carl. 2007. Has China Reached the Top of the Kuznets Curve? In *Paying for Progress: Public Finance, Human Welfare and Inequality in China,* eds. V. Shue and C. Wong, 29–45. London: Routledge.

Riskin, Carl, Renwei Zhao, and Shi Li. 2001. Introduction: The Retreat from Equality: Highlights of the Findings. In *China's Retreat from Equality: Income Distribution and Economic Transition,* eds. C. Riskin, R. Zhao, and S. Li, 3–22. Armonk, NY: M. E. Sharpe.

Romer, Paul M. 1986. Increasing Returns and Long-Run Growth. *Journal of Political Economy* 94:1002–1037.

Rona-Tas, Akos. 1994. The First Shall Be Last? *American Journal of Sociology* 100:40–59.

Rosen, Stanley. 2004. The Victory of Materialism, *China Journal* No. 51 (January):27–51.

Ross, H. 2005. *China Country Study.* Paper commissioned for the *Education for All Global Monitoring Report* 2006, *Literacy for Life.* Paris: UNESCO (available http://unesdoc.unesco.org/images/0014/001461/14608e.pdf, accessed August 12, 2008).

Rowe, William. 1984. *Hankow: Commerce and Society in a Chinese City: 1796–1889.* Stanford, CA: Stanford University Press.

———. 1989. *Hankow: Conflict and Community in a Chinese City 1796–1895.* Stanford, CA: Stanford University Press

———. 2002. Social Stability and Social Change. In *The Cambridge History of China* (vol. 9, part 1, *The Ch'ing to 1800*), ed. W. Peterson, 473–562. Cambridge: Cambridge University Press.

Salaff, Janet. 1973. Mortality Decline in the People's Republic of China and the United States. *Population Studies* 27(3):551–576.

Sargent, Tanja. Forthcoming. Revolutionizing Ritual Interaction in the Classroom: Constructing the Chinese Renaissance of the 21st Century. *Modern China.*

Sato, Hiroshi. 2003. *The Growth of Market Relations in Post-Reform Rural China: A Microanalysis of Peasants, Migrants, and Peasant Entrepreneurs.* New York: Routledge Curzon.

Scott, James C. 1976. *The Moral Economy of the Peasant: Rebellion and Subsistence in Southeast Asia.* New Haven: Yale University Press.

Sen, Amartya. 1999. *Development as Freedom.* New York: Anchor Books.

———. 2006. Conceptualizing and Measuring Poverty. In *Poverty and Inequality*, eds. D. Grusky and R. Kanbur, 30–46. Stanford, CA: Stanford University Press.

Shambaugh, David, ed. 2000. *Is China Unstable?* Armonk, NY: M. E. Sharpe.

Sherman, Rachel. 2005. Producing the Superior Self: Strategic Comparison and Symbolic Boundaries among Luxury Hotel Workers. *Ethnography* 6:131–158.

Shu, Xiaoling. 2005. Market Transition and Gender Segregation in Urban China. *Social Science Quarterly* 86:1299–1323.

Shu, Xiaoling, and Yanjie Bian. 2003. Market Transition and Gender Gap in Earnings in Urban China. *Social Forces* 81(4):1107–1145.

Shue, Vivienne. 1988. *The Reach of the State: Sketches of the Chinese Body Politic.* Stanford, CA: Stanford University Press.

———. 2004. Legitimacy Crisis in China? In *State and Society in 21st-Century China*, eds. P. Gries and S. Rosen, 24–49. New York: Routledge Curzon.

Skeggs, Beverly. 1997. *Formations of Class and Gender*. London: Sage.

Skinner, G. William. 2005. *The Spatial Logic of Uneven Development in Contemporary China*. Unpublished paper.

Solinger, Dorothy J. 1999a. *Contesting Citizenship: Peasants Migrants, the State, and the Logic of the Market in Urban China*. Berkeley and Los Angeles: University of California Press.

———. 1999b. Demolishing partitions: Back to Beginnings in the Cities? *China Quarterly* 159:629–639.

———. 2000. Sudden Sackings and the Mirage of the Market: Unemployment, Reemployment, and Survival in Wuhan, Summer 1999. Unpubl. ms. East Asian Institute, Columbia University.

Song, Binwen, Xiaogang Fan, and Huiwen Zhou. 2003. Shidi nongmin wenti de chengyin jiqi huajie duice (Reasons for Farmers Losing Land and Ways to Deal with the Problem). *Guancha yu sikao (Observation and Reflection)* 12.

Song, Shige. 1998. Shichang zhuanbianzhong de jingying zaisheng yu xunhuan (Reproduction and Circulation of Elites during Market Transition). *Shehuixue yanjiu (Sociological Research)* No. 3.

Sørensen, Aage B. 2000. Toward a Sounder Basis for Class Analysis. *American Journal of Sociology* 105:1523–1558.

Stacey, Judith. 1983. *Patriarchy and Socialist Revolution in China*. Berkeley, CA: University of California Press.

State Council. 2004. 2003–2007 Action Plan for Revitalizing Education. (March, 2004).

State Statistical Bureau of People's Republic of China. 1983–1987. *Statistical Yearbook of China*. Hong Kong: Economic Information Agency.

Stinchcombe, Arthur. 1965. Social Structure and Organizations, in *Handbook of Organizations*, ed. J. March, 142–193. Chicago: Rand McNally.

Sun Liping 2002. Shijian shehuixue yu shichang zhuanxing guocheng fenxi (Sociology of Practice and the Study of the Market Transition Process). *Zhongguo shehui kexue* (Social Sciences in China) No. 5.

———. 2006. Duanlie: ershi shiji jiushiniandai yilai zhongguo shehui de fencing jieguo (Fracture: The Structure of Social Stratification since 1990s in China). In *Dangdai zhongguo shehui fencing: lilun yu shizheng* (*Social Stratification of Contemporary China: Theory and Evidence*), eds. Y. Li, L. Sun, and Y. Shen. 1–35. Beijing: Shehui Kexue Wenxian Chubanshe.

Szelényi, Iván. 1978. Social Inequalities in State Socialist Redistributive Economies. *International Journal of Comparative Sociology* 1–2:63–87.

Szelényi, Iván, and Eric Kostello. 1996. The Market Transition Debate: Toward a Synthesis? *American Journal of Sociology* 101:1082–1096.

———. 1998. Outline of an Institutionalist Theory of Inequality: The Case of Socialist and Post-Communist Eastern Europe. In *The New Institutionalism in Sociology*, eds. M. Brinton and V. Nee, 305–326. New York: Russell Sage Foundation.

Szelényi, Iván, and Robert Manchin. 1987. Social Policy under State Socialism. In *Stagnation and Renewal in Social Policy*, eds. G. Esping-Anderson, L. Rainwater, and M. Rein, 102–139. New York: M. E. Sharpe.

Tanner, Murray Scot. 2006. We the People (of China) . . . *Wall Street Journal*, February 2:A10.

Tilly, Charles. 1984. Demographic Origins of the European Proletariat. In David Levine, ed. *Proletarianization and Family History*. New York: Academic Press, 1-85.

———. 1998. *Durable Inequality*. Berkeley, CA: University of California Press.

Tilly, Charles, B. Bluestone, and B. Harrison. 1986. What Is Making American Wages More Unequal? In *Proceedings of the Industrial Relations Research Association Annual Meeting*. December.

Time Asia. 2006. Seeds of Fury. *Time Asia*, March 5.

Tsang, M. C. 1996. The Financial Reform of Basic Education in China. *Economics of Education Review* 15(4):423–444.

———. 2000. Education and National Development in China since 1949: Oscillating Policies and Enduring Dilemmas. *China Review—An Interdisciplinary Journal on Greater China* 579–618.

U.S. Bureau of Labor Statistics. 2005. *Women in the Labor Force: A Databook*. U.S. Department of Labor. Report 985 (May). Accessed at: http://www.bls.gov/cps/wlf-databook2005.htm.

U.S. Department of Commerce. 1975. *Historical Statistics for the United States, Colonial Times through 1970*. Washington, DC: U.S. Department of Commerce.

United Nations Conference on Trade and Development. 2006. UNCTAD Handbook of Statistics Online. http://stats.unctad.org/handbook.

United Nations Development Program (UNDP). 2003, 2004, 2005. *Human Development Report*. United Nations.

United Nations Economic and Social Commission for Asia and the Pacific (UNESCAP). NA. Population and Family Planning in China by Province: Gansu Province. Bangkok, Thailand: United Nations Economic and Social Commission for Asia and the Pacific (UNESCAP). Retrieved 10/21, 2005. http://www.unescap.org/esid/psis/population/database/chinadata/gansu.htm.

United Nations Statistics Division. 2002. *Demographic Yearbook*. (http://unstats.un.org/unsd/demographic/products/dyb).

———. 1997. *Demographic Yearbook Historical Supplement*. (http://unstats.un.org/unsd/demographic/products/dyb).

Vallas, Steven Peter. 2001. Symbolic Boundaries and the New Division of Labor: Engineers, Workers, and the Restructuring of Factory Life. *Researching Social Stratification and Mobility* 18: 3–37.

Wakita, Osamu. 1991. The Social and Economic Consequences of Unification. In *The Cambridge History of Japan* (vol. 4) *Early Modern Japan*, ed. John W. Hall.

Walder, Andrew. 1986. *Communist Neo-Traditionalism: Work and Authority in Chinese Industry.* Berkeley, CA: University of California Press.

———. 1992. Property Rights and Stratification in Socialist Redistributive Economies. *American Sociological Review* 57:524–539.

———. 1995a. Career mobility and Communist Political Order. *American Sociological Review* 60:309–328.

———. 1995b. Local Governments as Industrial Firms: An Organizational Analysis of China's Transformation Economy. *American Journal of Sociology* 101:263–301.

———. 1996. Markets and Inequality in Transitional Economies: Toward Testable Theories. *American Journal of Sociology* 101:1060–1073.

———. 2002. Markets and Income Inequality in Rural China: Political Advantage in an Expanding Economy. *American Sociological Review* 67:231–253

———. 2003. Elite Opportunity in Transitional Economies. *American Sociological Review* 68:899–916.

Walder, Andrew, Bobai Li, and Donald Treiman. 2000. Politics and Life Chances in a State Socialist Regime. *American Sociological Review* 65(2):191–209.

Walder, Andrew, and Jean Oi. 1999. Property Rights in the Chinese Economy: Contours of the Process of China. In *Property Rights and Economic Reform in China*, eds. J. Oi and A. Walder, 1–24. Stanford, CA: Stanford University Press.

Wang, Fei-ling. 2005. *Organizing through Division and Exclusion: China's* Hukou *System.* Stanford, CA: Stanford University Press.

Wang, Feng. 2003. Housing Improvement and Distribution in Urban China. *The China Review* Vol. 3. No. 2 (fall):121–143.

———. 2005. Can China Afford to Continue Its One-Child Policy? *Asia Pacific Issues* 77:1–12. Honolulu: The East-West Center.

———. 2008. *Boundaries and Categories: Rising Inequality in Post-Socialist Urban China.* Stanford, CA: Stanford University Press.

Wang, Feng, and Tsui-o Tai. 2006. A Decade of Rising Poverty in Urban China: Who Are More Likely to Fall Under? Working Paper of the Center for the Study of Democracy, University of California, Irvine. No. 06–14.

Wang, Feng, and Tianfu Wang. 2007. Boundaries and Categories: Urban Income Inequality in China, 1986–1995. In *Social Change in Contemporary China: C. K. Yang and the Concept of Institutional Diffusion*, eds. Wenfang Tang and Burkart Holzner, 125–152. Pittsburgh: University of Pittsburgh Press.

Wang, Feng, Xuejin Zuo, and Danqing Ruan. 2002. Rural Migrants in Shanghai. *International Migration Review* vol. 36.2 (Summer):520–545.

Wang Haishen. 2004. Shidi nongmin de chulu yu xianshi (Ways Out for Farmers Lost Land and Reality). *Nongcun tiandi (The World of Villages)* 4.

Wang, Hong, Licheng Zhang, and William Hsiao. 2005. Ill Health and Its Potential Influence on Household Consumptions in Rural China. *Health Policy* (Cited version: In Press, Corrected Proof).

Wang, Sangui. 2004. *Poverty Targeting in the People's Republic of China*. Tokyo: Asian Development Bank Institute.

Wang, Shaoguang. 1997. *Decentralization: The Bottom Line (Fenquan de dixian)*. Beijing: Zhongguo Jihua Chubanshe.

———. 2004. China's Health System: From Crisis to Opportunity. *Yale-China Health Journal* Vol 3:5–50. Available on line at www.yalechina.org.

Wank, David L. 1999. *Commodifying Communism: Business, Trust, and Politics in Chinese City*. New York: Cambridge University Press.

Watson, James L. 1984. *Class and Social Stratification in Post-Revolution China*. Cambridge: Cambridge University Press.

Weber, Max. 1978. *Economy and Society*. Berkeley: University of California Press.

———. 1981. *General Economic History*. New Brunswick, NJ: Transaction Books.

Whyte, Martin King. 1985. The Politics of Life Chances in the People's Republic of China. In *Power and Policy in the PRC*, ed. Yu-ming Shaw, 244–265. Boulder, CO: Westview.

———. 1995a. From Arranged Matches to Love Marriages in Urban China. In *Family Formation and Dissolution: Perspectives from East and West*, ed. Chin-Chun Yi, 33–83. Taipei: Academia Sinica.

———. 1995b. The Social Roots of China's Economic Development. *The China Quarterly*, 144, 999–1019.

———. 1996. City versus Countryside in China's Development. *Problems of Post-Communism* 43:9–22.

———. 2000. The Perils of Assessing Trends in Gender Inequality in China. In *Re-Drawing Boundaries*, eds. Barbara Entwisle and Gail E. Henderson, 157–167. Berkeley: University of California Press.

———. 2002. Chinese Popular Views about Inequality. *Asia Program Special Report, Woodrow Wilson International Center* 104:4–10.

Whyte, Martin K., and Chunping Han. 2003. Distributive Justice Issues and the Prospects for Unrest in China. Weatherhead Center for International Affairs Working Paper, Harvard University.

———. 2005. Learning to Love the Market: Warsaw and Beijing Compared. Unpublished paper.

Whyte, Martin King, and William Parish. 1984. *Urban Life in Contemporary China*. Chicago: The University of Chicago Press.

Willis, Paul. 1982. *Learning to Labor: How Working Class Kids get Working Class Jobs*. New York: Columbia University Press.

Wilson, Richard. 2005. Political Culture and the Persistence of Inequality. *East Asia: An International Quarterly* vol. 22 (Spring):3–17.

Wolf, Margery. 1985. *Revolution Postponed: Women in Contemporary China*. Stanford, CA: Stanford University Press.

Wong, Christine. 2007. Can the Retreat from Equality Be Reversed? Assessing Fiscal Policies toward Redistribution from Deng Xiaoping to Wen Jiabao. In *Pay-*

*ing for Progress: Public Finance, Human Welfare and Inequality in China*, eds. V. Shue and C. Wong,12–28. London: Routledge.

Wong, Roy Bin. 1997. *China Transformed: Historical Change and the Limits of European Experience*. Ithaca, NY: Cornell University Press.

———. 2004. Relationships between the Political Economies of Maritime and Agrarian China, 1750–1850. In *Maritime China and the Overseas Chinese Communities*, eds. Wang Gungwu and Ng Chin-Keong. Wiesbaden (Germany): Harrassowitz Verlag.

Woo, E. T., and S. Bao. 2003. China: Case Study on Human Development Progress towards the Millennium Development Goals at the Submational Level (Background Paper for the Human Development Report 2003). New York: United Nations Development Programme Human Development Report Office.

Wood, Robert. 1985. The Effects of Population Redistribution on the Level of Mortality in Nineteenth-Century England and Wales. *The Journal of Economic History* 45(3):645–651.

World Bank. 2005. *World Development Indicators*. http://devdata.worldbank.org/wdi2005/section1_1_1.htm.

———. 2006. *World Development Report 2006: Equity and Development*. Washington, DC: The World Bank.

World Health Organization (WHO). 2000. *The World Health Report*. http://www.who.int/whr/en.

Wright, Erik Olin. 1997. *Class Counts: Comparative Studies in Class Analysis*. New York: Cambridge University Press.

Wu Jinglian. 2003. *Dangdai zhongguo jingji gaige (Economic Reforms in Contemporary China)* Shanghai: Shanghai Yuandong Chubanshe.

Wu, Xiaogang. 2002. Work Units and Income Inequality: The Effect of Market Transition in Urban China. *Social Forces* 80:1069–1099.

Wu, Xiaogang, and Yu Xie. 2003. Does the Market Pay Off? Earnings Returns to Education in Urban China. *American Sociological Review* 68:425–442.

Xiang, Huaicheng, ed. 1999. *Fifty Years of Chinese Public Finance (Zhongguo caizheng wushinian)*. Beijing: Zhongguo Caizheng Jingji Chubanshe.

Xiang Jiquan. 2005. Duanque caizheng xia de xiangcun zhengzhi jianshe (Political Construction in Rural Villages under Public Finance Deficits). *Xiangcun zhongguo guancha* (Observations of Rural China), 4. http://www.blsq.com/xiangcun/View.asp?ViewID=26.

Xie, Yu, and Emily Hannum. 1996. Regional Variation in Earnings Inequality in Reform Era Urban China. *American Journal of Sociology* 101:950–992.

Xie, Yu, Yang Jiang, and Emily Greenman. 2006. Did Send-Down Experience Benefit Youth? A Reevaluation of the Social Consequences of Forced Urban-Rural Migration during China's Cultural Revolution. Unpublished paper.

Xinhua News Agency. 2006. China Adopts Amendment to Compulsory Education Law. *Xinhua Online 2006* (June 29).

Xinhua News Agency. 2006b. Chinese Communist Party Says Membership Reached 70 Million in 2005. (July 4)

Xinhua. 2004. Survey of Chinese Officials' Opinions on Reform: Beijing Daily. *Xinhua News Bulletin*, November 29.

*Xin Jing Bao* 2004.07.05.

Xu Fuhai. 2002. Zuowei nongmin liyi biaoda fangshi de jieguo boyi yu xiangtu zhixu—Heibei shancun de tudi tiaozheng zhuang kuang yu nongmin fanying de diao cha (Returns to Farmers and Rural Social Order—A Survey of Land Adjustment and Farmers' Reactions in Mountainous Villages in Hebei Province). Unpublished Master's thesis. Department of Sociology, Peking University.

Yang, Dennis Tao. 2005. Determinants of Schooling Returns during Transition: Evidence from Chinese Cities. *Journal of Comparative Economics* 33(2):244–264.

Yang, Mayfair Mei-hui. 1999. From Gender Erasure to Gender Difference: State Feminism, Consumer Sexuality, and Women's Public Sphere in China. In *Spaces of Their Own: Women's Public Sphere in Transnational China*, ed. Mayfair Mei-hui Yang, 35–67. Minneapolis: University of Minnesota Press.

Young, Iris Marion. 1990. *Justice and the Politics of Difference*. Princeton, NJ: Princeton University Press.

Zhang Jing. 2001. *Liyi zuzhhua danwei (Danwei as organized interest organization)*. Beijing: Zhongguo Shehui Kexue Chubanshe.

———. 2002. Cunshe tudi de jiti zhipei wenti (Land Use Issue in Villages). *Zhengjiang xuekan* No. 2. 32–39.

Zhang, Junsen, and Yaohui Zhao. 2007. Rising Schooling Returns in Urban China. In *Education and Reform in China*, eds. E. Hannum and A. Park, 248–259. London: Routledge 2007.

Zhang, Junsen, et al. 2005. Economic Returns to Schooling in Urban China, 1988 to 2001. *Journal of Comparative Economics* 33(4):730–752.

Zhang Weiying. 1995. Gongyouzhi jingji zhong de weituoren-dailiren guanxi: lilun fenxi he zhengce hanyi (Relationships between Trustees and Representatives in Public Economy: Theortical Analysis and Policy Implications). *Jingji yanjiu* (Economic Research).

———. 1999. *Qiye lilun yu zhongguo qiye gaige (Theories of Enterprises and Enterprises Reform in China)*. Beijing: Beijing Daxue Chubanshe.

Zhang Yongle, and Qiudao Song. 2001. Zhejiang Y cun diaocha baogao (Survey Report of Y Village in Zhejiang, Student Report for Summer Practice Workshop). Beijing: Peking University. Unpublished.

Zhang, Yuping, Grace Kao, and Emily Hannum. 2007. Do Mothers in Rural China Practice Gender Equity in Educational Aspirations for Children? *Comparative Education Review* 51(2):131–157.

Zhao, Dingxin. 2001. *The Power of Tiananmen: State-Society Relations and the 1989 Beijing Student Movement*. Chicago: University of Chicago Press.

Zhao, Wei, and Xueguang Zhou. 2002. Institutional Transformation and Returns to Education in Urban China: An Empirical Assessment. *Research in Social Stratification and Mobility* 19:339–375.

Zhao, Yaohui. 1997. Labor Migration and Returns to Rural Education in China. *American Journal of Agricultural Economics* 79(4):1278.

Zheng Changgan. 1989. *Ming Qing nongcun shangpin jingji (Rural Commodity Economy in Ming-Qing China)*. Beijing: Zhongguo Renmin Daxue Chubanshe.

Zhou Qiren. 2002. *Chanquan zhidu yu zhidu bianqian: zhongguo gaige de jingyan yanjiu* (Property Rights and Institutional Change: Empirical Research of China's Reforms). Beijing: Shehui Kexue Wenxian Chubanshe.

Zhou, Xueguang. 2000a. An Institutional Theory of Reputation. Paper presented at Academy of Management Annual Meeting. Toronto, Canada.

———. 2000b. Economic Transformation and Income Inequality in Urban China: Evidence from Panel Data. *American Journal of Sociology* 105:1135–1174.

———. 2004. *The State and Life Chances in Urban China: Redistribution and Stratification 1949–1994*. New York: Cambridge University Press.

———. 2005a. Inverted Soft Budget Constraint: An Organizational Analysis of Extrabudgetary Seeking Behavior in Local Governments. (in Chinese) *Social Sciences in China* 2:132–143.

———. 2005b. Relational Property Rights: A Sociological Interpretation. (in Chinese) *Sociological Research* 2:1–31.

———. 2007a. The Autumn Harvest: Peasants and Markets in the Post-Corporatist Rural China. Unpublished manuscript. Stanford, CA: Department of Sociology, Stanford University.

———. 2007b. Can a Falling Leaf Tell the Coming of the Autumn? Making Sense of Village Elections in a Township . . . and in China. Chapter in *Growing Pains*, ed. Jean Oi, Scott Rozelle, and Xueguang Zhou. Under review at Brookings Institute Press.

Zhou, Xueguang, Nancy Tuma, and Phyllis Moen. 1997. Institutional Change and Job-Shift Patterns in Urban China. *American Sociological Review* 62:339–365.

Zhu, Muju. 2007. Recent Chinese Experiences in Curriculum Reform. *Prospects* 37(2):223–34.

Zhu, Yu, and Tingyu Zhou. 2005. Total Number of Migrants Doubled within 10 Years, Making Up More Than 10% of Total Population, in Xinhua Net, as Cited by China Web at www.china.org.cn/chinese/renkou/748584.htm.

Zweig, David. 1989. Struggle over Land in China: Peasant Resistance after Collectivization, 1966–1986. In *Everyday Forms of Peasant Resistance*, ed. F. Colburn, 151–174. Armonk, NY: M. E. Sharpe.

*A "t" after a page number indicates a table; an "f" indicates a figure.*